God Answers

A Daily Devotional for Christians

Lele Beutel

Lele Beutel loves to meet and chat with fans! Reach out to her at apedersen6@comcast.net.

Cover and book design by Publishing Hackers

Paperback ISBN: 979-8839801363
Ebook ISBN: 979-8-9902359-5-3

For those who seek the Lord's
hope-filled reassurance
during trying times

"Pray like this: Our Father in heaven,
may your name be kept holy.
May your Kingdom come soon.
May your will be done on earth,
as it is in heaven.
Give us today the food we need,
and forgive us our sins,
as we have forgiven those who sin
against us.
And don't let us yield to temptation,
but rescue us from the evil one."

—Matthew 6:9-13

Introduction

In 2001, I discovered a passionate love for God while experiencing great angst for the life of my son, who was diagnosed with lung disease. He bravely fought an ongoing battle for the next 12 years with resurgences of cancerous tumors as my daughter struggled with her own beliefs while starting a family. Both were removed from me, living in places far from home, so I often felt helpless to be involved in their struggles, even as I fought my own battle to nurture a new business.

In 2002, I wrote: "For many years, I sought God in bits and pieces, usually going to Him during the times when I was at my wit's end. Between my children's growing needs, an inevitable divorce, finishing college in my thirties, and working to establish myself in the business community, I had little time to seek out His presence or read the Bible, which I'd savored in my earlier Christian years. When I read a book called *Dining at the Master's Table, Learning to Hear the Voice of the Lord,* by Paul Norcross, I began to seek Him again, this time along with daily devotions and prayer. I felt I'd found my resting place."

Realizing how much more God could do for me if I would only take daily time to sit in His presence, I made a commitment to "go to my prayer closet" each morning. Since I found it difficult to sit in silence for very long trying to focus my attention on Him alone, I started by walking around a lake and listening for Him in the stillness. Then I'd spend time in my upstairs "throne room," where I got down on my knees spiritually. I read chapters from the Bible to set the tone for the day. And I asked God for direction. I threw my cares at His feet and prayed for people He put on my heart. As I learned to grow quiet, I began to hear His soft whispers.

The more I went to Him like this, the more I was amazed and thrilled to find that I could begin to discern His voice. I was so enraptured by this that I often forgot

1

what He said. So, I decided to write His messages down in a journal. Then I could be reminded of His words. Sometimes, months or years after writing what I'd heard, I'd reread the passages. It was these return visits that convinced me that the words were from Him. On August 1, 2001, my journal entry read: "There are those in this world who will try to bring harm, thinking they are right in their ways. These people suffer later for their injustices. They reap consequences to their actions. Do not be afraid of these people, thinking they may bring you harm or destruction. They can never touch your spirit..." Such timely words! The terrorist attacks came shortly after this message, on September 11th, and scarred all of us physically and mentally forever.

Spending daily time with Him changed my life in unimaginable ways. Things that used to bother me no longer caused me to struggle. And I began to more fully experience the fruits of the spirit: love, joy, peace, patience, kindness, goodness, faithfulness, gentleness, and self-control (Galatians 5:22-23) in new and wonderful ways. The following pages are excerpts from my journal entries between 2001 and 2021. They are words spoken to and from my heart. They are conversations between my spirit and God's.

I hope they bring you as much comfort, peace, joy, and hope as they have brought to me. But, most of all, that they inspire you to spend your own daily time with God seeking His words and will for your life.

Though my son passed away in November 2013, it's the words I reread from the Bible and in my journal that get me through the hardest days. I see now how God prepared me for this difficult time. He strengthened me and built me up in ways no one else could have. I'm alive because of Him, and I see hope in the future. My daughter prays again. And I know, because He told me so, that one day I'll be reunited with my beloved son.

–Lele Beutel, 2024

January

FOCUS:
LASTING LOVE

"Three things will last forever— faith, hope, and love— and the greatest of these is love."

—I CORINTHIANS 13:13

JANUARY 1
Thanks for this new day

"Light is sweet; how pleasant to see a new day dawning."
—Ecclesiastes 11:2

Me: Thanks, Lord, for this new day and new year. As I look toward You and whisper Your name, would You remind me of Your presence, the hope You bring me, and the peace I can have through You each moment? Would You convey to me the unspeakable joy, abounding love, and matchless grace I can experience through You? And would You show me more of how dynamic our combined efforts are and how I can overcome any challenge with Your help? Whether it concerns health, finances, relationships, work, or homelife. Show me more clearly how You can abound in and through me. Thanks for all You've done for me, for my family, and for those I love. You are my first love and will always be. Thanks for a spectacular new year! I love You.

God: Dear one, as the year begins, proclaim new promises for yourself. First, vow to honor Me in all you do by pledging to offer only your best efforts in every situation. Second, determine to start the day with prayer, but also to pray throughout the day. When opportunities are presented and needs disclosed, bring them to Me. Pledge to intercede for others because this opens doors and allows Me to work on their behalf. Third, rededicate your heart, your life, and your mind to Me. Lay out your dreams and goals before Me. Then, you'll see Me answer them in wondrous ways. I will work with you this year and in all the years ahead. Listen carefully to what I tell you because My words will serve you well. Every message from Me leads you to goodness, and you must hold tight to every word. You'll come to recognize My voice more as time goes on, and you'll grow accustomed to hearing it. You'll see a pattern emerge as I unfold greater insight to you. And you'll see how My words bring you a sense of calm. You'll begin to recognize this feeling as a sign that you're on the right track. Depend on Me to bring you what you need. Rely on Me for answers. Sometimes at night I'll speak to you and tell you things you need to know. Listen as I speak. I'll give you a greater understanding of yourself and others. My words will always bring good results to you and to your family. Open your heart, and let My words lead and guide you today and throughout the year. Come to Me for answers. I will never fail you. Because I love you.

To walk and talk with You

"I know the Lord is always with me. I will not be shaken, for he is right beside me."
—Psalm 16:8

Me: Lord, You've been with me since I was small. You watched over me, sitting near me when I was alone, caressing my thoughts with Your extravagant love, easing my fears with Your heart of mercy, and comforting me over and over with Your hand of hope. Thanks for that. Thanks for loving me when I felt unloved, teaching and guiding me, and showing me the meaning of Your grace. How often have You forgiven me? How often have You been patient with my shortcomings and mindful of my mistakes? And yet You loved me and gave me life. You called and blessed me time and time again. You led me to a belief in Your precious Son Jesus and in all He accomplished for me. You've always been there in the dark places. You're still with me when the pathways are too dim to manage. Be with me now. I need Your help to get through the next days, weeks, and months. Let Your strong hand guide me through the uncertain times. Open my eyes so I can see the spiritual side of life. Remind me of Your presence and mercy today. And continue to comfort me when I need reassurance that You're here with me. Speak to me, for I am listening for Your reassuring words. I love You.

God: Dear one, I love how you chose to believe in Me and My Son and refused to take other possible paths. I've always looked past your weaknesses. But remember, it's through these that I show Myself strongest. Reach for My hand when you need it. I can guide you through unchartered territory if you will let Me. Just ask. You may or may not like the answers I give you, but just trust Me to steer you in the right direction. I'm always beside you. I'm your best friend. I was there when your parents conceived you and I watched for you to live one day for Me. I needed you to reach those you'd touch for Me. I've chosen you to be My advocate in this world. You'll reach many, and I will show you how. Open your hands and receive My blessings. It's a new year—a time for rejoicing and seeing My great wonders. Make a new commitment—to seek Me diligently in the dark places and through the difficult people I bring to you. Go with Me a step higher because My ways are not your ways. Through places and times that are hard to bear, seek Me. And let My still small voice guide and direct you. I love you.

As You show me how Your love is enough

"I love you, Lord; you are my strength."
—*Psalm 18:1*

Me: Lord, help me see Your hand in my life today. Would You help me to be thankful for all I have, to see that I have all I need, and to recognize that all I have is because of You? Would You help me to use my time in the most profitable way today by looking to You for guidance? Would You strengthen my hands to be able to give more? Let me seek You in my heart and mind today, not reacting to others' negative words or comparing myself to those around me. May I glorify You through all that I do. Would You help me to act and speak from a heart of love and never react out of anger or self-defense? I want to serve You and do my best for you. I want to be Your servant—ready to minister Your love to others. Help me to be my best for you. Help me to speak only the words You give me—words of peace, joy, love, gentleness, kindness, goodness, meekness, patience, faithfulness, and self-control. I am Yours today, Lord. Work in me to will and to do of Your good pleasure. Open new doors and expand my territory so I can reach more. I love You.

God: Dear one, shine as you do, and I will bring you people who want to receive My words of wisdom and hope. I'll direct your steps and your ways. I will bring people you can minister to—those to whom you can represent My presence. This is my purpose for you—to touch many with and through My love. Other things will begin to seem as nothing. You see, My love is enough. Through My love, you will always have what you need. With My love, you can heal hearts. You can depend on Me, because I'm always ready to help and heal you and meet your needs. You can come to Me with an open heart and let Me accomplish these things for you. My strength is sufficient for you. It gives you power to withstand any evil. You never need to be faint in your mind or doubt My ability. Evil will confront you, but You can resist it with the words I give you. My Word always brings deliverance. Through it, you have power and boldness. Don't be afraid to speak what I tell you to bring justice and a blessing to those around you. Continue to pray for others, because this too is powerful. Never let fear grip you. I stand beside you always. You have My army at your fingertips. I'm here for you, ready to hear your prayers and requests. So, why be afraid? I love you.

To prevail over discouragement

"Don't be selfish; don't try to impress others. Be humble, thinking of others as better than yourselves. Don't look out only for your own interests, but take an interest in others, too."
—*Philippians 2:3-4*

Me: Help me, Lord, to put off any self-centeredness. I want to be more concerned and mindful of others' needs. Would You help me bring joy and hope to those around me? You are righteous and just. You concern Yourself with our needs and watch over us with a loving eye. You bring us our hearts' desires and meet our needs beyond measure. But still, we often seek our own ways and put our needs before others'. It's discouraging to me. I'm sure it is for You too! Help me to rise above my own selfish concerns. Release me from self-pity. Help me to give and not be offended or hurt when others don't give in return. Open their eyes to how blessed they could be if they tried to reciprocate. You're good, loving, trustworthy, and true. Help me to be more like You, to be Your beacon and fulfill Your will. And to love others as You do. I need Your strength for this. I love You.

God: My child, I give you mercy when there's none to be found. I give you grace when you don't deserve it. I give you love when no one else will. The best way to avoid selfishness is to open your heart and receive the blessings I give you so you can spread My love around lavishly. Come to Me with your whole heart and follow My lead. Then your rewards will be great, not just in this life, but also in the next. Seek My will, no matter what the circumstances. People will blow hot and cold depending on how they feel, and their responses will not always match your giving. But let Me be what you need. When you feel attacked or like forces are trying to pull you away from what you know is right, look to Me and ask Me for help. I'll reveal Myself more and more to you as you pursue Me. When you're distracted, I'll remind you of what to say or do. Listen eagerly, and you will hear Me. I long to speak to you. I love you dearly because you desire to know Me. This tenderizes My heart and brings Me great joy. And My joy overflows to you. I want you to experience it too. You see, I've known you from the time you were conceived. I've desired you as a baby in your mother's arms, when others didn't think much of you. I favored and pursued you from childhood because I love you.

And see more of Your heart

"But it was to us that God revealed these things by his Spirit. For his Spirit searches out everything and shows us God's deep secrets. No one can know a person's thoughts except that person's own spirit, and no one can know God's thoughts except God's own Spirit."
—1 Corinthians 2:10-11

Me: Lord, I turn my thoughts to You today, and I seek Your heart in every situation. Is there something I need to know? Something I need to do? Please show me! Reveal to me more of Your greatness and how wonderful You are! I experience joy in Your presence. I sometimes cry at the thought of You. My heart is embraced by Your loving friendship. Thanks for the wonderful gift of Your Spirit when I believed in Your Son and what He did for me. Thanks for showing me how You reveal more of Yourself as I pursue You. Thanks for taking me by the hand and leading me to Your quiet place. Thanks for teaching me about love and opening my heart to it. You alone are worthy of praise, and I'm thankful for You. You're always with me, stirring my thoughts and whispering in my ear. You encourage me when I'm depressed. You enlighten my eyes. Thanks for all You do for me. I know You love me as I love You, and Your love can't be measured. Thanks for opening doors and bringing me light and life. Open more pathways so I can share with others. Bring me before great men and women who can teach me about You. Help me to grow up in You so I can better serve through Your love. I love You.

God: Dear one, I'll take you higher, but each new step will be harder. You'll need to depend more on Me so you can encourage those I bring to you. At times, you'll need to love the unlovable and support those who seem unworthy. And you'll need patience. It takes time for My promises to be fulfilled. But they'll happen soon enough. In your lifetime, I'll call you to places and people, which I'll reveal as time goes on. I'll show you when and where you must go. You'll stand before people and affirm to them My desires. You've seen My blessings. Isn't it amazing what I can do for you and what I've already done? You'll see more of My might and love, for these are compounded to you as you walk alongside Me. I've done so much for you because I love you. And My love never fades. Like sunshine, it pours down on you and makes you shine even brighter. It brings you joy. Continue to radiate it to others. I love you.

JANUARY 6
And understand what You gave

"People are made right with God when they believe that Jesus sacrificed his life, shedding his blood. This sacrifice shows that God was being fair when he held back and did not punish those who sinned in times past..."
—Romans 3:26

Me: I want to seek Your face, Lord! And I want to serve others and bless those around me. I want to make a pathway for those who seek You. Help me to do all these things for You by receiving the love that You pour out to me. For I want to offer You as my daily sacrifice of love. I want to begin to understand Your ways more fully. I want to walk for You with each step I take so that I can produce bushels of new fruit for You. Lord, work in me today and help me to minister to others. Would You open the windows of heaven spiritually, mentally, physically, and financially, so I can offer more and more of You? Would You count me as one of Your faithful ones—a friend, supporter, and partner? Would You lead me to the places You'd have me go—courts or alleys, private or public places? Give me words to speak and remove far from me any feelings of doubt, fear, impatience, or frustration. Shower me with Your kindness and show me Your immeasurable mercies. Let me see Your works in ways I've never seen before, because I really want to behold the eyes and hands and feet and face of Your Son. I long for this. I love You.

God: Child, kindness is deep. It flows from a pure heart and blesses whoever it touches. Love is even deeper. True love, My love, moves like blood. It flows slowly so it can seep into every crevice and cover the torn places by forming a patch, or scab, for protection, healing, and comfort. My Son shed His blood freely for you to form a covering so you can be healed from sickness, heartache, pain, suffering, and more. As you walk in pureness of heart by showing heart-felt love to people, you represent My holiness. To be holy means to be "set apart," and this is how you set yourself apart for Me. I never ask you to shed blood for others; My Son already did this. But you can walk in love and offer it freely to others. My deliverance will follow. Holiness means that you move away from unkind thoughts, because this can undo the healing properties of My Son's blood. Your job is to bring a message of forgiveness and freedom from brokenness or unkindness. Convey this message using words of love. Remember His shed blood covers and protects from harm. I love you.

January 7
To overcome any threat

"And remember, when you are being tempted, do not say, "God is tempting me." God is never tempted to do wrong, and he never tempts anyone else."
—James 1:13

Me: Lord, do You test us sometimes to see what we're made of? Do You allow threats to come against us to see what we'll do? Enlighten me in Your ways. As a God of love, make Your ways clear to me, and enable me to glorify You, even in a sometimes-hateful world. Help me to be stronger than my feelings and mightier than my thoughts. Help me to forgive ungodly people and be able to thrive in their presence because I know how much You love me. Help me to see their potential and the reason for their existence and be able speak to them with Your words of wisdom. Help me to be a beacon of hope to them and show them Your way. Give me strength to overcome any negativity with the knowingness that You are love and that Your love will always supersede hate. I love You.

God: Child, do you doubt Me or My love for you? Am I not real to you? Why allow the concerns and false views of this world to prevail in your mind? Why focus on negative things and let them overwhelm you? Why allow people to make you feel anxious or worry about things you have no control over? Or doubt that I am a good God? Am I not a loving Lord? Am I not the supplier of all your needs? Didn't I form, make, and create you? If I did all these things, why would I want harm to come to you? As a God of love, I do allow you to make your own choices, whether good or bad. And wrong decisions can lead to regrettable repercussions. But, if you come to Me, I can work everything out for good. If you listen, you can hear My voice. If you look, you can see Me in what I've done. You can view Me in the things I've accomplished in your life. Think about what you've prayed for. You trusted Me, and I answered your prayers. People sometimes wonder why their prayers go unanswered. I can give two reasons: first, they don't believe I can deliver, so they arrange things their own way and don't listen for or watch for My answers. Second, they grow impatient and give up too soon, before the answer comes. If they'd wait, they'd see My response. You may not see My face today, but you can see Me in My works. Watch for what I'll reveal to you. For I am a God of love and I care for you. And I love you.

When I'm surrounded by hate

"If the world hates you, remember that it hated me first."
—John 15:18

Me: Dear Lord, I'm so tired of dealing with ungodly and hateful people. I grow sick of haughtiness, self-righteousness, and political divisiveness. Would You show me how to deal with people who thrive on spewing dishonesty and hate? Would You help me to see and speak as Jesus did, directed by Your love and not driven by emotions or hatred? I want to represent You. Help me to be who You want me to be. Help me to know what to say, but mostly give me wisdom in how to react when I'm confronted by chaos or lies. Guide me, for, without Your help, I can do nothing in the way that's needed. Work with and in and through me. Thanks! I love You.

God: Dear one, My way never ushers in rude disruption or hatred or retaliation. When you see these things, you know I don't abide in that place. Remember how My Son was confronted by the Pharisees? He recognized that their gods were belief systems that drew others away from Me and enabled them to control people and circumstances. Their "boxes" defined how others could safely exist in their tightknit realm so that they could maintain their own power. Do you see how people do this today? Often politicians and religious leaders lasso others with "guarantees" of safety and provisions if they will just follow their rules and speak as they do. So, instead of trusting in Me, people are lured into trusting in false ideologies. I hate this because it draws people away from Me and a relationship with Me. As a result, many wander aimlessly at the mercy of the power-seekers. At some point, a few will wake up to the emptiness of their promises. I will bring those who seek answers to you, and I'll unfold My wisdom so you can minister to them and offer them enlightenment. That's your purpose. Show them what I've given you—the strength of a belief and hope in My Son. Show them that if they come closer to Me, they can live abundantly and have joy, love, and peace. Today, press into Me with your thoughts, then your frustrations will disappear. Remember My love, how it reaches far beyond the heavens? This love is in you, and you can use it to heal and bring answers of peace. When you witness true love, you know that's where I abide, for this is My trademark and the emblem of My heart. You will find Me there. I love you.

As I follow Your breadcrumbs

"The LORD says, 'I will guide you along the best pathway for your life. I will advise you and watch over you.'"
—Psalm 32:8

Me: Dear Lord, how awesome You are! I'm amazed each day at how You chose me—picked me out and showed me Your favor. Was it because I was looking for You? Remind me of the ways You confirmed Your presence to me when I was younger, for I sometimes forget. Help me to recall how You stirred my heart, especially during the times I felt most vulnerable. I believe You knew I would believe, so you placed before me the things I would need—the "breadcrumbs" to find You. Lord, open my eyes now so I can see clearly what You have in store for me and my family. I want to rely more on You and see Your hand in every eventuality. Help me see the breadcrumbs You're laying out for me. I love You.

God: My child, I've always been near you, but you weren't always aware of My presence. Remember when you were 11—you fell off the bridge and almost died? I sent My angels then to hold you and prevent your death. After that, on the way to church, you gazed out the car window and asked Me why you were still alive. Then, when you were 12, you looked up at the stars and asked Me about the universe and if I was there somewhere. I confirmed My presence to you, even then. When you were 19, I led you to believers who taught you about Me and unfolded My Word to you. Remember when you were 24 and felt alone? You saw a rainbow and thanked Me for it. I smiled on you because you remembered Me. I've always heard your prayers, and I appreciate each one. You're special because I made you that way. I longed for your friendship way before you were born. I made the universe for you. I made the trees, the flowers, the birds, the fish, the animals, and even the air you breathe. Why wouldn't you seek to understand My ways and how I operate? You deserve a relationship with Me, the Almighty One, who seeks to lead and direct your ways! I've always loved you with an unspeakable love. Even now, I care for your needs when others don't. I stand ready to guide you and give you grace, mercy, and peace. More than a few small breadcrumbs, I lit a fire that blazes inside you. It's bright enough to guide you through any darkness. It brightens and lightens each of your days and burns throughout your life. That fire is My Spirit inside you. I love you.

JANUARY 10
Past the uncertainty

"The faithful love of the Lord never ends! His mercies never cease. Great is his faithfulness; his mercies begin afresh each morning."
—Lamentations 3:22-23

Me: Lord, will this be a significant day? Will You bring me some unexpected treasure? This day feels special, like the bursting forth of a ray through a cloud! Enlighten me, Lord, for I'm blind to Your kindness at times. I do appreciate the lovely sunrises, which appear just as I crest the hill on my morning walk. No wonder I love to see them, since they remind me of how You'll come from the east one day, and Your voice will sound like many waters. Help me to recognize this sound and hear when You're calling out to me. It was nice to hear the owl hooting as I crossed the dam and to see a few walkers and joggers along the way. Make it a joyful, special day of wonderful, unexpected blessings. Show me more of Your heart and help me to see others' hearts more clearly. Help me to see even deeper to the root of each person. Would You open my eyes so I can view things as You do and not be trapped by my own blindness or held captive by my own delusions? Help me to see with clarity so I can know when You're stirring up someone for a reaction that will lead them to You. Would You help me to not be offended or hurt by peoples' self-centeredness and to remember to pray for them! For they are just ignorant. Help me draw them closer to You and touch them in remarkable ways by looking beyond myself. Thanks for Your help! I love You.

God: Child, you are precious to Me, like a beautiful gem—a topaz. I view you as very special. As I wait for you, I prepare you. Don't you know that nothing happens by coincidence? Even the lovely sunrises are prepared just for you to see! Never doubt My intentions for you. Don't doubt My ways or allow uncertainty to hinder how I'm leading and teaching you. As you wait for Me, I will show you what to do next. One day, others will see you as you are in Me. Because I work on your behalf, I'm bringing you to a breakthrough. Watch and see. Listen for My words and My messages, and I'll enlighten you. I give you strength. I bring you peace and mercy. I bring you light and life. Never focus on peoples' negatives or allow them to discourage you. Focus on truth—My truth. Focus on love—My love. For this is the key to My infinite treasure. I love you.

14

And discover Your hidden treasures

"Who can find a virtuous and capable wife? She is more precious than rubies."
—Proverbs 31:10

Me: Dear Lord, I remember a trip my husband and I took to Croatia. I'd prayed for divine appointments and had a strange dream one night. I was in a beautiful setting where a young man sang an inspiring song. Something glittered in the dirt, and I bent down to uncover a ruby ring. Then I woke up. That morning, we ran into a couple we'd seen before at breakfast, and they introduced us to their son, a missionary in Macedonia, who came to see them in Dubrovnik. They asked if we could join them on a boat ride to an island, and we ended up sitting in a beautiful area overlooking the water. Suddenly, the son began singing a song. It was the one in my dream! Then, the father asked if he'd found a ruby yet, since the son worked in a Macedonian mine. As we walked back to the boat, I saw a sign that read, "More," with an arrow pointing to where we'd been sitting. That night, we sat with them at dinner, and the wife confessed that she and her husband were separated but had reconnected so they could both see their son here. My husband and I prayed with them for marital healing, and they both cried. At that moment, I realized what the ruby in my dream meant. "Who can find a virtuous woman? For her price is far above rubies" says Proverbs 31:10. It refers to a wife who blesses her husband, and this husband needed to rediscover the ruby he had! I shared the dream with them and how You'd led us to connect and pray for their marriage. So amazing! I love You.

God: Dear one, see how amazing life is when you pay attention and make yourself available to Me? I'll speak to you often, sometimes through dreams, but you need to be listening, and you may need to ask for the meaning of the message. I will always make it clear, but not always immediately. Continue to listen for My voice, for I have so much to say to you! I'll speak to you in little ways and in big ways too. As a child, you came to Me with your questions. Even now, you stay child-like in your faith and expectation for answers. I love that. When people seek Me more than the praise and recognition of the world, or the attainment of experiences and possessions, I can come to them and speak gently, but powerfully, in their ears. Sometimes in unexpected ways! I love surprises and mysteries. And I have the power to help and heal hearts. I will direct you in what to do for people and how. Just follow My directions. I'll open the right doors for you to the right people. I love you.

JANUARY 12
Whenever I feel weary

"Love is patient and kind. Love is not jealous or boastful or proud or rude. It does not demand its own way. It is not irritable, and it keeps no record of being wronged. It does not rejoice about injustice but rejoices whenever the truth wins out. Love never gives up, never loses faith, is always hopeful, and endures through every circumstance."
—1 Corinthians 13:4-7

Me: Lord, I need Your help to love, because, of myself, I can't love people the way You want me to! I grow impatient and frustrated, and I often feel like giving up on the difficult ones. I'm weary of people who whine, and I resent being a cheerleader for those who can't seem to move past their fears and complaints and bad habits. I want them to grow up and move on! Especially when they're oblivious to their own capabilities and unwilling to use their gifts and talents. Many times, they're incapable of managing their lives in away that benefits themselves or others. They don't recognize the obvious and are unaware of what it takes to get things done. They make the same mistakes over and over despite the red flags. Then others spend countless hours repairing what's lost in the moments. Help me to love those who choose to be victims. Help me to nurture their goodness. I love You.

God: Child, how do you think I feel? I watch as people make the same mistakes over and over again, ever learning but never coming to a knowledge of the truth (2 Timothy 3:7). My own people are destroyed because they don't understand Me (Hosea 4:6)! They go 'round and 'round the same mountain, just like the Israelites! It's hard to be patient and forgive again and again. I know. But, in this life, you'll need to learn how. Jesus's disciples were rough, uncouth, and ill-mannered souls. If you think you have it bad, you should've seen these guys! But the reason for that is that even My Son had to "pass the test" of forgiveness, patience, and love! His ministry was to the broken ones. He had to work with them and show them how to stand against the wiles of the devil. Imagine being the leader of such a group of mismatched fellows! He put up with them and loved them despite themselves. You can do this too. Let Me work through you to love the unlovable. Then, watch as they blossom and grow. They will if you love them the way He does. I love you.

16

But see Your boundlessness

"Give thanks to the God of heaven. His faithful love endures forever."
—Psalm 136:26

Me: How boundless is Your love, Lord! I really can't comprehend it. You, Lord, bring me up when I'm down. You lift me to new heights and give me strength. You encourage me when all hope seems lost. You infuse strength into me when I feel like I have nothing left to give. You're my all in all, my everything. Today, I give all that I have to You. It's Yours to do with as You will. Please show me how to be my best for You. I want to serve You in wonderful ways. Surround me with Your goodness, especially in the times when my heart hurts from pain caused by others. Would You help me to manage my life in better ways? I trust You to lead me, and I ask for Your guidance. Would You bless my work and my family with the blessings that only You can give? I see how You can bring good things out of bad choices. Lord, bring amazing results to me today, and send a special blessing to remind me of Your powerful but loving presence. How boundless is Your love, Lord! I love You.

God: Dear one, I love you. Never forget this. I love your heart and each step you take in My direction. I appreciate your determination to follow Me. And it hurts My heart to see you stymied by others' hurtful heedlessness. People sometimes speak from a place of imagined cruelty. This creates a destructive cycle that spirals like a cyclone that disrupts many lives. And it all stems from torn-apart hearts and minds disoriented by brokenness and unforgiveness, because people often expect from others the kind of love that only I can give. Remember, I will always lead you to good things. You'll experience renewed joy when you see who I place in your path—people who once doubted and wondered about Me. But because their hearts have turned toward Me, they will come to you for encouragement. Now, let My Word live in your heart. Let it dwell in your mind and flow like a river through you. Then, freely give what I've placed inside you. I'll speak more to you as you listen. Yes, I want you to take the time to hear My words of encouragement. Spend time in My sanctuary. I'm your Lord, your God. I give grace and joy and hope—more than you have room enough to receive! I give you boundless love because You are my special child. I love you.

January 14
In all that my heart desires

"The Lord will work out his plans for my life—for your faithful love, O Lord, endures forever."
—Psalm 138:8

Me: Lord, You're so awesome. Your name is magnified above all names. I enjoy our relationship more than any other on this earth because You never disappoint me. Instead, Your ways are full of surprise and delight! You reward me for the good I do and somehow make the bad things right again, even when I least expect it! Would You continue to reveal more of Your purposes to me? Would You help me acknowledge You in all my ways? Thanks for fulfilling all my heart's desires! Help me to share Your love with others and never be hurt or disappointed by their words or actions. Help me to see the good in people and to move on without regret when I know that what I've said or done is right because You inspired it. I know You're guiding me. Help me live out Your mercy. Help me see others as You view them. Let others find Your grace through me. Show me who You want me to reach. Would You make that clear? Help me to keep my mouth shut when I need to and to speak what You tell me when it's the right time and place. Help me to absorb more of You today. I love You.

God: Dear one, I'm preparing you for great things to come. Remember, what may seem small to you now is usually a big thing to Me. There are people who want and need to hear from you. I will reveal them to you. You'll recognize who they are. Some people may reject you, not because of anything you've done, but because they don't want to go My way. Remember, it's not you they dismiss. They renounce Me. Some have their own gods: time, money, glory, praise, pride, or self. There's little I can do for these. But I'll show you the faces of those who seek My will. And I'll give you the words to say to them. You'll be amazed at what I can and will do through you. I'll bless you more than you can imagine if you just trust Me. Continue to arm yourself with My Word and clothe yourself with My garments of praise. Wrap My love around your heart to protect it from any onslaughts. Only My Word brings peace and protection, mercy and understanding. Only My Word brings deliverance from oppression and bondage. Continue in My Word. That is My purpose and My will for you. I love you.

Because You're a true friend

"For since our friendship with God was restored by the death of his Son while we were still his enemies, we will certainly be saved through the life of his Son. So now we can rejoice in our wonderful new relationship with God because our Lord Jesus Christ has made us friends of God."
—Romans 5:10-11

Me: Dear Lord, sometimes I feel discouraged when I have a hard time connecting with other people. I know You're beside me every moment, but would You help me feel more encouraged by sending people who are more like-minded? Would You help me see You in a way that's undeniably real through the insight of others? Help me experience more of Your glory, might, greatness, and awesome wonder through individuals who love You as I do. But, more than anything, I want to feel in a greater way Your love and acceptance! I seek You today with My whole heart. I see Your Son's face in every cloud and watch for Him to come! I recognize Your hand in every tree and snowflake, and I wonder how You made such exquisite things. I see You in the hearts of some. Thanks for these. Bring me more true friends who crave Your presence, long for Your Son's return, seek Your glory, and want to bask in Your love as I do. I love You.

God: Child, you sometimes feel sad because you can discern things that others can't. I've blessed you with great spiritual insight to see things supernaturally—through My eyes. This gift makes you feel alienated at times because most can't see what you see. But you can use this gift to help others determine what's ahead. Many are frustrated because they can't understand what's happening around them. You can teach them how to pull from the spirit within them for help and guidance. You can show them how they can draw from their own supernatural strength to overcome the obstacles. Most people rely on their limited senses, and they grow very confused by what they see. In this world, it's hard to understand how I can work or move when so many movements they see lead to hardship, violence, and evil. It's difficult for most to comprehend the love I have and how I work on behalf of those who love Me. Believe Me that My Spirit in you gives you great capability for love, comfort, hope, and peace. When you feel alone or discouraged, open your hands and heart to Me. Hold your arms out to receive what I have to give you. And I will lead you to the ones who long for My true love. It's as simple as that. I love you.

JANUARY 16
Who understands me

"I have come as a light to shine in this dark world, so that all who put their trust in me will no longer remain in the dark."
—John 12:46

Me: Lord, I'm grateful for people who respond and approach me with kindness. I love those who show appreciation for the things I do. And I'm so thankful when anyone returns goodness or love. I just wonder about the people who act with little regard for others. They don't seem to realize that when they treat others poorly, they themselves lose out in the end. And they suffer because of a loss of love in their own lives. Lead me to those You love, Lord, who also want to love You. And if there are some who are rough around the edges, but You're still working on them, would You show me who they are so I can see their hearts the way You do? Would You give me what's needed to prepare for the coming years? Help me to be ever watchful. Show me how to introduce light during darkness, peace amid hostility, love when hatred abounds, hope in desperation, sacrifice out of selfishness, plenty in the midst of scarcity, and courage when there's fear. Show me more of You! Help me turn to You when I feel frustrated and don't understand. How can I love when others don't respond? I love You.

God: Dear one, it hurts My heart when people are unkind or hateful to any of My children. When they act this way, they overlook the blessings they could receive and are unaware of the negative consequences they bring on themselves. Then they wonder why they are lonely, unloved, lacking, or sick. They blame others because they need to cover up their own anger, neglect, laziness, unforgiveness, and self-hatred. They refuse to let go of issues, and they dwell on what's wrong with everyone and everything, instead of turning to Me to find what's good. The more your eyes are on Me, the more you can see wonderful results. I can bring great things to pass in your life, despite the unbelief or negativity of people around you! You will see My great works as you put My thoughts on in your mind. Just stretch out your arms and receive My blessings. Know that I'm with you, always working to bring about your heart's desires. So, open your heart and receive My blessings! My love is real and true. My love surpasses all other loves. It comes to you with no strings attached. Because I see you as you really are—beautiful! And I love you.

And shows me true greatness

"You can enter God's Kingdom only through the narrow gate. The highway to hell is broad, and its gate is wide for the many who choose that way. But the gateway to life is very narrow and the road is difficult, and only a few ever find it."
—Matthew 7:13-14

Me: God, I know the gate to You is narrow because it's compressed by pressure. Please guide me through it! For, of myself, I'm weak and unworthy. The only way I can travel successfully through life is if You walk alongside me. I know I've been critical and prideful at times. I've thought ungodly thoughts and acted in godless ways. Please help me to look more at You and assume more of Your ways of thinking. I long to be closer to You in every way. I know that Your Word exposes, sifts, analyzes, and judges the thoughts and intents of every heart. All things are open and exposed, naked and defenseless, in Your eyes. Instead of striving so much for fleshly perfection, I want to rest more in Your spiritual excellence. Refine me as Your warrior, so I can fight effectively for You. Lord, let me be what You are to me. Show me what true greatness looks like. Open my eyes to what I need to know so I can recognize the enemy's wiles. Cover me with Your love so I may cover others with Your kindness. I love You.

God: Child, I love how you seek Me. I know Your weaknesses, and I understand how they can cause you to feel like you are less than worthy. Many people feel like they are without value because they have had little or no affirmation from others. They either remain weak, defenseless, pitiful, and below par, or they create barriers to hide their true feelings of worthlessness. Some create illusions of self-worth by inflating and vocalizing their ideas and actions to prove that they are valuable and important. But you, by believing in My promises, can overcome all sense of irrelevance, even in the darkest hours. As you come to Me, you receive more of My assurances. But rehearsing My promises takes practice. It's like a sport or a game or a talent that you undertake. The more you practice, the easier it becomes. As each negative thought comes into your mind, repeat the words I give you to replace it. This is your defense. It's what makes you great. By thinking My thoughts, you can always overcome. This is how I refine you. I love you.

January 18
And surrounds me with love

"We know how much God loves us, and we have put our trust in his love. God is love, and all who live in love live in God, and God lives in them."
—1 John 4:16

Me: Lord, today lead me to places where You'd have me go. I know You'll tell me if there's something I must do. Stop me if I'm entering a harmful place or teetering at the edge of a dangerous precipice. Nudge me if I need to move on or go to a special person or place. Show me clearly the right direction, especially as I face uncertain times. Would You let me see what Your eyes see? Would You place me where You want me? Would You give me right words to say to those in my path? And guide and direct me? If I need to make changes, show me. Give me Your wisdom, for You alone are holy. Your mercy is everlasting to those who seek You. I want to approach You with My whole heart and seek Your ways in all I do. I want to love with a pure heart fervently. I want to give my whole self because of Your love shown to me. May it engulf and surround me. I love You.

God: Dear one, I'm always near to offer wisdom, insight, and direction. Listen for my whispers, for they are available whenever you need to hear Me. I'll bring you opportunities to speak, the right words to say, and the courage to do what I've called you to do. Just follow My lead one step at a time, and remember that I always work on your behalf. As you approach people, remember that it's often hard for them to look to Me, because they feel overwhelmed and engulfed by their own situations. My purpose is to break through the barriers and offer them aid—with your help. But they must trust you, and Me, and that's hard for many whose eyes are on their own needs and frustrations. The reason Peter began to sink in the water as he walked out to Jesus from the boat was because his eyes were diverted by the choppy water and not focused on My Son (Matthew 14:30). Depend on Me today for what you need. Lean on Me to bring you greater peace. The world is a troubled place, and many seek counsel from the ungodly. Many seek pleasure but can't find it anywhere. I alone can give you true joy, happiness, peace, mercy, and an anointing of grace. People will see these things in you. Then you can shine My bright love to them, and they won't be able to deny it. Then you can speak what I tell you. I love you.

As the apple of Your eye

"The Lord directs our steps, so why try to understand everything along the way?"
—Proverbs 20:24

Me: Lord, thanks for your mercy in how You've guided me through every situation. Would You reveal to me the unfolding plan of my life? Show me Your love in ways I can't deny, and work through me to touch others in greater ways to change the course of history. I want to be like Joseph and work with You in powerful ways. Though he ended up in a land far from his family, You moved through him to provide life and sustenance to Your people and many others. He was friendless and lonely, yet out of his forsaken condition he brought about mighty results by heeding Your voice and responding to You. Lord, I'm not sure why I'm here, and sometimes I feel out of place. I'm often far from my family. But when the time's right, and I've accomplished what's needed here, direct me to the places where I can be useful to You. I may wish things would happen faster, but I know all things occur in Your timing. Even though I'm not a "fast starter," or greatly honored, I know that You're with me, and You love me! And Your presence brings me unspeakable joy. I love You.

God: Child, Do you see how the story of Joseph is like the story of My Son? Though they were betrayed and suffered at the hands of ones close to them, they were able to save many people. They went as forerunners to prepare a place for you by rising to stand in the positions of honor where I set them: Joseph next to Pharoah and Jesus next to Me. And, with their help, I've chosen a bountiful place for you to reside one day. Like Joseph, you'll rejoin the family members you once lost. And you'll rejoice with Me in a place more beautiful than you can imagine! I've blessed and honored you because I love you so much! You're the apple of My eye, and those who love you also love Me. You've been near to My heart from the time you were conceived, and you were chosen before you were born. I've been after you for a very long time because I knew you'd respond to Me with your love! I cry when you cry, and I mourn when you mourn. When others can't see what I see in you, it's because they're blind. I'm preparing you for great things in this life and the next. Be patient. I hear and honor your requests and forgive your weaknesses. And My hand is on your life more than you can know. Have peace knowing that I'm always directing your steps. I love you.

When I try to be good enough for You

"Then the LORD answered Job from the whirlwind...."
—Job 38:1

Me: I dreamed about Jesus again, Lord. Oh, how I love Him! He was with me in a room, gazing lovingly at me as He waited. But I had misgivings. He was young and handsome. Darkly complected with dark hair and blue-green eyes, he had a short beard and mustache. He was so full of life! But I was concerned. He was half my age. I was old and dowdy, and I feared He would be disappointed in me because I wasn't really worthy of His love. But I still prepared to go with Him. My mother was with me, helping me pick out something to wear. I tried on a long, whirly skirt and twirled around in it a few times, but it didn't suit me. I found another skirt that was more understated and put it on. I pulled on boots, but the heels kept buckling under me. Finally, I discovered a solid pair that fit me well. I found a simple top that matched the skirt and shoes, and I was almost ready. But then I realized He was watching me the whole time and I felt very self-conscious! He'd seen how my body was—not toned or tan or sleek. Obviously, I was not in great shape. And yet, He still looked at me admiringly. He seemed to love me despite my disappointing lacks. What hit me most about the dream was how He loved me no matter how I looked or what I wore. He saw me as one who loves You, and so He loved me too. I love You.

God: Dear one, do you know what this means: "I answered Job from the whirlwind?" It means that when you feel like life is whirling around you like a skirt that doesn't fit right, and things seem to happen randomly and you question where I could be in all of it, I will come to you and show you how I'm there with you, even in the midst of your storms. And I will, if you look to Me, show you My deepest thoughts and feelings for you and the whys and wherefores of life, and your eyes will be opened, and you will see Me waiting there, beyond yourself and your plights. I do this for those who love Me, who will stick with Me even through the storms of life. When you are beset by worries and wonder where I am, I'll show up and you will see Me. Though you can't make out My face, you'll recognize Me through My Son—in a dream or a vision or a person or a thing that comes to you. I will be there, and you will see Me in that place. But you must wait for that moment of recognition. For I will linger near you and wait until you do. I love you.

Yet You make me feel adored

"You have captured my heart, my treasure my bride. You hold it hostage with one glance of your eyes, with a single jewel of your necklace. Your love delights me, my treasure, my bride."
—*Song of Solomon 4:9-10*

Me: Lord, like so many, I want to feel adored. Recently I went to a friend's funeral, and the one thing everyone recalled about him was how he adored his wife. I thought of my grandfather and his love letters to my grandmother. He wrote so many touching words to express his devotion to her. When I read through this special collection of memories, I cried. We all yearn to be adored by someone. Sometimes I feel I've never really experienced this feeling. Lord, I seek Your face in this. I seek Your touch and Your loving words. Would You be my lover and remind me of Your affection with mementos of compassion? Fulfill all my heart's desires with Your comforting and warming words of delight, especially when I don't feel loved. I enfold myself in Your encircling hands of kindness. And I embrace Your caring heart of mercy so I can help others feel Your adoration. I love You.

God: Dear one, I adore you as no other. And I will always take care of you as a husband, a friend, and a lover. For you are My beloved bride. And I want your heart for Myself. I am jealous of your love because I've sought you out from before you were born. Yes, from the very beginning I've wanted to prove to you how much I adore you! Lean on Me now, and I'll confirm My great love for you, even through people I'll bring to you who will also love and appreciate you. They will be kind and wonderful people of faith who are waiting to meet you! And you will experience new levels of peace and blessing and love from these people. What seems like a very big thing to you is often a very small thing to Me. What seems very insignificant to you is often very important to Me. Think in these terms. I'll show you when an event or a happening is important and what the true meaning of it is. Turn your eyes and ears to Me, and I'll always fill you with My love. Look around you. Let Me open your eyes to what is truly significant today. There are more people than you know who appreciate you. More than anything, know that I will always adore you as no one else can. I love you.

As my dear Mr. Darcy

"And may you have the power to understand, as all God's people should, how wide, how long, how high, and how deep his love is."
—*Ephesians 3:18*

Me: Lord, today You asked me why I enjoyed Jane Austen's books. My reply was, "Because the heroines see through the airs, the deception, and the pretention of others and can discern true character, nobility, and worth beyond what others can see. They are pursued by ones they grow to love because of their sincerity and trueness of character. In the end, they are won over by true love." I love to watch one of the last scenes in the movie, *Pride and Prejudice*, when Mr. Darcy walks out of a mist toward Lizzie Bennet, and she realizes how much she loves him because she sees his heart revealed. This reminds me of You and how You, over so many years, sought and won me over by Your love and sterling character. You revealed to me, little by little, my own worth and value and how much I meant to You. You showed me my rightful place in this world and the next. And, more than these, the extreme love You had for me. And this was more precious to me than any worldly thing, whether it was a possession, an honor, or a value set by people. Lord, You are my Mr. Darcy! Thanks for Your constant reminders of Your eternal love. I love You.

God: Dear one, do you know how much I love you? How I've pursued you for so many years? How I've fought for you and stood next to you during hardship and hurt? I will always fight for you. I will stop the mouths of roaring lions who come against you! I will give you wisdom and direction and show you where you need to be and when. I do love you and am near you constantly. I have been—always. I am by your side even now and especially when you are in the midst of a spiritual battle. I fight for you, along with My angels, who lift their swords at My direction on your behalf. When you stand for Me, I stand at your side. As you issue peace and love through words that I give you, I'm your greatest advocate. I'm your best friend. I'm your biggest fan. I'm your most ardent lover. And I love you.

  Who brings me insight

"Love each other with genuine affection and take delight in honoring each other."
—Romans 12:10

Me: God, help me to love others as You love me. When I feel rejected or spurned by people, help me to see the goodness in them. When they overreact with anger because of their skewed views, help me to understand and see through their eyes into their hearts. Often, I find that their outrage stems from something entirely different from the feigned object of their emotion. Would You help me to see and think as You do with the positive insight that ushers in understanding, kindness, and forgiveness? Help me to relinquish all negative and unkind perceptions of others to You. Then You can do with them what You will! When I want to lash out in retaliation or see someone get what they deserve, remind me of what Your Son did for me. Help me to be as merciful as You are. Thanks, Lord. I love You.

God: Child, there will always be people who reject you or walk away from you, no matter what you do or how much you try to help and bless them. You see, it makes them feel better about themselves if they make you look weaker than they are, because, if they can find fault with someone whom they perceive to be somewhat stronger or more "renowned," this proves that their own mediocrity is not so bad. Women are often more threatened by other women than by men. This is because they expect men to be different and better in some things, but if a woman excels, this means that they should be able to do as well as her. Don't take this personally. As you know, it takes great effort to accomplish anything. And it takes persistence to overcome hurt, envy, accusation, hatred, and anger. Many people become bitter instead of better because they don't want to change their thinking from negative to positive. You can overcome any bitterness with My help. You see how wonderful My love is when it's shared with others? You see how healing My love is and how it restores brokenness of any kind? Remember this as you spend time with people. My love helps, heals, restores, and brings wholeness. People try so hard to do things themselves. And when they can't accomplish what they've set out to do on their own, they become frustrated and angry. It's not until they experience My love that, for the first time, their eyes are opened, and they truly see Me. And then they begin to understand life and who they really are. I love you.

When I feel alone

"God places the lonely in families; he sets the prisoners free and gives them joy."
—*Psalm 68:6*

Me: Lord, I sometimes feel alone. I sometimes feel betrayed and forgotten by others. There are times when I think there is no real love anywhere. People show love when they think it will serve their own purposes but when I really need to hear from them, they are nowhere to be found. Sometimes I feel disheartened and dismayed. I feel left behind. I know You desire my love and trust and attention. Would You remind me of this? I offer these to You now. I apologize for not always coming to You when I should. I do need You, and I'm thankful for You, though I don't always tell You. Thank You for being there for me and for always answering my prayers. Thanks for life and all You do for me and for others. Thanks for Your presence, for it is real. Thanks for being with me today. Thanks for showing me Your favor and love in unforeseen ways. Thanks for Your blessings and help. Thanks for helping me to help others who may feel the same way I do. You are faithful. You are light. You are love. Thanks for being near when I need You. I love You.

God: Dear one, you can see how fickle people are. That's why you can never stake your life on the words of those who won't listen to Me and are led by their own emotions and needs. People who are motivated by self, and oblivious to others, unknowingly hurt people like you because they are careless. They react out of pride and self-defense. And often they are offended by little things. Don't let them affect or control you. If you're not sure how to respond to them, turn to Me! I'll guide you. Never act out of fear of possible reactions or retaliation. Only I can know what will work and what won't. You can't base your plans on a fear of rejection. Base your aims on My guidance. Act out of a love for Me, knowing I will always steer you in the right direction and give you what you need. Let Me lead you with mercy and forgiveness. Let Me be your "white knight" to lift you up and cause you to be great in My eyes! I'm your king of caring and your knight of kindness. I bring you peace, and I shower you with lovingkindness, even when others can't and won't. People will often disappoint you. But I am steadfast in My love for you. I bring you wonders that are beyond the ways of this world. The world may let you down. But I never will. I love you.

But I press into You

"And I am convinced that nothing can ever separate us from God's love. Neither death nor life, neither angels nor demons, neither our fears for today nor our worries about tomorrow—not even the powers of hell can separate us from God's love."
—Romans 8:38

Me: God, today reveal Your presence as I read and reflect on Your peace, Your pleasure as I work, Your joy through ordinary tasks, and Your love through my conversations with people. Would You lead me into a more dynamic way today? And guide me in all I do so I see Your face in every encounter? Would You allow Your blessings to fall on me like soft rain showers of kindness? And then shine down on me and through me with rays of sunshine that can break through any clouds of darkness? Would You show Yourself to me in unexpected moments with splashes of love and beauty from unforeseen sources? Would You ease my mind and comfort me when hurtful blows are aimed against me? And remind me, when I feel angry or hurt by people, that it's never personal. Show me their heart and why they might be upset or offended. Help me to always look to You for guidance so I don't react or get hurt by others' actions or reactions. You alone can heal. Let me feel Your healing hand now and throughout the day. Thanks, Lord. I love You.

God: Child, as you press into Me, you bear more fruit and gain greater peace, joy, and love. You're doing a great job, and I'm so proud of you! Keep pressing into Me, and I'll keep helping you to shine your light despite any hardship or persecution. Now, gain more access to Me by rejoicing and thanking Me for all you have. Know that I made the heavens and the earth for you. I made the trees, the flowers, the birds, the fish, the animals, the insects, the air—everything! Why wouldn't I be real to you? Why wouldn't you seek to know and understand My ways and how I operate? Why wouldn't you desire a relationship with Me, the Almighty One, the One who stands in your presence, seeking to lead and direct your ways? I love you dearly with an unsurpassable love. I care for your needs, even when others may not. I stand ready to guide you, to give you grace, mercy, and peace. I defend you. I heal you when others aren't there for you. And My love never fails. Seek My reality—My great love for you. I love you.

To see Your tender mercies

"Lord, don't hold back your tender mercies from me. Let your unfailing love and faithfulness always protect me."
—Psalm 40:11

Me: Thanks, Lord, for getting me through another day. You're my protector, my fortress, and my guide. Lead me today over treacherous paths, up jagged cliffs, and through swamp-filled valleys to the safe harbor of Your arms. Let me bask in Your love and the sweet fellowship of Your tender mercies. You're my friend and my love. You give me comfort when there's none to be found. Help me to walk with You and to bring Your merciful love to others. Would You show me how to best operate so that I can glorify You in all I do? Let me clearly see the garden you've prepared for me, and Your flower-strewn walkway to get there, when I feel like I'm surrounded by thickets of thorny bushes, attacked by biting ants, and I can't seem to see clear of them. Thanks. I love You.

God: Child, do you see how special you are to Me? Do you understand your purpose and why I created you? Have you noticed the delights and wonders I've surrounded you with that are meant to bless you? So, why do you feel sad for yourself? Don't you realize that I made so many wonderful things for your fulfillment, and that I have your best interest at heart? Place your ear to My lips, and let Me whisper to you sweet words of comfort and hope. Turn your eyes to Me, and see My face looking adoringly at you. You're My sweet child, and I love you more than words can say. I delight in how you sought My love, even when you were surrounded by people who denied and rejected Me. Know that I always work on your behalf to bring you plenty during hardship and to spare you when others faint from fear. I want you to rejoice amid the world's desperation. Depend on Me as I open doors and bring you people who are hungry to hear of Me. You can show them who I am and how they can grow closer to Me. Follow My directions today and you'll see My great mercies. I have a plan that will last forever—one designed to bless you beyond your imagination! Lean on Me now. Let me steer your course toward wonderful and amazing things. Let Me lead you to truth. Be patient and remember that all things work together for good. It's hard to envision now. But one day you will see. I love you.

Through a white duck

"How sweet your words taste to me; they are sweeter than honey. Your commandments give me understanding; no wonder I hate every false way of life. Your word is a lamp to guide my feet and a light for my path."
—Psalm 119:103-105

Me: Dear Lord, thank You for this new day. Open my eyes to see everything as You do. Help me to experience it with Your heart and insight. This morning, I saw the white duck again in the same place near a dock on the lake. He had his head tucked under a wing, but he lifted it to watch as I walked by. He was alone and I wondered if he'd been rejected by the more colorful mallard ducks who swam nearby. I felt sad for him and hoped he would be able to join in with the other ducks. It made me think of Your Son and what He must have felt like when He walked among people. He knew He was unique and would never fit in with them. Help me to have compassion on others, Lord, and be sensitive to those who might feel rejected or alone or misunderstood, because they are different. Help me to open my mouth when the time is right so I can utter Your words of acceptance and love. You are a great and mighty God, and I adore You. Thank You for Your Son, Jesus, and for His sacrificial life and love for me and for others. He is worthy of all praise. Thanks for offering Him as You did to us. I'm amazed by You. Would You help me to understand and love as You do? I love You.

God: Dear one, can you love the unlovable just as you love that duck? Can you be patient with those who are different and not so smart or those who may have imperfect bodies or minds? It takes true love to be able to do this and a great willingness to help those less capable than you are. How can you love the stubborn, the rebellious, the hateful, the offensive, the opinionated, or the weak? It's hard. Jonah realized this. But, like him, you can. And I can help you. Today, as you go out, don't forget about My promises to you, for they are real. Turn your ears to Me and listen. Turn your eyes to Me and see. You'll meet some who seek Me as you do and some who long to hear and know Me but don't know how. You can bring them the new light of My Word that brings life and hope. You can speak into their hearts. I will reveal many things to you as time goes on, but you must turn your eyes and ears to Me. Then you will see, more and more, just how real I am to you and to others. I love you.

And how You make this fire very big

"I am the light of the world. If you follow me, you won't have to walk in darkness, because you will have the light that leads to life."
—John 8:12

Me: I glory, Lord, in Your magnificence, power, and might. I praise You for all You've done for me! You've provided for all my needs and brought me friends and family who love and appreciate me. You're unbelievable, Lord, how You open doors beyond my imagination, how You see what's in my own heart when I'm blind, and how You surround me with good things beyond measure: flowers, fragrances, colors, textures, and beautiful sunrises and sunsets. Thanks for bringing me here and for sparing my life. Thanks for Your precious generosity in every way—spiritually, mentally, physically, and financially. Now, this one thing I ask: How can I find and follow You wherever You may lead so I can bring others with me to your light? I think of Karen's servant, Farah, in the movie, *Out of Africa*. When she went on safari, he would go ahead of her and light a fire so she could find him and the camp in the darkness. He loved her dearly and wanted to be with her wherever she might go. So, when she was leaving him and Africa, he said, "You must make this fire very big so I can find you." Lord, would You make Your fire so big and so bright that we can find You, even when our eyes are blinded by the darkness? I love You.

God: Dear one, whenever you turn your eyes to Me, I will be there. For I'm your light-filled redeemer. You are singular in My sight, and you have a special place in My kingdom. In the Body of Christ each person plays a unique role. Some are My arms, some are My legs, and some are My hands and feet. You are My eyes. Open them wide so you can see what I want to show you. Because I will make Myself known to you and direct you to those who also need to see Me. I will lead you, but you must listen for My directions. Then you will know which way to go. Around every corner are new paths. It's like walking through the woods. You can't always see what lies ahead, but, as you move ahead, I'll guide you. Now you can only see for a short distance. But, if you'll hold My hand, I'll lead you. There may be roaring bears beside the path but, with Me, you'll always be safe. And, if you lessen your grip and lose sight of me, I'll keep a big fire blazing to light your way to Me. I promise. I love you.

So I won't feel alone

"Never let loyalty and kindness leave you! Tie them around your neck as a reminder. Write them deep within your heart. Then you will find favor with both God and people, and you will earn a good reputation."
—*Proverbs 3:3-4*

Me: Lord, I sometimes feel frail, weak, and imperfect. I often confront thoughts of defeat, hurt, rejection, and exclusion. Would You take me to a place where these things don't exist, where I no longer feel like this? Sometimes I see friends or family members get together, and they exclude me, and this makes me sad. Would You show me how to think and feel in these situations? I'm tired of feeling rejected. Who are my true friends, Lord? Are there any out there? Show me! Let today be a blessing, where time spent is joyful and true friends resurface. People often seem oblivious to others, including me! Help me to see as You see. I know You want to strip me of unkind thoughts. Help me to think as You do and to pull from Your treasure trove of love. Give me joy unspeakable. Lead me to those who seek You as I do. Uncover Your lovers, for I am blind and need Your eyes to see them. Sometimes I need Your encouragement, Lord. I love You.

God: Dear one, don't be discouraged by others' neglect. Continue to love, for love covers many shortcomings. It's in My love that you'll find your answers. These situations are not about you. They're about people who put their own needs first and don't understand how this affects others. I will work in these situations to bring about good. When people are unwilling to combine their efforts with Mine, I find others to work through. I'll bring good people to you so both you and they can be blessed. When people are filled with fear of loss or control, they make bad choices, and they say and do hurtful things. It's only in faith and trust that right decisions can be made. Today, walk in love and kindness. Let mercy prevail through you. I'll bring greater understanding, and you will prosper. Don't worry. Let Me bring you rest and peace and comfort. Let me bring you the love you deserve. Focus on Me and My will and I'll direct you. Let My arms of joy, love, and peace surround you. I love you.

And can see Your hand of mercy

"I pray that your love will overflow more and more, and that you will keep on growing in knowledge and understanding. For I want you to understand what really matters, so that you may live pure and blameless lives until the day of Christ's return."
—*Philippians 1:9-10*

Me: Continue Your conversations with me, Lord, for I yearn to hear Your voice and feel Your presence. And help me to be more like You in every way. Lend me Your healing hand today so I can minister as You would to others. Open more doors and give me Your strength to walk through them. And reveal to me what I need to know in each moment. Enlighten my understanding. Show me clearly how to discern good versus evil. It must bless Your heart when people really listen to Your words and then follow through! Let me touch Your heart today by hearing and doing things for You. I realize Abraham wasn't always perfect. At times he misled others, listened to his wife instead of You, and negotiated with You. But You loved how he came to You with his whole heart. Oh, that I might connect with You in the same way, Lord! Show me how deep is Your love! Open my eyes so I can see You and Your hand of mercy more clearly. Thanks, Lord. I love You.

God: Dear one, how I love you! You've come so far! But remember that you're always in a battle for your thoughts. The adversary wants you to focus on evil so he can render you incapable of bringing good things to yourself or others. Don't be fooled. Shortcomings, imperfections, and falsehoods will always surround you, and you may succumb to them at times. But I can use these for good if you will let Me. Take every thought captive, and give it to Me to deal with. Don't try to analyze what you hear or see. Only I know what's true, so come to Me for understanding. This will take a great burden off your shoulders and your mind. Keep your ear close to Me, and I'll tell you what you need to know. The world is filled with anxiety and turmoil. People strive endlessly to solve problems by smoothing over rough edges and recreating what I've already made to be good. Only through Me can you have real peace or understanding. This is not a profound thought or a new revelation. Through Me you can have grace and mercy. Let My healing hand be on you and let Me bring you peace today. I love you.

JANUARY 31
Even when I make mistakes

"The Lord is righteous in everything he does; he is filled with kindness."
—Psalm 145:17

Me: It's the last day of the month, Lord. Will I look back on these days with fondness? Will I wish I was here again? Help me to enjoy the days I have so I never regret things I've said or done. I want to rest in Your love and know that You work all things out for good. Help me to remember I can trust You to be there in every moment for me so I can have great joy in any circumstance. Help me to live each day to the fullest, love with my utmost, and depend on You to meet every need. That way I will never worry about tomorrow or yesterday. Because I don't want to regret past mistakes! Lord, be near me today, and help me to rest in an awareness of You. I pray it's a prosperous and blessed day, full of Your promises, peace, and protection. Open new doors to me. Show me Your continued kindness, and enlighten me to a greater understanding of Your love. Let my words be Your words so I can continue to drip honey on the hearts of those around me and bring them closer to You. I love You.

God: Dear one, can't you see that My hand is in everything? What you think of as mistakes are all part of a grander design. I can use even what you perceive as a small thing to build something great. You must begin to understand that what you view as misdirection or mistakes are used for my greater purposes. I've known about these things from the beginning, and I've outlined and designed a good path for you to walk on. I want more and more of your heart. So I arrange ways to bring you closer to Me. You can begin to understand more about how I work by spending time in My Word. Pay attention to the stories, for they reveal different parts of Me. I'll send messengers to you from time to time. They'll bring you words of encouragement, healing, peace, and hope. I'll remind you that I surround you with My love. You'll be awakened from sleep at times. When you are, I'll tell you to pray for specific things. I may show you people and situations to lift up in prayer. You are My prayer warrior, so partner with Me to best use your abilities. I'll reveal many things to you, but you must listen. Remember, when you pray, you bring My kingdom to earth by enabling My power to proceed from heaven into situations. Through prayer you can change the direction of the winds that blow from evil to good. I love you.

February

**FOCUS:
FAITHFUL FORGIVENESS**

*"Make allowance for each other's faults and forgive
anyone who offends you. Remember, the Lord
forgave you, so you must forgive others."*

—1 CORINTHIANS 15:58

I wonder how this can be

"You light a lamp for me. The LORD, my God, lights up my darkness."
—Psalm 18:28

Me: Lord of heaven, earth, the stars, the planets, and all the people who've inhabited the earth, please allow me to see Your purposes in a greater way and to know You in ways beyond my imagination! On a recent walk I looked down at the marred sidewalk, and You told me that this was how I saw myself. I often focused on my shortcomings, You said. But You don't see me this way at all! You look inside and view me very differently. You see my spirit and my heart and all that is good in me. How can this be, I asked, since I have so many faults? You explained that, because You are light, You see what You are—light. And, the more light I allow into my life through prayer and drawing closer to You, the more it emanates through and from me. It's my reflected light that You see. Darkness from unforgiveness, bitterness, anger, pride, and hatred blocks the flow of light and affects my ability to walk by the spirit. Getting rid of this darkness by repentance, or asking You for forgiveness, is crucial for survival, You explained, because it prevents me from having health spiritually, mentally, and physically. The more I walk with You, the brighter my light can be. Let my light shine today, Lord! I love You.

God: Dear one, it's during the quiet moments, when you see nothing happening, that the most is actually occurring. That's because it's during these times, when you're wholeheartedly seeking fellowship with Me, that you're employing My greatest power. As you come to Me, I'm able to work in and through you. It's by looking at Me, and letting My light flow through you, that you can see more of My glory, power, and might. After He prayed, Jesus fed multitudes with a little bit of fish and bread. He walked on water, healed the sick, and delivered the destitute and broken—all after He spent time alone with Me. During your times with Me, I will give you great ideas to help you accomplish your purposes on earth. Each moment with Me brings a precious opportunity to believe and act. And see miracles. Remember My Word and how powerful it is. It brings light and life. It ushers in healing, abundance, grace, mercy, and peace. I am the Father of light. I always promote joy and give understanding. I alone can separate light from darkness. Walk with My light today. Live My mercy. Heal through My forgiveness. I love you.

And how to deal with people

"The Lord is for me, so I will have no fear. What can mere people do to me?"
—Psalm 118:6

Me: I feel ill at ease today, Lord. Maybe it's because of the lack of integrity and deficit of caring I see in so many people. I watch more and more respond with cruelty, anger, hatred, abruptness, and impatience. I also see people running after influence, wealth, or control with little consideration for those they take advantage of to attain it. These things bother me. Would You help me be strong and remember to pray when I see deception, dishonesty, and lack of integrity? I find my own fear of reprisal and lack of willingness to act very bothersome at times. And I sometimes worry that people will be offended by my outspokenness, so I don't say what needs to be said. Help me to overcome this angst. I grow weary of those who won't confront their own negativity and brokenness. Maybe they don't care? Show me how to deal with this lack of concern. And my own. Help me to hear You clearly during these times and to give a proper response that can change people's attitudes and lives for good. Thanks for Your forgiveness for my failure to act when prompted and how You make all things work for good. I want to speak Your wisdom when it's appropriate. I love You.

God: Dear one, remember when I showed you Ezekiel 3:5-8, and I told you that I called you to minister to stubborn people? Sometimes these are the very ones I pursue as My bride. Their hearts may be hardened because they've listened to the wrong voices, but I continue to work on them. And it may take time. When people complain to or about you, it's often an excuse for not receiving what you or I have tried to tell them. They may not listen now, but, eventually, they'll come to themselves and realize that the real problem lies in their own lack of humility or willingness to fight through their fears. Someday, some will return and thank you for what you tried to show them. Men are conditioned to fight and work through their pain or fear; women sometimes run from their problems or try to manipulate people or situations to change their circumstances. You are different. One day you'll see why I placed you where I did and the impact you had on so many people. You try to work through your own fears, but sometimes you still worry what others think about you. I'll help you with this fear too. I love you.

   As I struggle

"Since God chose you to be the holy people he loves, you must clothe yourselves with tenderhearted mercy, kindness, humility, gentleness, and patience."
—*Colossians 3:12*

Me: God, thanks for preparing me so I'm able to answer people's questions. Would You protect and overshadow me so that the credibility of my words—Your words—is never reduced to rubble by unbelief, skepticism, blindness, hatred, jealousy, or anger? Would You show me the true hearts and areas of entrée, and help me to love people despite their negativity or lack of acceptance and agreement? And forgive me for my need to trust at times. Forgive me for my frailty. Forgive me for my humanness and weakness. Because sometimes I forget that my strength and power come from you alone and not from myself. I'm trying to be more like You and to represent Your good will in everything I say and do. I want to only think Your thoughts of others, to not react with impatience, and to speak only Your words. But I struggle. Would You show me how to deal with people who try to control others through rudeness, unkindness, intolerance, and manipulation? Show me how to respond, what to say, and when to speak. Help me to shine Your love and presence always. Thanks for this, Lord. I love You.

God: Child, sometimes people are so focused on their own point of view that they're blind to what really matters. It's not you! It's them! This is their problem, not yours. Forgive and love as best you can. When this fails, move on! Remember, you were once lost, but now you're found. You once squandered what you were given, not knowing the treasures available to you. Now, your eyes and ears are open to what is real. Now, you're enlightened spiritually and mentally. And you've received so much of My abundance. Don't squander it by throwing your pearls before swine. Don't waste precious time. You must continue to walk forward into the light, where you'll see others like you. It's a path toward greater wisdom and wonder. Continue toward Me and the magnificent beauty of My Word. Shine my peace. It's in you to give and to share. Don't let others' unbelief and discouragement push you down or make you feel small. I love you no matter what you do. I stand by you and uphold you. I already forgave you. Remember—you were lost. But now you're found. I love you.

To live forgiveness

"If you forgive those who sin against you, your heavenly Father will forgive you."
—Matthew 6:14

Me: How sweet it is, Lord, to sit and converse with You, to get Your feedback and answers, and just to hear Your voice! Thanks for Your help in dealing with people. Thanks for standing up for me, mediating for me, and supporting me! I've been frustrated not knowing how to be patient at times, especially when people overlook important things and end up hurting themselves and others. I've known few who were merciful or patient with me, so I ask You how I can have these qualities toward others? I desperately need Your help with this, because it's difficult for me to handhold others when no one ever did this for me! Not even my parents, who expected me to problem-solve, figure things out, and achieve perfection on my own. So, Lord, would You be my teacher? Would You show me how to be a better leader, mentor, guide, boss, spouse, mother, colleague, friend, etc. Thanks. Forgive my impatience. Help me, for I'm not sure how I can do these things. I can't, without Your help and guidance. Thanks for being patient with me. I love You.

God: Dear one, you've always struggled with forgiveness and letting go when others, through fear, lack of concern, or self-interest, looked past you or reacted harshly to what you said or did. Sometimes people, because of self-involvement, don't want to be included in your life or to hear what you have to say. Sometimes they don't see what you see as important. To them, it lacks appeal. But I see your heart. I see how earnestly you try to include and be included and how much you yearn for a close-knit family. I do too. True fellowship with people means more to me than you can fathom. I made mankind for this reason. I long for your attention, and I want to serve and help and guide you. As you turn your thoughts and attention to Me, you will understand more thoroughly My nature, which is good. All beneficial things come from Me. I created the earth for you to bless you and bring you great joy. Continue your fellowship with Me, for it is great joy to Me. Through it, you'll begin to know more deeply My love that is poured out to you. And you'll begin to understand how to forgive as I do. And many you touch will respond to your overriding love and forgiveness. I love you.

When some never come through

"Oh, what joy for those whose disobedience is forgiven, whose sin is put out of sight!"
—*Psalm 32:1*

Me: Lord, forgive me for my unforgiveness. Help me to pardon when people don't come through the way I wish they would, when non-responsive eyes greet me, and when efforts aren't made to reciprocate with kindness or thoughtfulness. I know I must forgive, but it's hard at times, Lord. I know people often mean well, but sometimes they seem oblivious to me and to others. Help me to overlook their faults and be able to see the goodness in them. Show me how You see them. What should I expect, and how do You view them? Help me to see as You see. Help me to be kind and to do things Your way, even when I don't feel like it. Show me how I can love the unlovable. Help me to forgive and move on. Teach me how to better help those who need healing and a helping hand. Sweep me up into Your sweet, encouraging, loving arms today, Lord, so I can overflow these things to others! I love You.

God: Dear one, I'm a God of mercy. Come to me with an open heart, and I'll refresh your mind and thoughts and expectations. I'll give you new ways of viewing things, including people who are hateful and abusive! I'll heal your heart from any unforgiveness. Listen to Me, and I'll work with you in incredible ways. I'll tell you amazing things that are beyond your comprehension! When you ask to be able to forgive others, I'll give you ways to accomplish this. Your requests enable Me to work in and through you. Your faith from Me produces the power needed to overcome any wrong thinking. But you must also ask for forgiveness for yourself—for your own lack of mercy. And remember all the things I've pardoned you for! People are imperfect. They'll make mistakes and sometimes behave improperly, sometimes even offensively. You must forgive them and move on in your heart. Don't anchor your thoughts on their disrespect or unkindness. Leave them to Me. But you must absolve their actions and try to understand their hearts. I'll help you with this. Using My power, you can do this. Work with others as I work with You—as with children who have innocent hearts and minds. Don't ever assume evil in those around you. I'll always reveal their true nature and their real heart if you ask Me. You see, so many times people are oblivious to or focused on their mistakes and weaknesses, and they are ignorant of their great strengths. I love you.

But You show me how

"I am praying to you because I know you will answer, O God. Bend down and listen as I pray. Show me your unfailing love in wonderful ways."
—Psalm 17:6-7

Me: Lord, I often feel remorse for the moments I've wasted in regret and anger, bitterness and spite, unforgiveness and hate. Would You help me not to focus on actions and thoughts that don't glorify You or help me to have Your peace and joy and love? I want to move forward with Your help! Would You show me how to magnify You in all I do today so I can become a better, bigger person? I want to be able to rise above strife, unforgiveness, and senseless words and behaviors. Help me to use my time most profitably by doing what needs to be done to best serve Your people and bringing glory to Your name. I am weak. Help me to be strong enough to stand upright before You. Speak to me and pour Your anointing wisdom and power and love all over me. Thanks, Lord. I love You.

God: Dear one, don't fret or worry over past mistakes. Allow My peace to wash over and cleanse you. Let My Word heal and strengthen you and bring you wonderful peace and joy. You worry about small things. Don't allow what's diminutive to grow so large that it takes over your thoughts. Lift it up to Me immediately so I can handle it for you. I want to do this for you. You don't have to problem-solve everything. I am your wise God, and you can come to me for answers. I'm also a God of mercy and forgiveness. Allow My love to reign in your life and take preeminence over all the little worries and fears and regrets. Focus on My forgiveness. During distress, it's easy to forget Me, but that's the time you need Me the most! That's the time to turn your heart and mind and thoughts to Me, because I am the One who can heal and deliver you. Only I can bring great peace and calm, even amid turmoil. Only Me. Now, lean your ear to Me and let Me speak kind and loving words to you. Let Me ease your mind and your soul. I can do this because I'm a loving God. I forgive those times you forget to come to Me and listen. I'm ever near you, ready to help and hear and serve you. You need only ask. Never forget I'm always here. And I love you.

FEBRUARY 7
By revealing Your heart for me

"Take delight in the Lord, and he will give you your heart's desires."
—*Psalm 37:4*

Me: Dear Lord, I need to know that my dreams are also Your dreams for me. I understand that if the direction I choose is of my own inclination, I can only go so far. And I will only be able to accomplish my goals through my own efforts and ability. On the other hand, if my dreams are also Your dreams for me, I will have access to Your supernatural power to be able to fulfill them. And I want so much for my efforts to glorify You. Would You open my eyes to what I need to see? Would You clearly show me the path You're paving for me? I'm sometimes frustrated at not seeing the fulfillment and fruition of my own plans. And I wonder if they're just mine and not what You want for me! Forgive me for my mistakes if my eyes have turned away from Your focus for me. I want to best serve You and be able to help others. But sometimes I'm admittedly sidetracked by my own or others' disappointment, and I grow frustrated with my inability to accomplish my plans. Just show me clearly if I'm on the right track! I want my life to be an example of Your gracious greatness and amazing ability. Because I love You.

God: Dear one, the fulfillment of great dreams requires patience and perseverance. It may even demand your blood, sweat, and tears. But often these are the ones most precious to you, to Me, and to others. When My Son gave His life for you, it required His all! But see how precious a gift He gave and what the results were? Now, you can be part of a spiritual family alongside those who understand the cost of that sacrifice. Accomplishing significant and meaningful dreams always requires some sacrifice. When you give your all, the return to you will always be beyond your expectations. I'll show you how, but you must listen during your weakest moments, when you're tired and drained and pushed to the extreme. The greater the goal, and the more it affects others' wellbeing, the more you must fight against spiritual forces to achieve it. The accomplishment of such a goal can be a wonderful example to others, because it encourages them to strive for their own dreams. Today, focus on Me, not on what's around you. Look for the ways I can help you reach your heart's desires. Remember, I can bring you closer to accomplishing your dreams, which are also My desires for you. I love you.

FEBRUARY 8
And how You want me to reign with You

"If we endure hardship, we will reign with him."
—*2 Timothy 2:12*

Me: Lord, over and over You show me how You make lemonade out of lemons. I read about the women in Jesus' lineage, and I realize that so many of them were viewed as outcasts by the people of their day. The list includes Tamar, Rahab, Ruth, Bathsheba, and even Mary. Lord, You constantly show me how it's by Your grace alone that I can receive Your blessings. It's not by my own or others' accomplishments, acceptability, or esteem, but only by my belief and trust in You that I can have access to Your power and ability and healing grace. And I see, as I sit here feeling at times broken and unworthy, that it can only be by Your hand that I'm made whole or deserving of You. I need Your help today, Lord, to break through the barriers that surround me. For only You have the power to lift me up or set me in the right places. Would You help me to forgive myself and others for how far we've fallen away from what You intended for us? And restore me to Your place of grace and peace. Thanks, Lord. How I love You.

God: Child, My intent is that you will reign in My kingdom with Me. To prepare you for this, you must endure many tests. Of course, I'll be with you to help you so that you can pass these trials. One test is for submission to Me in all things. You've wondered why wives are asked to submit to their husbands, when you know I've made all people, regardless of sex, race, or class, to be equal in My sight. But there's a special test for women because of the fall. You see, Eve was tempted by pride. She began to think of herself as more competent than Adam, because she listened to the enemy, who enticed her to believe that she knew better than him and Me. When she ate the apple, she said to Adam, "See, it didn't hurt me at all. And I think I'm smarter now." And Adam, who loved her, listened. Women are the same today. They tend to think they're smarter than men and are often lifted up by pride. Then they strive to prove that they can do things better. Because of Eve, I give them this test to see if they can submit to authority and to Me. That's the challenge for them and also for men. The real test is if any can be humble enough to submit to one another in love. If you can pass this test, you have come a long way and are much closer to being ready to reign in My kingdom alongside Me. Let's pass this test together. I love you.

And embrace Your treasures

"He has removed our sins as far from us as the east is from the west."
—Psalm 103:12

Me: Lord, forgive one who spoke unkindly to me recently. And pardon me if I said something I shouldn't have said in return. Bless him, Lord, and work in his life so that he has peace and can overcome bitterness. Awaken him, Lord, to what a relationship with You is really like. It's not just about reading words on a page or hearing a teaching preached. It's a heartfelt reality where one can hear Your whisperings and feel Your nudgings. Let him be swept right off his feet with love and a desire to know You as his dearest friend! Only then can his heart be healed. Help me to arise and love despite others' cynicism. If I need to love one who isn't ready to reciprocate, show me how. Help me to abide in Your peace. This day is Yours, Lord! You're mighty beyond my understanding. You fulfill my dreams and give me vision. Open my eyes and let me see You as You are in all Your glory! Would You help me to know You for who You really are? Forgive me for not living up to Your desire for me at times, Lord. You are gracious. You are kind. You are plenteous in mercy. Help me to manifest Your wonderful attributes to others. I love You.

God: Child, of course I always forgive you. Your sins are as far from Me as the east is from the west. And it's nothing for Me to do a small thing for you. It's like stopping a rain shower when I've created the heavens and the earth! I made you. Don't you realize how much I want to bless you, and others, and make you joyful? Continue to come to Me, for I'm always available to you. And I can do so much more for you as you forgive others. I can reveal more of My treasures to you. Seek me throughout the day. You'll find Me, sometimes in the least likely places. I'll bring people to you who love you as I do. Shake the dust from your feet when some oppose you. You're My child and I love you more than I can express. You give Me great joy, just as your own children or grandchildren do when they tell you how much they love you. Let Me direct you in all your ways and bring you My great joy. Look to Me for answers, thoughts, strength, and the keys to open life's doors. Look to Me for messages of hope and peace and love. Look to Me to give you the light you need. Then I can show you the way clearly. I love you.

FEBRUARY 10
And see heaven with my heart

"You quieted the raging oceans with their pounding waves and silenced the shouting of the nations."
—Psalm 65:7

Me: Lord, thanks for getting me through each day! Help me to make it through today too! You're awesome, powerful, and mighty. Would You shine Your love and grace through me to those who are merciless? Would You help me to focus on You when I'm in the midst of a storm? Remind me to be kind when tumultuous waves crash around me as people hurl accusations or offensive insults at me and act out of ignorance. Help me to forgive them. Because You're my inspiration. You give me direction. You show me how to ebb and flow with Your love. You show me how to gracefully ride at the top of every wave that mounts against me. Give me Your strength and power to continue to surf with Your power, Lord! Protect me from the evil forces that try to undermine my good intentions. Show me their wiles and how to overcome them with Your Word. You are love, light, hope, forgiveness, and peace. You give rest when I need it desperately. Help me to have a peaceful day by seeing what I need to see. You're awesome, Lord! I love You.

God: Child, heaven and hell are determined by the heart. I give all people choices, and I watch to see what paths they choose. Then I determine the best place for them. If they continuously reject Me, even after I've offered them love and help out of miry messes.... If they continue to choose the enemy's darkness instead of My light.... If they take the devil's hand instead of Mine consistently.... I consider all these things. My own hear My voice. They follow My steps and come to know My ways. The kingdom of heaven is not attained by perfection but through a willingness to serve and become more like Me. It's as simple as that. My followers will be with Me for eternity. Others will not. They will be reserved for judgment in a place they've willingly chosen. Now, don't be distracted by the choices of the people around you. These diversions can trip you up and cause you to swerve away from your destination, like roadblocks or hazards that pop up unexpectedly. They will try to steal your thoughts and keep you from focusing on Me. Watch and be vigilant. Listen attentively to what I tell you. I'll warn you. But you must listen and heed My words. I'll always prepare you to face tumultuous times. I'm preparing you even now. I love you.

So I'm never swayed

"For you look deep within the mind and heart, O righteous God."
—Psalm 7:9

Me: Lord, my heart hurts and it's hard to reach up to You for healing. Because I feel crushed. I don't want to be swayed by the words people speak. I don't want them to pierce my heart the way they often do. Would You show me Your thoughts about the hearts behind the words? You told me once that there would be "Judases" in our lives. They'd be people close to us who'd betray our confidence and trust. The adversary infiltrates their minds with evil thoughts and uses them to try to hurt or suppress us. In every situation, let me seek Your protection and the wisdom I need to overcome this kind of betrayal. You're the only God of love, peace, and joy. Show me how to resist the evil and abide in Your peaceful place. I know You're preparing me for something. Show me what it is. I trust You, Lord. Others will fail me. Only You prove to be trustworthy. Forgive me for straying from Your ways and closing my ears to You at times. Help me to listen more closely to Your instructions. Help me to resist destructive and discouraging words. I want to hold true to You. I want to adhere to Your Word and heed You in each moment. I want to forgive. I love You.

God: Child, yes, I'm absolutely preparing you for something! People will rise up against you—some of them close friends and family members. But I want you to be prepared by equipping yourself with a greater knowledge of Me so you can resist these attacks. I'll defend you when others try to crush you. Some will speak evil of you and denounce what you've done or said. As long as you follow My instructions, and speak what I tell you, they'll be proven wrong. You'll be tempted to react with anger to their hateful words, but if you follow my lead, their words will crumble and become like dust that is swept away by the wind. But you will stand firm if you continue to trust in Me and realize that I'm always working on your behalf. I continuously move to bring you what you need. Only believe and trust that I'm able to do this. Your prayers are precious to me. They are like valuable gems. Never belittle your time with Me. It's priceless. Remember, your requests for help, healing, and strength will open doors for your heart to remain strong and for Me to be able to heal it. Then you can forgive. I love you.

Because I can see His face

"And they will see his face, and his name will be written on their foreheads. And there will be no night there—no need for lamps or sun—for the Lord God will shine on them. And they will reign forever and ever."
—Revelation 22:4-5

Me: Lord, I cried when I read in the last chapter of John how Jesus appeared to Peter and John and the other disciples on the beach, after He'd died and risen from death. I thought about how they must've felt overjoyed to see Him again and be able to sit with Him and share a meal. How their hearts must have melted with adoration and appreciation and awe! How their minds must have been overwhelmed to see His face and to realize that He really had risen, just as He said He would. I yearn for the time when I can sit with Jesus by a fire and eat and talk and share and ask questions and get to hear His responses! I hope this will happen sometime soon. I long to see Him and touch Him and be in his presence. We can talk daily, because of Your Spirit in me, but I still long to gaze upon Him. Lord, could today be the day You let me behold Your Son? I love You.

God: Dear one, I know you seek My Son's face. It's there—in front of you. The answers are there too. And there are many who seek to know and see Me, just as you do. Bring them My message of love and hope. Many look everywhere for it. Remember Jesus's words to Peter as they sat on the beach by the fire? He asked him three times, "Do you love me more than these?" Then, he said, "Feed My lambs. Tend My sheep. Feed My sheep." I'll bring you lambs to nurture. Watch for these. You're My messenger, so bring them My message of peace. Do you love Me? Then seek Me when you rise up and when you lie down. Do you love Me more than these? Then, as My disciple, seek Me at all times! Because I'm always there to be found. I open doors and show you what you need to know each and every day. Do you see how Jesus forgave Peter there on the beach for denying Him before His crucifixion? You can also forgive those who've hurt you. I've already dealt with them. But you—have peace and joy in your own heart. Then your mind can be clear to focus on where I want to lead you—to My lambs, My sheep. Never seek recompense through vengeance. That's My job. I'm a God of peace, hope, love, and joy. As you continue to seek Me, you will find me. And there you'll also find My Son. And behold His lovely face. I love you.

When You take me up to Your mountain

"Who may climb the mountain of the Lord? Who may stand in his holy place? Only those whose hands and hearts are pure, who do not worship idols and never tell lies."
—*Psalm 24:3-4*

Me: Lord, You're my Lord. Help me to see things through Your eyes without being so distracted by the things around me. I'm thankful that the little things that used to upset me no longer rile me the way they used to. Would You help me to see in an even greater way how You view things? Help me to forgive people for their slights and see them the way You do. And help me to forgive myself for my own failures. I see now that often mistakes are part of Your plan. Would You help me to see beyond the things that try to get in my way? Take me up to Your mountain so I can see the sights You want me to see and have Your overall scope of things. For You have a 360-degree view and can see the world with "3D" vision. My sight is obscured. Open up my vision, and draw my eyes to what You want me to see! Thanks, Lord. You're awesome. How I love You!

God: Dear one, remember that I desire your love more than anything. Today, direct your thoughts to Me as you work so I can show you what I see. I know how tired you are at times. But you must endure to the finish. I'll bring you needed rest and joy along the way. I understand the difficulties of life—dealing with unkind and unhappy people. Know there are many who appreciate you and will always feel this way. For these I've placed you where you are. You've begun to rely on Me more. Because of this, things don't rattle you as they once did. This makes Me happy. I continue to work on your behalf to strengthen you and bring you people who want to hear what you have to say. Focus on what I show you about them, for many seek My counsel, and you can lead them through the door to My truth. Listen to Me so I can protect your heart. And I'll help you to forgive. Bend your ears to Me, and I'll tell you wonderful things that will melt your heart. I'll open your eyes so you can shine My love to those I bring you. I'll caress you with My peace and warm you with My love. Breathe deeply the pure air of My Word, like the fragrance of a lush pine forest. Let My joy run through your veins, heal your mind, clarify your vision, and strengthen your spirit. Lean into My arms as I lead you up to My mountain! I love you.

And show me a day of forgiveness

"I know the one in whom I trust, and I am sure that he is able to guard what I have entrusted to him until the day of his return."
—*2 Timothy 1:12*

Me: Dear Lord, it's Valentine's Day. Let it be a day of love and forgiveness. Let it be a day to understand and know Your heart in a greater way. I thank You for my many earthly loves. Thanks for bringing them all into my life and blessing me mightily through their presence. Thanks for all the things I learned from each friend along the way. Their words and actions and presence encouraged me and brought me more wisdom. Would You help me to be to others what some have been to me? Help me to forgive their shortcomings and place them in Your hands, because You can encourage them more than I can. Let this be a miraculous day of blessings. Help me to surround others with Your love by heartening them with Your vision. Help me to focus on Your words and be able to accomplish what matters most. You're able and willing to do all You've promised. You're a ready source of power, might, strength, confidence, healing, and faith, and I thank You for these gifts! You alone give goodness and abundance. You alone help in times of trouble and lift me up when I fall short. I can turn to You with my whole heart, and Your message is always clear. You never disappoint me. You'll always be my first love. I love You.

God: Dear one, today is a special day, not because it's Valentine's Day, but because I love you so much. Do you see how meaningful your prayers are to Me? Do you see the power behind your petitions as I take them into My own heart? Your bended knee is awesome to Me! When you ask, I always hear and honor your requests. Know that You're My princess, My bride! I'll always give you the strength you need to accomplish what's needed. I have the power to do this. Today, rest in Me, and let Me work for you. You see how I have. And you'll continue to see Me work on your behalf. All things are in My hands. Don't worry. I forgive your shortfalls. Today, you'll see the signs of My great love, mercy, and grace toward you. Today, open your ears and hear My mighty words. Spend time in prayer. Let the light of My love shine all over you and penetrate the deepest parts of your heart. See its magnificence as I lead you step by step on this journey. Believe and see that I love you.

And fill me to overflowing

"I know all the things you do, and I have opened a door for you that no one can close. You have little strength, yet you obeyed my word and did not deny me."
—Revelation 3:8

Me: Lord, I seek You today with my whole heart. I look to You for guidance, because I know You're my only true source for it. Would You give me the strength to serve and to be as much of a blessing as possible to those around me? Help me to be a source of peace and joy for others. Help me to seek You in all I do and to soak up Your wisdom like a sponge. I want to absorb as much as I can from You so that others may sit and gain more understanding from me. Let me be a vessel for You—one that is filled to overflowing with Your mercy and kindness so I can pour these out to those who are thirsty. Forgive me for my judgmental attitudes. Pardon me for speaking and thinking negative thoughts. Help me to speak peace, favor, and kindness, and to never focus on what is not Yours. Help me to get through my obligations with great ease so I have more time to spend with You. Thanks for a blessed day that's brimming over with Your promises, possibilities, and protection. I love You.

God: Child, how precious you are to Me! I adore your prayers and how you listen and wait for Me to answer. I am ever with you, always hearing what you have to say and rejoicing in what you are learning. Bend your ear a little more to Me today, for I have many special things to say to you. I will pour out Myself to you and bring many more people to you to bless, refresh, and enjoy. Only I can do this. Call on Me today, and I will show you great and mighty things—things you hadn't known or understood before. But you will now. Ask Me as you meet with people throughout the day what to say to them, and I will tell you. Come to Me, and I will show you answers to your deepest questions and explain what you are seeing. Depend on Me, and I will preserve and keep you as the apple of My eye. Listen as I give you words to speak—life-giving words. My Son lived in a "small" place, but see how His ministry affected so many around the world? His love overflowed the boundaries of Israel. You can also live in one place but reach many for Me! I will help you with this. I love you.

So I can live courageously

"For the word of God is alive and powerful. It is sharper than the sharpest two-edged sword, cutting between soul and spirit, between joint and marrow. It exposes our innermost thoughts and desires."
—Hebrews 4:12

Me: Lord, would You show me how to give freely when I only want to be with You? Show me how to have grace when others require so much of my time. Demonstrate to me how to have mercy when I feel pressed by others' problems and impatient with their demands. Show me how to be Your "manna" for others when, like Moses and Jesus, I just want to spend time with You on a mountain somewhere. Reveal how to do Your will freely when I don't feel like sharing so much of myself. Show me how to see You more clearly and live Your will more courageously. Demonstrate how to forgive when people have wronged or hurt me unthinkingly. Show me how to listen and learn from You when You speak in my ear and give me direction. Signify how to love as You do and see Your good works in others. You are lovely. You are kind. You are awesome. And I love You.

God: Dear one, you can't always control the things around you, including others' actions or reactions. I'll make it clear when you should serve and when you should spend time with Me. Sometimes people will be offended if you say "no." And sometimes you must, because they need to become hungry enough to come to Me on their own. They need to realize that you aren't God. Sometimes they won't understand you or who you represent or why you don't have extra time for them. Don't worry so much about others' choices or attitudes, even when you think their decisions might negatively impact you. You've seen how I work on your behalf. People can choose whatever they want. And neither you nor I can make them go a certain way. But I'll always arrange things to bless you and make a way when there seems to be no way. Even when people try to pull the wool over your eyes or whisper behind your back, I'll reveal their thoughts and intentions so that you're aware of what's really going on. That way you can make wise decisions regarding your own life as You stand with Me. You see how I work out all things to be a blessing for you? Don't worry about others' plans or actions. Have peace in everything. I want what's best for you and your family. You are My precious one and My love. And I love you.

   As You cover for me

"Keep watch and pray, so that you will not give in to temptation. For the spirit is willing, but the body is weak!"
—Matthew 26:41

Me: Father, would You help me to recognize what I need to focus on today? Help me to acknowledge those things that I most need to learn so I can survive and thrive. Lock them into my mind so I can easily bring them to remembrance, especially when I'm distracted by people. Energize my mind so I can retain what's needful. Would You cover my mistakes and smooth over the areas where I fall short? I need Your healing touch in my life. Forgive my worldliness at times, when I wander away from what's good and meaningful. Sometimes I get carried away. Bring me back to Your center, Your "bull's eye," and help me to focus on what is necessary. Today is in Your hands. Make it a great day. Open new doors and give me Your strength to walk through them. You are a God of mercy and kindness. You touch my heart in special ways when I need it most. I love You.

God: Dear one, I am with you. I fight for you. And I forgive you. Come with Me up to the mountain. I will wait for you there as you're made ready. I'm preparing your heart now, cleansing away any impurity and unforgiveness. Let Me fight for you. Remember, it's not all up to you. So lean on Me. I'll reclaim what was lost to you! Look to Me for this. I'm working on your children's hearts too. And they will seek me. For I am your supplanter, succourer, and special friend. I'm the One who makes you secure and wise. I'm with you always, granting you peace, mercy, love, grace, kindness, gentleness, and faith. I'm all these things for you, to you, and in you. Today, come to me often for insight. I'll always listen and respond to your requests. Let Me enlighten you with My words. Incline your ear to Me, and hold Me close to your heart. You breathe because of Me. You notice and help others, because I inspire you to do these things. There are times you don't feel like obeying Me. Let Me give you strength by rushing through your veins. It's My Spirit that gives you what you need to act. Let it flow through you. Don't be blinded by what you see in the world. There is only darkness. Come to Me often—to My light. Know that, like My Son, you're the source of My delight. I love you.

And ease my heart

"So let's not get tired of doing what is good. At just the right time we will reap a harvest of blessing if we don't give up."
—*Galatians 6:9*

Me: Lord, today I'm especially tired, because I must make up for those who failed to do what they agreed to do! They either forgot or procrastinated or just didn't show up! Sometimes I feel overwhelmed, because I can't do it all by myself. Often, I'm overlooked by co-workers, family members, and friends, especially in the times when I need their help the most! I feel like there's no real caring or desire to give on their part. They're too self-focused. It saddens me and makes me want to throw in the towel. A few have extended a hand to me at times, and for these I'm extremely grateful. But I can name them all on one hand! And it's usually the people I least expected who come through for me. Would You help me to rejoice in You and be glad and have strength and courage to carry on? I need Your wisdom and reassurance to be able to see past others' lacks. I need Your help when I see things left undone or neglected, and it bothers me. Show me how to deal with these frustrations. Would You ease my heart and take care of these things so I don't have to? Would You help me to forgive? I love You.

God: Dear one, like you, I'm also disappointed by people's lack of consideration for others. And I understand why you feel this way. People often don't see the needs around them, because they're so focused on their own lacks, anxieties, or needs. Self-focus or focus on the wrong things brings an oblivion to the most important things right in front of them. When you're confronted by this blindness, turn to Me and I'll give you My own thoughts on the matter—what's really going on. I'll show you what to do and how to do it. And, though others neglect their own talents, abilities, or responsibilities in this life, I can use these opportunities to prepare and teach you. Don't worry about how you can accomplish things or who will help you. I'll always provide what you need when you need it. You can't control others, but you can lean on Me for help. Never be anxious about what may happen because I'll be there with you! I love you.

Through Your wellspring

"But those who drink the water I give will never be thirsty again. It becomes a fresh, bubbling spring within them, giving them eternal life."
—John 4:14

Me: Dear Lord, You're merciful and forgiving. You're just and mighty. You look on our lives and seek our love. You lean toward us in times of trouble to help and sustain us. You bring us grace and love and joy each day as we look to You. You heal our bones, our flesh, and our thoughts. You're faithful—a God to be depended on. You're strong—a God to be leaned on. You're forgiving—a God who overlooks our shortcomings and helps us to pardon others. I thank You and remember You in my thoughts. I know You're near—closer than I can imagine. I bring my cares, my worries, and my sorrows to You today, Lord, because I know You hear me. Would You forgive me for the times when I've grown impatient to see Your plan unfold before me? When I later saw how You arranged things and made things happen in the best way possible, I felt sad at my lack of faith in You. I could've avoided so much hurt and pain over the years by trusting in You more! Forgive me. Help me today to seek Your will and to turn to You in every situation, instead of listening to my own feelings. Today, guide me. For You are my dearest friend! My best ally! Take my hand and lead me. I desire Your company above all else! I love You.

God: Dear one, within you is a wellspring that brings you continuous grace and mercy. Through it, I provide supernatural ability that wells up from this perpetual spring within you. It gives you needed strength. It revives and renews you with a refreshing that comes from Me. It gives you courage, energy, and love. It heals and leads you to the most beneficial places and people—those who'll be a blessing to you and want to be blessed by My Word spoken by you. Let it comfort you. Let it guide your body and mind so that you never end up wandering into places that can cause you harm. It will help you focus on My promises—the positives I've chosen for you. It will bring you peace and hope and a certainty of forgiveness. It will cause you to be a "change agent," so you can transform the atmosphere around you through your presence. It will help you to push away the negative words and circumstances around you. All with the help of My wellspring within you. I love you.

That assures me of Your presence

"See, I have written your name on the palms of my hands."
—Isaiah 49:15

Me: Lord, would You heal this crack in my heart created by harsh words spoken? Would You help me to move past unkindness to be able to forgive and to see Your mercy in a greater way? Let the words spoken in hatred and self-centeredness be silenced in my mind. Remove them far from me. And let me be as You are—a joy-filled blessing. Forgive my weaknesses and help me to overcome my shortcomings with Your power. Let me be the warrior You've called me to be, ever ready to fight for You and not against You. Show me the battles I must fight and how to fight them. Arm and strengthen me, Lord, for I sometimes feel overwhelmed by the things I must do. And give me Your wisdom to handle them. I need Your peace. Lord, in Your quiet way, assure me of Your presence. Help me to flow in and through Your love to others and to shine with Your oil-rubbed anointing. Help me to accomplish all that I need by lifting away from me any burdens that have settled on my shoulders. Help me to reach into people's hearts to touch the hidden places of hurtfulness. And give me greater revelation as to who and what I'm dealing with. You're my Lord and my King. And I will praise You. I love You.

God: Dear one, it seems hard at times to remember that I am ever near you, but I assure you of My presence. Remember who you are—the daughter of the King! Sometimes it's hard to turn your thoughts to Me and praise Me for what I've done, especially when some come against you and cause your heart to hurt. When you're caught up in daily tasks, you may forget who I am and how I surround you, but I do. I stand by your side, ready to fight for you. And I never forget about you. You may lose sight of Me. But you're always on My mind. Your name is even engraved in My palms! Remember that people who forsake you or come against you also forsake and reject Me. They usually blame others for their own problems and are never satisfied or happy. Their souls are sick, because they're unable or unwilling to seek Me with their whole heart. Never let them bring you down or cause you to be discouraged. Remember, I love you.

And comforts me

"All praise to God, the Father of our Lord Jesus Christ. God is our merciful Father and the source of all comfort. He comforts us in all our troubles so that we can comfort others."
—*2 Corinthians 1:3-4*

Me: Lord, may Your kingdom come and Your will be done here on earth as it is in heaven. I want so much to behold Your supernatural works here on earth. Would You embolden me to believe in Your promises in such a way that I can help You to release them here on earth? I think about Joseph and how, even when evil was unleashed on him, You worked it all out for good for him and for so many. You somehow used evil to bring about Your promise of a Messiah who came from the Israelites. When people are cruel and thoughtless and hateful, or they simply ignore Your words, You still work their intentions or actions out in a way that fulfills Your promises. Would You help me to see as You do—beyond the bad to what You can do because of Your greatness? Please use Your soothing hand of comfort and Your gentle caress of lovingkindness to work through me so I can effectively minister to others. Forgive me for shortsightedness, for jumping to conclusions, and for allowing negative thoughts to capture my mind. Pardon me for the times I've reacted with anger to people who were upset because they were hurting. Thanks for giving me positive words to speak and the ability to see beyond the superficial. I love You.

God: Child, lean on Me today and consult Me in everything. Move forward with a renewed spirit, and watch as I work all things out for good. I'll do this as I've promised. You see the Big Dipper early in the morning as you walk, or at night when darkness covers the sky. Imagine it pouring My blessings all over you so that they flow out from you. If you remain in My presence, you'll avoid negative and hurtful thoughts and be released from their entanglements. In the world, you're bombarded mentally and physically. You can rebuke the ungodly thoughts so your mind is at peace. Then your body can relax and be refreshed for a new day. Throughout the day, when you're accosted by unpleasantness or unkindness, let your mind be at peace by meditating on My Word. Only I can bring you light and life, deliverance from sickness, freedom from unforgiveness and negative reactions, and bright rays of hope. I love you.

Through a bird's eye view

"For you are my hiding place; you protect me from trouble."
—Psalm 32:7

Me: You, Lord, are my sanctuary. You're my hiding place from harm. You keep me hidden in Your nook of kindness so that I'm protected from evil and the storms of life. Cover me now with Your great might and glory so I can abide beneath the pinions of Your wings. Help me to feel safe in Your arms and to not be afraid to say "yes" and respond to Your call. Prepare me to take steps forward for You. Bless these steps and let me never forget that You're beside me. Would You remind me continuously of Your presence so I never forget Your mercy and goodness? Oh, that I might never doubt Your hand of plenty and how You've always provided for me! You see me as I am in all my ignorance and weakness, yet, with Your amazing compassion, You accept me as I am—knowing little or nothing. Me, with all my imperfections! Help me in my blindness to have Your great insight. From my hiding place in Your mountainside, give me greater glimpses of Your vision, glances at Your light and love, and a bird's eye view of Your faithfulness and forgiveness. How I long to see the magnitude of these and to be able to view things as You see them. I love You.

God: Dear one, during trials and storms, I am with you. When others forsake, disparage, or demean you, I am your hiding place from harm. I alone am faithful. I alone remove your faults as far as the east is from the west. I'm aware of your weaknesses, but I never want you to focus on these. I don't. I see your strengths and work with you to build on them. I see who you really are and what you can do. I alone bring you joy and peace and reassurance. Turn your thoughts to Me, for I want to speak to you clearly and inform you of My hidden secrets, including the things I want only you to know. I'm your informant—the One who clarifies the hidden reasons for things and the secret ways of people. I'm the One who enlightens and brings you wisdom. I'm your guide—the One who clears a path and leads you to reality. I'm the One who takes you by the hand and brings you to My sanctuary. I'm also your lover—the One who holds you and wipes away your tears. I'm the One who soothes your fears and loves you unconditionally through good and bad times. Let Me be these things for you. I long for it. I love you.

As I stand in the gap for You

"I looked for someone who might rebuild the wall of righteousness that guards the land. I searched for someone to stand in the gap in the wall so I wouldn't have to destroy the land, but I found no one."
—Ezekiel 22:30

Me: Lord, today You reminded me not to look down on people who seem weak or incapable or inadequate, because these may be the very ones You are sending to me so I can speak into their lives! You remind me how You "searched for someone to stand in the gap in the wall," which represents Your protective barrier against the damaging forces of the world. Lord, You called me to stand in this gap for those teetering on the edge, because they feel hopeless and helpless. And Your hand in my hand may be what's needed to catch them before they fall. Would You help me to be strong enough to help them? I stand on this wall, and I hold out Your hand of hope. Give me strength to continue. Help me not to focus on their weaknesses, but on what You see in them and what You've called them to do. Forgive my impatience. Forgive me if I've caused some to turn back. Let Your way live through me. Remind me of Your grace, mercy, kindness, love, and gentleness. Thanks. I love You.

God: Child, can you comprehend how much I truly love you? I appreciate you as My "watchman on the wall" (Ezekiel 3:17). Yes, My Word says that I value weakness (2 Corinthians 12:10). It's through fragility that I can show My greatest strength and perform My best wonders by supernaturally working through the least likely people to will and to do of My good pleasure (Philippians 2:13.) My home is in you. Pull from within, for that is where your strength comes from. Seek Me there, for that is where I abide. The adversary will try to use weakness for his own purposes. He'll take an offense or a slight and blow it out of proportion. He'll emphasize people's shortcomings instead of their strengths. By doing this, he promotes his evil agenda to sway people's hearts to his own way of distortion and lies. Those who heed his lies have no root in Me. They justify their own lacks by pointing fingers at others and exaggerating their faults. My spiritual leaders and warriors have always been attacked in this way. But I'll always advocate for you. I'll defend you. I'll stop the mouths of the liars and support you as you stand for Me on the wall. Because I forgive and see the best in you. And love you.

With my head on Your shoulders

"Now I will take the load from your shoulders; I will free your hands from their heavy tasks."
—Psalm 81:6

Me: Lord, is there anything I need to ask Your forgiveness for? Any areas of my life where I need to "come clean" before You? I know sometimes I'm oblivious to my own faults. It's easier to point out the ways others fall short and how they get on my nerves! But I know I mustn't pick out their "splinters," when I might be carrying loads that I'm burdening them with, like stacking logs on their back. Take my hand, Lord, and lead me up to Your mountain over paths of peace through the world's peaks and valleys. I want to go where Your light always shines and Your love always reigns, no matter what! Would You carry me when I feel small? Hold me up, and help me with these burdens. Let me rest my head on Your shoulders for a while as we walk. Let me be a beacon for You, reflecting the glory of Your presence. I know my attitude about things makes all the difference between a joyful day and a stressful day. Lord, show me how to have great joy today and every day and to be able to understand how, with You, it's never hard! Would You give me a special blessing, something unique that reveals Your presence in a greater way? And please forgive my lacks. I love You.

God: Dear one, you know that I love you. As you go about your day, remember I'm always ready to speak to you and give you encouragement. Patience is hard for you. Apply My hand to your heart when you feel an urge to rush to judgment. Remember, I'm the final judge, and I'll remind you if you're being unjust. Discernment is good, and I can show you many things, but leave all the judgment to Me. You may struggle with this, but I will help you. The people I send to you may catch you off-guard. Their appearance may throw you, but see into their true heart. And be ready. I'll prepare you and give you the words to say. They'll want to believe, and you can build their trust in Me. You see how precious life is? Remember, I can help you keep this fragile life alive through wisdom. If you trust Me, I can guide and bring you right results. I can protect you. Because I know you and how you best operate. I inspired the book of instructions. If you trust in Me, I can help you to live abundantly. Life with Me is sweet. You can always rest your head, and your burdens, on My shoulders. And know that I'll support you. I love you.

So I can see what matters most

"And be sure of this: I am with you always, even to the end of the age."
—Matthew 28:20

Me: Lord, so many things distract us from loving and getting close to those who desire our love the most. Work and busyness often side-track our focus from intimacy with those who want and need us. This includes You! The drives and desires of this world are the main culprits. Lord, help me to see past these to You alone. Would You forgive me for allowing distractions to keep me from being closer to You and my loved ones? Would You help me to look beyond the insignificant things to seek You more and more? Let me always remain in the palms of Your hands. Help me to know You in a deeper way as my continual guide and source for joy and peace. Help me to seek You in every situation, in every corner of my life and at every turn. Sometimes I feel neglected by people I care about. And I hope others don't feel lost and alone because I've overlooked them. I see ones I care about seeking others for friendship or love, and I feel sad. Help me not to feel hurt by their neglect or oversight. These feelings are ghosts from my past—lingering memories of past slights that resurrect painful thoughts. Help me to move on, to grow past them, and to seek You in all I do. Heal the sore spots in my life, and help me see things as You do—by way of the spirit. You're such a blessing to me, Lord. You're always there. Help me to seek Your face today, free from all the crazy distractions! I love You.

God: Child, days and seasons, times and hours.... It will all seem like a blur to you years from now. What matters so much to you now will be forgotten tomorrow. Don't dwell so much on what you think is important for this moment in time. Focus on what will last for eternity. I'll show you clearly which are the distractions and what is most significant to spend your time contemplating and doing now. I'll make it clear when there are people to attend to in the present. Remember, you'll be rewarded for the works that can't be burned with the fire of the Word that refines and purifies. Speak the comfort of My words to others, including your loved ones. Bring them a message of peace and hope and the wholeness brought to them by My Son and all He accomplished for them. Only My Word can heal and amend what once was torn apart, including your heart. With it you can forgive and focus on what's advantageous in the long run. I love you.

And know how to react

"I believe in your commands; now teach me good judgment and knowledge."
—Psalm 119:66

Me: Lord, would You forgive me for being judgmental? Pardon me for being accusatory. I know this is not my job. Show me how to speak to others who turn their backs on me and wash their hands of You. I'm especially disturbed when I see people who say they stand for You living in a way that disregards Your Word and what is clearly the truth. It makes me feel both sad and angry, and I'm not sure if this is my own or Your anger I feel. Show me. Help me to understand how You work with people like this, and how I should react to them. I know You love them, and I want to love them too. I remember how Your Son loved the woman caught in the act of adultery, when the religious leaders were ready to stone her. I think about the woman at the well whose life was riddled with sin, yet Your Son reached out and touched her. I don't want to be like the Pharisees, who were ready to destroy people for falling short of their rules! I want to love. I want to forgive. But I also know that You see sin as sin and make no excuses for it. Because of unrepented brokenness, some will never inherit Your kingdom. This seems severe. Help me to recognize things as You do. I know I can pray and put people in Your hands. Help me to understand how. I love You.

God: Child, is sin a light thing? Is it a small matter? No. Sin, which is disobedience or "missing the mark or bulls-eye," causes grief and leads to death. Willful disobedience causes shame and degradation. Can it be forgiven? Yes. But it still has consequences. The more responsibility a person has, the more I hold him or her accountable. Sin is never insignificant, but I count it more heavily in those whom I've called to be My leaders and representatives on earth. Understand this. Not everyone experiences severe consequences to their behavior immediately, but My expectation for obedience is greater in those to whom I have given greater responsibility. Remember, My Son died so that every sin of those who believed in Him could be forgiven. Do you understand? When you're tempted, there's always a way out. And you'll feel a prompting by the Holy Spirit to avoid any wrong turns. Let Him show you how to deal with your sin and that of others. He's always there to direct you. I love you.

To be able to overcome offense

"Forgive your people who have sinned against you. Forgive all the offenses they have committed against you."
—1 Kings 8:50

Me: Lord, I come to You again with an angry and hurting heart. And I'm having a hard time figuring out how to move past these feelings. Would You replace the hurt and anger with Your joy, love, and peace? Would You help me to forgive and move forward? Let me see clearly what You want me to see and how You perceive things. I know You want me to be larger than offense and able to see past it to what's really in peoples' hearts. Show me how. Help me not to be overcome by things that offend me and to be able to rejoice when others receive greater blessings than me, especially after I've given so much. I guess I feel offended because I know how hard I've tried! Let me fully face You as never before, seeing what I need to do to be released from this anxiety, fear, unforgiveness, and bitterness. Let me love more fully and trust You when I feel hurt or offended. Help me to love those who seem to overlook me. And help me move to a greater level of love. I love You.

God: Child, remember that only I can truly meet your needs. Don't get down on yourself by thinking you may not be doing what you need to or you may not be good enough. You do more than most people. Rely more on Me to accomplish what's needed. I want you to see past how you think or feel and be able to view yourself more as a servant. Don't worry when people who seem less worthy receive the promotions. Don't let others' actions, haughtiness, anger, or lack of acknowledgement bring you down or pull you off track. See past their ignorance and lack of understanding. When you know who you are and how valuable your life is to Me, then you'll begin to see that people without an understanding of Me often fall from their pedestals, especially if they're placed there undeservedly. Eventually people who don't belong in certain positions will be replaced with people who should inhabit that space, because it's rightfully theirs. I'm the vindicator. Know that I will promote and lift you up at the right time and place and give you what's meant for you. Right now, I'm working on your behalf to bring you success and prosperity so that you have more to give. Be encouraged. Have peace in your heart. Know that I will always show you how because I love you.

And focus on the right things

"Fix your thoughts on what is true, and honorable, and right, and pure, and lovely, and admirable. Think about things that are excellent and worthy of praise."
—*Philippians 4:8*

Me: Lord, would You help me to forgive and be forgiven by others? Help me to see good and not evil in people. Help me to focus on Your truth, not the frustrations, day to day. Show me how to think and speak only what is good and profitable and lovely. You're so awesome, Lord! And Your Son's life was such a shining example of living out Your Word in a positive way, even when He was confronted by negative people! It's only through You that my life has meaning, luster, brilliance, or joy. It's only with Your help that I can stand or endure a fall. You set me on a pedestal when I myself am nothing. You raise me up and give me strength. You surround my moments with hope and shower my days with kindness. Help me to pour out Your love to others. Show me more clearly Your purposes for me and the direction You want me to go. Thanks for being there for me. Help me to see everything through Your eyes. I want to please You, Lord. Because I love You.

God: Child, I love you and walk beside you daily. Don't fret over mistakes or inappropriate words you might have spoken. I'll help you by correcting what you think are mistakes and smoothing over misstatements. Listen as I speak in your ears to remind you of My love and tell you that you're so very special to Me. I'll continue to open divine doors for you and show you clearly what you must say to the people I place in front of you. It may seem at times like they don't hear or see you, but I'll open their eyes more and more by making you appear bigger and more important and prominent, so they can't ignore what you say! Right now, you're a hidden gem, set aside for future purposes. Let Me heal your heart of any lingering grief or pain. Let Me console you with My love so that you can better express love to others. Don't beat yourself up for what you consider to be flaws or slips. I will correct them. Lean on Me. Just continue to trust. And take time each day to put on the encouraging thoughts from My Word. That way you can replace anything negative with all things positive. I love you.

As You clarify My job

"Finally, all of you should be of one mind. Sympathize with each other. Love each other as brothers and sisters. Be tenderhearted, and keep a humble attitude."
—1 Peter 3:8

Me: Lord, You're my buddy, my comfort, my joy. Thanks for Your reassurances and blessings. Thanks for family and friends who patiently put up with my moods. I know you're trying to give me what I need. Let me not stand in Your way. You know best what I should be doing, and I trust You. Thanks for peace apart from this world. I pray for more of that. Today, forgive my merciless attitude at times. Pardon me, Lord, if I've wronged anyone. Forgive me if I haven't been just in my dealings. Or if I haven't spoken or dealt fairly. Forgive me for the times when I didn't fight for people who fought for me. Help me to better serve those in need. And pardon me for not acting sooner when You prompted me to proceed. Please make things right for me and those I may have neglected, and correct any wrongs I've done. Turn things around for good. I put my life in Your hands, and I ask for Your guidance. I long to hear Your voice. Please speak to me, and give me a singular blessing that I know can only come from You. Would You acknowledge me in some special way, beyond my own ability or actions? I want to see Your love in a greater way. Others lack the ability to comfort, love, give assurance, or be there when I really need them. You alone have always been there for me. You've stood by me when others have failed. Thanks for Your constant presence in my life. I love You.

God: My child, watch your thoughts and your words. Be careful what you say and how you speak. Some in this world are Mine and their hearts are being made ready, even though you don't understand their mannerisms or actions. They're called as My children, and I'm teaching them just as I'm directing you. Your job is to forgive and accept them for who they are, even if they are a bit rough around the edges. Be tender with them. See into their hearts, and help them to perceive My ways. They may be misled or lack understanding, but you can help them. I'll show you how. Don't take their words personally or as an affront against you. Understand that they are doing the best they can with what they know. Show them kindness. This always brings healing. Remember, love covers a multitude of sins. And that I love you.

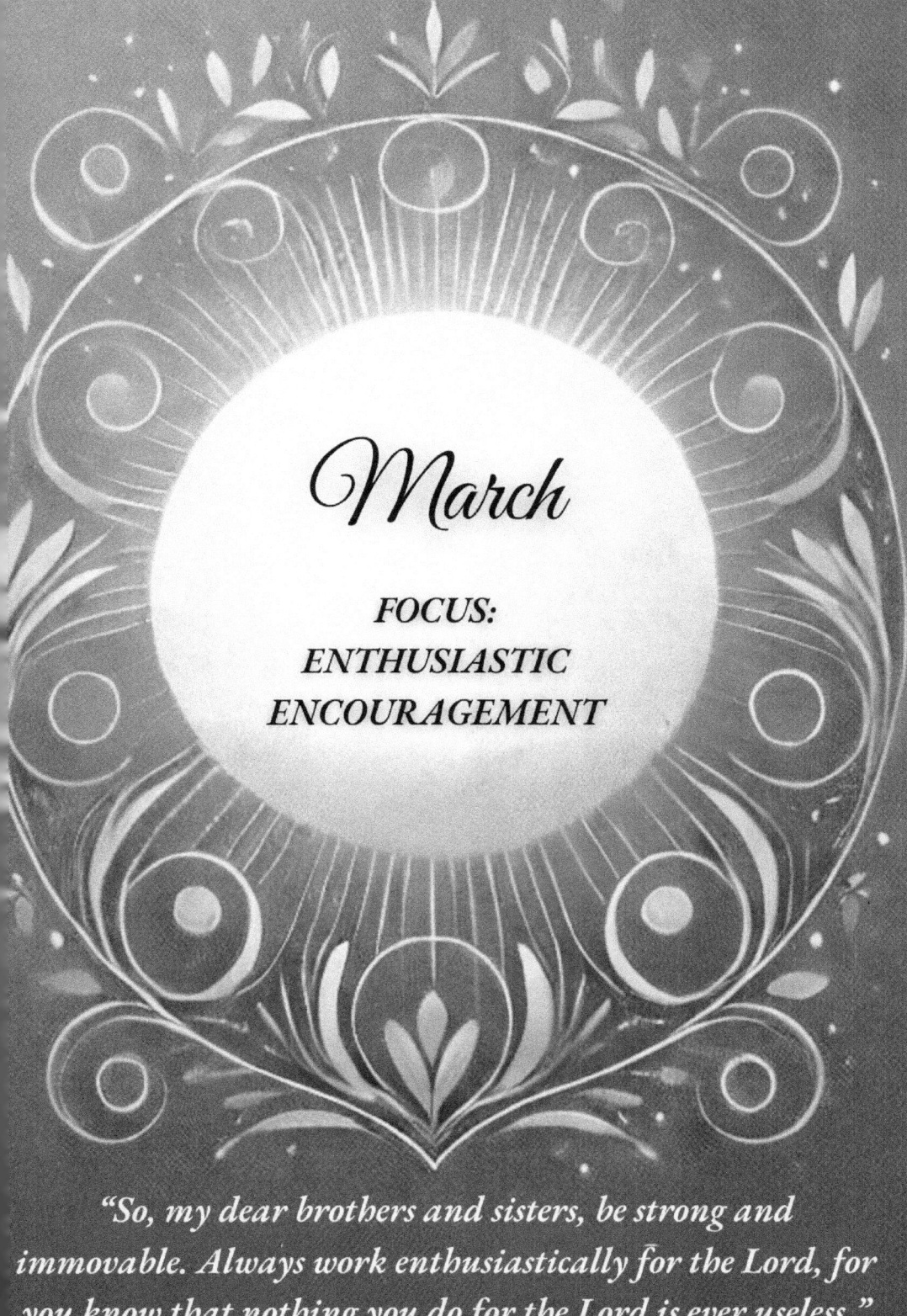

March

FOCUS:
ENTHUSIASTIC
ENCOURAGEMENT

"So, my dear brothers and sisters, be strong and immovable. Always work enthusiastically for the Lord, for you know that nothing you do for the Lord is ever useless."

—1 CORINTHIANS 15:58

MARCH 1
Me—bold as a lion?

"The wicked run away when no one is chasing them, but the godly are as bold as lions."
—Proverbs 28:1

Me: Lord, You've made my way prosperous. You've blessed me bountifully, and I thank You for that! You've enlightened my eyes and given me peace. You've blessed my children and watched over them. Would You give me fearlessness today to face any fear and come out shining in a way that glorifies You? Help me to be bold and ready to deliver Your message whenever You call on me to speak. Open my ears to Your sweet whispers, and help me to hear Your every word. Then give me courage to act! You alone inspire me with what I need each day. You alone are my sufficiency. You alone are my help in times of trouble. Help me to lean on You continuously. Help me to never forget Your promises. Help me to never neglect to praise You, especially during the times when I feel like things aren't going the way I'd hoped they would. Thanks for Your unspeakable gift of love. Thanks for Your divine grace and mercy and peace heaped plenteously on me. I love You.

God: Dear one, some say, "March comes in like a lion, goes out like a lamb." My Word says that, with Me by your side, you can be bold as a lion and bring great deliverance to My people at any time! Allow Me to work through you to "roar" fearlessly at the enemy so that he's always frozen in his tracks. See yourself as a great defender of the faith. Then My people who hear My Word spoken can receive it as lambs. And together we can shepherd them and bring them to glory, might, and dominion over the earth. My Son was the first lamb slaughtered for your deliverance. Because of His boldness, I glorified Him. And I will reward your courageous actions one day. See yourself as valiant and able to bravely carry out My assignments each day. Step by step, I'll help you overcome every fear. Things like going to new places, facing unexpected life changes, losing a child or a parent or a spouse, entering new situations, making mistakes, or being rejected by others may cause you concern. But, as you lean on Me, I'll obliterate any worry by showing you how I walk boldly beside you and take care of every situation. One day, you'll look back to see just how I delivered you from everything that once stole your peace. But you must trust Me to direct you, even when you feel threatened. I love you.

Or a mighty "yes" person?

"For all of God's promises have been fulfilled in Christ with a resounding "Yes!" And through Christ, our "Amen" (which means "Yes") ascends to God for his glory."
—2 Corinthians 1:20

Me: Lord, how special am I to You? I wonder sometimes why I've never had a visitation from Your Son or from an angel, like Paul or Mary or Daniel once did. This morning, You asked me if I'd paid attention to the times when people were visited by angelic beings. You showed me that You only send angels or Your Son to those who need special encouragement and confirmation of Your presence so they can fulfill a divine mission. The actions You require of some on earth often necessitate extraordinary courage in the face of great opposition, rejection, hatred, terror, persecution, sacrifice, torture, or death. You give people visitations when You're preparing them to do something supernatural. Those You call to perform these measures are those You know will say "yes" and follow You to overcome unspeakable obstacles and do what's needed to accomplish an assignment. Lord, help me to be a "yes" person. Today, help me to do exploits for You. I love You.

God: Dear one, I love your eagerness to do what's needed and your hunger to know and understand My will in your life. I know that life lived through a belief in Me is not always easy. Sometimes you struggle because you're not sure when it's My voice you hear or when it's your own. I'll continue to teach you, but you must listen. Bend your ears toward Me. Often it's My voice you are hearing. I'm a ready Lord. I want to bring you answers. Hold My hand, and let Me lead you as a shepherd leads his flock. I can minister to you in ways you never imagined. Turn more to Me in your thoughts, and let Me whisper to you My loving words of kindness and love. I'm always available to bring you healing. The more you praise Me, the more I can do My job, which is to bring deliverance through you. I'm your Lord, and you're My beloved disciple. You're a chosen one. Never forget this. I sought you out because I saw your heart and realized your desire to know Me. I knew you would believe. You've always been very special to Me. You're blessed because of your belief, and so are your children. Don't forget to listen for My voice. I may not send angels today, but I will come and speak to you. Is that good enough? I love you.

When I just want to know how to lead

"If your gift is to encourage others, be encouraging. If it is giving, give generously. If God has given you leadership ability, take the responsibility seriously. And if you have a gift for showing kindness to others, do it gladly."
—Romans 12:8

Me: Lord, once You showed me the difference between being a boss and being a leader. You told me that I must be a leader, though I didn't always think of myself this way. Bosses manipulate, You said, and tell people what to do. They push people around and try to control them and make them do what suits their own purposes. Their determinations are often motivated by their own likes or dislikes. On the other hand, leaders inspire others by their example. They direct with suggestions, motivate by showing how to do what's in others' best interest, create vision, and incorporate truths that make sense to the people they're leading. Lord, would You teach me how to lead? Show me how. Only You can do this! I love You.

God: Dear one, do you see how I defend My people? I come to their aid when they turn to Me with their whole hearts and seek My will. Jesus was an excellent example of a leader. Glean from his teachings through the Gospels. If you read the book of Esther, you can see how a prominent woman, who did not see herself as a leader, stood up for My people, and miraculously saved them, at an opportune and crucial time in history. At the urging of her cousin, she acted courageously, and she bravely turned the tide for My people, who were threatened by an insanely jealous political leader. When anyone attacks or accuses My people dishonestly or viciously, I will always defend them! I chose David, and many enemies came against him—those who desired power, control, and favor. That's what happens in this world. When I lead you and call you out to fulfill a purpose, as I did David, enemies will try to undermine your efforts. But, if you persist as David did, by seeking Me and My help, I will guide you through hardship and persecution. Remember that My main purpose for you as a leader is to bring others to My light, including your own children and grandchildren. And never forget that I love you.

MARCH 4
Without throwing my pearls before swine

"Whatever you do, work heartily, as for the Lord and not for men, knowing that from the Lord you will receive the inheritance as your reward. You are serving the Lord Christ. For the wrongdoer will be paid back for the wrong he has done, and there is no partiality."
—*Colossians 3:23-25*

Me: Lord, would You answer this question for me? Why do people, whom I've spent so much time caring for, turn away and seek the same advice or help from others? Why are those whom I've poured my soul into the most often the very ones who betray me by kowtowing to people who really don't care for them at all? It baffles me. And it's hurtful and painful. Would You show me the ones who deserve more of my effort? And point out those who'll waste my time by never doing what I've suggested or being thankful for what I've given! I don't want to expect something in return, but I do want to make sure I'm not throwing my "pearls before swine." I ask that You open the floodgates, and pour out a blessing I don't have room enough to receive, so I can give to the worthy ones. I seek Your favor. Show me Your hand of mercy and grace, and where Your kindness lies. You're my savior. And I love You.

God: Dear one, you are precious to Me. You're My light-filled one. So, stop beating yourself up over these things: how you might've wasted your time, things that happened in the past, and people with inappropriate responses to your efforts. Remember that nothing you give is ever wasted. I use every loving effort for good. My way is always the way to blessings. Walk in it. Take My hand and let me lead you. The path may not always be clear, but I'll lead you through uncertainty to greater clarity. I'll always come through for you. People will not always do as you'd hoped they would, but I'll never disappoint you. Don't burden yourself with guilt, bitterness, or worries about misused time. Was the help Jesus offered to people always received with thankfulness and appreciation? No! So, rely on Me to work on your behalf. I am trustworthy. I will reward the kindness you deserve. I can make whole what's lacking—in you and in others. Put your life in My hands and let Me bring you what you need. Open your heart and mind to My abundance. Be encouraged by Me when you feel discouraged by others. I love you.

And still be able to see Your hand in the stars

"When I look at the night sky and see the work of your fingers—the moon and the stars you set in place—what are mere mortals that you should think about them, human beings that you should care for them? Yet you made them only a little lower than God and crowned them with glory and honor."
—*Psalm 8:3-5*

Me: Lord, how amazing You are! Nothing is too hard for You. I see Your face in each day's dawning and Your hand as I watch the moon and stars appearing. I see You in the masterful way You taught all Your creatures to understand their places in this world. I see You in the intricacies of vegetation and how we ourselves are made. Would You teach me as You have all your creation? I want to turn to You with my whole heart and mind and instinctively know more about You! Besides understanding more about myself, would You help me to recognize those who want to comprehend Your ways as I do? I long to connect with those who want to gain more knowledge of Your truth. Show me the light in their eyes and the glow in their hearts, and give me the right words to say. Thanks for those You bring, and for this moment, this hour, and this special time. I love You.

God: My child, people are limited by their ability, background, surroundings, beliefs, and understanding. I don't expect more from those who do the best they can with what they have. Some will overcome great odds and leave everything they have just to come to Me, because they see the wonders of My world. But many will never respond to My call, because they lack the desire, the heart, the courage, or the will to pursue Me. I will show you a few to focus on with prayer and encouragement. With these you can share the purpose of My calling and the awesomeness of My ways. Sadly, many will walk away to seek their own agendas. They may want to control their surroundings, so they can manipulate the outcomes. They may want Me to fit in with their beliefs. It will take time for some to accept Me because of the webs they've woven. Others will come when they realize that their minds have been overtaken by the world's irrationality and fear, and they desperately want to be released. My plans will always be achieved in the end, and I will show you how, together, we can accomplish them. I love you.

And be efficient with my time

"Throw off your old sinful nature and your former way of life, which is corrupted by lust and deception. Instead, let the Spirit renew your thoughts and attitudes. Put on your new nature, created to be like God—truly righteous and holy."
—Ephesians 4:22-24

Me: Dear Lord, this Spring I want to experience life anew with You, because You are a God of endearing peace and adoring love. You are a God of enduring strength who honors humility. You meet my needs and shower me with lovingkindness. I praise You for Your ways, which are always above mine. I praise You for Your gentleness as You minister to my heart. Let me experience unspeakable elation today, Lord, as I enter this new season of springing joy. Would You help me to see more of Your abounding miracles, signs, and wonders? Let me feel Your sweet delight as I recognize Your face more and more in the world around me. Help me to be in the right place at the right time. Lord, direct my steps and my speech, and remind me that You are there through a soft touch or a kind word whispered. Spirit of God, I need Your encouragement. When I feel uncomfortable or constrained, remind me to look for You. Give me greater courage to bless others without fear of how I can give more of my time or accommodate them. Or how they might respond. I long for more hours to spend with You. Help me through this day! I love You.

God: Child, renew your mind by putting on My thoughts. Refresh your peace by focusing on the words I give you—both written and spoken. Reassert your love for others by growing closer to Me through My Son. Rekindle your joy by experiencing fellowship with Me through My believers, who also rejoice in Me. Rebuild your strength by relying on My God-given power. Reanoint your hands by clasping Mine so you can touch, reach, and bless others. Remove your anxieties by trusting in what I tell you. Replace your fears with My courage, ability, and authority. Remember that I loved David, not because he walked perfectly before Me, but because he loved Me passionately. What I love most is your steadfastness and your persistence. You are like a streetlight that flickers a few times but then grows brighter! You remind me of a star shining through overhanging clouds—the only one people can see in the dark sky. Your light is constant. I love this about you. Let your light continue to shine as a beacon to others. I love you.

MARCH 7
And know You as my soulmate

"There is no longer Jew or Gentile, slave or free, male and female. For you are all one in Christ Jesus."
—*Galatians 3:28*

Me: Dear Lord, when I read Your Word, it seems like men were more honored and esteemed than women throughout history. But, You assure me, You value women as much as men, and women will be seated near Your throne and reign along with You one day. Lord, how I would love to be one who sits next to You. How I long to behold Your face shining like a beacon and Your body adorned with gem-laden, beautiful, and glorious attire! How I look forward to bowing down before You and kneeling at Your feet! As each day passes, draw me closer to You. Would You reveal to me Your most precious secrets? And let me be Your confidante, Your friend, Your soulmate? I long for this. Open my heart more and more, and the hearts of my family members, especially my children and grandchildren. I realize more each day that if I submit to Your will, and don't worry so much about my own needs, You will supply me with more than I could ever ask or think. Show me today Your will, and give me the strength to do it. Help me to focus on what's needed, so I can give honor to You always. Guide me and direct my steps. I love You.

God: Dear one, men and women of every race and class and nation are equal in My sight. All can become one with Me through My Son and My Spirit. I'm working even now to will and to do of My good pleasure among many. See My hand in every situation. Trust Me and see My mighty power and grace in your life. I love you dearly, and I want to show You how much. You are precious to Me and, although you don't see yourself this way, I do! I sought you out as a child. I saw your willful desire to serve and to accomplish much, and I longed for you! I wanted you as one of My own. So, I pursued you. I whispered in your ear and gave you inspiration, thoughts, even desires. I saw in you an ability and willingness to give to others, and I loved this about you. I longed to work in and through you. Even now, I guide you to give and to serve. I will continue to tell you things you need to know. Don't ever think I'm not beside you, encouraging you and giving you hope. I will take care of you and your family. Never fear. Even now, I work to stir up the desires of those closest to you. It just takes time. Keep asking. Keep speaking. Keep telling them about Me. I love you.

The One I can fly away with

"If I ride the wings of the morning, if I dwell by the farthest oceans, even there your hand will guide me, and your strength will support me."
—Psalm 139:9-10

Me: Lord, You gave me another amazing dream where I was meeting with a group of people around a long table. One man at the table was very engaging, and I wanted so much to be acknowledged by him, because he spoke with such authority. An older man walked in and sat at the far end of the table next to him. I could tell that he was the younger man's boss because of his demeanor. These two had a tremendous presence of wisdom and knowingness. I wanted so much to be recognized by them both. I asked them a question about how to deal with difficult people, and the younger one responded, "What do you think is the best way?" I replied that I always tried to see peoples' hearts so I could make right choices regarding them. The two men looked at each other when I said this, and I wondered what they thought. When they got up to leave, a woman whispered to me, "I think they like you!" I replied, "Well, I like them!" I followed them outside to a small plane on the ground with three tracks in front of it. I wanted to go with them so very much. But then I woke up! Lord, show me the meaning of the dream. I love You.

God: Dear one, the first man was Jesus. The second one was Me. If you recall, when I got up to leave, you held out your hand to Me and said, "My name is Lele." I looked at you, puzzled, and you realized that, of course I knew your name! But then Jesus came over and held His hand out to you and said, "My name is Jeff." The name "Jeff" is like "Jesus" and comes from the name Godfrey, which means "God is peace." He wanted to show you My peace and bring serenity to your heart and mind. He approached you to show how much He appreciated you. Instead of being sad that people may not acknowledge you or your most important life-role, I want you to see your value to Us. I want to encourage you to speak into others' lives and help them understand their true worth. You ask so often to see My Son's face and, in this dream, you did. The three tracks on which the plane sat were the ways We can come to you: as Father, Son, and Holy Spirit. Through Us, you are complete. The plane is the symbol of the way all things are transported between heaven and earth. You will be on that plane one day. I love you.

MARCH 9
As I wonder how long You want me here

"Lead me by your truth and teach me, for you are the God who saves me. All day long I put my hope in you."
—Psalm 25:5

Me: Lord, today I look forward to seeing Your face, hearing Your voice, sitting in Your presence, and knowing You as You've known me. Would You let me be as one of Your favored and honored ones, Lord? Would You give me courage as I face earthly challenges today? Remove my fears and concerns so that I can trust in You more and more. Give me strength so I can be bold and brave as I tackle each moment You offer to me. I wonder at times how long my life will last, and then I say, "Lord, let it be as long as You need me here!" Lord, it seems that those who walk closer to You sometimes have fewer days on this earth. Is that to avoid the evil? Is it because You've seen from how they've lived what they can do, and it's enough to determine their role in the next life? Is it because they've achieved what You sent them to accomplish? Show me. And help me, like Enoch, to walk my remaining days in Your fellowship as I put my hope in You. Thanks! I love You.

God: Dear one, do you see how I'm preparing you? Do you see how I encourage and strengthen you? Don't be discouraged by death or the loss of those close to you, for their spirits await your arrival. When the trumpet blows, you'll rise to meet Me, and them, in the air! Then we'll all be together forever, and you'll see their faces once again, and You'll rejoice in Me and see what I've planned for you and everyone who comes to Me. It's easy, in this present world, to get bogged down by time and space, and to worry about the past, present, or the future. Those are all nothing to me. I live for all time, and you will too, because you believed in My Son. One day, you'll see the loved ones you've lost, and you'll smile and rejoice in their love and in Mine. One day, you'll see the people you've known or read about who knew Me and died. You sometimes feel sorrow and despair. I understand. It's hard to feel joy when you can't see what I have in store for you. But you must trust Me. I'll lead you down quiet and peaceful paths and guide you to places you've never seen. And you'll meet people who long for Me as you do. Don't feel discouraged. Just follow Me. I love you.

MARCH 10
To live among other clueless sheep

"Then Jesus said, "Come to me, all of you who are weary and carry heavy burdens, and I will give you rest. Take my yoke upon you. Let me teach you, because I am humble and gentle at heart, and you will find rest for your souls. For my yoke is easy to bear, and the burden I give you is light."
—Matthew 11:28-30

Me: Lord, I sometimes feel exhausted. Would You give me strength and encouragement? Enlighten me and show me what to do and how to do it! I've obviously taken on too many burdens that aren't my responsibility. You're my wonderful guide and my chief shepherd. Lead me as one of Your stupid and clueless sheep! Show me Your presence so I know You're here. Do something wonderful for me today. I need it, Lord! Whisper in my ears, and make Your words very clear. For I need Your help to discern which responsibilities are mine and which ones aren't. Thanks for reminding me that many burdens aren't mine to bear. Set me free from others' false assumptions, and help me to understand that only You can heal and meet my needs. All I can do is what I know to be true from You! And I don't know everything. So, others must forgive me for being imperfect and not living up to their expectations. I must forgive them for their weaknesses too. Help me with this! I love You.

God: Dear child, you've been on My heart and in My thoughts. I understand your discouragement, and I'm aware of your frustrations. I'm with you, supporting you and giving you peace and grace and guidance. I surround you with My love. Today, you'll see this love more than ever through a few. Watch for this. Today, I'll be with you to give you strength. Others may not believe it, but I can do this for you. Just look to me. Yes, I'm your chief shepherd and I do lead and guide and take care of you always. Put your life in My hands, and I'll be with you to comfort and encourage you, for I have much in store for you. I have so many things prepared for you! Trust me in this. Today, lean on Me for direction. Today, allow My hand in all you do. Hear My words, and act on them. Then you will see mighty signs, miracles, and wonders. There are more people to pray for. I'll bring them to your mind. And I'll always show you which burdens are yours to bear and which are not. I love you.

MARCH 11
Especially when I feel discouraged

"Why am I discouraged? Why is my heart so sad? I will put my hope in God! I will praise him again—my Savior and my God!"
—Psalm 43:5

Me: Dear God, today I ask for freedom from self-pity. At times I feel sorry for myself, when family and friends are nowhere to be found, and I need to know someone's there for me. I also sometimes succumb to the stronghold of rejection, when recognition for the things I've done is withheld, and my efforts to give go unnoticed and unappreciated. Then, my heart hurts, and I feel like retreating into a cave or sitting sadly under a lone broom tree, like Elijah, and waiting for my time to end. Do You withhold acknowledgement because You want me to turn to You for recognition? You always reassure me through Your words that You never forget about me, even if others do. And I know that, when I turn my eyes to You, You'll encourage me with love as no one else can. Help me to recognize Your wonderful kindness and remember that You're always near. Help me to come to you with an open heart and seek You diligently, especially in the dark times of discouragement. I love You.

God: Dear child, one day you'll sit beside Me. Then you'll be fully aware of My light-filled love for you, because You'll see Me looking down at you through adoring eyes. And you'll realize that the recognition you deserved was always there—from Me. You recall the pain you felt when people abandoned you in moments of vulnerability. And you ask Me why this occurred. I want you to know that it's always the work of the adversary, who wants to cause a deepening rift or crack in your soul to try to make you unable to reach the very people I'm calling you to touch! Rely on me for healing, because I will come once and again to embrace and restore you to wholeness. When you feel let down and rejected, turn your heart to Me. You were never meant to be a victim, as some imagine themselves to be. You're more than a conqueror, and you have the victory through Me. I'll work with you in greater ways to lead you to those who also feel like they've been belittled for who and what they are. The hurt you experience when some are self-absorbed is real, but, one day, you'll forget all about it, because your life will be so glorious and amazing as you sit beside Me. I love you.

MARCH 12
As I seek Your certainty

"For God is working in you, giving you the desire and the power to do what pleases him."
—*Philippians 2:13*

Me: God, You're the Lord of righteousness—goodness from right living. You bring certainty and hopeful expectation, no matter what the world offers. Would You help me to hear Your words more clearly today and to know what direction to take in every moment? I see how the adversary prods and pokes at my weak spots so I'll make mistakes and blurt things out inappropriately. Then he tries to highlight my missteps to belittle and humiliate me. Lord, give me strength to resist this kind of evil intent. Let me always fall into Your hands of mercy and depend on Your ability, never my own. Help me to refrain from anger when I'm pushed so that I always walk in Your wisdom. When people are unkind, disrespectful, thoughtless, or cruel, help me to be an example of Your love by walking in Your light. Reveal to me their true hearts so that I never take their unkind words personally. Be near me today and always. I love You.

God: Dear one, you are My child, and I love you. I work in you to will and to do of My good pleasure, always. This is because you are a chosen one. But, because the adversary knows this, he tries to pick on you. He focuses on your weaknesses and tries to make them look bigger and more prominent than they are. Those who listen to him fall into his trap and become his mouthpiece. Don't mind them. Know that I'll always stand up for you. Seek Me, because I'm always there to guide and direct you. I will steer you away from harm. Listen to your spirit, for in it lies your "true north." When you feel unpeaceful or uncomfortable, it's because there's something you need to do differently. It's My way of getting your attention. Heed this inner voice. You're never far from the truth. It lies inside you. You'll get better at discerning My voice the more you listen closely, for I am always with you. I love you.

To make up for my stupidity

"No, dear brothers and sisters, I have not achieved it, but I focus on this one thing: Forgetting the past and looking forward to what lies ahead, I press on to reach the end of the race and receive the heavenly prize for which God, through Christ Jesus, is calling us."
—Philippians 3:13-14

Me: Lord, thanks for getting me through the difficult and stressful times. Thanks for somehow working out even seemingly bad things for good and giving me wonderful outcomes in the end. Thanks for always making lemonade out of lemons. Thanks for showing me clearly how to overcome fear and negative situations. You are so awesome, and I praise You for all you do! Would You continue to help me? Show me more of Your greatness in times of tension and anxiety. Help me to see through my own blindness and inability to Your shining face smiling down at me. Lord, I need more of Your wisdom to compensate for my stupidity. Help me to celebrate the truth with Your power, joy, peace, and love. I need Your help now. I want to see that I am in the right place at the right time for the right reasons. Help me today to do more than I ever dreamed of! You're awesome, Lord. Thanks for directing my steps. I love You.

God: Dear one, do you remember a time when things were easier, simpler, and not so complicated? Remember when the number of things to be concerned about were fewer? Even then, you experienced stress, but the pressure was over different matters. Distress isn't brought about by the number of responsibilities or cares you have. It's brought about by focusing on the wrong things—what you don't have instead of what you do have. In other words, the negatives instead of the positives. Sometimes you may think, "If only I had this or that, then everything would be great." But this is never true. You have all you need right now to deal with each and every situation you encounter. Focus on this! Then you'll see My mighty hand in all you're going through. And you'll realize that everything always does work out for good. My hand is mighty in power toward you. My strength is sufficient for you. As you step forward, step out with faith. Then you'll see the gates spring open and blessings pour down from the windows of heaven. Just wait and see! Trust Me. Don't be afraid. For I'm fighting for you. I stand beside you as we face every eventuality. Because I love you.

But then You honor me

"I will honor those who honor me, and I will despise those who think lightly of me."
—1 Samuel 2:30

Me: Lord, last night in a dream I was alone in a large group of people, when a young man stood up. I could tell that everyone, especially the women, admired him. He made announcements and gave out assignments. I was shocked when he called me up and presented me with a beautifully painted platter. He asked me to take it to the general. I told him that I didn't know where to find him. Then a woman next to me pushed herself forward and abruptly announced that she would take the platter to the general. She grabbed the platter from my hands and turned to leave. But, as she left, I called out that she was missing something—a key that I held securely in my pocket. Without it she wouldn't be able to get in to see him. When I said this, several people in the crowd snickered as she walked away. The young man then turned and handed me another platter and told me to take it instead. This platter was less impressive than the first one, and I wondered how well this one would be received by the general. When I finally arrived at the right location, I stepped up to a sliding glass door that was immediately pulled open for me to enter. I introduced myself and was ushered in to see the general. Everyone there was happy to see me, and I was ecstatic to have found the right place and to be welcomed so joyfully. Then I woke up. Lord, show me the meaning of all this! I love You.

God: Dear one, others may think you are unable or incapable of presenting something of value to Me or anyone else. They may say you don't measure up to their "standards," and that you are separated from those "in the know," who wield more power. So, they look down on you, because they don't understand My great love for you. They may not believe that I could appreciate or honor you as I do, or that I would choose you. After all, in their minds you don't deserve such honor or regard. They think they have more right to pursue and be rewarded with My assignments. So, they try to confiscate the charges I've intended for you. But, they will always lack what is truly needed to gain entrée to Me. Only I can give true access to My presence through a belief in Me. Remember, I have angels watching over you and guarding all that I've given to you. No one can steal away what I've meant for you. So, never fear. I love you.

And shift all my "stinkin' thinkin'"

"Unfailing love and faithfulness make atonement for sin. By fearing the Lord, people avoid evil."
—*Proverbs 16:6*

Me: Lord, today is the Ides of March. This day of celebration once signified a new annum, where "ides" referred to the first full moon of the year. Let me count it as a new beginning by setting a precedent to live wholly for You as I reflect on and claim Your promises. I want to draw closer to You and see how You can work through me in greater ways. Lord, would You help me to be more of a servant by doing things in a way that honors You? Lead me to help others find their way to You too. Help me to be Your ambassador by shifting all my "stinkin' thinkin'" to the peace, grace, and mercy of Your loving thoughts. Heal my heart of any hurt, and let me see more of Your faithfulness in extravagant ways. You are my vindicator, my rewarder, and my ever-present supporter when others fail me. Let me be merciful when people walk away and make their own plans. Be near when others fade away. Forgive those who turn against me, and help me to love them in spite of their actions. May I look only to You, Lord, for this is my desire. I love You.

God: Dear one, today can be a turning point for you. I'll pour out many blessings to you, as I promised. But you must remember that, when you believed in My Son, you were set apart for My purposes. Through Him, you were forgiven for your past separation from Me. Your life was redeemed by His blood that was shed so your life could be bought back from the wiles of the adversary. Now, to live in a way that represents Me, you must resist evil. Flee from it. Withstand any temptation of falling into the trap of judgment and condemnation and self-pity. I'll weed out those who reject Me, but I'll also bring many who want to hear about Me. For now, combat the lure of focusing on evil that's done, especially to you. Oppose the temptation of dwelling on peoples' offenses. This focus is ungodly, and it leads to heartache and hurt. Allow love and light to be magnified in your life. Focus only on good, and the results of goodness, in your life and others. Move away from evil and those who dwell on it. Then, it will flee from you. It will lose its grip on you. And you can show yourself as holy. I will help you with this. Let Me be the ultimate judge. I love you.

MARCH 16
When all I can see is sadness

"No, I will not abandon you as orphans—I will come to you."
—John 14:18

Me: Lord, I see loneliness, powerlessness, and sickness in the lives of so many who don't know You! And it makes me sad! Would You draw them closer to You somehow, so they can know You in a greater way? Enable them to see You as I do—as a dear friend above all friends. Bring them along, like a horse to water, so they will thirstily seek out Your counsel and receive Your deliverance. Be near them so they can overcome their depression, loneliness, fear, rejection, pride, and self-pity. So they are not so discouraged. Open doors, Lord, for me to be able to reach into their hearts. Thanks for Your help during times when I myself feel alone. You've always come through with Your mighty hand of comfort by encouraging me when I needed You the most. Thanks for being a friend when others have failed me. Show me more of Your wonderful friendship today, and help me reach those who want to be closer to You. You're the provider of all good things. You bring deliverance, comfort, and wonderful blessings. Thanks for this! I love You.

God: Dear one, today, as you look out at the people I send your way, see Me in their faces. Watch for Me to accomplish My purposes through them. As you look for Me in them, you'll be surprised and amazed, because you'll see My face revealed. Instead of seeing them as they are—weak, sad, sick, unkind, thoughtless, helpless, and worn down by the world, you'll see them as I want them to be—strong, purposeful, light and life-filled, capable, and sound in body, soul, and spirit. You'll be surprised at what you view if you just look for Me in them. And remember that some are looking for you to save them, but that's not your job. You can lead them to Me, but your responsibility lies in pointing them in the right direction. Never let people put you in My place by making you the object of their worship or reliance. Your friendship is a precious gift, but, like any gift, people can take it or leave it. Those who discard it have done themselves a great disservice and will regret this later. You can offer it, but don't take offense if they refuse it. That's their choice. If they choose to move away or appeal to others to give them support, that's their choice. Don't take it to heart. Remember, I'm your best friend—always. I love you.

But then I remember St. Patrick

"The Spirit of the Lord is upon me, for he has anointed me to bring Good News to the poor. He has sent me to proclaim that captives will be released, that the blind will see, that the oppressed will be set free."
—Luke 4:18

Me: Lord, thanks for St. Patrick today. Thanks for how he brought Christianity to a nation. I'm sure You'll reward him for all his efforts! Let me be a light, like him, to those around me, so I can bring Your message of hope to many. Let me speak of Your mercy and love, as he did. Today, would You remind me of your grace and what St. Patrick accomplished? Lord, continue to teach and work through me. Give me needed strength to accomplish Your will and be able to bring Your encouragement to others. Today, I'm very grateful for those who committed their lives to stand on a belief in You. I praise You for steadfast hearts of service. I thank You for those who choose to stay where they are and press in and bow before You, and for those who want to learn to live out Your ways despite the world's pressured messages. Lord, deliver us from evil, and let Your will be done. Oh, that Your kingdom might come soon! I love You.

God: Dear one, whenever you turn your thoughts to Me and recognize My presence, power, and love, you are blessed. People are often anxious and distressed because, instead of acknowledging Me, they allow the cares and concerns of this world to drive their thoughts. Then, they become captivated and trapped by the lures of worldly worries. Some want more and more but end up with less and less. Some pray, but when I try to answer their prayers, they walk away from My voice. They end up wallowing in self-pity, self-loathing, and self-centeredness, as they follow people's voices and demands to try to deal with their own problems. As a result, they collapse into the same old pits over and over again. Pray that I can work in their hearts to will and to do of My good pleasure. I desperately desire to set them on high, by My side. But if they resist My calling, I can't help them. I sadly watch as they become entrenched in an abyss of sorrow. I love them as I love you, and I want the best for all people. You can help Me. Like St. Patrick, you can bring deliverance with My power-filled words. The good news you bring will release captives, open the eyes of the blind, and set free the oppressed! I love you.

March 18
And seek that kind of success

"And Samuel replied, "Speak, your servant is listening."
—1 Samuel 3:10

Me: Dear Lord, I ask for Your hand of grace and favor. I ask for Your abundance through My life, so I may have more to bring to Your House. You're the supplier of all my needs. I put my trust in You alone. Would You reveal to me those who truly seek You and want to know You? I want to serve You by leading those with a real desire to understand how to walk successfully in this world. I want to show them how to thrive in this life. Show me how to help them to understand and apply Your principles of success, Lord. I want to be a better teacher and leader by representing You in all things. Speak to me as You did to Samuel so I can hear Your voice clearly and be able to remember and share what You have to say. Help me to direct many more to You. I love You.

God: Dear one, I complete you through My gift of Holy Spirit. It's by way of My Spirit in you that you can begin to recognize My voice, because it's a sort of "channel" through which you can hear me. I will remind you that you are capable because you believe in Me and My Son. Our authority is your authority and you're able to "take the reins" of any situation by declaring and dispatching My promises. My words enable you to use My power to override any negative situation. Your weaknesses will always remind you that you must depend on Me. All I ask is that you do your best by devoting yourself and your efforts to Me. I will do the rest. In whatever you endeavor, do it as if you were doing it for Me. Then your works will always succeed. You can expect great things when you use the power of the spirit inside you. Don't worry about what will happen and when. I will bring you what you need when you require it. Come to Me with an open and thankful heart, and I will bring you abundance to share. My ways are above your ways. Trust in Me for yourself, your children, and those you lead—spiritually, mentally, and physically. I will work to open their eyes so they can see more clearly. Continue to minister to them with My love, and expect to see more than you ever imagined. But it will take time. Rely on My timeframe. I will come through for you. Now, seek strength from your spiritual "spring." I love you.

MARCH 19

With warriors who fight alongside me

"The armies of heaven, dressed in the finest of pure white linen, followed him on white horses."
—Revelation 19:14

Me: I ask for miracles today, Lord. I know something great must be about to happen. Otherwise, why would I be attacked so vehemently? Sometimes I feel like I need fellow warriors to fight alongside me. Would You reveal Your purpose in all this? Show me what You have in mind. How will You lead me, and in what direction are You taking me? Let this be a "miracle month." I implore You. Though I see nothing within view to prosper my way, bring me amazing abundance as needed. Help me to be in the middle of Your will so I can accomplish what You've designed me to do in ways beyond my expectations. You've always been good to me, even when I didn't deserve it. Today, I need your mercy and grace. I seek Your hand in my hand to guide and direct me. Overshadow my heart, and rain down Your drenching love until I'm saturated by it. Let Your mercies bubble up through me to others. I love You.

God: Dear one, I'm setting before you people who are being prepared to one day fight in My army. It'll all be clear later. For now, don't take people's offenses personally. I'm culling and pruning the character of each one. And you're seeing the results as dark natures are exposed, confronted, and stripped away, so they can be replaced by My light. Continue to pray for the ones I indicate to you. These are the ones I'm grooming for My army. I need your help with this. You can recognize them. They're the ones who desire to know the truth and want to see through the deceptions of political power, promises of safety and comfort, position, honor, wealth, and ideological achievements. They are those who seek to love even when they are faced with treachery. They avoid spewing venom to serve their own purposes. I chose you as a spiritual warrior, because you sought Me out. Stay faithful in the little things so I can give you more responsibility. As time goes on, you'll see your purpose more clearly. Now I need you to identify other warriors and minister to them. Some will falter, and some will advance under pressure. Seek those who are rooted, grounded, and unmoved by reproach or rejection, which are the weapons used by the enemy to try to defeat them. Strengthen your heart in Me. I'm bringing other warriors to fight alongside you. Watch and listen and pray. I love you.

MARCH 20

In this amazing place

"Because of God's tender mercy, the morning light from heaven is about to break upon us...."
—Luke 1:78

Me: Thanks for Your wonderful blessings, Lord, to bring me to this time and place! Thanks for being near me, even during the time when I walked away from You. At one stage, I thought I must go my own way to be free of heartache in a desperate situation. But You stuck with me and pursued and sought after my heart—continuously. Thanks for the people You placed in my life, who showed me how wonderful a relationship with You truly is. And for those who surrounded me with unconditional love when I felt unlovable and unacceptable. Would You continue to reveal Yourself to me in Your amazing ways? Unravel Your plan like You did with Joseph, after he found himself in another land, sold into slavery. You taught him so many lessons about how to trust and rely on You, even in prison. He must have thought himself forsaken at times, but, in the end, he realized how You meant it all for good. Out of evil, You worked out great blessings and a way to save Your people. You make good out of anything the devil intends to hurt us. It's all in Your design. Help me today to see Your hand in it all. I know You always stand up for me. I love You.

God: Dear one, today brings the beginning of Spring, and you've started to see the buds emerging on the tips of the tree branches. You're energized by the birds' chirping and the squirrels' bounding about as you walk. Remember how you identified the Eastern Wood Peewee singing outside your window last Spring? You watch the tops of crocuses as they sprout up again around the trees. You're happy to watch the new births and miracles of life resurfacing. And you appreciate once again all I've done for you and everyone who enjoys this resurfacing of life. Praise Me in this moment! Thank Me for everything I do! Because it's a wonderful time of joy! Let your lips sing of My goodness. Give thanks for My mercy. Rejoice! It's a time to celebrate! Salute another year of experiencing My love and mercy, My heart and kindness. Be glad that it's another day closer to My Son's return. Rejoice! It's Spring! And, one day, the "Dayspring," who is My Son and the Morning Star, will return to earth to shine, enliven, and brighten the new earth continuously. For this you can look forward and be grateful. I love you.

As You bear me up in Your quiver

"He has hidden me in the shadow of his hand. I am like a sharp arrow in his quiver."
—*Isaiah 49:2*

Me: Lord, thanks so much for Your mighty signs and wonders. I look for them every day, because I know they are just as real now as they were in the book of Acts. Let me see more of them in my life and others', because I want to clearly see the fulfillment of Your revelations. I want to draw closer to You, so I can be a purveyor of Your promises. Thanks for showing me how. Help me to be quick to respond to Your voice and instructions. I don't want to be a "loose cannon." I want to be a sharp arrow in Your quiver as You, the accurate archer, aim me to strike through the right targets. Would You help me to hit Your bull's eye every time, with Your steady arm directing me? Let me be one of Your arrows of love. Reveal to me those who seek You, so I can penetrate their hearts precisely. Bear me up and carry me swiftly. And I will go wherever You direct me. I love You.

God: Dear one, there are people in your midst who long to know the truth. Be bold to speak it. You'll encounter some who desire the rest and refreshing that only I can offer. Deliver it to them on a silver platter. Some want healing—physically, mentally, and spiritually. You can minister this to them. You don't need to go very far to see or find them. They're an arm's length away. Put out your hand and be bold to deliver My message of love, peace, healing, and truth. I'll send you as My best arrow of love to pierce through the thick layers of hate and fear slathered over them by the world. I will give you words to speak at the right moments to penetrate the dark film that coats their hearts. But remember that most people come for what they think they want. They may not seek to receive what they really need, which is what you can give them. People are very short-sighted. They only see their immediate needs. I pursue many who walk away after they get what they ask for. Few come back for more. Remember the 10 lepers Jesus healed? Only one returned to thank Him for the miracle of healing. And he received complete wholeness as a result. Though many don't understand what you offer them now, some will turn and return to you later. I love you.

To aim at those far away

"But the love of the Lord remains forever with those who fear him. His salvation extends to the children's children of those who are faithful to his covenant, of those who obey his commandments!"
—Psalm 103:17-18

Me: Thank You, God, for this day being a blessed day, full of Your promise, Your peace, and Your love. Thanks for working in me to will and to do of your good pleasure, especially in the moments when I feel like I'm missing out. Thanks for encouraging me. I often feel Your presence, and I want to fully experience Your love. Would You extend my encounters with Your intimacy? I asked You recently why I'm not surrounded by the love of children and grandchildren like others I know. I often feel sad, especially after visiting with friends or relatives who are always encircled by their families. They share pictures and memories during visits, and I feel sad that my children and grandchildren are so far away. I can only spend small tidbits of time with them, and I miss out on so much of their lives. Thanks, Lord, for helping me with this. I love You.

God: Dear one, don't imagine that I'm separating you from your family. It's just that I've had other more imperative purposes for you. Some people are blessed with family members who surround them continuously. But I haven't wanted your time to be so taken up. I need you to spend your time in prayer and study, because I want you to reach others with My hope. Your family will be touched in other ways. Your children will rise up and call you blessed, even though they're far away. I'll give you precious time with them both now and later. Every compressed encounter will make a difference in their lives. So don't be discouraged. I'll multiply the love and the days you've lost. Many will seek you, including your grandchildren, as they grow older. And, one day, you'll spend eternity with them! Most people never realize life's true potential, even though they're surrounded by family. They're oblivious to the greater world around them and the world to come. They never hear Me speak from within them to guide, direct, and prepare them. Heaven is within their reach, yet they trod down a narrow path that leads to a dead end. You can show them another way—a better way. This is your purpose. This is your focus now! I love you.

And watch as You pick up my slack

"So take a new grip with your tired hands and strengthen your weak knees."
—*Hebrews 12:12*

Me: God, sometimes I feel frustrated because I'm tired of picking up the slack for other people. Would You help me to be supportive of others when they stumble time and time again? And be able to enlighten them when they can't see what's right in front of them? I wish that people would take more responsibility for themselves and others. But they make foolhardy mistakes that sometimes lead many astray. They pose the same questions over and over, and, though I repeat back the same answers, they act like they can't hear me! And I feel like screaming. But, instead, I turn to You and ask for Your help. Would You give me patience and appropriate words to say? It really is so tiresome. I feel like I'm surrounded by hopeless people with endless requirements, and I'm left with little time to do my own work or to spend time with You! Help them to rise up, Lord. Help them to be strong and wise and make right choices. Help me to use wisdom and discernment as to which burdens to take on and which ones to let go. Help me to not feel exasperated. I can't be everyone's eyes and ears continuously. Help others to rely more on You. Help me to trust that You'll take care of me when I'm surrounded by needy people. I give them to You! I love You.

God: Dear one, you want people to "step up to the plate" and pay attention to what's needed, but they themselves often feel inadequate and unappreciated. Look on them with love and compassion, even when they seem to be overly needy and irritating. Sometimes people can be infuriating. When My Son was in the garden, before His crucifixion, He wanted so badly for His disciples to stay awake with Him and pray. This didn't happen. He was disappointed, but He acknowledged their weakness and forgave them. People are weak. They often don't think right thoughts and are undisciplined mentally, physically, financially, and spiritually. They're imperfect. Even the people you think are nearly perfect aren't. They're usually the ones with the most imperfections. They just know how to conceal their faults better. Forgive and give them another chance. They feel badly and may not even know they missed their opportunity to hear good advice. Continue to speak My words. And I will always give you the encouragement you need. I love you.

And pursue me

"Don't copy the behavior and customs of this world, but let God transform you into a new person by changing the way you think. Then you will learn to know God's will for you, which is good and pleasing and perfect."
—Romans 12:2

Me: Dear Lord, I often feel like I don't belong. I've thought that I don't fit in because I'm not like other people. Looking back, I see how I was always in a war for my life and my soul! And the people who came against me were set up to sidetrack or discourage me! They didn't really know me or who I was, yet they spoke accusingly against me. Lord, I see how the adversary uses people who are broken to try to disrupt the lives of those You are calling. As I read through my journals and reflect on Your words, I'm amazed at the fulfillment of Your promises in my life, despite my hurt feelings. Thanks for pursuing me all these years! You're awesome! Continue to show me Your own good purposes. I understand more about You now, and I see how You've called me. It all seems surreal, but I understand now how You completed the promises You made to me over the years. It blows my mind. Life with You is beyond belief. Thanks for Your presence and reassurance. Thanks for making my life fulfilling and exciting. I see how there can be no better way than Your way. I love You.

God: Dear one, it's only just begun! I'll bring you to more people and places than you can conceive of now. Just wait! See how I've already "loosed your heel," as I promised, by setting you free from debt and unforgiveness and the pain caused by others? I continue to release you from financial, mental, and physical burdens so you can be free to live and give to others—those I'll bring to you. I promised I would pour out to you blessings beyond your imagination. And you'll see more divine connections in the future. Continue to seek my purposes for you. You may often feel alone, because I've set you apart from this world. I have always sought you out and desired to reach and touch your heart. I knew you'd continue to believe in Me, even when others tried to attack you with their words. And I love your persistence. Often, it's when people are separated from others that they will come to Me with their whole heart. You did. Never allow your loneliness to give you pain. Remember, you're never alone or rejected by Me. I accept you always. I love you.

Then send me out as Your messenger

"When we tell you these things, we do not use words that come from human wisdom. Instead, we speak words given to us by the Spirit, using the Spirit's words to explain spiritual truths."
—1 Corinthians 2:13

Me: Dear Lord, I want to be a special representative for You! Help me to be like Elijah and Elisha, who walked with You during times of extreme national upheaval and political corruption. I want to stand against the forces of evil that continuously attack what is good. Only You can see what lies ahead. Guide and direct me. I long to act for You with the miracles of Moses, the strength of Samson, the sagacity of Samuel, the devotion of David, and the joy of Jesus. Stir me up and embolden me to speak Your words without hesitation. Show me Your insights like You did with Ezekiel, Daniel, and John. I'm Your willing vessel. Work with me! Mold me into a beautiful urn so I can pour out Your spiritual oil freely and abundantly. Just as Isaac prophesied about his son Joseph in Genesis 49:25, "Bless me with the blessings of the heavens above and the watery depths below." Though enemy archers attack and harass me, may my bow remain taut and my arms strengthened by Your hand so I'm able to protect Your people from harm. I love You.

God: Dear one, you are a spiritual warrior and a watchman for Me. You can alert people of My warnings and bring them strength to fight the world's battles. Your voice is powerful—it brings light and life as you speak what I tell you. My Word is like a two-edged sword—it can break through any wickedness and deception. Use My weapon as often as possible to disperse darkness and separate it from My light. I'll bring people to you who seek your counsel. Speak My words to them and bring them consolation. Only My Word offers hope. With My sword, you can divide and conquer and be as powerful and effective as any prophet who's lived. I've set you "on a hill," as I did My Son, so people can see you and hear your light-filled stories. You'll become known as a storyteller—one who gives encouragement with accounts of My wonders in your life. As you age, store up your miraculous encounters of deliverance. Preserve them for future generations. As you recount them, some will hear and rejoice. Some will be set free. I'll work through you, because you are My strong messenger. And I love you.

MARCH 26
And give me the courage to face them

"So we can say with confidence, "The LORD is my helper, so I will have no fear. What can mere people do to me?"
—Hebrews 13:6

Me: Thanks, Lord, for this new day when I can relax in Your presence and praise You for Your wonderful works! Thanks that I can overcome anything in ways beyond my imagination. More and more, You keep bringing me people who desire to know You. But they are often weakened by fears and desperately need help, guidance, and encouragement. Lord, I often don't feel like I'm the right person for this job, but this seems to be part of Your calling for me. You showed me that, as it says in Ezekiel 3:5-9, You chose me because I'm strong-minded enough to deal with them. Though some rebel against You, I can resist them with Your help. When some come with qualms or misgivings, would You give me Your pure heart to be able to bring them back to You? Open my eyes to see clearly their needs, desires, and longings. Let me be able to help them by revealing Your true nature in ways they've never imagined. Give me the wisdom and courage I need to speak. Thanks for being my strongest advocate and ally, and for standing up for me. I love You.

God: Child, each day is a new day to serve and to offer love to others, especially those who are broken and hurting. As your "maître d'," I show you how to "carry the tray" and be the best servant to all. Follow My example. I'll always work in you to will and to do of My good pleasure. I'll give you the strength, mercy, kindness, and ability to help those I bring to you. You see My calling for you—to help the weaker ones mentally, spiritually, physically, and financially. Like the prophetess Huldah did for King Josiah, your ministry involves speaking prophetic words over people, including many women. You're a hidden gem. You will reach many in My name. But you must be selective and hear My counsel as to who to speak to and which of My divine secrets to reveal and when. Some will come to you when they realize how far they've drifted from My Word and how estranged they've become from Me. When their eyes are opened, and they see how their children have forgotten Me, they'll call on you to come and deliver a message of hope and tell them what to do. Then they'll call on you, like some requested Huldah, to offer My words to save them and their children. I'll show you how to speak and what to say. I love you.

MARCH 27
While I wonder how You must feel

"And this hope will not lead to disappointment. For we know how dearly God loves us, because he has given us the Holy Spirit to fill our hearts with his love."
—Romans 5:5

Me: Lord, now I understand how You must feel when You extend Your hands to people and offer them all You have, yet they turn their backs on You! It must be so frustrating to watch them struggle and wallow in self-pity, pride, hurtfulness, sickness, sadness, poverty, and then suffer death, when You can set them free! You have so much to give us, and yet we often refuse to turn to You for help. This morning, I felt frustrated when a woman I'd reached out to with answers to her dilemma walked away from me and turned to others for help. They helped her a little, but I knew I was far more able to meet her needs. Yet she refused my help. It was baffling. And I know how You must feel when people turn to everyone else except You! It's painful to watch. Would You show me how to help those who want my input? Enlighten me so I can see as You do and not blame myself when I feel rejected or spurned. Help me move on and be able to work with those You send me. Bring humble people and prosper my way so I can bless them even more. Unveil my eyes to Your view. I want to trust You in each moment. And see You swing open many more amazing doors. I love You.

God: Dear one, your heart is heavy and sometimes burdened. This is because you allow your mind to be diverted from Me, and then you lose the true focus of what I can do for and through you. Trust Me that, even now, I'm working on your behalf to bring you wonderful people who will trust you and Me. These are the people I want you to help with My Word. They will listen, so speak boldly! Tell them what you know—what I have placed in your heart. They want your insight and wisdom. Give it to them. They'll come to you with open ears and hearts. Don't begrudge those who don't respond to you or return your calls. These are people who aren't ready to hear, because they're still enmeshed in nets created by the enemy. They're ensnared with concerns and worries. They're not ready now, but they may come later. When they do, speak My words of deliverance, hope, and love. I'm your helper. I'm by your side and ready to give you what you need. Don't despair. I never do. I love you.

MARCH 28

As You lead me one heart at a time

"For God, who said, "Let there be light in the darkness," has made this light shine in our hearts so we could know the glory of God that is seen in the face of Jesus Christ."
—2 Corinthians 4:6

Me: Oh Lord, only You can give answers that soothe our hearts and give us peace. Only You can offer us meaning and lift the shadows from our eyes. Only You hold the key to our future and help us to understand it all. Now we see things so very darkly. We live in shadows and obscurity. Then, we'll see You as You are. Oh, give me a small glimpse now to sustain me! Let me see Your face, even if it's through the hearts of people. Let me be a part of You as You are a part of me. Help me feel Your presence, see as You want me to see, and speak what You tell me. I want to be obedient to Your will. Help me to see my feelings for what they are and be able to better read others' thoughts and intents. And help me to see their hearts, especially if they appear to be adversarial or contentious, when You have other purposes for them. Thanks. I love You.

God: My love, I'll bring people to you one at a time. I'll set them before you for prayer and words of encouragement. And I'll help you see their hearts clearly. In your mind's eye, you'll be able to discern a transparent view of their spirit. With this insight, you can determine the degree of their radiant glow—or how close their hearts are to Mine. Those who shine with a brilliance that illuminates their actions are the ones who are red hot for Me. They deeply desire to know Me in a greater way. Those who shine with a more subdued light may accept a belief in Me, but they haven't pressed in to know Me. They may grow hot in their love for Me later but haven't yet. Those without faith shine very little light and emanate a very minimal life glow. These are lukewarm in their desire to know their true purpose. They just exist. They merely survive. Those who emanate "darkness" have blackened hearts. These work for the adversary and serve his purposes. Their malicious words and evil actions betray them. I'll always show you peoples' hearts if you turn your eyes to Me. And when I show you the "glow," speak the words I give you. You can change their lives by offering direction, peace, prosperity, grace, mercy, and so much more! I have more to do with life and its direction than you can imagine! Trust Me. Because I love you.

Even as I feel "put out"

"I have chosen to be faithful..."
—Psalm 119:30

Me: Lord, some people think that if things don't come easily, they just aren't meant to be. This may be because they don't want to subject themselves to discipline, change, or greater responsibility. So, they do what seems easiest. They continue on the same path of least resistance so they don't have to expend too much effort. They blend into the scenery, because they're afraid of what others might say about them. And they react hyper-defensively if they suspect that someone might be suggesting a change in their lifestyle. As a result, they turn their faces from the only One who truly loves them and can give them what they want: love, peace, joy, the desires of their heart, health, comfort, provision, satisfaction, and encouragement. You're all these things and more, Lord. How can I help people like this to see You more clearly? You've taught me to refrain from fault-finding and complaining and to look for what You can teach me through even the roughest and harshest of people. Show me when a relationship is no longer beneficial for Your purposes. I need Your guidance with this. Thanks for renewing friendships that should be restored and ending those that are no longer advantageous. And, in Your mercy, help me to be nonjudgmental and noncritical. Thank You, Lord. I love You.

God: Dear one, people will come and go. They're sometimes unfaithful to those who've tried the most to help them. And it's easy to feel "put out" by those who demand your time and patience when they're in need but never reciprocate your thoughtful regard or even say thank you. Some don't want to expend the effort to make the changes in their lives that would set them free! But you can be faithful! Be consistent in your dealings with people, even when they turn against you or away from you. You can still be kind, even when thoughtless people are self-centered, self-involved, and rude. It's good to stay in one place for a while, because the people who may not appreciate you now will one day remember your kind ways and come to look for you when they need you. Let Me bring good people to you—the ones who want to change and learn about Me. I'll do this in miraculous ways. You'll be amazed. They'll come, because I'll lead them to you. They'll seek your advice and counsel. Let Me give you the right words to speak to them. And you'll be encouraged by the outcome. I love you.

MARCH 30
And I try to hide

"God blesses those who are humble, for they will inherit the whole earth."
—Matthew 5:5

Me: Lord, what a blessing it'd be to have more time to relax and be refreshed in You! You've always been so good to me. You answer my every request and meet my every need. You love me when I feel unloved and call to me in my hiding place when it's time for me to come out! Like Elijah, I sometimes feel like burrowing down deep to separate myself from the world's hurtful ways. I seek a cave, like him, to wallow in self-pity and self-soothing. But then, You whisper to me and ask, "What are you doing in there? Why are you hiding?" Lord, I seek my own quiet place sometimes to read and write and reflect. Is that wrong? I do love being by myself with my own thoughts at times. But I know You want me to seek out others to minister to, with Your help. You've shown me ways to lead people to You through prayer. My hands are before You now. Fill and direct them. My eyes seek You. Would You give me Your insight? My feet wander. Give me direction and the right path to walk on. My arms reach out. Embrace me and give me Your peace to spread. Thanks. Today, open doors so that I can help others spiritually, financially, mentally, and physically. Lead me. I'm Yours. Oh, let me see and hear You more clearly too! I love You.

God: Child, you seek Me, and sometimes you don't know where I am. And so, you hide, because you don't see me in the harshness of people in the world—those who turn against Me or try to conceal themselves from Me. But there are places you can find me when you're not in your secret place. I'm in the lowly. I'm in the meek. I'm in the least likely people you'll encounter. I'm even in the forlorn places and the areas that are bleak and sad. I'm in the ones who come to you with yearning eyes, who seek love because they feel rejected. I'm in the humble ones, who won't lift themselves up with self-righteousness. I'm in the forgiving and benevolent ones who seek peace. Those who are prideful and arrogant won't enter My gates. Nor will those who think they have all the answers and don't dare come to Me for counsel or advice. Only the searching and humble ones can enter My presence. Seek these! I love you.

But You take me to places I'd never dream of

"Do not be afraid or discouraged, for the LORD will personally go ahead of you. He will be with you; he will neither fail you nor abandon you."
—Deuteronomy 31:8

Me: Lord, You've brought me so far! You've taken me beyond my imagination to places I'd never have dreamed of. Your mercies, kindness, and love are beyond comparison. Thanks for answering my prayers and preparing me for every turn in this journey. The prophetic words, dreams, and visions have all changed my life and brought my faith to higher levels. They've given me strength to fulfill Your calling. Today, lead me through doors beyond my imagination! I've spoken for You. I've offered Your message to those whom You've set in front of me. I've presented Your gifts. But sometimes I'm discouraged by a lack of response. Why do people choose to stay in a place of fear, where they're trapped by bars of their own choosing? Why do some choose to live with sickness or pain, when they could be delivered? Only You can give real peace or healing. When others decide to stay in broken places, would You guide and give me the right words to say? I seek Your wisdom. Lead me now to people who want to hear about You and receive deliverance! I love You.

God: Dear one, remember, it isn't you that people reject when they turn away from the hope you offer. It's Me. People filled with fear of rejection, failure, or abandonment often won't try to overcome these things. Instead, they submit to them and make little effort to go beyond life as they know it. They blame Me or others for their lacks, instead of seeking reasons for their condition, or trying to find ways to overcome it. People who stay in ditches of their own making often point at others as the reason for their muddling. They remain where they are because they've chosen this half-life of victimhood. They want to stay dependent on other people. They grow angry or bitter when others won't step up and compensate for their lacks. Their god is helplessness. It's a lifestyle they've fallen into and a spirit they choose to worship. You can direct them to another way, and encourage them with positive thoughts based on My Word, but they must decide to follow that way. Remember, fear causes barriers. You can speak love, truth, joy, and healing. And someday, hopefully, they'll decide to join you on your overcoming journey. I love you.

April

FOCUS:
WONDERFUL WISDOM

"For the Lord grants wisdom! From his mouth
come knowledge and understanding."

—PROVERBS 2:6

APRIL 1
I want to be like Brother Lawrence

"I will praise you, Lord, with all my heart; I will tell of all the marvelous things you have done."
—Psalm 9:1

Me: The first day of April! Wow! Thanks, Lord, for Spring and the semblances of it—the delightful daffodils, crocuses, and buds on the trees. Thanks for being there for me when I need you so much and for being my constant companion, guide, leader, and life-giver. Thanks for meeting every need beyond my expectation and for bringing great joy out of sorrow and fulfillment out of lack. You've never disappointed me! Help me to continue to grow in Your love in this new season. Would You show me how to praise You in all I do like Brother Lawrence? He's one who served as a lay brother in a monastery in Paris in the 1600s and is remembered for his intimate relationship with You. Even as he did menial tasks, he worshipped and praised Your name. Would You remind me to turn my thoughts to You in thankfulness, even in the moments when life feels hard and unrelenting. When the job I'm doing grows tedious and boring with no end in sight, jog my memory to all the things You've done for me. Help me to reflect You moment by moment as I look into Your face and manifest it to others. Thanks for Your joy and peace and wisdom today! I love You.

God: Dear one, yes, I can give you greater wisdom and insight, along with endurance and joy, as you turn to Me more and more. Depend on Me for these. I can give you greater peace and sound thoughts, and I can free you from all fear. Come to Me, and let Me ease your mind today. Give Me your cares and worries. Allow Me to smooth over the rough edges and calm your heart. I alone can do these things. Don't worry so much about people and what they think. It doesn't matter in the scheme of things. They'll come and they'll go. Only My Word will prevail. It alone brings constant joy. It alone offers wisdom. Sink your thoughts into the deep waters of My loving words. Let your heart settle into My lavish sands of devotion as My warm, healing waters wash over you to assuage and calm you. That's what My peace is like. That's the comfort of My ways. Let your heart be at peace; let it be calm. Only by anchoring it in My Word can this be accomplished, because, through it, I can draw you to Myself like a magnet and surround you with My love. I love you.

And have great wisdom

"But when the time of perfection comes, these partial things will become useless."
—*1 Corinthians 13:10*

Me: God, sometimes I do things without waiting for Your direction. Would You forgive me? Sometimes I want to see things happen more quickly, and I forget to look to You. Forgive me for this. I want to walk in Your ways because mine are frustratingly fruitless. Your course is lined with gorgeous trees loaded with good fruit. Help me to recognize Your path and see clearly when I wander beyond it. Help me to wait until I know Your insight on a matter so I can follow Your heart in all I say and do. You've shown me that if I grow impatient or angry, I'll likely lose Your focus and the opportunity for which You called me. I must be careful to walk with You so I can touch the hearts of those You point out to me. With Your Spirit in me, I can know the time and the place for everything and be a greater wooer of Your Word. Lord, I need Your help to know when to speak so I can warn people about the things You tell me. But I need to know when to withhold my words. Give me wisdom on the timing. You are wise. You are kind. I love You.

God: Dear one, life can be tumultuous. It can be full of busyness and the unending needs and wants of life. But you can be at peace if you remember to turn to Me and surrender your thoughts moment by moment. I can warn you when your efforts might be fruitless—a waste of your time. Time is precious. It can be easily stolen and never returned. Time on earth is valuable because it's limited. Be sparing with it and never careless. How you spend each moment using your gifts and "talents" will determine how you'll live in the next life. Treat time as a gift from Me. And let Me lead you in the best ways to make use of it. To do this, calm your mind, especially when there's chaos, so you can hear from Me. Because, through Me, your choices will always be the right ones in every situation. You may be tempted to view time alone with Me as wasted time. But it's in these tremendously valuable moments that I can be closest to your thoughts. In these quiet mental moments I can answer your questions and ease your mind. It's when you can see and hear Me most clearly. It's the most precious time you have each day. I love you.

APRIL 3
So I'm never a victim

"Joyful is the person who finds wisdom, the one who gains understanding. She will guide you down delightful paths; all her ways are satisfying."
—Proverbs 3:13,17

Me: Dear Lord, let my words be salted with Your wisdom. Let my hands hold Your mercy. Lord, this day is Yours. May my actions please You, and may I shine Your love to others and bring them Your peace during trials and turmoil. Let kindness and forgiveness pour from my lips. Lord, from what I've seen, You never place us in situations indefinitely where we must depend on others for help. You want us to "grow up," so we can abound toward others. When I had no job or money, You always provided what I needed, though often it came in unexpected ways. I've never felt like a victim because I couldn't reach the right destination or attain the right ends. In time, if I was patient, You always led me down the best path to where I belonged, if I listened and followed Your lead. The only times I ended up in the wrong places were when I took a detour from what You clearly showed me. Today, as I go out into the world, give me wisdom as I deal with needy people who don't know or understand Your abundance and grace. Sometimes I meet people who are perpetual victims. Give me the right words to speak to help them overcome their challenges and mindset, so they can see themselves in a new way—Your way! I love You.

God: Dear one, people's level of faith is always tested by the situations they encounter. Those who react with fear, complaints, blame, or self-pity haven't submitted themselves to Me. And some respond to your attempts with verbal outrage. They may walk away or act out through accusations, finger pointing, avoidance, or losing themselves in their own or others' lacks. Many don't recognize these as signs of rebellion against Me. Every person deals with fear. The world teaches it, so everyone reacts to it in one way or another—by avoiding it, submitting to it, or overcoming it. I can teach you how to conquer it. And, with My guidance, you can help others surmount it too by speaking to them the words I give you. As you seek to do My will, I'll bring you greater wisdom. Seek My way of faith so you can see the blessings I have in store for you. I love you.

Or afraid of what others think

"Fearing people is a dangerous trap, but trusting the Lord means safety."
—Proverbs 29:25

Me: It's been a stressful week, Lord. Thanks for helping me deal with it by working things out for good. You always ease my mind. Would You remind me to turn to You for advice? I want to respond to Your promptings. Today, thanks for peace no matter what happens. I want to use my time wisely and focus only on what's needed. I lean on You, Lord. Would You show me the way I must go and how to avoid distractions? I see how Jesus walked with You in the Gospels. He didn't care (maybe He did, but He learned to look to You so He wasn't discouraged) what people thought of Him, because that was not His focus. When He spoke in the synagogue in His own hometown, he was bold to say the words You gave Him, and He rebuked people for their lack of trust. They tried to kill Him by pushing Him off a cliff, but He escaped their clutches. Oh, that I would never worry about what others think of me, or what they might do to me, especially when they angrily reject or overlook me. Help me to only care about what You think of me. I want to only focus on how I can fulfill Your will for my life. Thanks, Lord. Work through me today. I love You.

God: Dear one, some people will get upset and angry because they have no substance—nothing to fall back on. They "strain at a gnat" (Matthew 23:24), because they haven't built a foundation on Me. They don't spend time in prayer and praise, nor do they give thanks for what they have, so their minds are susceptible and undisciplined. And they grow "thin-skinned." They can't stand pressure of any kind and falter at any sign of opposition. Don't be afraid of them. What can they do to you? Remember, I supply your needs every day. I hear your requests and stand by you. I hear your prayers and work on your behalf. So, never be afraid of people and what they think of you or what they might do to you. Come to Me with a pure heart today. I alone can give you strength and wisdom in times of stress. I alone can give you courage in threatening times. Lean on My help for your daily needs, and I will support you. Can you encourage these people who live in so much fear? Sometimes, if they want help and are willing to change. Because overcoming fear will take great effort, as you know. But some will want to be overcomers. And I will show you who they are. I love you.

APRIL 5
While You protect me from the storms

"You fools! You know how to interpret the weather signs of the earth and sky, but you don't know how to interpret the present times."
—*Luke 12:56*

Me: Lord, thanks for protecting me from the terrible "weather" of our times and for leading me where I need to go so I avoid harm. You constantly watch over me, and for that I'm thankful. It's awesome how You direct my steps without me knowing where You're taking me! Thanks. Lift me up, Lord, and set me on high—wherever You are! For I long to sit with You on Your magnificent mountaintop! Would You help me to see from Your precipitous view and understand all that You see? Show me the direction I need to take—what things I need to focus on. Give me needed wisdom, and direct me, Lord, so I can best guide others. I submit to You. Keep me safe, and place me in the right place at the right time. I'm in Your hands, Lord. And I can see them solidly on my life. I love You.

God: Dear one, weather's a tricky thing. It's determined by winds and clouds and pressure. When warm air comes, it forces cold air out. It's hard to know how you'll be affected when so much is determined by unforeseeable conditions and patterns. It's just like this with the movement of My Spirit in this world. You may speak My Word, and people may or may not be ready to receive it, depending on worldly pressures and conditions. They may have been persuaded by others, or they may feel that it doesn't "fit" with their thinking about how things should work. As a result, it may be hard for them to accept or understand your words. People can be hot or cold, just like weather. When they're hot to receive your words, it's because their hearts have been prepared. If they're cold, it's because they've been strongly affected by evil "winds." These drafts blow in and create false thoughts that produce inappropriate actions. Some people are more affected by them than others, especially if their hearts have not had the time (or the opportunity) to be tenderized by My love or guided in their understanding of Me. They may be hardened by events or evil words spoken by people around them. Your job is to change the direction of the winds from hurtful to good. You can change the "patterns" of weather in peoples' lives by speaking and living My love. My Word spoken with kindness can bring great deliverance into their lives. I love you.

And help me to focus on You

"For the word of God is alive and powerful. It is sharper than the sharpest two-edged sword, cutting between soul and spirit, between joint and marrow. It exposes our innermost thoughts and desires."
—Hebrews 4:12

Me: Lord, sometimes it's hard to go out into the world, where I'm constantly confronted by people's needs. If I don't focus on You, the frustrations can become overwhelming. I feel like I must appease so many who are filled with anger and bitterness. I must listen to their complaints, chart out their hopes and dreams, and finally console and pray for their hurts. Sometimes, I think I must convince them of things of which even I'm not sure! Lord, give me needed strength and wisdom, for it's hard to bear. I feel I need a break at times because it's exhausting! And when I do have time to rest, I think I must spend more time making up for others' lacks. It never ends! I know You must laugh, thinking of all You've put up with from me. It all must seem so tedious! I do pray that every day could be like that one sunny day when I sat in a café overlooking the turquoise sea that surrounded Santorini Island. Each one would be filled with light and life and joy and peace as we watched life's boats drift in and out of view. No one would complain or get upset. Everyone would be content and agreeable. And all would share in love unequivocally and praise You continuously for what You've done! It would be so wonderful! I love You.

God: Child, My Word can cut through any mess! It's as alive and real today as it ever was! If you'll read it every day, you'll begin to discover within its pages the heartening courage you need to face anything. It will give you the wisdom and insight you need to deal with any stress, whether it comes from people or situations. Its promises of hope, peace, love, joy, and deliverance are life-giving and easy to understand. Encourage others to read it too, so they can begin to understand My ways through My prophets' messages. My Word reaches into hard to access places, surmounts walls, and penetrates barriers. It cuts through the most overwhelming obstacles and softens the hardest hearts. It tenderizes and caresses. It brings peace and makes clear what seems super confusing. It also brings joy, love, and a new heart. Read it every day, and your life will begin to change, especially as you apply it to your daily situations with people. It will also help you to recognize what is real. I love you.

APRIL 7
So I can hear, "Well done!"

"So humble yourselves under the mighty power of God, and at the right time he will lift you up in honor."
—1 Peter 5:6

Me: Dear Lord, I have my goals—things I'd like to see happen. But I'm not sure if they are part of Your plan for me. Would You make clear which ones You have placed in my heart and how I can reach them? You alone have the answers and know what's to come. Open my eyes to Your view and how You see the people and things around me. You're a great God who fills me with joy and delight. Through Your wisdom, You bring strength and honor. Lift me up to where You want to place me in Your timing, and demonstrate how to continue to live and serve You. Forgive me for my lack of understanding and humility at times. Remind me to speak honorably of others so that I never focus on their shortcomings or failures. Reveal Your view of things, and help me to speak only Your words. I want to live for Your glory so that my goals fit with Your purposes. You're my confidante, Lord. I may never be recognized for what I've done while I'm here on earth, but my heartfelt desire is that, one day, You'll draw me to You, set a crown on my head, gaze into my eyes, and say, "Well done, daughter, friend, love, partner, bride, and one who is lovely to Me." I look forward to that amazing day! I love You.

God: Dear one, don't be distracted by the things of this world. Keep in mind, there are many diversions out there, and often they're meant to trip you up, avert your attention from what's truly important, steal your joy, and cause you harm. They are like roadblocks or hazards that come up suddenly and unexpectedly. Watch and be ready for them. Listen attentively to what I tell you, because I'll always try to warn you so I can prevent you from experiencing harm and lead you to what is good. I can make provisions for you, but you must pay attention. Heed My words and the nudgings in your spirit. I'll use these to alert you. I'm preparing you even now. How your goals fit in with My plan for you will become more and more evident as time goes on. But you must trust Me each day to reveal how I can incorporate all that you are and what you can do into tough situations, so they are tolerable for you and for others. Think about Joseph in Egypt and what I was able to do through him. Remember, I can work in you every day to will and to do of My good pleasure. You are precious and valuable to Me. And I love you.

APRIL 8
From my best friend

"For God wanted them to know that the riches and glory of Christ are for you Gentiles, too. And this is the secret: Christ lives in you. This gives you assurance of sharing his glory."
—*Colossians 1:27*

Me: Lord, thanks for the friends You've surrounded me with. You show me that all things work toward Your purposes and that the things we thought were coincidental were actually meant to be threads in the pattern of Your divine design. We're all a part of this grand masterpiece, even those who turn away from us and from You. I looked out my window as I drove to the store today, and I wondered how people can exist without You. How can they bear to live without any purpose or meaning and without a true source to turn to for unconditional love? What a desperate way to live! They're continuously disappointed by the betrayal and neglect of others! Even those in our own families won't always be there for us. How can we depend on anyone but You? Thanks for being my best friend, Lord. Put Your heart in mine so I can see things in a greater way today! I love You.

God: Dear child, it's written: "Eye has not seen, nor ear heard, and no mind has imagined what God has prepared for those who love him (1 Corinthians 2:9). That speaks of the mystery, the accomplishment of "Christ in you, the hope of glory." Remember, Jesus is inside you now, working to will and to do My good pleasure through you. Rely on Him for advice and counsel. Let Him speak to you and direct you through His Spirit inside you. He will. Today, let Him lead you into a fuller understanding of life with Him. It's a more beautiful existence when it's lived from within. Through this spirit in you, I can be ever present, ever available, and ever by your side. It's your light, your life, and your true being. It's your inspiration, your meditation, your identification, your transformation, and your transportation into My kingdom. It's your freedom from desperation, your separation from this world, your indication of what is most holy, your differentiation from everyone else, your familiarization with the true family to which you belong, and the personification of a most awesome God—all within you! Congratulations for accepting this great gift into your heart! I love you.

Who helps me see my true self

"He makes me as surefooted as a deer, enabling me to stand on mountain heights."
—*Psalm 18:33*

Me: Lord, help me to see things I could never see on my own. That way, I can more effectively encourage others. Would You open my eyes so I can focus more on You? Because You're a God of mercy, peace, and forgiveness. You bless me with Your love, and You work all things out for good. Thanks. You remind me of Your love and how You enjoy talking with me, as I do with You. I want to think Your thoughts and see myself as You see me. You continue to show me each day just how You view me. To You, I'm a warrior. Help me see this! You remind me of how the things I've thought and imagined came from You! So often, You inspired in me the words to speak and gave me the boldness to utter them. And when some turned away, you made clear that they just didn't want to change. They wouldn't listen because they defended bad behavior instead of turning to face the truth. "How they respond is not your responsibility," You said, whenever I blamed myself. And then You reminded me of the people who despised and rejected Your Son and the prophets. Show me those who do want to hear, Lord! With Your help, I seek these. I love You.

God: Dear one, I've always been by your side. And I've often directed you to those whom others ignored or rejected. Once you wanted to be "popular," but that wasn't My desire for you. I wanted your heart and for you to know that others' approval would never suffice. I still pursue you. Because you're My warrior bride. When you're alone and feeling sad or slighted, that's when I'm closest to you. Remember My Son's Sermon on the Mount, when He said, "Blessed are the poor in spirit, for theirs is the kingdom of heaven?" You're most blessed when you seek Me in grief or pain or sorrow. Know that I'm always with you in the hard times. I give you sure footing when paths seem slippery. Today, you'll see My mercy, grace, and kindness as you focus on giving. My hand is a hand of blessing— it blesses what it touches. I overflow with promises. My fingers hold the truth. I can relinquish this to you as you reach up to Me. Walk with Me by placing your toes inside My toeprints and your heels inside Mine. Remember, My way is a way of peace, hope, and mercy. A way of love. Never forget this. I love you.

APRIL 10
So I can reach people

"Be strong and courageous, and do the work. Don't be afraid or discouraged, for the Lord God, my God, is with you. He will not fail you or forsake you."
—*1 Chronicles 28:20*

Me: Dear Lord, yesterday a young man asked me how I bring Your words and my beliefs into the workplace. I shared about the things You've taught me over the years, and the ways You speak to me, so I can reach the hearts of those who come. Thanks for bringing me people who want to know You and aren't afraid to stand up for You against all odds. Would You help me to do what's right for those I meet today? Would You give me direction so I can lead them to Your truth and light? Would You enlighten me so I can clearly see what You see? Advise me on how to help them, for I need Your guidance to be able to best place these divine appointments in Your hands. Lord, You are powerful and all knowing. Give me clear direction. Thanks! Open my eyes and ears to what is right and what is true. Guide me through difficult moments when I'm not sure what to say. And warn me of any worthless words or conversations, for at times I've been caught unaware. I love You.

God: Listen closely, My child. It's often through the most difficult situations that I'm able to work My greatest wonders. My ability to work comes only through people who are willing to give of themselves, even in adversity, to bring about what I need accomplished on the earth. Think of Noah and the ark he built, Moses bringing deliverance to the Israelites, Esther's bravery to speak up for the Jews, and Mary's willingness to care for My Son when most thought He was illegitimate. Through disparity, I can work miracles. This year, you'll experience challenging times, but, in them, you'll see Me at work. Through opposition, you'll experience great joy. Trust Me and let Me work on your behalf. My voice comes from within you. Listen closely, so you can hear as I speak softly through your spirit. My words are there for you to learn from. Sometimes I'll tell you of people and enlighten you as to who they are, where they've been, and why they are the way they are. Sometimes I'll tell you about places and who's been there before you. Other times, I'll warn you of events and people's motives. Whether you are at work or at home or anywhere else, listen closely for Me. I love you.

APRIL 11
And still have rest

"And the Spirit of the Lord will rest on him—the Spirit of wisdom and understanding, the Spirit of counsel and might, the Spirit of knowledge and the fear of the Lord."
—Isaiah 11:2

Me: Thanks, Lord, for Your promise of the spirit of wisdom and understanding, counsel and might, knowledge and "awe." Thanks that these can rest on me, just as they rested on Your Son, because He lives in me. Would You lead me as my good shepherd? I know You want me to rest in Your counsel. Open new doors, and grant me needed wisdom as to how to proceed. Lord, be my guide and my shepherd, so I can proceed with Your heart of hope, grace, mercy, and peace. Thanks for loving and blessing me, even when I don't deserve it. Be near, and get me through the hard days, when I really need Your strength. I'm grateful for Your blessings and Your light that strengthens and heals and brings me grace. Be with me today as I encourage those in need. Grant me peace during trials, and sharpen my senses so I can see clearly. I want to see as You do. Open my eyes and show me people's hearts so I can better help them. I love You.

God: Child, I've touched and blessed you. I've given you a lot because you trusted and asked. Now it's time to give to others. It's time to stretch yourself by relying on Me for strength and wisdom. You've come far, but I'll lead you farther still. That's My plan. Some may feel threatened and turn away. That's their choice. You just love, love, love. Show My grace, even when others don't deserve it. Demonstrate My wisdom when they mock, betray, slander, gossip, get angry, or just ignore you. If you can do this, you can be victorious in anything. You can rise above all to a unique place of honor. It's hard, I know. My Son had to do this. He faced many who were unkind, hateful, angry, and treacherous. You may face the demons of those who hate you, because you stand for Me, and they see Me in you. It's these who cause the unrest you see around you. If you can see past their words of hate, you'll see what's behind them. Move on. Never be discouraged. I'm with you, and I'll reveal many things to you. There's so much you don't understand now, but I'll teach you little by little, in the same way a child learns. As you begin to handle new things, I'll reveal more to you. I love your heart and your eagerness to learn. I love you.

APRIL 12
In my role as a spiritual midwife

"He saved us, not because of the righteous things we had done, but because of his mercy. He washed away our sins, giving us a new birth and new life through the Holy Spirit."
—Titus 3:5

Me: Lord, today You showed me that I'm a sort of spiritual midwife. My job is to help others birth their dreams. My role is to lead them to Your gate, where they can enter Your kingdom and proceed to their true destiny. Some will choose to step inside the entryway, and some will walk away. My job is to prepare them to go in, to coach them through it, then to encourage them on the other side. Once they're born again, I can teach them how to nurture their new "baby"—the spirit inside them. Like a midwife, I can instruct, strengthen, enlighten, and guide them. Would You teach me so I can better direct them? I need Your wisdom so I can best help them navigate through life. I need patience and endurance to fulfill Your mission, and courage and fearlessness to speak and act. I need You to show me how to reflect Your love moment by moment so I can gaze on Your face and reflect it to others. I love You.

God: Child, what you're doing is what I desire. You're affecting multiple lives—more than you can know. And you'll touch many more. I'll bring an abundance of fullness through your life. I'll grant you greater wisdom. I'll enlighten your understanding with hope and augment the assurance of My presence. What I can do for you is a small thing to Me. To you it may seem enormous, but to Me it's miniscule compared to what I'm able to do and who I am. Remember this as you go about your business today. Let Me lead you forward. This is not your final resting place. You're here for a while to bring My message of hope to others. Many seek to find Me, but don't know where to look. They're lost, like sheep without a shepherd. You know the truth, but few really do. Share My Word with them. But don't be surprised when some veer away from it. They hear what's spoken in the world and are swayed by the lies. They may move away, but you will bring some of them back. How I love you! Don't blame yourself for others' lack of zeal or interest. Come to Me and make yourself available. That's all you can do. It's never your responsibility to save them. You can't. Leave them to Me. And remember, I love you.

APRIL 13
And know that my life matters

"God chose things despised by the world, things counted as nothing at all, and used them to bring to nothing what the world considers important."
—1 Corinthians 1:28

Me: Would You help me, Lord, to be bold to speak Your Word and courageous in ministering Your presence, even when events and situations seem to point to crises and alarm? Recently many in this world were exposed to a global pandemic, and now other terrifying events have occurred. The news creates great uncertainty of so many things, including the possibilities of dearth and death. People react in different ways, and many live in fear of repercussions. You've directed me so often, including in what to do day by day, so that I'm not afraid. Thanks for this affirmation of Your presence. Would You continue to teach me, in every situation, how to act wisely? I want to demonstrate to others that if they'll stick with You and listen to You in every situation, they'll always end up in the right place at the right time. You're above it all. You give wisdom and courage, strength and honor, blessings and joy. Thanks for these today. Thanks for Your hand of guidance as I go from moment to moment and place to place. Bless my friends and family. Give them health and strength, peace and wisdom. I love You.

God: Dear one, consider your life, and the impact you have on so many people. Consider how short life is and how meaningless are so many of the things people focus on, which, after several years, are forgotten. No one remembers who did what or why. Time is brief, so don't focus on what the world deems as important now. In the end, it amounts to momentary concerns and insignificant matters. Spend your time on what counts most for eternity. There are lives to be saved—people who need to understand that they are bought with a price through the life of My dear Son. They can have eternal life because of what He did. But someone must tell them. Don't be afraid to speak. What are you afraid of? I'll give you the right words to say, with wisdom in how and when to speak. And I'll place you where you're needed—at the right place and time. You can be bold, knowing that fear is not from Me. It's of this world. Focus on what matters most—I love you.

APRIL 14
While You draw me closer still

"In my search for wisdom and in my observation of people's burdens here on earth, I discovered that there is ceaseless activity, day and night. I realized that no one can discover everything God is doing under the sun. Not even the wisest people discover everything, no matter what they claim."
—Ecclesiastes 8:16-17

Me: God, how can I ever be like You? How can I ever aspire to walk like Your Son? How can I ever die to my selfish desires and live just for You? I want to live for You by laying aside all blame, anger, bitterness, wrath, envy, hurt, accusation, pride, and fear. Would You help me to see more clearly Your will and how I can do it? And to walk in Your path? You're a great God, worthy to be praised! You're a Father of love, light, wisdom, and justice. Help me to walk in Your amazing ways. Let me be as one who hears and always obeys You, Lord. If there's something You'd have me do, make it clear to me! You say You're training me, and I'm closer to where You'd have me now. Draw me closer still! Make it clear if there's more I can do! Thanks for the opportunity of today and for bringing me to broken people I can encourage. I'll listen for Your direction. I love You.

God: Dear one, you can accomplish so many things as you seek My direction in your life. Even now, consider your life and the impact you've made on so many by listening to Me. Consider how short life is and how meaningless are most people's accomplishments. I can't motivate people. But I can put a fire under them by placing them in situations to stir them up so they will act. Many build structures, like houses, gardens, monuments, buildings, and statues, to honor themselves. But, after many years, people forget who they were. Life is short and time is brief. Remember that the more you listen for My voice, the more you'll discern it. And each moment spent with Me brings you closer to experiencing new levels of intimacy with Me and greater breakthroughs. Don't blame yourself for the times you didn't turn to Me for advice. Remember, I work on your behalf to right any wrongs. I can do this for you as you trust in Me. To make the most of the years you have, never be afraid to speak. Or to love. For many need to see Me through you. Many are blind because few will bring words of hope to them. I'll give you wisdom and always have your back. I love you.

APRIL 15
Through taxing days

"There was a man named Jabez who was more honorable than any of his brothers.... He was the one who prayed to the God of Israel, "Oh, that you would bless me and expand my territory! Please be with me in all that I do, and keep me from all trouble and pain!" And God granted him his request."
—*1 Chronicles 4:9-10*

Me: Lord, today is "Tax Day," or, as some might say, "a taxing day." Thanks for helping me to be mentally strong and able to mentor those who come to me for guidance. Would You get me through this day with tremendous peace as I work on other's behalf? Give me clarity as I worship and acknowledge You today. Enlighten my eyes so I can envision what You see. Open My ears so I can detect what You hear, even as the world throws curve balls right in my face! Help me to sense what You feel too. Lord, You're powerful and mighty. Work within me today to be Your messenger of peace. I want to be where You need me to be. Show me. Teach me. Share Your heart with me in greater ways as I work and move about from place to place. With Your guidance and wisdom, help me to expand my territory and keep me from trouble and pain, as you did for Jabez. I love You.

God: Child, I'll alert you to the promptings of the spirit so you can grow to recognize them. Then you'll sense My directions and hear My whisperings. When you feel uneasy about things, that's your spirit nudging you and trying to get your attention. Heed the warnings. When you feel unpeaceful, that's Me letting you know the truth about a situation or a person. My messages are vivid and clear. Just listen for them. Following Me may be hard, because your mind may argue with your spirit, but you can take control of your thoughts by leading them captive to My words. The more you heed Me, the more peace you'll have. Know that I never intended people to confine themselves indefinitely to places of prayer. The purpose of prayer is action. My aim is to set people among others whose lives they can change. The disciples in the Acts of the Apostles went out among the people to bring them the Good News, after they'd spent time in prayer. They didn't remain isolated for long. That's why I love the prayer of Jabez—for expansion of one's "territory." I surround you with good things to enjoy and share, not to hoard in isolation. Don't forget your main purpose, which is to live for Me, as a light in this world. I love you.

So I can tune into the sound of Your voice

"Look, I am sending you out as sheep among wolves. So be as shrewd as snakes and harmless as doves."
—*Matthew 10:16*

Me: Lord, last night I dreamed that I was sitting in the courtyard of a foreign restaurant that overlooked a parking lot. A waiter suddenly put up a screen to block my view of the cars. Just then a man on the other side of the screen screamed for everyone inside the restaurant to stop and drop their pants, or he would kill us all! I couldn't see him, but I froze, not knowing what to do. You abruptly ended the dream and said, "This is why you need to be more familiar with My voice! In this situation I had the waiter place the screen there to obstruct the man's view of you so you'd have just enough time to hide under the table before the killer could see you." You told me that I was too distracted by the things around me, and I needed to focus more on hearing Your voice during the day, especially when I was surrounded by people. If I'd just practice listening to You more often, I'd be prepared for situations like this. I thought of the day before, when I was at an art fair with my family, completely absorbed with viewing the artwork. I realize the importance of what You just showed me, and I want to learn how to be more aware of Your warnings. Would You help me with this? I want to hear Your voice clearly so I can be aware of what's around me. I love You.

God: Dear one, always be wary and vigilant, no matter where you are. Listen closely for My words and turn your ears to Me. Let Me make things clearer to you, including who you should approach and where you should go. I'm ever-present. I can see everything. I'm your most intimate and ardent friend. I can give you wisdom and understanding. Today, spend time seeking Me. Be aware of the two "frequencies" you can tune into. You can call one the "hate channel" and one the "love channel." The hate channel is controlled by the adversary, who echoes and repeats vile messages via willing people and the media. If you let his reports grip and control your thoughts, they'll lead you to a life of extreme bitterness and selfishness. If you listen to My "love" channel, you'll hear messages of kindness, forgiveness, self-control, gentleness, goodness, faithfulness, peace, and joy. Remember this to-day as you experience the world around you. And that I love you.

APRIL 17
And withstand offense

"He has showered his kindness on us, along with all wisdom and understanding."
—*Ephesians 1:8*

Me: Lord, You explained to me why people verbally belittle others. It's how some contend in the natural realm. When they can't use physical means to get ahead, they use combative or manipulative words to thrust themselves forward. By finding fault with those whom others look up to and perceive as good or courageous, they think they will make themselves look smarter and better. This is never your way. People may honor and flatter those they choose, but I know that only Your praise and placement will prevail. Lord, would You help me to move far away from propaganda and innuendo that undermine and weaken Your purposes? Today, help me to listen more to You and recognize Your will in everything. I put this day in Your hands, Lord. Help me to use wise words when I speak. Enlighten my eyes to Your view of things and people. Where do they really stand? I want to live for You alone. I love You.

God: Dear child, I'll help you move away from the hurt caused by people who belittle others. I'll show you how to guard your heart from those who won't focus on their own issues or need for Me. Some invent lies. That's the nature of the flesh that has no desire for change or humility. You can be different when you refuse to demean others. People will see this and be dumbfounded. The only explanation they'll have is that something is unique about you. Some may think you're "weird," but then they will wonder when they fail to see any truth or goodness in the evil around them. People won't come honestly to Me when they think that My light might dispel their own darkness, and they're afraid to change. If they fear that their faults might be revealed, or their weaknesses exposed, they'll hide behind their own stinging criticisms of others. You must move away from those unwilling to revise their bad behavior. My nature is to forgive, bless, and heal. So, when you hear people speak evil of others, just ask, "Can God forgive that person?" If the answer is "Yes," then say, "If God can, then we can too!" This answer will stop the mouths of the critics. You see how wonderful My Word is and how applicable it is! Let Me help you with people like this! I will deepen your understanding, so you'll always know how to respond. I love you.

While I work as Your gatekeeper

"The gatekeeper opens the gate for him, and the sheep recognize his voice and come to him. He calls his own sheep by name and leads them out."
—John 10:3

Me: Lord, You reminded me recently of my calling as a "gatekeeper." *Gotques tions.org* says, "Gates are mentioned often in Scripture, and gatekeepers were an important part of maintaining order in ancient societies. Gatekeepers were guards stationed for protection at various kinds of gates, which could be city gates, palace gates, or temple gates. Ancient cities had high, thick walls around them to keep out wild beasts and invading armies.... A gatekeeper had to be trustworthy and alert for any signs of trouble. A gatekeeper lax in his duties could bring ruin upon an entire civilization, so the idea of gatekeeping implies alertness and security. The keeper of the gates...is none other than the Lord Himself, as He guards our mouths, preventing us from unwise speech." As I read the book of Nehemiah, I see how gatekeepers guarded the sacred city and the temple against unholiness. They kept foreigners from illegally selling wares for monetary gain inside the gates on the Sabbath. They also made sure tithes were received and stored properly in the storehouses for the priests' benefit. Would You teach me more about this calling and how I can guard against unholiness inside Your gates? I love You.

God: Dear one, I will work with you to teach you what being a gatekeeper means in this life and the next. I'll show you what guarding My Word and My people means. Part of this training is learning how to deal with people who judge you because they themselves are being judged. Only My Word can reach into corners and penetrate barriers. It will cut through even the most difficult obstacles and overcome even the hardest hearts. Like butter, it softens, tenderizes, flavors, and even heals! It brings peace. It also ushers in joy, rejoicing, love, and a new heart. Use it like butter. Spread it thickly over every hurtful action or word and over every unfair criticism or judgment. Let it sit in the open, where it can become soft and user-friendly. For it is the ultimate healer. Apply its saltiness to your words and deeds to bring savor and flavor. As My gracious gatekeeper, spread it lavishly and lovingly over others' shortcomings. I love you.

APRIL 19
Your wannabe hero

"The godly people in the land are my true heroes! I take pleasure in them!"
—Psalm 16:3

Me: Dear Lord, one day spent with You is worth so much more than many years spent apart from Your presence. Wisdom comes only from Your Word. Grace is Your miraculous gift to us from Your Son. Mercy is poured over us through Your anointing Spirit. Peace issues in with Your presence. A day walking with You far exceeds many days of walking alone in this world. Recently I read a book about the life of Hans Christian Anderson, and I was impressed by how he prayed, and how You so wonderfully answered his prayers. It's a story of one who pressed on, came to You for assistance, and succeeded through persistence. Thanks for this example of living faith. So many similar real-life stories surround us. Sadly, often they're hidden from us! You're a great God, full of mercy, grace, peace, truth, and wisdom. Your love abounds toward us, even when we don't deserve it. Would You reveal more of your heroes to me today, Lord? And help me to be one of them. I love You.

God: Dear one, I'm the Lord your God. I don't change. I'm always the same. The things of the world will adjust from day to day. But My Word never does. And the words I speak to your heart will never contradict the Word I gave to the prophets. Through them, I can lead you moment by moment, just as I did Abraham, Isaac, Jacob, David, and My Son, Jesus. They're the essence of faith and the underpinning of heroism. Just listen for them. For they can lighten your way through any dense fog, and, with them, you can command the obedience of any storm. They enable Me to guide you in the same way I directed other heroes, so you can accomplish courageous deeds. With them, I can carve a path through any thorny wilderness and steer you through any threatening jungle. I will place godly people in your life to speak My words and confirm My purposes for you, so you can do what needs to be done. Never ignore the signs or landmarks I place along your path as you draw closer to Me. Watch for these building blocks of faith, so you never make a decision out of fear or guilt. You can always operate out of faith in your journey by using My words as your guide. I love you.

And watch as You blow down Your blessings

"This I declare about the Lord: He alone is my refuge, my place of safety; he is my God, and I trust him. For he will rescue you from every trap and protect you from deadly disease."
—Psalm 91:2-3

Me: Lord, would You protect me from every evil thing? Would You construct Your hedge of protection—Your holy fence—around me, so only those things You permit can enter? Would You place Your angels near me so that nothing unworthy can come near me? Separate me now from those who wish to do me harm, and from those who seek to accuse me wrongly. I think about the Lord's Prayer, especially this part from Matthew 6:13: "And don't let us yield to temptation, but rescue us from the evil one." Some have said this really means "lead us away from testing or temptation" (*bibleref.com*), because James 1:13 says You never entice people to sin. Mainly, Lord, give me boldness so I'm never intimidated by the enemy. Give me great insight to be able to see into people's hearts and wisdom as to when I should speak and what I should say. Show me how to avoid evil attacks, Lord. Guide my steps and protect my paths. Pour down Your blessings of peace on me. Thanks! I love You.

God: Dear one, you know I'm always near you. Just call on Me, and I'll be there. I work daily to protect you by warning you of danger. Some who enter your life will try to bring you harm, but others will want to mend your heart of any hurt. I'll help you to discern both good and evil intentions. The amount of help I can bring you is determined by how much you want to believe and receive from Me. I'm preparing many, just as I've been preparing you, for service now and in the next life. I need more willing workers like you, because many unsettling things will happen before My Son's return. Incline your ears to Me and I will tell you what to expect and what to do. You can help prepare the way. Many need to hear My message, and You're My willing messenger. I want you to be ready, for I will open up the means to speak and rain down favor on you at My appointed times. Be patient, for I'm working now on your behalf. Continue to work as you have, looking for opportunities to be My "weathergirl" to change the direction of the winds in peoples' lives. My Word is like a tornado that can uproot wickedness by replacing tumultuous torrents with showers of blessings. By using its power, you can help control the winds and bring sweet storms that can blow away any evil. I love you.

That prepare and strengthen me

"Stand your ground, putting on the belt of truth and the body armor of God's right-eousness. For shoes, put on the peace that comes from the Good News so that you will be fully prepared. In addition to all of these, hold up the shield of faith to stop the fiery arrows of the devil. Put on salvation as your helmet, and take the sword of the Spirit, which is the word of God."
—Ephesians 6:14-17

Me: Who, truly, is a friend like You, Lord? Who is there when I need help but You? Who stands by me when I need support but You? I'm sometimes exhausted by peoples' demands and needs, and I just long to rest in You. When people let me down, You remind me that I can't control them or their choices. As hard as I may try to be a friend, people will still ignore and desert me and make promises they can never fulfill. But I can always count on You! You never disappoint me. When people tire me out, You refresh my soul. You open doors beyond my expectation and drench me with Your downpour of blessings. Thanks for how You answer my prayers and give me more than I could ever ask or imagine. You're a great God. You alone deserve my worship and praise. Thanks for all You do and all You've done. And thanks for Your timing in the fulfillment of Your promises. I love You.

God: Dear one, I see you as My anointed warrior. And, as My beloved one, I've equipped you with all the armor you'll ever need. Remember that you're connected to Me like a branch on a tree. As you draw from Me, You'll receive My sweet sustenance that strengthens as it flows through you. It's like life-giving ambrosia for your soul. When you approach situations, without leaning on My life-source, you cut off My power that can surge through you. With My help, you can do exploits—heroic feats. As my warrior, I'm training you to overcome obstacles, so you're never stymied by them. Today is a day full of promise and hope. Minister to My people. Bring them peace and joy. Bring them My love as I succor you. You're great, because I made you this way. You're wise because I infuse you with wisdom. Everything has a purpose. Let me reveal this to you over time. Trust Me. I love you.

APRIL 22
While I dig for rare treasures

"Wise words are more valuable than much gold and many rubies."
—*Proverbs 20:15*

Me: I will seek You early, Lord, even before the sun peeks over the rim of the earth. For I crave Your words, which are more precious to me than fine gold or silver and worth more than diamonds or rubies. You're dearer to me than any good friend. You're my father, and I look up to You. I seek Your wisdom and encouragement. You're in my heart, and I listen for Your words to direct me. Thanks for the examples of faith You've showed me over the years. Thanks for how they've blessed me as I've attempted to walk with You. I think of Corrie ten Boom's recollections in *The Hiding Place*—of how some days may seem insignificant, like her time spent as a young woman teaching and leading other young people, but those years were all a part of Your preparation for the challenges she faced later on, when she was interred in a Nazi prison camp. Show me how You guide me now, Lord, and give me strength and wisdom to face each day, especially future challenges. Like Corrie, I have a strong will. Would You help me to use this trait for Your glory? I love You.

God: Dear one, My Word is a jewel shining brightly in a dark and gloomy world. Seek it, then hold it high above you so others can see its glowing truth. For it is light and life. It brings beauty out of ugliness. Those who seek it early will find it. But, like digging for lost treasure, those who wish to find it must make every effort, because its discovery does not come easily. I search for those who will value a relationship with me. And I dig and pan diligently for even one ounce of fine gold. And, to those precious "nuggets" I find, I reveal My innermost secrets. Because you've sought me continuously, I have great plans for you. Follow My lead. For I'm sifting, sifting. Don't be surprised when some walk away. Because I'm sifting, sifting. And I want you to work with those who are eager to meet the challenges. These are those who are willing to withstand the fine filters and measures of My sifting. Like you, they're strong-willed, and they'll heed your advice as they search for Me. These are the hidden gems I treasure. I'll inspire you with words of wisdom for them because you are hand-picked—sifted through My love. I love you.

And see how You're the Lord of light

"This is the message we heard from Jesus and now declare to you: God is light, and there is no darkness in him at all."
—*1 John 1:5*

Me: Lord, You are powerful and perfect in all Your ways. You showed me once that You produced the world from what You are: light. Using the dynamics of light, You formed, made, and created all that we can see, and even can't see, including the universes, the stars, and the planets. When I watched "Journey to the Stars" at the Hayden Planetarium in New York City years ago, I cried, because I saw how You, in Your genius, fabricated it all! How perfect is the earth and how beyond our comprehension is what You've done! Would You show me how You did this? I long to see Your wonderful workings, and how it all came into being. Broaden my understanding, Lord. Open my eyes to comprehend more. I want to be an integral part of Your amazing plan. You lighten and liven this dark world. You beam down on us as we walk and talk with You. You love our friendship, and, for this purpose, You made us. Your love is pure, transcending human kindness. We should seek this end—to remain in Your love and be surrounded by it. You are magnificent—a God of light and life. Oh, that we could understand Your wisdom. Help me to see as You do. I love You.

God: Dear one, your world is like looking at the surface of a lake. You can see the shiny surface and the waves, but it's hard to see what lies beneath. At times the water seems clear; at other times it's murky. Water is heavier than the air around you. And the atmosphere that surrounds you is heavier than the space where I exist, which is made up of light particles. I operate within a different sphere that moves faster, like the speed of light, than any movement you can see. Your world is "thicker," like water is to air. My world is lighter and weightless, like light is to air. Light and darkness operate differently. I exist within light. The adversary can't, so he inhabits darkness. Remember, light moves faster. "Dark" thoughts come from the heavier darkness. The adversary uses darkness and dark thoughts to bring evil to the world, including sickness and death. "Light-filled" thoughts come from Me, and I can work with them to will and to do of My good pleasure. Through My light, I can heal and deliver from darkness. As you learn more about light and darkness, and see its reality, it will all make more sense to you. I love you.

Who shows me how to be wise

"If you need wisdom, ask our generous God, and he will give it to you. He will not rebuke you for asking."
—James 1:5

Me: Lord, today please reveal more of Yourself, so I can see Your greatness in unique and wonderful ways! And show me how to reach greater levels of intimacy with You. Lead me, so I can look back and know You were there all along! Touch my family and those who struggle to find You. Reveal Yourself to them in ways they can't deny. Your confirming words are such a comfort and blessing to me! I yearn for them each day. They speak to me in ways that nothing else can. Thanks for Your Word that heals, delivers, directs, encourages, and enlightens my understanding. Let me be like Solomon, who attained great wisdom from You. Let me be known for my insight imparted by You. And shower me with Your patience, humility, joy, and peace! I want to be able to warn and help others to prepare for the storms. Once You showed me a picture of a bird in a nest in a tree that was blown about by gale force winds. Yet the bird sat peacefully undisturbed. Help me to be like this bird, Lord! Give me fearlessness, courage, strength, and wisdom, especially when dealing with chaotic situations. Thanks so much, Lord! I love You.

God: Child, within you are such hidden treasures! Remember how I told you once that you are like a prism that can reflect all the colors of the rainbow? That is a perfect picture of the variety of qualities that reside inside you. I've given you missions that are unique to your abilities. As you follow My lead, I'll reveal My plans for you more and more. And everything will fall into place. You'll see the great results of My blessings over time. Life through Me will flow from you in ways you can't even imagine now. And you'll live in peace, because I'll open your eyes and heart and mind to what I have in store for you. I'll download more of My wisdom as you open your heart to Me. Just watch and see! I'm always with you and near you. There will be times when you feel alone and left to yourself. Know that, even more so in these times, I am with you. I can steer and guide you. Just turn your thoughts to Me, because I desire to speak to you and for you to hear Me. I'll always show you where I want you to be. As time goes on, I'll unfold to you more of My promises and prophecies. And you'll see their fulfillment and begin to understand just what they mean. I love you.

APRIL 25
When I'm weary of spinning my wheels

"He gives power to the weak and strength to the powerless."
—*Isaiah 40:29*

Me: Lord, today I desperately need Your strength. I feel tired and weary. Would You let me see more of Your goodness and experience more of Your power? I feel like I'm continuously stepping in for those who are unable to do what needs to be done. They leave more for me to handle. Help me, Lord, to follow Your will and use Your wisdom. Show me how to be just and fair and kind, to recognize when people are doing the best they can, and to be thankful for what others can do with their capabilities. Would You also demonstrate to me how to have peace in my heart, how to help those You lead me to, how to have the courage to do Your will, how to listen more to Your sound advice, and how to follow Your directions? I also need Your fearlessness to speak up when I need to. Give me stamina and wisdom today, Lord. And help me to focus on what You want me to see and do, so I don't spin my wheels on unnecessary things. I love You.

God: Dear one, I'm your father, mother, sister, brother, and your lover. I'm the family you've always wanted, and the help you've always needed in desperate, and not so stressful, times. Remember that it's often the less able people—those who aren't "on top of things"—whom I can most easily work with. They're the ones who recognize their neediness and want hope and change. Many considered Joan of Arc simple-minded, but her thoughts were uncluttered, so I was able to work with her and give her needed information to help save an entire nation! Less complicated people are often the ones most open to Me. Never despise the weak. I put them in your life for a reason. I've made you strong and wise in certain areas so you can inspire and lead others. When you feel like you're incapable, then I'll send people to help you in the areas where you need it. When you pay attention, I'll always give you guidance. And I'll give you endurance too. From My written Word, you'll learn about people like Abraham, who overcame great obstacles by turning to Me in times of trouble. Remember when he had to compensate for Lot's inabilities and lacks? I'll lead you to other examples of faith today. You'll grow to appreciate fellowshipping with ones who also stand with Me, and this will bring you needed insight and strength. I love you.

But still want to see things clearly

"My eyes grew tired of looking to heaven for help. I am in trouble, Lord. Help me!"
—Isaiah 38:14

Me: I feel stronger today. Thanks, Lord. You did promise strength in weakness. But I still need Your direction. Would You help me to see more clearly how I can use my time most effectively? Where do my talents lie? I've wondered why You didn't call me as another Joan of Arc, coming and going in a blaze of glory! Then You reminded me that, from the time of my youth, I desired a family and children. And You wanted for me what I wanted. Now, You give me another choice: long life to see my grandchildren grow up and have some influence over them, or a shorter life with greater impact on many. Lord, I leave this up to You. Whatever You decide is fine with me! Right now, help me to hear You clearly and to know what to do next. Guide me to best help those around me. I often feel frustrated, because I can't do everything. I find my focus drifting and then wanting to do nothing but read, pray, and write. I would love to take a "sabbatical" and just reflect and spend time with You, but I don't know if this would be the best use of my time or the most productive way to spend it. Show me how to do what You've planned for me. I love You.

God: It's hard for you now, dear one. You worry about the use of your time, because you don't see My promises coming to pass yet in your life, and you wonder when you'll see answers to your prayers. Continue to trust Me. Remember that My will is not for you to strive to get something from Me but to merely receive what I've already made available to you. I want you to be like a branch attached to a tree, and allow Me to provide for all your needs. Let Me nourish and sustain you. Without Me, you'll shrivel up and die. So, rest more in Me. Be faithful to what you know of Me, and look daily for My promises to be fulfilled. Because they will. I'll show you clearly the direction you need to go now and what I've called you to do. Today, seek My words, and be bold to speak and follow them. I'll always be there for you. Today, seek My hand to lead you and others to a clearer understanding of Me, which always brings deliverance. My Word is real. Watch and continue to pray for answers. I love you.

APRIL 27
As a godly leader

"Tell the godly that all will be well for them. They will enjoy the rich reward they have earned!"
—Isaiah 3:10

Me: Dear Lord, would You bring us people like Asa in the Old Testament, who brought a nation back to You? Would You raise up godly men and women, who'll step up to the helm of our country, raise their hands in praise, and stand tall for You? We need freedom to worship You! But many flounder, because they're manipulated by other peoples' agendas. Release us from the corruption that's abounding around us! Let Your Word reign supreme through godly voices! Give us the power to fight spiritual battles in troubled times. When others let us down, may we stand up for You. I know, even now, You're teaching me to be strong, to be wise, to resist evil, and to be capable, even when people or events hit me between the knees. Would You help me to not be afraid, or overly disappointed in people, when I am struck with adversity? And to be able to see and support clear leaders? Give me Your wisdom, Lord. And remind me to pray for others, especially those in charge. Thanks! I love You.

God: Dear one, the world will always disappoint you. That's because people don't have a clue what real love or leadership looks like. They imagine what they think is real, but, without an understanding of My ways, they end up being prideful, power-hungry, self-promoting, and greedy. But you can recognize true love and leadership. Because you've experienced both, you can teach others about them, no matter what the circumstances are around you. You can rise above the world's hateful voices by living out My higher level of love, which is selfless, comforting, kind, giving, merciful, and gracious. I love My Son, yet I was willing to watch Him be betrayed, scorned, persecuted, tortured, and killed. He endured it all! Imagine what it would be like for you to see this happen to your own child. It was heart-breaking. But I knew the end result would be the deliverance of many. One sacrificial gift, so that anyone who desired it could have eternal life! This is an example of love and leadership—the ability to see beyond oneself into the hearts of people because of a willingness to serve and give one's life for the benefit of many. Be My servant by expressing My love to others. See beyond their words into their hearts, and remember that most people can't see as you do. I love you.

In a darkening world

"Light shines in the darkness for the godly. They are generous, compassionate, and righteous."
—Psalm 112:3

Me: Lord, thank You so much for Your mercy, which You've shown to me over the years. Thanks for how You've shown me how to survive and overcome adversity through the examples of so many in the Old Testament, who suffered through oppressive regimes and the onslaughts of foreign attacks. Even now, in a world that grows darker, You continue to work through people who trust You. Would You help me to depend on You amid persecution, accusation, defamation, and personal attacks? Help me to rely on Your ability to open the right doors to reach people's hearts. You've entrusted me with so much! Help me to be a good and faithful steward of Your gifts. Show me how to seek and follow Your directions in all I do so I can manifest Your power each day. I want to be prudent as I counsel others, so they're never led astray. Lord, let me be Your wise servant. Thanks for Your hand in this today. I love You.

God: Dear one, you can always trust Me, for I am trustworthy. I give grace to the humble and wisdom to those who seek it. Pursue My ways, because they'll always prove to be fruitful and profitable. In all your efforts, trust and allow Me to show you My great mercy and power. I forgive, even when you feel like you're unworthy of any forgiveness. And My path is always peaceful. As you meander down it, I will always clear away the debris so you can find your way to Me. Following Me may feel hard at times, especially when you're faced with difficult choices, or when people dissuade and distract you. Whenever you lose your way, because you're diverted by noxious things that make you feel wobbly and uncertain and unable to see clearly, just call out to Me. I will be there. I'll help you to regain your vision—your ability to see clearly. I'll help you to trust Me again, so you can know how simple things really are. I'll redirect you to your "true north." With My wisdom, you're a fortified wall as in Jeremiah 15:20: "They will fight against you like an attacking army, but I will make you as secure as a fortified wall of bronze!" I give you strength to stand and walk through adversity. And, as My wise steward, you can release My truth and power! I love you.

As I think about where You are

"God's voice is glorious in the thunder. We can't even imagine the greatness of his power. He directs the snow to fall on the earth and tells the rain to pour down. Then everyone stops working so they can watch his power."
—Job 37:5-7

Me: Lord, my memories of spending time with my children when they were young are so very precious and meaningful to me! How thankful I am to have had these special times. Thanks for these enjoyable moments, Lord, and for the life-sparing ones too. You snatched me from destruction early on and saved my life many times. You pulled me from several pits and showed me the path to Your wonderful ways. Thanks, Lord. Sometimes I wonder, "Why am I so privileged to have had every request granted, every prayer answered?" I hear stories of people whose lives are cut short, who lack peace and joy, who never experience real love, and others who suffer continuously. And I wonder if they ever looked for You, Lord. I wonder if they are lost because they never found out who You are. I wonder if their hearts have been hardened by life. Show me clearly. All I know is that You've always, always been there for me, meeting my needs and helping me when I needed it. Thanks. I love You.

God: Child, can you see My face? See it there...in the trees, in the flowers, in the plants, in the birds, in the fish, in the animals, and in the people you love and who love you. See it in the stars, the planets, the air you breathe, the rivers and lakes and oceans, the sand by the seashore, even in the dirt between your fingers as you plant pretty flowers. See it in the life-giving seeds, the bulbs, the leaves, the fruit and vegetables you eat, the crystal-clear water you drink. See Me there, because that is where I am. I am all around you, although you can't see Me. But you can know Me, because I make up all that is real and all that is beautiful. I move and I breathe in everything you know and love. I am in all the things that bring you peace and joy. That is who I am. That is where I am. And anyone who searches for truth, who seeks true love, who wants real meaning, or the ability to explore and fathom inexhaustible wisdom, can find me. I love you.

While You deliver me from evil

"Yes, and the Lord will deliver me from every evil attack and will bring me safely into his heavenly Kingdom. All glory to God forever and ever! Amen."
—2 Timothy 4:18

Me: Lord, would You help me to know how to handle people who try to control me or others? Would You show me how to work with those who find fault and blame everyone and everything else for their lacks? Teach me how to deal with people who want to make others do what they done. Give me Your insight, Lord, on how You see these people and how I should view them. Show me how to have peace despite their manipulative methods. I want to feel Your presence and to know You are near, no matter what's going on around me. Help me with these things, Lord. Help me to lead others more effectively. And know when it's appropriate to set suitable boundaries with some. If there's something I need to see more clearly, open my eyes. Thanks for this day being a productive day. Show me Your path, and help me to walk on it with wisdom. Reveal to me which gates to enter and which to avoid along the way. I love You.

God: Child, you're talking about a spirit of control. Some people want to establish and maintain their territory, their personal space, and they fear that others might steal it from them. It's a dread of losing power or dominance. Their biggest concern is giving up part of themselves, or that someone else might "one up" them and be seen as more important or esteemed. This fear is accompanied by pride, hatred, jealousy, acts of aggression, and control. You can even sense the "fir" rising on their skin, like a territorial dog or cat who doesn't want to give up its space or supremacy. Those most susceptible to this spirit are people who've lost a loved one or been abandoned or abused. As a result, they're easily threatened by others and may become jealous of your placement. I'll show you what you need to know and do. Don't worry about anyone who tries to obstruct you or cause you harm. No one can stop My plans for you! The adversary will try to distract you by confronting you with vicious people. He wants to make you think that My purposes are worthless and weak. His desire is that you "shrink back" in fear. But, My way will always prevail! Just know that I can give you wisdom in any situation. Remember, people can make their plans, but if they're not a blessing to you and to others, I'll get in the middle to obstruct them! Trust that I want the best for you and your family. Even now, I intervene for your good. I love you.

May

FOCUS:
PRESENT PEACE

"In peace I will lie down and sleep, for you alone,
O LORD, will keep me safe."

—PSALM 4:8

MAY 1
Wherever You lead me

"Even in old age they will still produce fruit; they will remain vital and green."
—*Psalm 92:14*

Me: Lord, it's May Day. How glorious is this new season! I see flowers blooming and green grass shooting up and leaf buds exploding all over the trees. Thanks for life that springs up from the barren ground! While visiting my daughter in Portland, Oregon, in the Spring one year, I enjoyed sitting high up on her deck, looking out over a densely wooded hill. I peered down through the trees and watched every day as an elderly man worked tirelessly in his small yard planting things throughout his stair-stepped space. The man had a modest, but very appealing, wood-sided home with a moss-covered roof. A small patio extended from his back door and was surrounded by meandering plant-lined paths that wound around beneath the trees. In the evenings, he turned on a soft outdoor light that glowed down over his patio as he worked. At night, when the weather allowed, neighbors gathered around to chat with him on the road in front of his home. I imagined myself living there, retired and happy like him. Thanks for how you've always fulfilled my dreams beyond my imagination. I'll follow You anywhere, because You've proven Your love to me. Reveal to me little by little Your plan for my life. And show me what You have in store for me. I want to live in Your presence always. And I'd be at peace with You wherever You lead me. I love You.

God: Dear one, My peace is always with you—in your heart, in your soul, and in your mind. It flows through you and can give you needed rest. It can bring you closer to My heart. My love can also emanate from you to touch peoples' hearts. Through it, I can work miracles and bring healing to you and to others. Let Me show you how. When you trust Me by listening and acting fearlessly on what I tell you, you'll begin to see windows of heaven opening up. Things will begin to change around you, as you allow My power to work through you. Know that I'll always provide for you, and your life will be a blessing, even in old age, as you lean on Me. Only let your heart be My house and your body My temple. As My love shines out from you, people will see it, like the warm light that glowed from the old man's home. And it will attract people like moths. Continue to shine My love. Hold onto My peace. I love you.

I know it's the best way

"Keep putting into practice all you learned and received from me—everything you heard from me and saw me doing. Then the God of peace will be with you."
—Philippians 4:9

Me: I seek Your peace, Lord, in every thought I hold. I seek Your love, Lord, in every word I say. I seek Your gentleness, Lord, in everything I do. I look to You today, and I ask for Your input in each effort I make. Would You help me to not feel anxious when I'm around people, especially those who seek to control me? Give me the right words, so I can reach into their hearts and offer them comfort and peace. I want to be able to lead in a more effective way. If there's a better way, a better place, or a better time, please show me. You, Lord, are righteous. You watch over me with Your power, might, dominion, and holiness. You bless me mightily. Thanks for being here now for me. Thanks for blessing my day and helping me to maintain Your peace. Help me to be loving and kind. You give me the strength and wisdom I need! Thanks, Lord. I love You.

God: Dear one, by centering your thoughts on Me, you'll gain more of My peace. Focus on the words I give you, because they will be there when you need them. Follow in My steps, and know that I'll never burden you with problems as others do! Don't let the naysayers steal your peace or destroy your joy. Don't let them move you from where I've placed you. Be kind and show mercy, but never allow others to bind your mind or unravel your ties and connections with Me. People who try to disturb your peace fear losing control. They think that by pushing their own opinions forward they can "win." They fear that when someone else looks better than they do, it might mean that they're losing their own identity, because people are focused more on someone else's goodness or ability! So, they think they must put them in their place to reestablish a pecking order. Don't be afraid of them! Avoid trying to please them, because they are never satisfied, no matter how much you try to give. Follow Me to peace. Remember, people-pleasing leads to anxiety. I'm Your burden-bearer, so come to Me for all the heavy lifting. I'm in this time. I'm in this day. And I will direct you as you listen for My words. I whisper to you, and I hear Your prayers. I make up for the losses you experience. I'll show you what to say and what to do so you're ever blessed. I love you.

May 3
Even when life feels uneasy

"For this world is not our permanent home; we are looking forward to a home yet to come."
—Hebrews 13:14

Me: Lord, looking back, I've often felt uneasy, anxious, and unsettled. Maybe it's because my mother always seemed unpeaceful and restless. She was never satisfied with her surroundings and sought satisfaction elsewhere. The grass was always greener somewhere else. And so, we moved a lot! Maybe she sensed that there was no real home for her here on earth and that her real home lay "beyond the blue." Her restlessness rubbed off on me. Over the years I've often felt this way—like things weren't quite right. Lord, give me peace where I am, and help me to feel content. Show me my place in this ever-changing world. How can I glorify You now, where I live? Thanks, Lord, that I can always magnify Your name in everything I do, wherever I am, so I can bring glory to You. I love You.

God: Dear one, why feel unsettled? Why be concerned? Do you believe I am with you and that I have My hand on every detail of your life? I do. Believe this. Even the bad things will be used for My purposes. And My plan will come to pass on this earth, regardless of the evil you see. I have you where you are for a reason. There are those you can help and guide. You'll know who they are. Will things get worse? In some ways, yes. But I'll show you what to do and what to say, and I'll always take care of you. So don't worry. I'll let you know when to let go of things and how to have more time for what's important. Wherever you are, I'll set you up as a beacon so others can be drawn to you like moths to light. They'll know they can get a real, clear view through you. They'll see Me in you and recognize the truth you speak. If you feel restless, it's because your spirit is nudging you to pray. If you don't know what to pray for, you can pray "in the spirit," and I'll reveal more to you. If you feel uneasy, I'll show you where to go and what to do. Your spirit may yearn for another home, an eternal "house." But no matter where your heart and soul abide, I'm with you. Trust Me. You may feel unsettled at times, but never be afraid. Because, as you walk, I'll always reveal the right way to go. Take life a step at a time. It'll all become clearer as you go. I'll put a light out along the way so you can know which path to take. It'll always be bright enough for you to see. Just open your spiritual eyes. My way is never difficult if you just trust in Me as we go. I'll pave the way. Follow Me. I love you.

MAY 4
And I want to "surf on Your wavelength"

"Your eye is like a lamp that provides light for your body. When your eye is healthy, your whole body is filled with light. But when your eye is unhealthy, your whole body is filled with darkness. And if the light you think you have is actually darkness, how deep that darkness is!"
—Matthew 6:22-23

Me: God, let today be a peaceful day. Lord, You're always with me, and I really appreciate this! Help me to look to You when I'm feeling pressured, because I often forget Your indwelling ability to work on my behalf. When I'm confronted with negatives, I tend to "freeze up" with panic. I forget to allow Your peace to reign. I search through my own thoughts for answers, instead of looking to You for the right response. I listen to others' opinions, when I really want to serve You in greater ways. When I'm challenged by fear or chaos, would You help me to remain at peace and remember to look to You, so I can better help myself and others? Would You remind me that I have what I need in every situation? Would You make me aware of what's necessary, so I don't miss the opportunities You're providing? Some things don't come in the way I expect them, and I often miss what's truly important. Help me to see what you want me to see, Lord. I desire peace, but I also need more wisdom and discernment. Thanks for these, Lord. I love You.

God: Dear one, My peace passes all understanding. My love heals and grows deeper as it's applied. My grace forgives and My mercy soothes and smooths over any problem that arises. My bounty brings abundance to you as you receive and share it. Turn your face to Me. Let Me warm your soul, shine through you, and radiate from you. I am the way. I am the truth. I am the light. And it's all about "light connections." The more tapped into My light you are, the more I can use you by making you aware of your surroundings and what needs to be done for yourself and for others. You're often distracted by things around and within you, including your own thoughts and misgivings. When you listen to the wrong voices, you can't hear Me. When you tune into Me and My words, then I can help you identify the needs around you. It's like tuning into the frequency of a radio station. When you hit it just right, you can easily distinguish the words and sounds. Then you can freely "surf on My wavelength." I love you.

MAY 5
So I can budget for best use

"Seek the Kingdom of God above all else, and live righteously, and he will give you everything you need."
—Matthew 6:33

Me: Lord, thanks for showing me how to be disciplined enough to stay within my budget. I feel good about that. Help me see more ways to do this and be able to curb my spending on frivolous things so I can have more to give. I really need Your guidance with this. I want to pay off all my debt and have more to offer others, including the church. Show me how. I want to best manage my finances and always live within my means. You've said I'm a giver and I do love to give gifts to others. I want to always be able to do this. Would You reveal to me clearly the best use of my money—where I'm overspending and where I need to cut back or give more? Would You bring me new peace and reconciliation in this area, so I feel like I'm doing things Your way and not my own? Let each day be profitable in every way—financially, mentally, physically, and spiritually. I want to have overall peace in every area of my life. Including these. I love You.

God: Dear one, trust Me. I'll help you pay off all your debt, little by little. But don't deprive yourself while trying hard to accomplish this in your own efforts. I'm greater than this, and I care about you. I will always be your true source. Don't burden yourself by having a scarcity mentality, like so many do. I'm the Lord of abundance. Stop fretting over your needs and lacks, or where you may fall short. Things will happen, but maybe not in your timing. It may take time to undo what's been done, but it will get done. I promise. Don't worry so much. I will give you clear direction as to how to "dig out" of any hole you find yourself in. You'll always find Me in the little things—the details where you didn't imagine I'd be involved. I'm concerned even with your finances. My ways are beyond the ways of people. My ways are above, and you may sometimes not understand them. But I see beyond what You can see in your little sphere of here and now. Prepare your heart to receive My words, for I will give you many unique messages. I'll answer your questions and guide you, even in what to spend and how to spend it. I'll also show you ways to prosper and abound, if you'll act on what I tell you. Listen for My words today so you can be at peace in every decision you make. I love you.

MAY 6
In Your place of peace

"God has told his people, 'Here is a place of rest; let the weary rest here. This is a place of quiet rest.'"
—Isaiah 28:12

Me: This morning, I feel refreshed, Lord, like I'm on reprieve from a battle. I feel renewed, calm, and peaceful. I left especially early this morning to walk around the lake. I watched as the orange fingers of the sun reached between the purplish clouds that hung in billows above me. The wind blew to make itself heard and caused the tree branches to sway wildly above me as the leaves clapped as if applauding my efforts. It wrapped around my neck like a scarf and tried to muss my hair as it whispered loudly in my ears. Two flags flapped and danced in the breeze and a lone dove cooed from across the street. I could hear the black-capped chickadees chirping in the distance. The calm before the storm. Thanks for this time to mend and heal, Lord. I now have greater strength to face the day and wisdom to address concerns. To see as You see, and to be as You are. I feel a gradual release me from my frustrations, though I wonder if You feel these things too. I can see You in a more expansive way, remember to seek Your input, and to pray for those You bring to my mind. To be honest and unafraid of what others may think of me and more concerned with how You view me. To emanate peace and kindness, truth and love. Thanks for Your magnificent goodness and for this special time of refreshing. Touch me, direct me, and give me continued peace. I love You.

God: Dear one, let Me fill you completely with My peace and replace any anxieties or tensions. Let Me guide your thoughts and share tender moments with you, like this one, for that is My greatest desire! I seek your companionship, your heart, and your love. Because you look for Me, you can find Me. Even in nature. And you can discover how I love and care for you through the things I've made. How I only mean good for you. The glorious sunrise...this was a small token of what is in store for you! The wind with its surreal ways. One day, you'll see so much more...the glory of a new world that's created just for you. It will be filled with beautiful hills, valleys, streams, waterfalls, and foliage unlike anything you've ever seen! It'll be a place of wonderful joy and peace and rest, populated by those summoned to live there. There, you'll be reunited with those you miss so much. And every day will be a day of refreshing, even more than this one! How excited I am to show you this lovely place! I love you.

After I fall short

"The Lord gives his people strength. The Lord blesses them with peace."
—Psalm 29:11

Me: Dear Lord, I feel bad, because I often fail Your tests. I sometimes miss the opportunities to help when You present them to me. I'm sorry. Other times I get impatient or angry when people don't follow through in the way I hoped or expected them to. Then I confront the ones I love with what I perceive as their shortcomings or lacks, because I feel exasperated. Help me with this. I don't want to bring pain to others. Touch me with Your strength and patience and help me to overcome in the places where I fall short. Thanks for Your tender mercies and for easing my mind and settling my heart through Your supernatural gift of Holy Spirit. Thanks for giving me Your peace in every situation so I can forgive others. Would You help me to see past their faults into their hearts? Through Your love, show me how to be a good example. Help me to seek and offer Your kindness and never presume unkindness from others. I want to seek only You. Because I love You.

God: Dear one, I look beyond what you view as failings, and I see them as growing experiences. Nothing in life is wasted. And I love to watch as you grow into a keener spiritual awareness and understanding of My ways. Open your heart more and more to Me. Then I can surround your heart with My supernatural peace. Remember, peace only comes from Me. It's the result of My gift given freely to My children. Allow it to flow through your spirit to others. You'll never find true peace in this world. When you face chaotic times, events, people, and situations, don't let them steal away what I've given to you. Hold tight to this peace so you can walk with freedom from fear, worry, and anxiety. Breathe in My peace by inhaling the energizing reality of My presence in you. Give hope and encouragement to those around you by showing them this "fruit." Many crave it, because they're surrounded by turmoil. Guide them as I lead you, and more opportunities will present themselves to you. But be wary of accusations or blaming. These are not from Me. I'll always take care of you and those who come to Me. Though mistrust may abound, it won't affect you if you stand fast with Me. And I will cover your needs and protect you from harm. I love you.

MAY 8
And long for Your blessings

"Now may the Lord of peace himself give you his peace at all times and in every situation. The Lord be with you all."
—2 Thessalonians 3:16

Me: Lord, it's so wonderful to have time to enjoy Your blessings and not feel rushed by life's demands. I know You commanded such a day each week, so I don't feel guilty taking it! Would You help me today to get through what needs to be done so I have time to rest and be at peace in Your presence? I need Your help to focus on what is necessary. Help me to walk in Your ways and manifest Your fruit of the spirit (Galatians 5:22-23). Lord, help me to maintain peace when people come to me for advice and then walk away, unwilling to consider my words. This reaction leaves me feeling rejected and blamed for their failure. It makes me feel like I've fallen short in my ability to help them. Help me understand why people are the way they are. I love You.

God: Child, when you allow peace to reign in your mind, you'll experience complete deliverance from worry about what people think or how they react to you. Then you'll experience rest. Peace can reign when you bring your focus back to Me. This requires moving your mind away from what confronts you to what imbues you. You can tap into My peace inside you by spending more time away from people and alone with Me. This time allows you to direct your thoughts to what I've given you so you can experience more of My peace. You'll also experience greater joy and manifest more love and understanding. Others sense your anxiety when your worries govern your thoughts and actions, and they resist you. Let them sense your peace. Let them see your joy and love. Then they'll flock to you. But, first, start with more quiet time with Me to nurture peace of heart and mind. As it grows in your life, your responses will change, and you'll manifest more of the fruit of the spirit, which will overflow from you to others. Then, they'll listen to your words, because they'll see something far different in you than what they see manifested from others in the world. But remember that some will always turn away from your words, because they want to blame others for their failures. Don't take their responses personally. They may be seeking a savior, but be unwilling to come to Me! Their failure lies in their own heart or lack of it. I love you.

And wonder who's to blame

"The nations will see your righteousness. World leaders will be blinded by your glory. And you will be given a new name by the Lord's own mouth. The Lord will hold you in his hand for all to see—a splendid crown in the hand of God."
—Isaiah 62:2-3

Me: Lord, I pray for our leaders—for humility, wisdom, courage, and divine inspiration so they can make right choices. Cut through the clutter and expose those who seek to lead with ulterior motives. Uncover the truth that's buried beneath hidden agendas. I pray for boldness to speak of You and fearlessness to hold forth Your words. Would You spare our country for those who are righteous and want to live for You? Watch over us, our homes and businesses, our families, and all that we have for the sake of the elect. Thanks for peace in our land, even when we're surrounded on all sides by threats and conflict. I so desire the day when I'll see You reign on this earth! Enlighten me now more and more on how it will be so I can have a wholehearted vision of what that day will look like, especially during the times I feel discouraged with the failing leadership I see around me. Show me and others how we can live in peace so that we can freely enjoy plenteous and joy-filled lives with You here on earth. Raise up righteous leaders we can support, and bring revival to our nation! I love You.

God: Dear one, I see people individually. Nations are made up of individuals. A nation can be blessed if enough people seek Me in it. And life is far bigger than a series of events. It is made up of experiences and choices made by individuals. People often blame leaders for their misfortunes, but they don't realize that the most important thing to Me is how they react to the circumstances. Leaders come and go. Some are good, some are evil. But I want to see what each person will do during trials. Do they finger-point, or do they trust Me to see their way through? I'm always looking for warriors who can pass life's tests. What are you made of? I'm searching for those who'll rise up and overcome, people who'll serve with loyalty, obedience, and trust, who won't forsake Me when times get tough. Don't blame circumstances or leaders for the bad things. They happen for a reason. An adversary lurks behind what you see. Trust and believe that I will work in and through you and others to will and to do of My good pleasure. This will bring peace to you and to your nation. I love you.

As I give my all

"The Lord is my shepherd; I have all that I need. He lets me rest in green meadows; he leads me beside peaceful streams."
—Psalm 23:1-2

Me: Thanks, Lord, for a little reprieve, a little rest, and a little comfort during a tempest! Thanks for showing me Your merciful ways and for restoring my wholeness and health. Would You help me to view things as they are and to envision what only You can see? You alone are holy. You alone are almighty. Open my eyes, Lord. Be my vindicator, and authorize me as your priestess and princess in the places where You'd have me go. Prepare me with Your heart of justice, mercy, and truth, so I'm never afraid of what people might say or do to me. May I always have a heart of courage to carry out Your will! Set Your truths in my mouth and a willingness to carry out Your purposes in my heart. Then I can help You to bring Your kingdom closer to earth! You alone are my true friend. You alone provide for my needs. You alone are my comforter. Thanks for Your comfort now. Continue to lead me down paths of righteousness and guide me toward Your truth, as I walk with You beside peaceful streams. Show me how to lead others with Your fearlessness. Show me what is acceptable to You, for I desire Your blessings. I want to sit at Your feet, gaze at Your face, and listen to You speak as we rest together in Your green meadows. You are my Lord, my king, my love, my all in all! I love You.

God: Dear one, life can be tumultuous. It can be full of busyness and unending needs in your own life and in the lives of others. Despite it all, you can be at peace if you just surrender everything to Me in each moment. I'll warn you when you're entering dangerous or unprofitable territory or when the things you are attempting to do are a waste of your time and effort. Time is precious. It's something that can be easily stolen from you, and it's something you can never recoup. Time on earth is limited. So guard it. And remind others of this. Each moment counts toward the rewards you can expect in the next life. Each one is a building block for what your life will look like for eternity. How you spend moments here will determine what your assignment will be later. Treat time as something precious—a guarded gem. Because it's very valuable. And allotted time for rest and refreshing with Me is imperative for your survival. I love you.

And remember her love

"Honor your father and mother. Then you will live a long, full life in the land the Lord your God is giving you."
—*Exodus 20:12*

Me: Dear Lord, thanks for Mother's Day and the memories from past years that fill me with joy. Thanks for conversations and sweet times that mean so much to me now. Thanks for all my mother did for me as I grew up. Would You forgive me for the bitterness I have felt because of her reactions to me? In spite of my struggles with her sometimes-controlling nature and desire to direct life, You've helped me to see her goodness and to love her despite her shortcomings. I know she always did the best she could. Help me to remember the good times we spent together and how she helped me to be a better person. Thanks for opening incredible doors of understanding about her life—the things she had to bear in her youth and the hardships she survived. Help me to see her as You do and to understand what she endured. Thanks for reconciliation in needed areas and for being able to love and show mercy toward her. Please unveil the mysteries of her past more and more to me, so I can understand her better. Help me to forgive her. And to be more appreciative of her life. And, finally, to be at peace with her in all my memories. Thanks. I love You.

God: Child, your memories of your mother are sometimes painful. Your mind turns to hurtful words and situations, and you have a hard time seeing all the wonderful things she did for you. More than you know, she was by your side when you were totally unaware of it! If you could see how much she treasured you when you were born or realized all the little things she did for you, you'd be completely bereft of any unforgiveness. You must forgive her humanness. She was a person with lacks like everyone. You can recall when she was kind, when she took time for you, and the many times she cared for you. Remember how she met you at the airport when you came home from college? How she took you shopping for clothes? How she planned a trip to Europe so you and your sister could experience the world? Remember when she thanked you for introducing her to My Son and to Me? Focus on these wonderful memories of her life. I love you.

MAY 12
That helps me endure the storms

"Pray in the Spirit at all times and on every occasion. Stay alert and be persistent in your prayers for all believers everywhere."
—*Ephesians 6:18*

Me: Lord, I need Your lucid eyes to see. I must remember, as often as I breathe, that You're near, even as I'm confronted by people trying to control every aspect of my life. I need Your help in this increasingly corrupt world to know how to survive and live freely for You. How can I express my belief in You openly without persecution? Would You lead me, Lord? Confirm Your power in ways that are beyond my imagination! Would You give me the grace to shine, even when the going gets tough? Let me feel the warmth of Your light that can penetrate through any area of darkness. Show me how to exude Your humility and love, even with those who are haughty and hateful. Give me mental strength to do what's right, and physical energy to be what You need me to be in every situation. Help me to remember Your wonderful ways of mercy, kindness, forgiveness, blessing, helpfulness, goodness, joy, and peace. Let my words be a blessing to those around me as I present Your peace and ministering mercy. Your name brings strength and hope. You bear me up when I feel weak. Work through me to will and to do of Your good pleasure. You're a merciful God. Help me to hear Your whispers so I can emanate Your grace. And to courageously stand as others buckle and bow under fear. I love You.

God: Child, people grow anxious and fearful when they sense there's something missing. They realize things aren't going the way they should and that there are things happening that they can't justify or understand. They can't put their finger on what's really amiss, and this bothers them. What they're missing is Me. When you feel uneasy, it's not because you've done something wrong, but because I'm prompting you to pray. Do as I tell you. Pray in the spirit. When you don't know what to pray for, your spirit will guide you. The words you receive will bring you understanding and guide you. Follow My lead. Reach into your spirit, and listen for My words. They will uplift you and bring you peace when you face the storms. They will give you what's needed to lead others away from fear and anxiety toward peace, even in a broken world. They will always be there when you need them. I love you.

MAY 13
And be reminded of Your presence

"They are like trees planted along the riverbank, bearing fruit each season. Their leaves never wither, and they prosper in all they do."
—Psalm 1:3

Me: Lord, I remember when I didn't know You the way I do now. I recall the anxiety and worry I experienced most of the time. Every night I used to rock myself to sleep, and, when I felt stressed, I'd rock back and forth in place. This seemed to be the only way I could relieve my anxiety. But I no longer need to rely on this method to calm me down. Because I've found that You give me the peace and joy and a love I need in each moment. As I've drawn closer to You, I'm able to hand off each new care to You. And, through You, I can know life as You meant it to be lived—in constant peace. Thanks for the words You give me each day. I love our conversations! You've clarified so many things and assured me that You're taking care of everything. Would You help me to draw even closer to You? I want to be even nearer to You in my thoughts, words, and actions. I know You want to entrust me with more responsibility, and I want to show myself trustworthy with all you bring to me. Continue to teach and show me how to best deal with what You send. Thanks, Lord. I love You.

God: Dear one, you move with Me like a tree that easily sways whichever way My Word goes. I delight in this. I love your willingness to lean on Me. I want to extend your branches and spread them out, so they can cover even more people. This is My desire. And I want you to see what others may not be able to see. I want you to be able to recognize My treasure, which is hidden to many, so you can more effectively guide them to it. I want to reveal even more of Myself to you. But I can only do this when you rest in me—like the bird you once saw sitting solidly in a nest in the middle of a storm. Remember, life is precious. People originated from the dust, and I breathed into them life and gave them a soul. If you trust in Me, I can help you sustain this fragile life with health and wisdom and love. If you trust in Me, I can lead and guide you and bring you right results. I can protect you, but you must trust Me. I made you. I formed you. I created you. I know you and how you can best thrive, even amid adversity. I inspired The Book of instructions. My prophets wrote it with My guidance. Remember, if you trust Me, I can help you to live abundantly. Life with Me is sweet. It's peaceful. It's calm. It's precious. I love you.

So I can release my rebuttals

"But the fruit of the Spirit is love, joy, peace, patience, kindness, goodness, faithfulness, gentleness, self-control; against such things there is no law."
—Galatians 5:22-23

Me: Dear Lord, why do I react so negatively sometimes? Why do I feel angry, bitter, and sometimes unforgiving? I sense negativity in others and ready myself with rebuttals to conversations that never happen! I anticipate evil confrontations and prepare possible responses. Let me see as You see—inside others' hearts. Help me understand why people question Your words and what fears lurk within them. I want to see what motivates them and what hurts cause them pain. And to lead them closer to You and be able to advise them more effectively. Help me to discern and know more because of You. Show me more of Your heart. Help me to feel Your joy and experience Your peace. Help me to reflect Your love and emanate Your kindness. Help me to forgive. When I'm sad, help me to see You more clearly so I can discern Your presence and live in Your great love by reflecting it to others. I love You.

God: Dear one, begin a new day today with My Word at the center of your heart, your mind, and your actions. Remember that the words you speak reflect what's in your heart. When your heart is at one with your spirit, you can emanate My essence and bear witness to My wisdom. Then the "fruit of the spirit" becomes clearly evident in your life. Only through My Spirit in you do you have access to this fruit. And it gives you supernatural ability to manifest each aspect of it. Then, My love through you is true love. My patience through you is true patience. My kindness through you is true kindness. My gentleness and goodness through you are the "real deal," as are self-control, faithfulness, joy, and peace. These are all the *fruit of the spirit*. You can strive through the flesh to display these attributes. But, only through My Spirit in you can you fully embrace and demonstrate the true fruit. When your heart connects and intertwines with My Spirit, then these characteristics become an integral part of your thoughts and actions. And, you can overcome sadness and feel My joy and peace at any moment! I love you.

And know that I'm enough

"And don't be concerned about what to eat and what to drink. Don't worry about such things."
—*Luke 12:29*

Me: Lord, draw me closer to Your presence today, especially when I'm feeling over-whelmed. Sometimes I lose sight of how great You are, and I focus on insignificant things. I may be consumed with how I can have enough, be enough, or do enough. And this stifling anxiety makes me feel super-burdened at the times when I want so much to be available for You. I remember You telling me once that I needed to take off the "savior" hat. "That hat belongs to Me!" You said. You understand my desire to help others, but You also don't want me to hinder their dependence on You. Would You help me to direct my thoughts to Your ability and willingness to give of all that You are? Would You show me how to focus on You regardless of my circumstances and realize that You'll always be there to provide for my own and others' needs? Release me from this focus that steals my thoughts and causes me so much concern. Help me to look to You. Open new doors for me to release Your amazing message of peace. I love You.

God: Dear one, you are always enough for Me. And, with Me, you'll always have enough and be enough. So, stop worrying about how you'll be able to deal with things! Let Me manage your needs and your life. I'm the God of all resource and abundance. You worry too much about how you'll accomplish this or that. Let Me be your comforter, supplier, and provider. Aren't I your true husband? Aren't I your true father? You never need to worry or fret or focus on things. Let Me take care of them and you. You've seen how circumstances can engulf you and steal your thoughts. They can eat up your time and leave you with little to show for it. Always lean on Me, because I can bring you real peace. I can open your eyes to what you need to see and your ears to what you need to hear. I'll give you answers and the responses you need to give. Trust Me. I'll lead you to those who want to hear your words and be able to trust as you do. This is your calling: to pray for and minister to those I bring to you. You can do this anywhere, anytime. And I'll give you words that will bring peace, comfort, and light to those who need them. I love you.

But realize I can't live without You

"When doubts filled my mind, your comfort gave me renewed hope and cheer."
—Psalm 94:19

Me: I can't forget You, Lord, because You're always near me, beside me, and inside me. I can't ignore You, Lord, because You're an integral part of my very being. I can't walk without You, Lord, because You alone guide and strengthen me. You're my sufficiency. You're my redeemer. You're my comforter. You alone bring me great peace. I can't live without You, Lord, because You're my succorer and sustainer in every situation. You've told me You adore me. Thanks for that, Lord! Can You remind me of how present You are today? Can You be even nearer through my thoughts and actions? With You, I have great peace, and I need Your peace today. As Moses asked in Exodus 33:13, "If it is true that you look favorably on me, let me know Your ways so I may understand You more fully and continue to enjoy Your favor." I pray this today, Lord. I love You.

God: Dear one, you know that I love you. Rest in Me now. Our time together is always a time of great comfort and peace. You've been in spiritual warfare, because you've been praying for so many people. Continue your prayers, but rest in Me and allow Me to fight for you, for them, and for your children! Lift them up to Me and let Me take them from your hands. Depend on Me to bring what's needed. I can do this. Let me replace your burdened heart with physical, mental, and spiritual strength. Don't be anxious about what lies ahead. Step by step, I'm always with you. I'm in it all. You see how wonderful life is when you trust and allow Me to work on your behalf? See how delightful My ways are when you depend on Me? As you walk with Me, you'll see great and mighty things. As you grow closer to Me, you'll see My ways more perfectly and benefit from My many promises to you. Continue to put your thoughts and actions in My hands. Continue to rest in My peace. Continue to speak and heed My words. I will melt your heart with My love and kindness. And you'll experience My comfort. Then, I'll work My mighty works in you and through you. Just trust. Others will follow suit as you lean more on Me. I love you.

  When I'm tired of worrying

"Don't worry about anything; instead, pray about everything. Tell God what you need, and thank him for all he has done. Then you will experience God's peace, which exceeds anything we can understand. His peace will guard your hearts and minds as you live in Christ Jesus."
—Philippians 4:6-7

Me: Lord, remind me that my job is to seek *Your* approval. My concern should never be whether or not I can please people! They may find fault with me, but I know You love me! And my goal is always to gratify You. Would You help me with this, Lord? When I was young, my parents were always so concerned about "what the neighbors would say or think!" Please release me from that fear of disapproval by others and concern about what they might think. Set me free from these worries, Lord! You remind me not to focus so much on temporary things but to set my mind more and more on what pleases You. Help me to do this. I know I shouldn't get caught up in anxieties and trivialities. And I don't want to worry so much about things that I can't control. I want to trust more in You, knowing that all things will happen in Your timing and for Your wonderful purposes. Supply me with what I need, Lord. I am so tired of worrying about these things! I love You.

God: Dear one, I understand. Allow Me to work in you. When I tell you it's time to rest or to move on, follow My lead. If people are offended or don't understand, that's not your responsibility. You can't please everyone. Some will be upset, because you aren't there when it's convenient for them. Or they might not like how you did something, because it wasn't the way they would have done it. If people are upset when you aren't what they want you to be, they will need to learn how to deal with it. You can only be what I've made you to be—no more and no less. You can only fulfill what I've called you to do—no more and no less. Let me show you what this looks like. Then, you can experience My peace. You can tap into it any time by focusing on Me and what I can do for and through you. Then you'll see My power reflected to people who have eyes to see. Think of Me. Then you'll have My peace that passes all understanding. Reality lies in Me, not in this world, which is uncertain and chaotic. Someday, you'll fully understand what I'm telling you now. Don't put so much stake in the things of this world by worrying about what might happen or what others think. Certainty can only be found in Me. In Me alone. I love you.

MAY 18
And I want to just focus on Your peace

"You will keep in perfect peace all who trust in you, all whose thoughts are fixed on you!"
—*Isaiah 26:3*

Me: Lord, I realize that I seek perfection in my own life and in the lives of others. This is a source of frequent frustration for me. Would You help me to see through Your eyes so I can know how You view things? I'm sometimes exasperated with My own and others' lacks. But I know we're all imperfect, because you want us to realize how much we need You! Only You are perfect. Help me to help those who seek as I do to live like Jesus. I see people who say they believe in You, yet they are very judgmental, unkind, and unpleasant. And I wonder if I come across that way too! Recently I read about a denomination who rejected a famous author who was a member of their church, because she said she "wrote down what she heard from God." To them, that was sacrilegious. I wondered what they thought of the Old Testament prophets like Moses or the New Testament disciples like Peter and Paul. Lord, help me to love the way You do and to live as Jesus lived! Help me see as You see, not through critical eyes that pierce and slash out of blindness, but through eyes of love and appreciation. Help me never to condemn, but to love wholeheartedly. I love You.

God: Dear one, I've touched, blessed, and prospered your path by using the imperfect pieces of your life to create perfection. Allow Me to show you how to think about things. I'll draw you to the ways of My Son when you begin to be frustrated by what seems to be lacking. I'll help you recall how He worked with imperfect people to bring about perfect results. When you feel impatient, because you want quick and easy answers, remember that My ways are timeless, and I have all the patience in the world. There are no limits with Me. All My workings are part of an overall plan. And your life is an integral part of it. As you seek Me, your eyes will be opened to what is truly perfect. You'll see how everything fits, and how I've used your faults and failings as part of My design. People may not acknowledge you for what you've done. It doesn't matter. My rewards are greater than this. Look for Me in unexpected places. I'll show you how to view things as I do. I'll give you a heart of mercy and peace. Breathe in and let My peace enfold you. Let it be an integral part of you. Never let it go. Look to Me again today for strength and consolation. Look to Me. I will give you nonjudgmental words of encouragement and a way to peace. I love you.

But other things demand my time

"Always be humble and gentle. Be patient with each other, making allowance for each other's faults because of your love. Make every effort to keep yourselves united in the Spirit, binding yourselves together with peace."
—*Ephesians 4:2-3*

Me: Help me, Lord, to live life as You intended it to be lived, but to still have enough time and energy to help others. Show me how to balance work and family life so that I have time for You, time for myself, and needed time with others. Sometimes I struggle with trying to solve other people's problems. I try to reassure them and give them hope. Would You show me when this is a good use of my time and when it's not? Sometimes I feel I need more time to rest, read, walk, and talk to You. But I'm confronted with needy people, who want my advice, help, or just time to talk and share about things. I begin to resent them when I start to crave some solitary time. Show me how to best deal with these feelings. I want to do Your will but still maintain peace. Give me Your wisdom. How can I bless people, but graciously excuse myself when it's necessary? I know You bring many to me for a reason. How can I help them without taking on their burdens? Sometimes I need time to unwind so I can be refreshed by Your presence. Jesus went up to the mountain to pray when people surrounded Him. He found a way to escape when others demanded His time. Show me how He did this without offending people! I love You.

God: Child, you'll feel burdened and pressed by people when they're using you instead of coming to Me for assistance. It's imperative that you have special time with Me daily—for your own sanity and continued health. Time with Me is life-giving. It's essential. I'll help you with this, but you must listen for My leading. People were sometimes offended when My Son went away to the mountain to pray. They didn't understand. They even went out to find Him! You can't control peoples' reaction to what you do. I'll make it clear when you should serve and when you should spend time with Me. Direction from Me will always lead you to greater peace. I'll pull at your heartstrings when I want you to follow Me to a quiet place. When you follow Me, you will always have the time you need for the important things. I love you.

MAY 20
And I feel regret

"Each time he said, "My grace is all you need. My power works best in weakness." So now I am glad to boast about my weaknesses, so that the power of Christ can work through me. That's why I take pleasure in my weaknesses, and in the insults, hardships, persecutions, and troubles that I suffer for Christ. For when I am weak, then I am strong."
—2 Corinthians 12:9-10

Me: God, sometimes I feel regret for the people I've tried to help or "redirect," but failed. I disclosed what they needed to know and offered them advice, but they ignored what I said, so I watched them fall again and again. Even after persistent warnings, my son continued to smoke, then suffered many years from lung cancer. Clients who walked away from my advice later endured financial hardships. Did I do the best I could for them? Were my warnings enough to prevent disaster? Could I have done more for them? Help me to see things as You do. Open my eyes to be able to understand so I can speak the right words to bring people to Your truth. If they need compassion or a listening ear, make this clear to me. But if they don't want to follow through with my guidance, help me see into their hearts the way You can. It's so easy to judge a person, or a situation, based on appearances. Help me to see beyond the apparent to what lies beneath. I place each new encounter in Your hands. I love You.

God: Dear one, I love how you trust Me in ways others find difficult. When people fail to trust, they may attack you for having the faith they lack. They may blame you for their inability. Don't take this to heart. It's not your fault. Through these situations, I'll show myself strong on your behalf. To many, small matters seem unimportant. But to Me they never are. I care about the little things, like how you treat others, what you do for people, and when you listen to Me. During these "small" moments, I do My best work, for the little things add up to big things. You'll even begin to see how small things can be life-changing. When you feel the most desperate to help, but can't, that's when I can show Myself strongest. When your mind goes to things you feel you should've known or done, it's easy to dwell on your weakness. Let Me show you what you need to know. I can be your source for inspiration and help you see through to the truth. Just trust Me. I love you.

Until I understand that You are good

"And let the peace that comes from Christ rule in your hearts. For as members of one body you are called to live in peace. And always be thankful."
—*Colossians 3:15*

Me: Lord, the school year is almost over. I heard the bus rumbling up the street this morning, and I watched the kids on the corner as they eagerly clambered onto it. They chattered and giggled and jostled each other as they crammed through the door. I thought about how they must be gearing up for the last day of classes. Then I heard the birds singing around me, and I realized that they were oblivious to the bus, the children, or the end of school. And I wished I could feel all this joy as I prepared for the day. I wanted to be able to sing and laugh as I faced the onslaughts. I think of how Jesus's days were filled with stress. And I want His peace throughout this day. Maybe if I focused more on His return? Like the kids who anticipated the last day of school and the beginning of Summer vacation! I recently watched a teacher's presentation where she lay on the floor and moved her arms and legs like a roach on its back, unable to turn over. "This is how most Christians act!" she said. "People say they want deliverance, but they lay around waiting for someone to pull them up or turn them over." Am I like this? Just waiting for someone to come and set me free? Remind me of Your promises, Lord! And the hope of Jesus's return! I love You.

God: Child, why do you think those children were so happy? Or the birds? Why could they sing when they didn't know where their next meal would come from or how they'd get it? Could it be because of their focus? Maybe, instead of looking at what today may bring—hardship or stress—they just knew that, one way or another, they'd have what they needed when they needed it. Small children are usually carefree, especially if they have parents or guardians who take good care of them. Birds don't get stressed out, because they focus on what they know—that they will find a meal. People tend to be the only worriers in nature. Because they focus on the wrong things. Instead of believing that I am a good God who will provide for them and take care of them in this life and the next, they listen to the lies that I really don't care and that I am an "absentee landlord." What do you believe? Are you thankful for each day's provision? Are you excited for My Son's return for you one day and the adventure that lies ahead, kind of like the kids' anticipation for Summer vacation? I love you.

MAY 22
As I sense Your nearness

"I am leaving you with a gift—peace of mind and heart. And the peace I give is a gift the world cannot give. So don't be troubled or afraid."
—John 14:27

Me: Lord, how time flies! Today I thought fondly of clients I'd served as a financial advisor. When I met some of them years ago, they were already older, and many ended up moving into care centers. I recall going to see several and praying for them before they died. I was able to lead a few to an acknowledgement of a belief in Your Son and assure them of eternal life. I took one client, Nell, out to lunch for her 100th birthday. It meant so much to her! I held her hand as we walked back to the car. Within two years she was gone. I look forward to seeing her and the others again one day. People will come and go over time, yet I know You'll always be beside me. I am thankful for that. It makes their passing a little less painful. Especially knowing they'll be waiting for me. Thanks for always being there for me. And for the opportunity of getting to know these precious souls. Be near me today as I go about my business. Pave my way, and open more doors, so I may direct more people to You. I want to see more of Your great love exuded to others, along with Your peace and joy. I want this for my family too. So I can spend the next life with all of them around me! Thanks for how You continue to remind me of Your presence. I love You.

God: Dear one, I see you as a precious gem, like a ruby or a diamond. Like an "adamant"—a legendary stone that can't be broken, you have strength and persistence (Ezekiel 3:8). The belt of truth you wear keeps you from being shattered when you're faced with devastating and painful losses. And the world will always present these. Like the fiery ruby, you're zealous to overcome, because your heart glows red with My courageous love—like a burning flame. I'm even now bringing you new people to tell My story. You'll see them more and more. I've blessed your family, and I will continue to bless them. My hand is on them for good. I will always deal mercifully with them, because I love you. Be at peace today, knowing how I shine on you and bring you encouragement. Know that I'm always here for you. Have My peace in your heart—a peace beyond anything this world can offer. Let it heal any semblance of brokenness and soften any scars. Direct your thoughts to Me, and you'll know My presence in a greater way. Obey My words, and you'll experience My love, joy, and peace. Come and let Me acknowledge you in a way that others can't. I love you.

While You knead me

"You will show me the way of life, granting me the joy of your presence and the pleasures of living with you forever."
—Psalm 16:11

Me: Lord, thanks for reminding me of what's most important when I need to remember! Recently I was confronted by a very irate woman who blamed me for her own mistakes. Then a man who came into my office reacted violently to the picture of a famous person I had on my desk. Apparently, he disagreed with this person's views and hated him! In both cases, I was able to control my rising indignation and resist giving an angry and inappropriate response by turning my mind to You for help. You showed me things I needed to know in both situations and what was really driving their anger, so I could focus on how to respond. I told the woman I was sorry she was upset, and I asked for her forgiveness for anything I'd said or done wrong. Immediately her voice softened, and she accepted my offer. In the case of the man, You told me to ask about his wife, and I discovered that she was in the hospital. He was upset and worried, so I comforted him, and his anger was replaced by tears. Thanks, Lord, for reminding me to be a servant with a helper's heart. Thanks for teaching me how to handle so many situations with love. Would You help me to always exude Your peace by turning my focus to You? I love You.

God: Dear one, My Word prepares your heart for peace. It works in the same way as a baker, who kneads the dough to make bread. In My case, it's living bread. Like the baker, My Word makes your heart ready to receive and radiate the warmth of My love. As you work it into every chamber of your heart, you begin to exude My peace as your heart pumps My life-giving "blood" through every vein and muscle and tissue of your body. It enables you to deal with any situation that confronts you. As you knead the words deep into your thoughts, they begin to replace bitterness and unforgiveness and anger, including others' irritation. Then you can manifest My love, goodness, kindness, self-control, gentleness, faithfulness, patience, joy, and peace, no matter what the situation. Moment by moment and day by day, establish My Word in your heart. By this you will be prepared with lasting peace and comfort, no matter what the circumstance you find yourself in. I love you.

MAY 24
And show me how Your ways are higher

"For just as the heavens are higher than the earth, so my ways are higher than your ways and my thoughts higher than your thoughts."
—Isaiah 55:9

Me: Lord, we're nearing summer, and the days have been so pleasant. Thanks for that! Breezes through my window brush against my face and remind me of all You've created for us! As the birds sing outside, I watch as two baby blue jays grow in a nest that's embraced in the elbow of our pear tree. Nurtured by their parents, they are almost ready to stand. Their necks crane and their beaks open wide whenever a parent comes near. Soon, they'll fly away. What a miracle it all is. Thanks for all You do for us, Lord, and for the many kinds of birds, animals, fish, and plants You designed to bless us, with so much variety. I look forward to the day Your Son returns, because I know the next heaven and earth will be even more spectacular than this one. I look forward to seeing You and understanding more about You. Would You enlighten me today, and remind me of Your presence? Would You bring me greater peace as I look out at Your miracles, especially when the world seems so chaotic? Speak to me so I can know You're very near. I love You.

God: Dear one, My ways are always above your ways. And My thoughts are above your thoughts. What I can do may seem way beyond what You can wrap your mind around. But when you turn your ears to Me, you'll hear My whispers of love and hope for the future. Lean your thoughts closer to Me throughout the day and know that I'm beside you, even within you, ready to treasure everything you share with Me. As you listen, I'll tell you great and wonderful things. I'll reveal to you what's behind what you see. Lean your heart even closer, and I'll share some enlightening words with you. Focus on Me, and you'll see My ways more clearly. I love you, even when you feel unloved. I show you mercy, especially when you don't think you deserve mercy. When you look at Me, and away from the world's darkness, I can enliven your peace. Let My light shine through you more and more. This happens as you turn toward Me. Then you can lead others to Me and offer them My light, mercy, peace, and hope. Lean back into My everlasting arms today, just like the little jays in the nest. Know that I, your father, will be there to provide what you need when you need it. I love you.

   When my energy's sapped

"For he knows how weak we are; he remembers we are only dust."
—*Psalm 103:14*

Me: Lord, thanks for more peaceful times with You! I really need Your continual presence and guidance. I especially need Your help during times when I feel pressed and overwhelmed by the problems and needs of the world around me. My energy gets sapped when I give in to the things that demand more and more of my time and leave less and less time for the things that are most needful, like time to reflect on Your words and listen for Your voice in the stillness. Would You show me how to best use my time, Lord? How can I graciously decline the persistent pleas of people or things that demand my precious time and drain all my energy? Usually the moment-stealers are not worth what I spend on them. They're like leeches that try to suck all the life out of me and then demand more! They never change their needy ways so they can rise above their lacks! I want Your wisdom, Lord, to be able to serve and give. But I'm most desperate for Your guidance! Thanks for Your help, Lord. Thanks that You are never like these time-sappers. You give to us and never leech our energy with unnecessary or needless requests. I love You.

God: My love, sometimes you feel pulled by people and resentful that they use up the precious little time you have. You feel like you're throwing away your spare moments on meaningless or trivial pursuits. It's all relative. Remember, your life is eternal. And understand that your future is not just determined by proactive choices you make. It's also measured by how you respond, whether it's to things you consider trivial or things that seem more meaningful. The times when you're "squeezed" are the times I really look to see what you'll do. Do you react with frustration, impatience, or anger to the demands on you, or do you pull from your spirit the fruit inherent in it: love, joy, peace, patience, kindness, faithfulness, gentleness, goodness, and self-control? These are the nitty-gritty things I look for. Yes, I'll show you how to graciously avoid those who only sap your energy and time—the ones who gobble up anything you can offer with no intention of changing or giving back. I understand your frustration with these. But, as long as you're in this world, you'll be confronted by them. I'll guide you in these situations so you can handle them with wisdom. I love you.

MAY 26
I feel helpless

"Are any of you suffering hardships? You should pray."
—James 5:13

Me: Dear Lord, when I'm confronted with a dire situation, emergency, or "face-off," my mind freezes up, and I become mentally paralyzed. Would You show me how to overcome this? Would You help me to "go with Your flow" and move easily with Your Spirit when I'm challenged? I can recall many situations when I was faced with a statement or question about You, but my mind froze so I couldn't respond in a reasonable or appropriate way. Later, the words came to me, but it was too late. I want to be able to be mentally and spiritually agile, so I can respond quickly and know exactly what to say or do. I don't want to be distracted from Your purposes. In quiet times, I can pray and be peaceful. But when I'm confronted by chaos, it's hard for me to focus. I'm getting better, but I have a ways to go! Teach me how to do this so it becomes "second nature" for me. Help me to overcome my immediate reaction—mental paralysis—so I'm able to "deliver" in any situation. Thanks for Your help with this. Lord. I love You.

God: Dear one, I'm always near you. I'm only a heartbeat away. Just ask, and I'll tell you what you need to know, no matter how chaotic your surroundings seem to be. Your purpose is prayer *because you are a prayer warrior*. Practice focusing on Me each day in every situation, then, when emergencies occur, you'll be prepared, and your first reaction will be to look to Me for answers. As you become proficient in focusing on Me, I can show you how to pray and act in every situation. I've given you this power—to prevent harm from coming to you or to the people you encounter. You can relieve pain and prevent death through simple and immediate requests. A small prayer is very powerful. It's like a mustard seed—tiny but able to bring mighty results. Let Me continue to work in you and teach you how to focus on Me and pray effectively. We've begun a good work. Nourish it like a tree that can blossom and produce good fruit. Through prayer, you'll realize peace and oneness with My purpose. When you're unpeaceful, it's a sign you're distracted from your design—prayer. It's through this that you can find peace and reassurance of My presence. You can learn to hear My voice and come even closer to Me. Focusing on Me and refusing to be distracted by the world is the key! Yes! I love you.

And want You to break in

"I have told you all this so that you may have peace in me. Here on earth you will have many trials and sorrows. But take heart, because I have overcome the world."
—John 16:33

Me: Lord, every day I see people inciting violence, promoting terror, and disrupting peace in the world. Can You show us Your will for our country and how we can live peacefully with one another? Can You protect us from evil and those who plan evil against us? You are the God of peace and love. Only You can give clarity. Give us clear directions now. With elections coming up, I and others wonder what to do and who to vote for. Do any have good motives and the best interest for our country? Please make it clear. Today, as I go out into the world, open my eyes to what is going on and why. Enlighten me so I can see Your face in it all. Would You break in and unite more people who want to lean on You? You're a wonderful God and a great Lord. I desire You above all else. Help my family to see Your greatness. And to understand Your grace and mercy. Help me to be merciful in all my words and actions. Oh, to trust You in everything I do and to be able to acknowledge Your greatness through it all! I love You.

God: Dear one, I'm placing you strategically in front of certain people. Watch for them. You'll know them when you see them. They're the ones with longing in their eyes, whose hearts glow red with passion for Me. They may be hidden from others, but I'll show you who they are, and you'll recognize them. Because, like you, they yearn for a world beyond this one. Open your mouth and speak the words I give you to reach them. Today, open your heart and mind to Me, and I'll share unspeakable things with you—special secrets between us. Just listen. As the days go by, there will be less and less freedom as governments try to take more and more control under the guise of "safety." People will be motivated by fear, and, because they don't know how to trust in Me, they'll seek safety as their god. They'll think it's an entitled right that's owed to them, and they'll seek it at any cost. They'll even be willing to sacrifice their own freedom and children to attain it. They'll end up kowtowing to the government, because of its offers of security, while thinking this will bring them needed peace. But it won't. Speak honestly with people as I direct you. With the time you have, guide others to bring them to My place of victory, love, and peace. I love you.

To help me have confidence

"So we can say with confidence, 'The LORD is my helper, so I will have no fear. What can mere people do to me?'"
—*Hebrews 13:6*

Me: Lord, when I look back at the mistakes I've made, it makes me feel sad. And I worry that someday I may overlook something really important, and everyone will be sorely disappointed in me. God, I know I'm not perfect, but You are! Would You replace this anxiety with the certainty that You'll work everything out for good? I don't want to be afraid of making mistakes! I want to be able to act confidently, even boldly, and make choices that lead others to You, knowing You'll always back me up no matter what happens! Help me to overcome this worry over others' expectations. I need Your help in this, because I can't do it myself. Deliver me from these concerns and take them from me! Help me to do my best and to never focus on possible slip-ups or shortcomings. Help me to see what I need to see today and every day. Open my eyes to be able to trust You in a greater way. And to see clearly how I can bring value to You and to others so that I have Your peace. Thanks. I love You.

God: Dear one, I love your heart and desire to be My partner. I've longed for this! And I need you for this purpose. You feel "empty" and lacking at times. You sometimes feel inadequate, because you don't know what to do or how to pray. I'll help you with this. In time, it'll be more "third nature" as you connect more with Me through your spirit. I'll remind you of your desire and teach you. As I've told you, your responsibility is to deal with each moment by looking through My eyes. You can't control others or their reactions to you. But you can pray and act as I lead you. Mainly, you must focus on Me, not on yourself and your shortcomings. I'm a ready counselor, and I give you all you need to make right choices. Don't fear what others might think of you. They may speak shrilly or try to make you feel inadequate. It's only air. I make you capable to succeed. Just trust in Me and look to Me for answers. Don't weary yourself with anxious thoughts. I water the barren places and cover the areas you might have missed. I fill in the gaps, smooth over the flaws, and mend the broken places of your life. Today, remember how Jesus made you whole and perfected you by what He did. Then look to Me with thanksgiving in your heart. This will cause you joy and bring you confidence and peace. I love you.

And learn how to breathe

"Be still, and know that I am God!"
—Psalm 46:10

Me: God, help me to "be still" in You, and to be able to clearly hear Your voice. Today, teach me about this, Lord. You are exalted above all else. You made us and all that we can see. Wouldn't You know our hearts and understand our fears and sadness more than anyone else? Wouldn't You be aware of our enemies—those who dislike us—as well as those who love and support us? You reward and bless those who follow Your ways and believe in Your Son. You love us despite ourselves and our faults. You're our support in times of trouble. Strengthen me now, Lord. Give me the ability to carry out what's needed today so that I'm mentally sharp to remember Your Word. I crave Your peace, Your grace, and Your kindness, because sometimes I feel weak and less than capable. My body is fragile and not so strong at times. I need Your encouraging and healing hand to do my best today. Give me rest and strength and health physically, and peace mentally and spiritually. Then I can help myself and be able to lift others up too. I love You.

God: Dear one, I'm always near, but you are sometimes so very busy! Take time to stop and listen, and you will hear from Me. I long for your ears to pause and listen. Just take a few moments to hear what I have to say to you today. I'm always available, and I will direct you. I'll bring you healing when you need it, if you'll just come and sit with Me. Expect this. Have confidence in Me and My ability. Remember that I'm always with you. Never doubt My presence. Breathe in and feel My breath of life. I'm all around you. I'm in your mind and in your thoughts. I'm in your heart. So don't be afraid, because you can flee from worry! Give your ears to Me, and I will calm your heart with My peace. Talk to Me, and I will discuss many things with you. I can do this because I am God almighty. Don't be afraid to listen and do what I tell you. As you heed My words, you'll gain more confidence in Me. For I am trustworthy—a God who can be trusted. Relax and lean on Me. As you open your heart to Me, I'll lead you in your speech and tell you what to say. I'm closer than you can imagine! Let Me touch your heart and open your eyes. Let Me lead you to glory. Just trust Me. Come closer and listen with your spiritual ears. Breathe new breaths of peace by way of your spirit. For I love you.

As I watch You clear away the debris

"I love your sanctuary, Lord, the place where your glorious presence dwells."
—Psalm 26:8

Me: Oh, that I could always remain in Your secret sanctuary, Lord! Last night a terrible storm raged outside. It sounded like a hurricane, and it threatened to damage all the trees and plants in our yard, so I lay in bed and prayed for the winds to subside. I asked for surrounding peace. I wanted a miracle. When I got up, I was amazed to see all our tree limbs intact! And every flower and plant still standing as before! Thanks for this, Lord! I've felt unsettled lately, like I was being blown around by that storm. I've felt restless and pulled, but I don't know where to go. I want to spend more time with You, and I know You want that too, but then come the interruptions. Would You clear away the storms and work with me so I can have Your constant peace? Would You quiet my thoughts and show me clearly how all the precarious pieces of my life will eventually fall together into a well-designed puzzle? Guide me to Your peace. Enlighten me with Your wisdom. You can see the future. I can't. So, remove the debris left by the storms, and clear a path to You! Make it all plain to me. I need Your help, Lord. I love You.

God: Dear one, sometimes you feel like you're sitting in a boat in the middle of the sea, patiently waiting out a lull in the storms so you can be carried forward to your destination. Soon you grow impatient because you see nothing happening. During these times—the storms and the lulls—I'm at work to will and to do of My good pleasure. You can't see it, but I'm always working. People think that if they don't see an answer to a request right away, or something happening, that I've forgotten about them. This isn't the case. I'm always at work behind the scenes. In your case, I'm moving to answer your prayers. When you turn your heart to Me, I love our conversations. And I'll always lead you to where you need to be. Just trust Me in this. Each day is a new day—one to be treasured and enjoyed with thankfulness. As you go, I'll bless and direct you. Don't worry about where you're headed or what might happen later. I have it all planned out, and I intend for you to have a good future with many wonderful benefits. Don't fret about other people or who will be around for you. I'll have the right people there at the right moments. All things will work out together for your good. Trust Me and see. I love you.

MAY 31
As my God of peace

"I think of God, and I moan, overwhelmed with longing for his help."
—Psalm 77:3

Me: God, I don't understand how people can be so stupid as to make up their own gods to worship. Please show me if I am ever in awe of anything more than You! You made the heavens and earth. You formed, made, and created us. How can we be so blind as to think that any other god could know more about us than You do? You are our sustainer, creator, and protector. You give us light and life. You created the air for us to breathe. Why does mankind continually stray from You, when You make it so clear as to how we can be blessed and prosper? Forgive me if my thoughts wander far from You at times and if I depend more on people's abilities than on Your wonderful and capable expertise. I want to know You as Moses did—face to face as a friend. I want to be like Jesus, who walked and talked with You continuously. You are my closest ally. My dearest friend. And I can depend on You. Help me to draw closer to You and be able to hear Your voice always, especially when You're trying to get my attention! Then I'll know true peace. I love You.

God: Child, see how I bless My children when they come to Me with a pure heart and seek My face as you do? See how I answer prayers when you submit them to Me? I love My people and long for them to seek Me in the depths of their hearts. The people who seek other gods are always disappointed and lost in their ways. Their idols draw them to death. Whenever you see oppression and killing, there are always false gods involved. Whenever you see hardship and uncertainty and continuous failure, be certain that those involved have not sought My face. They may "pray," but what they worship are systems and ideologies created by people. They seek gods of their own making and the dictates of their own hearts. They don't seek Me. I can bring them life, love, joy, forgiveness, quietness, prosperity, and goodness. I am the God of peace. If people fight for what is rightfully theirs, it doesn't make them wrong, but My deepest desire is that they seek Me so I can vindicate for them. My words are near to you. Just listen and you will hear them. I desire your presence with Me because I love your heart. I understand what you long for. I long for this too. Continue to trust in Me so I can work in your life to bring about your deepest desires. I love you.

June

FOCUS:
HEAVEN-SENT HEALING

"O Lord, if you heal me, I will be truly healed; if you save me, I will be truly saved. My praises are for you alone!"

—JEREMIAH 17:14

JUNE 1
I wonder how I can trust anyone

"Who is like you among the gods, O LORD— glorious in holiness, awesome in splendor, performing great wonders?"
—Exodus 15:11

Me: Lord, why do attacks come from those we want to trust? Why do some people hone in on our vulnerabilities so they can hurt us? Shouldn't the people closest to us be the ones who protect us? Why must I always be the armor-bearer to preserve relationships? It makes me weary. Sometimes I wonder if I can trust anyone with my heart. Feeling as I do—frustrated and "done" with a few people—show me how I can be holy as You are holy. I know that "holy" means that I am separated from others in the world, because I'm devoted to You. Help me to represent You daily and be able to view others as You see them. Help me to be perfect in Your sight, even when others don't see me that way. You are holy. You are perfect in all Your ways. You are worthy to be praised. Help me to be like you. Help me to be led by You in all things and to place my feet in Your feet, even when I don't feel like it. Direct me in all things, Lord, so I can be healed of any unforgiveness. And able to love. I love You.

God: Dear one, people are often ignorant of how their words hurt other people. They speak meaningless things without thinking. Sometimes they use words to demean others so they can feel better about themselves. This never works. Only words that come from Me can lift others up or move people forward. Only actions done with My heart will strengthen and encourage others. Motives acted on apart from Mine will deplete, depress, and demean what I intended to be good. Only I can protect and heal hearts. Only I can build up what has been torn down. Only I can make you holy. Why is this important to know? Because being holy means that you are set apart from this world through your belief in Jesus. Being holy also means that you can have My peace. It means you can have My forgiveness, which comes from the sacrificial love of My Son, who died for you. It means you can have healing, which comes from My love living inside of you. Holiness comes because of the precious blood of My Son shed for you. When others try to demean you with their words, remember My Son's blood poured out for you, because it has the power to cleanse and heal your heart. Through it, you can be holy. I love you.

JUNE 2
Then I recognize the rainbow connection

"Your own ears will hear him. Right behind you a voice will say, 'This is the way you should go,' whether to the right or to the left."
—Isaiah 30:21

Me: Lord, how thankful I am for how You speak to me, even in my dreams! Last year I dreamed that I was singing *The Rainbow Connection*. As I did, people poured into my room to set up for a special event. When I woke up, I started to cry when I remembered that this was one of my daughter's favorite songs, and her birthday was approaching. I knew You'd put this tune on my heart for a reason. She'd been sad because of circumstances that surrounded her, and I considered singing it to her over the phone. But then I had another idea. I found someone to go to her house and deliver a singing telegram! So, on her birthday, a woman dressed up as a telegram delivery person went to her house and sang it for her. And it made her cry. I thought about how this song might have touched and reminded her that You've never forgotten about her. It might have even healed her heart. The song's lyrics are apropos for any who are searching for You: "Why are there so many songs about rainbows and what's on the other side? Have you been half asleep, and have you heard voices? I've heard them calling my name...." Thanks for how You show me special ways I can touch others' hearts! And bring healing. How I love You!

God: Child, you've begun to taste a bit of My creativity and what I can do for you and your children. Yes, I can work through you in unbelievably surprising ways that are "outside the box," for I am a great God. I'm able to lead you into even greater opportunities for bringing messages of hope. I'll work through you and give you ideas about how to reach into peoples' hearts in unique ways to bring about miraculous healing, one dream or vision at a time. In this case, you were able to touch your daughter's heartstrings and bring her one step closer to understanding how I work. She might question the reality of miracles, and say they are all coincidences, but she can't deny them when they happen to her. With others, I'll enlighten you by revealing what's inside each person so you're never blind-sighted by them. It'll always be clear to you. But you must open your spiritual eyes and let me guide you. Keep on watching and listening, for I will continue to lead you in astounding ways. I love you.

JUNE 3
As I stand alone

"I never joined the people in their merry feasts. I sat alone because your hand was on me."
—Jeremiah 15:17

Me: Dear Lord, I've wondered why I'm so often left to my own devices. Why do I end up alone so much of the time? Why have my children moved so far away that I don't see them or my grandchildren very often? You're a gracious God, full of mercy and kindness. You're just and mighty in power. You look on my life and seek my love. You lean toward me in times of trouble to help and sustain me. You bring me joy each day as I look to You, even during quiet moments when I'm alone with You. You heal my bones, my nerves, my mind, and my thoughts. You're trustworthy—a God I can depend on. You're strong—a God I can lean on. You're merciful—a God I can go to for all my needs, especially when I feel like I'm missing out. I thank You every day, and I remember You in my daytime thoughts and nighttime dreams, because I know You're nearer than I can even imagine. I can bring all my cares, sorrows, anxieties, and concerns to You. So, help me today to understand why I'm so often by myself. I love You.

God: Child, do you see how I separated you out, even from your youth? Do you see how I placed you by yourself so that I could get your attention and somehow reach you? Think about Robinson Crusoe in the story by Daniel Defoe and how he found Me on an island. When you have these "alone times," there's always a purpose for them and a reason that emanates from them. I need to speak to you. Then I can remind you of My love and heal your hurt places and be there for you when others have gone away. Don't resent theses times and wish that someone would come or call you. These may be just the times when I need you to pray or to listen or to write down what I tell you. Seek Me more and more, especially during these times of potential purpose. You're My prayer warrior, and I depend on your intercession for others, so I can bring to pass what's needed in their lives and throughout the earth. Listen closely today in the silence. Turn your face to Me so I can tell you My dreams and desires for you and for others. For these are very precious moments. I love you.

June 4
And feel You lift me up

"For the Lord is the one who shaped the mountains, stirs up the winds, and reveals his thoughts to mankind. He turns the light of dawn into darkness and treads on the heights of the earth. The Lord God of Heaven's Armies is his name!"
—Amos 4:13

Me: Heal me, Lord. Place Your healing hand on me and soothe my aches and pains. Rub Your calming balm all over me so it penetrates every pore! Like a bird, help me to fly free from my physical and mental limitations. You know how I've always dreamed of flying. Show me how I will one day! For I long to soar like a bird above the problems of this world and tread with You on the high places of the earth. You're my protector and my true love. Thanks for choosing me. Thanks for standing with me and being my constant friend. Thanks for Your encouragement and for being these things to and for me. Give me strength and peace to run my course and succeed with Your help. Give me needed rest, refreshing, and refuge when I need it. Show me more of Your miraculous healing. Direct me to what I can and should do. Thanks for Your help! I love You.

God: Dear one, My healing hand is on you, even now. Release your cares, worries, and ailments to Me. Let Me soothe you with My tenderness and My healing balm. My hand heals and strengthens. It repairs all your broken and torn parts. I can lift you up when you're falling and restore abundance to you when needed. But you must take hold of it. Imagine yourself walking down a path beside a crystal-clear, rushing stream. The weather is pleasant, and a breeze brushes by you and whispers through your hair. You hear My voice in the wind, and I tell you comforting words about how much I love you. You sit on a rock by the stream for a while, and you breathe in the fresh, invigorating air. You watch trout as they jump across the water to reach insects that hover nearby. You hear birds singing in the trees. There's a cardinal, a bluebird, a robin, a dove, a black-capped chickadee, and a whippoorwill. You recognize their calls. Then, you hear My voice murmuring to you: "Don't fear, My child. I'm your father and I love you. Release all your cares to Me today. Let them go. Surrender your worries and fears also. Let Me soothe you with My healing touch. I can lift you up. Allow Me to do this for you." Relax and breathe. Close your eyes. Get up and walk on, refreshed. Then, realize you're healed. And see how much I love you.

JUNE 5
So I can feel Your heart

"The Lord your God will delight in you if you obey his voice and keep the commands and decrees written in this Book of Instruction, and if you turn to the Lord your God with all your heart and soul."
—Deuteronomy 30:10

Me: Lord, I want to be more alert to the sound of Your voice. To be better at responding to what You tell me. Awaken in me more and more an intense awareness of You and the ability to hear You distinctly throughout the day. I long for this. Especially in times of distress, when people and things pull at me, I want to feel Your Spirit moving through me in greater ways. I want to feel steeped in Your presence. I imagine myself being submerged into Your healing waters and feeling the warmth of Your whooshing waterfall as it showers down over me. Its power flows over, around, and even through me, and it vitalizes every part of me! The more I rely on You as my power-source, the more I find myself enlivened by Your love, exhilarated by Your strength, and invigorated by the way You work through me. Then, I can display Your peaceful presence and calm amid any storm, because I'm not dependent on anything but You. Let this day be Yours, filled with Your glory. Show me the fullness of Your ways, especially when others doubt You. Lead me with Your love and help me to minister to others. You know the way. I don't. Lead me, Lord! I love You.

God: Dear one, give Me your heart. I will guard it. Give Me your soul and your thoughts. I will treasure them. Relinquish your cares and your worries to Me. I will heal you and bring you great peace. But first, you must come to Me with your whole heart and let Me work in you a masterpiece. Let Me paint over you and show you off as My radiant warrior, saturated with My colors and glowing with My light and brightness. I can redo you with My strokes. I can decorate you so that you grow more and more beautiful as My Word shines through you. But first, you must give Me your heart. Then, when ill words surround you, I can easily brush them away. Like magic, they'll disappear. When others make you feel forsaken or pushed aside, I will embrace you with My love as you bask beneath My pinions. You're always in My heart and ever in My sight. And I will always protect your heart when you offer it to Me. Because I love you.

And see You as my defender

"It is for freedom that Christ has set us free. Stand firm, then, and do not let yourselves be burdened again by a yoke of slavery."
—*Galatians 5:1*

Me: Lord, remind us of our true history and the ones who fought so hard for our freedom. Today was D-Day in 1944, and I think of all the young men who died to preserve our liberty. From a heart of service and a determination to free those who were being oppressed, they gave their lives. Normandy harbors 10,000 graves where 150,000 American soldiers were wounded. Many Germans also died or were wounded there. War sprang up from pride—a belief that one race of men was better and more deserving to live and rule than others. It came from a hatred seeded by fear. Lord, strengthen our hearts so that, even in the most desperate moments, we can forgive, trust, and act out of love for You. Even when the world grows harsh and makes it hard to survive and thrive, remind us not to rely on our own feelings or react with animus to words spurred by hatred and blame. Protect us from evil. Let our thoughts be Your thoughts, not those of the enemy whose aim is to steal, kill, and destroy. May we be led by leaders who are motivated for Your service and not by worldly glory and power. Only when we work for You can we attain true freedom and be healed as a nation. I love You.

God: Dear one, My Son fought in a constant war—a battle for the hearts and minds of the people on earth. You also fight in a continual conflict. Those who contend for the other side oppose My Son, Me, and you. These are those who worship other gods and are used by the enemy, who tries to manipulate them. Because of opponents, you'll experience trials in life. You'll suffer at times because of people who reject and deny your belief in Me. But, along the way, you'll find faithful companions who pursue what you do. You'll love and appreciate them, and they'll delight in you. Some who seem to want what you have will betray you, but I'll warn you by showing you their hearts and intent. Finetune your ears, and remember to ask Me before you trust your heart to anyone. I know you're developing this ability. Remember, I'm your guide. I'll lead you into all truth. Trust Me for this. I'll show you how to help others. And I'll always have your back. Stay close to Me and listen for My voice so together we can bring healing to a land that grows desperate. I love you.

JUNE 7
Who reminds me

"For God was in Christ, reconciling the world to himself, no longer counting people's sins against them. And he gave us this wonderful message of reconciliation."
—2 Corinthians 5:19

Me: Lord, how can I honor You in all I do? Would You remind me today when my thoughts turn away from You? Stir my heart when my words aren't Your words! I want to show deference to You in all I do. Today, remind me to listen for Your voice so I can thrive on Your love. I want to set my heart to follow Your voice so I can avoid life's pitfalls. Forgive my mistakes and the times I've veered far away from You. Heal any hurts or wounds I've inflicted on others. Today, I thought of a girl in my 6th grade class named Cynthia. She was Jewish, unlike so many in my Episcopalian school, but we had something in common. We shared the same fervent zeal for the Beatles. We'd go together to their movies, scream our heads off during the shows, then talk incessantly about them. She was my Beatle-manic friend. But, for some reason, in the 7th grade, I decided I wanted other friends, maybe ones more popular. One day, as we got ready to board a school bus, she asked if we could sit together. I said, "No," and I went to sit with someone else. I still remember the look on her face. She was devastated. And I regret dismissing her kind friendship to this day. Lord, forgive me for the times I've left people who wanted a friend behind. Repair what's been torn apart in my relationships. Thanks for healing those whose names You give me in prayer. I bring them to You, the One who hears and answers prayers. I love You.

God: Dear one, I'll give you new chapters to expand your story along the way. Often they'll include the ways you resolved old conflicts, faced broken friendships, and repented of past mistakes. Keep looking to Me, and remember how much I love you, despite your failures. And know that I give you the strength you need for each new season you enter. Today, rest in Me and let me work in and through you to heal your own and others' wounds. Lean on Me, and I'll bring you hope and peace, which you can spread around you. Bring Me all your cares and concerns, and never give into others' or your own despondency or despair. You can overpower any feeling of falling short with My love issued through the refreshing, medicinal nourishment of My Word. Because it heals. It restores. Remember My promise to you—that I *will* open floodgates and pour you out a blessing that you will not have room enough to receive! I love you.

To spend more time with You

"Seek his will in all you do, and he will show you which path to take."
—Proverbs 3:6

Me: You, God, are my redeemer, my savior, and my friend. Through You, I can find peace. You give me mercy and abounding grace. You forgive my wrongs and direct me to right paths. Your love abounds beyond any limits and lasts forever. Would You remind me of the good days when I walked with You, and You led me down fragrant, flower-strewn paths and conversed so freely with me? This You do so well. I think of all the years I walked with You around the lake near our house, and you showed me so many things along the way as I prayed. I have so many memories of the sun stretching its orange and red fingers over the water as I passed the ducks and geese along the shores. Though my heart was at times sorrowful, You were always there to heal and direct me. You give me hope and courage to face evil and the injustices of this world. You give me strength to endure so I can be available for others when they seek help. Remind me to speak of Your healing to those who need to hear about it. And tell me what to say. How I long for this! You are merciful and wise. I'm not always. Give me Your words of grace that heal. I love You.

God: Child, how much I do love you! How much I enjoy our times together! How much I cry for you when your heart aches or when you experience pain and sorrow! How I long to heal you and *can* when you turn to Me! I often wait for you. In the meantime, I use everything for a purpose. Even bad things, horrific events, and wrong choices. All are used for good. Everything is woven into the grand design I'm creating. Nothing is ever wasted. Step by step, I'm showing you My plan for you. Because I'm always beside you. Though you can't see My face, I'm smiling on you. In all your ways acknowledge Me, and I will bring you peace and healing. I'm joyful when you think of Me during the day and when you ask for Me in the night places. These times bring me great pleasure. Let Me help you more. I can. I will as you come to Me. Because I long to partner and plan with you. You'll be surprised at what we can come up with when our hearts are bound together. Turn to Me. I'll speak to you as often as you turn and listen for Me. I also love our walks together. I love you.

Because You feed me

"Jesus replied, "I am the bread of life. Whoever comes to me will never be hungry again. Whoever believes in me will never be thirsty."
—John 6:35

Me: Oh Lord, only You can deliver! Only You can supply our needs. Would You always provide for me? Today, You reminded me of what I've come to learn—that You sustain us with Your food physically, mentally, and spiritually. And when we profane our bodies, minds, or spirits with adulterated foods, we become sickly and weak. Your will was always that we would prosper and be in health (3 John 2). We make ourselves sick by eating the wrong food. Teach us what we need to know to live, survive, and thrive, Lord. Give us good and healthy provisions so we can be healthy in every way. In Eden, every food available to Adam and Eve sustained and enabled them to have a closer relationship with You. Nothing there would hinder or harm them, as long as they followed Your directions. We lose vitality when we turn from You and Your guidance. You created food for our benefit and health, even to prevent death. It's up to us to listen to You and follow Your advice on what is good to eat and drink mentally, physically, and spiritually, and what is not. All in moderation. Overexposure and lack of balance in anything can cause sickness, harm, and death. Teach us how to use what You've given us for good! I love You.

God: Beloved, you know that I love you. You see how I give you so many things for good, and how I instruct and lead you to the right use of everything, whether its physical food or information. Often, the more a thing is adulterated and changed, the less beneficial it becomes. All things must be used properly as intended and in the right balance. Everything was meant for a purpose and a reason. When things are misused, I can still make whole what's been broken. I can heal—physically, mentally, and spiritually. Rely on Me for this. Turn to Me when you experience pain, and let Me show you how I can make it right. If it's a hurt caused by unkind words, let Me heal it through reconciliation. If it's illness caused by toxins, come to Me for cleansing. If it's mental healing you need, seek Me for answers. But if people continue to feed on poisons that cause harm, after I've healed them, they set themselves on a course to their own demise. But I'm still a God of mercy. I love you.

JUNE 10
As I seek healing

"Don't call everything a conspiracy, like they do, and don't live in dread of what frightens them. Make the Lord of Heaven's Armies holy in your life. He is the one you should fear. He is the one who should make you tremble. He will keep you safe."
—Isaiah 8:12-14

Me: Lord, heal our land. Open blind eyes so people can see when what they're accepting as real is really a lie! Help us to come to You with our whole hearts. And help our children to recognize what's true, so they can turn to You. For only You are good. Only You can reveal what's real. Lies and degradation are evil. Greed and corruption suppress justice. Let me with open arms receive and share Your goodness. Show me today how I can tread, even soar, with You, never tempted by wrong thinking or evil, but understanding the difference between what is false and what is real. I want to be able to see inside people and understand their thoughts, so I can steer them closer to You. Lord, let me always turn to You for insight and the ability to discern the words and actions that cross my path, for You are my refuge, my high tower, my help, my sanctuary, and my rock. Be near and guide me. Open my eyes to what You wish me to see so I can help bring healing. I love You.

God: Dear one, remember when I gave Moses My Ten Commandments? What was the first one? "You must not have any other god but me" (Exodus 20:3). Why was this so important? Few people think through the outcome of worshipping other gods, so they willingly bow down to gods like money, power, fame, desires, etc. How deceived they are! They feel like they've "arrived" if they have what it takes to be successful in the world's eyes. Yet their hearts and hands are broken, because they focus on everything but Me. They want what others have, and they spend their time imagining ways to get more, so they can appear to be better off than the others. This is a sad life! They've created their own prisons! Yet, they could fly with wings like eagles and be free if they'd just look into My eyes and hear My voice and walk a little while with Me. Then, I could show them how much more there is to life—how they're meant to live, who they truly are, and how they can soar with gratitude. Remember, only I can deliver and set people free from the world's burdens. And I have the power to heal lands and make nations free and prosperous when the citizens turn their hearts to Me. I love you.

June 11
And never grow too old

"O God, you have taught me from my earliest childhood, and I constantly tell others about the wonderful things you do. Now that I am old and gray, do not abandon me, O God. Let me proclaim your power to this new generation, your mighty miracles to all who come after me."
—Psalm 71:17-18

Me: Dear Lord, sometimes my body aches and I seek Your healing hand. Would You spread Your soothing fingers over me and let me feel Your comforting touch? Even as I grow older, would You restore my body to vibrancy with Your healing balm so I can feel Your powerful presence? And heal my mind with Your peace. Whisper in my ears again and again, so I can hear Your melodious and peace-filled voice. You alone are strong and mighty. I am weak and powerless without You. As I age, I wonder how useful I am to You. Would You lift me up, and help me to stand in Your abiding strength? Open new doors, Lord, to places and people and things, and demonstrate Your love to me in ways beyond my imagination. I want the pure love that comes only from You. Touch my heart so I can continue to give Your love as though it was from You. Would You help me to extend Your healing hand to others too, so they can know You as I do? You're a mighty Lord. Give me strength to serve today. I love You.

God: Dear one, I'm here. I'm always present. And today is a day for healing. Today, release your fears and cares and worries to Me. Release any physical bondage that may have taken hold of you because of these. Release the aches and pains in your body and let Me heal you. Today, lean on Me, for I'm the One who delivers and makes you whole, no matter how old you are! Lean on Me, and I will lead you to the answers you seek and open your eyes to the needs around you. Then you'll see My hand of might on your life and the lives of others. Allow Me to do this for you. Do you see how I can work even with very broken and imperfect people to move My purposes forward? The people I work through aren't always the ones you might expect. Often, My promises are fulfilled through people whom others think less than likely because of their age. Think about Noah, Abraham, Sarah, Moses, and Naomi in the Old Testament, and Simeon and Anna in the New Testament. How old were they when they saw My promises fulfilled? How old are you? I love you.

To reach those who don't know who they are

"But blessed are those who trust in the Lord and have made the Lord their hope and confidence. They are like trees planted along a riverbank, with roots that reach deep into the water. Such trees are not bothered by the heat or worried by long months of drought. Their leaves stay green, and they never stop producing fruit."
—Jeremiah 17:7-8

Me: Lord, You've called me to minister to those who don't know who they are, because they've been misguided by those who don't know Your love. Sometimes this is hard, especially when they have terrible underlying problems based on torn-apart family lives that cause them to lash out in anger and hate. Many are deceived in their beliefs about themselves, and they fight to defend or release an illusory image. They need You desperately, but they don't know how to stop the record that keeps playing in their mind. They battle deluded thoughts that reel on and on. Would You show me how to love these ones who are so broken? How can I help them break the terrible record that drives them to live a false life? Lord, show me how to help them! And protect my heart from bitter reactions and hateful outbursts. Remind me not to react in anger by forgetting who the real enemy is. Let me see as You see with Your understanding. Only Your way will suffice. Today, may my buffer by Your peace, joy, and love—all working together so I can act for You. Let me represent You in all things so I can bring deliverance and healing to those around me. I love You.

God: Dear one, I'm delighted in you and your desire to serve Me. Do you see how I've anointed you with good things because you chose to love what I love and hate what I hate? Do you understand that your life confronts those who don't choose goodness or honesty, and they are sometimes offended by you because of this? It's not you that makes them mean-spirited. You understand that their evil thoughts are influenced by others. Keep on living and speaking the truth. You've seen how things become clear when you listen to Me and speak the words I give you! Nothing can disrupt your fellowship with Me if you don't allow it to. I'll shine My light so you can discern where words or actions are coming from and how to break the negative cycles. It can be a cruel world. Lean on Me for direction. I'll protect and heal you when needed. I'll fight alongside you and safeguard you with My peace. I'll show you how to encourage those who seek My hope, healing, and confidence. I love you.

With the help of Your heavenly knighthood

"The LORD of Heaven's Armies is here among us; the God of Israel is our fortress."
—Psalm 46:7

Me: Lord, it would be so easy for me to stay here all day with You. I adore our times together, especially when we talk and walk together at sunrise around the lake. It's hard to return home and get ready to go out to fight life's battles. Today, would You stay near me as I go? You showed me once a vision of Your heavenly "knighthood," as in Luke 2:13, when a heavenly host appeared to shepherds in the fields. Teach me more about this angelic host, Lord. Show me how to fight for those You've entrusted to me and when I should call on the help of Your angel army for supernatural power. How do I bless and work with people who need You? I don't want to waste Your precious resources on those who don't want to change or grow up in You. You're my only guide, and I'm realizing how You protect me and always work on my behalf. You encourage, strengthen, bless, bring abundance, and heal my heart in every stressful encounter. Thank You for being with me today and for all You do for me. I love You.

God: Dear child, one day you'll behold with your spiritual eyes my heavenly host or "knighthood." Some on earth have seen it: the shepherds in the field at My Son's birth and Elisha with his servant in a time of need (2 Kings 6:17-20). When it's necessary, I reveal this amazing army to certain individuals to give them strength and determination. Just remember, My forces in the heavenly realm are available whenever you need them! Know that when you give Me your heart and soul by relinquishing your cares and worries to Me, you also allow Me to bring you great peace and deliverance. Then you can see amazing and wonderful things! When you come to Me, and let Me work through you, you begin to see how your life becomes a miracle and a masterpiece! As you trust in Me, I illuminate your life and make it radiant so that you can reflect My spectacular, rainbowed colors. You begin to glow continuously with My light and brightness. I enliven you with My strokes, paint over the broken places in your life, and make you ever more beautiful. I can radiate from your very soul. But these things can only happen as you continuously give Me your heart! I love you.

As I linger with You

"The Lord passed in front of Moses, calling out, 'Yahweh! The Lord! The God of compassion and mercy. I am slow to anger and filled with unfailing love and faithfulness.'"
—*Exodus 34:6*

Me: Dear Lord, would You pass in front of me? Would You allow me to see You, or, at least, glimpse a little view of You? Would You let me linger with You so I can sit with You at least for a while? And feel You place Your warm blanket of mercy over my shoulders? Can I loiter long enough to feel Your hand in mine as I look into Your eyes? For I desire You more than food and crave You more than life itself! Oh, to see Your face, Your smile, and to understand Your every thought! Like Mr. Darcy in *Pride and Prejudice*, I know You work behind the scenes like a spurned lover at times, trying to bring peace and healing. You want to offer us hope, lavish us with Your hidden love, and win our adoration. How can You forgive me for all the times I looked away from You, when You sought my attention? And You still pursued me! Thanks for forgiving me. Thanks for healing me. Thanks for all You've done for me and how, even now, You fight for me! You saved me and gave me life. I love You.

God: Dear one, look into My eyes, for they are gazing adoringly at You right now! You'll be surprised, as you look closely, what you *can* see. When you peer into and through My eyes, you'll see a different view of everything. Because, deep inside them lies My perception of the world around you. You'll begin to see the inner workings of places and people and times beyond yours. You're never limited when you view things through My eyes. For they're all-seeing and all-knowing. They can see everything! They can lead you to places where you can minister in My name to people who seek the truth. Look forward to this, for I'm preparing you even now. Take life a day at a time, and seek My point of view more and more. For I'm the Lord your God. I alone bring deliverance. I alone am all-powerful and all-just. My love for you exceeds every expectation. You can't find this kind of love in the world. I bring you peace and healing, and I answer your prayers. Open your heart and your mind to Me. Let Me whisper in your ears, heal your heart, ease your pains, and bring you comfort. I am the Lord your God who adores you. I love you.

In a calming cabin

"And this righteousness will bring peace. Yes, it will bring quietness and confidence forever. My people will live in safety, quietly at home. They will be at rest."
—Isaiah 32:17-18

Me: Dear Lord, as I sit and rest, I reach deep inside for a place of peace. And as I breathe in to tap into Your Spirit, I see a place I've seen before in my mind's eye. It's a room in a fragrant-pine log cabin where a cushioned chair with a soft plaid throw welcomes me invitingly to sit by a fire. Warm flames burn brightly from logs placed inside a rustic limestone fireplace that reaches up to the ceiling. A rough-hewn wood mantel is set among the stones and holds a few meaningful pictures. Enveloped by a glow that pervades the room, I gaze at the morning sunrays that stream through the windows and highlight a colorful Indian rug that lays in front of the fire. The sight of it warms my heart. My grandparents had a rug like this one in a cabin just like this. And I spent many pleasant summers with them there. I sigh as I sit with the memories, and I ask, "Would You bring me here again and again when I feel the world trying to steal parts of my soul? I want so much to sit with You at least for a while as I breathe in draughts of Your healing nature in this cabin. Would You shed Your light on the dark places and clear away the thorny brush that blocks my way, so I can follow You to this peaceful place more often?" I sigh again and say, "I love You."

God: Dear one, like the sun's rays, My Word is a light that lightens your path and brings comfort. It gives needed wisdom and insight. It offers healing. Never be anxious or troubled, because I will always show you a way through the darkness when you turn your eyes to Me. And I'll lead you to My "cabin of peace" anytime you want to return to it. In years to come, you'll see good and bad things, but, through them all, you'll see My will fulfilled. Look to Me for the promises that will be fulfilled. My Son will return one day, and everything will be in harmony as it was meant to be, and all will work together for good. Be patient as I work things out little by little. And never worry or wonder how you can help yourself or others. For I'm a God of abundance and grace, and I'll always exceed your expectations. Trust Me to work in your life and provide needed healing. I'm here with you now. Sit with Me awhile today, and remember who I am. I'm the Lord your God who loves you. I alone can bring you to My place of peace, no matter where you are. I love you.

As I reach my hands up to You

"He heals the brokenhearted and bandages their wounds."
—*Psalm 147:3*

Me: Hear me, Lord. I need Your touch today. My heart requires supernatural strength, which can only come from You! Would You give me wisdom and patience with those who can't seem to direct their own lives and have little confidence in their own ability? Would You help me to forgive and see good in those who are so broken that they're blind to their own strengths and oblivious to others' needs? They stand on foundations that crumble and lean on walls that collapse with the weight of their burdens. They depend on those who seem less broken than they are but are actually empty, leaking containers. Lord, give me insight as to how to deal with people like this today without feeling discouraged and drained. Many show no motivation to grow or to accomplish anything. They're so self-absorbed with their own problems that they can't offer support to anyone else. I want to be a giver, not a taker. Show me how to be a good example. What words can I use to touch them? I reach my hands up to You for help. I love You.

God: Dear one, come to Me with your frustrations, and I will take them from you. Don't worry about what you're not doing or the negative responses of others. Let Me take care of the naysayers, the lost ones, and the non-plussers! I alone can give you peace and refresh your soul. My touch is penetrating and healing, and I can repair what's been ripped apart, whether it's something in you or in others. I can remove what doesn't belong there. So, reach your hands up to Me, and I will send My delivering power down through you like an electric current. At night, when you feel a rushing through your veins, that's just Me, cleansing and making you whole again. I'm a God of healing. I heal your heart and give you needed strength and patience. Remember what resides in you—My Holy Spirit. It's behind every part of you. Take care of your body by ministering to your mind with the power of My Word. Your body represents Me and My Word living in you. Take good care of it, for it's a gift from Me to you. Release your cares to Me and allow Me to meet your needs. Then, we can reach and touch the needs of others, even the nay-sayers. I love you.

JUNE 17
So I can leap with Your joy

"But for you who fear my name, the Sun of Righteousness will rise with healing in his wings. And you will go free, leaping with joy like calves let out to pasture."
—Malachi 4:2

Me: Lord, would You help me to be strong enough to overcome? You're my hope and my song in the night. Lead me to Your way and help me to be what I need to be for others. I sometimes feel weak and need Your healing hand to land on me! Help me to rise up so I'm strong and healthy. Lord, would You make it clear to me what's from You and what's just fearmongering from the world? Protect me from the things that bring harm or weaken my ability—physically, mentally, or spiritually. Steer me away from anything that's not from You. Lord, screen my every thought and filter my every action. Thanks for touching me now with Your soothing hand of blessing and healing. Pour down more of Your power to me, for I long to hear You in every moment and be able to soak in Your presence. Then I can leap with Your joy! Thanks for Your strength and protection today. I love You.

God: Child, I am near you always. Look to Me, for I will show you more of My beauty and joy. I've taught you about peace, and you experience more of it now than ever before. Do you see how I'm leading you? Do you see how far I've brought you? Or how things don't disturb or steal your peace the way they once did? Within you are remnants of anxiety. These will eventually be released too. Sometimes you still worry because you remember past failures and regrets, or you think that your body is breaking down as you age. Don't listen to the world regarding these things! It will only fill your mind with fear of health issues and diseases you might get. Listen to Me and My Word. Come to Me for health and healing. I can give you these, along with peace. Yes, it's right to visit a doctor you trust for help when you need it. I've called many to this profession to minister healing in different ways. But, you must use good judgment and discernment, and ask Me first when you have questions. I will always answer you, and I will guide you so you can make right choices regarding your health. I love you.

And see where it all comes from

"Here now is my final conclusion: Fear God and obey his commands, for this is everyone's duty. God will judge us for everything we do, including every secret thing, whether good or bad."
—*Ecclesiastes 12:13-14*

Me: It's interesting, Lord, how people put all their efforts into working and accomplishing things to receive recognition, praise, honor, money, acclaim, love, property, and more, only to end up disappointed with life. Their feeling of coming up short becomes evident when they express sarcasm, vindictiveness, anger, bitterness, hatred, etc. And they blame everyone and everything else, when they could get all they ever needed or wanted by simply going to You! Their shortsightedness is manifested through health problems, loss of material things, estrangement by family or friends, and loss of jobs or job satisfaction. They don't realize that it all could be fixed if they just understood who You are and what You could do for them. So many problems would be avoided! I think about Solomon, who wrote the book of Ecclesiastes, after he'd experienced every blessing and benefit in life, yet he was exasperated by the elusiveness of it all! In the end, he realized that nothing but awe for You and Your Word really mattered in the end. Lord, You're the author of every blessing. You're the healer, the provider, and the One who completes us. Thanks today for health, prosperity, and abundant blessings. Bless my family and friends, and reveal to them more of Your greatness. I love You.

God: Dear one, you're realizing how prosperity, health, and blessings come from Me. People often think that if they just work harder, they'll have more. It doesn't always work this way. Yes, it's true that laziness is a curse. People who are unwilling to put forth any effort suffer for their lacks and usually blame others for it. True and lasting prosperity always comes from Me. You can labor and have many things, but the enemy can come and steal away what you've expended so much effort to achieve. If you follow in My steps, I can help you to succeed and have no lack. I can also protect what you've worked so hard to attain. Let Me ease your burden and give you rest. Never be anxious about what you'll have to eat or drink or wear or how you might appear to others. I'm your father, and I will prosper your way and give you good health. I love you.

JUNE 19
So I can live to praise You

"God showed how much he loved us by sending his one and only Son into the world so that we might have eternal life through him. This is real love—not that we loved God, but that he loved us and sent his Son as a sacrifice to take away our sins."
—1 John 4:9-10

Me: Dear Lord, in the book of Exodus, Jochebed made a little boat and placed her son in it. How hard that must have been for her to watch another woman take and raise him as her own! But her son Moses became the great deliverer for Your people! And You remind me of Your goodness to my son. I gave him up when he moved away. I gave him up when he got married. I gave him up when he succumbed to cancer. Lord, make it all up to me, as You did to Jochebed and Mary and others whose sons were taken away from them at an early age. Let my son's children be mighty leaders for You! I think about what You gave up for us. Thanks for Your precious Son, whom You loved more than I could ever love my son! You were willing to give Him up so we could come to You as blameless ones. What an awesome gift! Thanks for how You set Him up as a mighty mediator. Thanks for what He did to spare me the unbearable effects of loss and pain, so I can live to praise and please You, and be able to receive Your healing hand. I love You.

God: Dear one, yes, I was grieved to watch My Son die, just as you mourned when yours suffered and passed away. But Jesus is with Me now, interceding for you. And you will rejoin your son one day because of My Son. I allowed Jesus to go through this because I knew what this would make available to people like you. And remember, He was *willing* to go through it for you. Now, what a friend you have in Him! Don't ever forget this. He's your source of inspiration and joy, your guide, your first love, your healer, and your friend. He sought you out and bought for you eternal life. He stands beside you. He guards your heart and protects you from harm, so you need never despair. Don't allow disappointments to dissuade you from His love, or Mine. Remember who stands with you. He's your shield. He's your comforter and the answer to all life's problems and worries. That's who He is for you. And He wants to protect and heal your heart as your best friend. For He loves you. And He loves your son more than words can say, just as I love you.

Because I see what matters most in the end

"Now we see things imperfectly, like puzzling reflections in a mirror, but then we will see everything with perfect clarity. All that I know now is partial and incomplete, but then I will know everything completely, just as God now knows me completely."
—1 Corinthians 13:12

Me: Lord, I thank You for watching over me and my family and for bringing us through troubling times. You are magnificent in Your blessings and profound in Your mercy. Help me now to speak Your wisdom and lead others to You. Help me to avoid the temptation of repeating lies, gossip, or criticism of others I may not even know. Help me to bring healing with my lips and breakthroughs with my touch. Only You can help me with this. Only You can do these things through me. Only Your love matters in the end. I want to help others with Your hand of mercy. Open doors and give me the strength and insight to walk through them. I love You.

God: Dear one, you've seen how quickly time passes. But your understanding of life is still obscure. One day, you'll see Me face to face. Then, you'll understand how time really works and what eternity means. You're right to think that what truly matters is My love. Anyone can recognize this. People come to understand Me in different ways. They see and believe the truths that are most meaningful to them. Some people deliver My message in a box by confining it to a set of rules. But My Word is boundless. It is many-faceted and comes through a variety of messengers. But it's still the truth. Understand that no one group has a complete understanding of My Word. When people devote time and effort to reading it, they understand more, but no one can know everything. Only I know it all. That's why I say, "Now you see through a glass darkly." It's like you're looking through a window to the outside, and the glass is fogged over. The more you read and listen to My Word, the more film is removed from the glass. But no one except My Son has seen clearly. Keep this in mind. Every view is tainted. How each person lives is according to the limited understanding he or she has acquired. My rewards are based on how well people walk out what they understand. I want them to have a greater knowledge of the truth, but this can only be attained when they come to Me and ask for understanding. Do you see? This is how it works. I love you.

JUNE 21
And how You minister love to us

"So the LORD must wait for you to come to him so he can show you his love and compassion. For the LORD is a faithful God. Blessed are those who wait for his help."
—Isaiah 30:18

Me: Oh Lord, sometimes I feel so weary of this world! I'm tired of the division and hatred I see. So many speak against each other, instead of working to bring healing and unity. And I see so much finger-pointing and corruption of the values I hold dear. Even teachers spew hatred toward groups of people and distorted information about heroes of our past. They ignore the things that can unify us. We need Your help, Lord. We need Your hand in our lives to show us how to come together. The only places I see unity these days are in the gatherings where people lift their hands up to You in praise and worship. I pray that more people will find their way to these places and to You. How can I help in this effort? How can I bring more to You? Lord, I need You now more than ever to give me comfort in times of anxiety and uncertainty. Fill me now with Your joy, peace, and love. Thanks for Your guidance and protection for me and my family. Fill me with wisdom to do what You need me to do. And sharpness of mind to see what You want me to see and courage to follow through. I love You.

God: Dear one, do you recall the song, *Turn Your Eyes Upon Jesus*? Or the verses, "Oh, soul, are you weary and troubled? No light in the darkness you see. There's light for a look at the savior. And life more abundant and free." When you turn your eyes to Me, you come to My fountain, the wellspring of life, where your mind is renewed and your soul is refreshed. It's where the spirit is invigorated and strengthened. Come to Me when you need answers, when you're uncertain, and when you're afraid. Come to Me when life deals you blows, or when you feel shipwrecked, disheartened, or discouraged. Come to Me when all seems lost, and you haven't the strength to go on. Come to Me when you see others flailing, and you haven't any answers. Come to Me when you feel adrift on a sea of uncertainty. I alone can strengthen, renew, uplift, hearten, and give you hope. Though you can't see Me now, one day you will, and your eyes will be opened. And Your heart will thrill in My presence! Now you see dimly. But I am here, and I want to help you. But I wait for you to come. So come now with your hurting heart, and I will mend it. I love you.

As the only antidote to hate

"Therefore let us stop passing judgment on one another. Instead, make up your mind not to put any stumbling block or obstacle in the way of a brother or sister."
—*Romans 14:13*

Me: Lord, all of life's connections amaze me! Each of us affects someone else, who, in turn, influences another. And the people we might think are insignificant are sometimes greatly used by You. We might speak into someone's life who can touch many people in unbelievable ways! Lord, would You help me to speak life-changing words to others today? Show me my own value and if I've somehow brought others closer to You. You've clearly shown me how I mustn't look critically at others, because I don't know their true worth in Your eyes. Whenever I've criticized people for not responding in the way I thought they should, You've often sent those very ones to perform some act of kindness that confronts my judgment. You remind me of Your grace continuously and how I can pray for people instead of criticizing them. I love You.

God: Dear one, remember that when people have a "dim" (lacking My light) view of themselves, they often attack others so they can feel better about themselves. Love is the only antidote. Kindness is the medicine that can cure others' feelings of self-loathing, which bring bitterness and hatred. "Small and belittled" thinking of themselves or others happens when people live in cages. Through the wires of the cages, they reach out and try to claw at others who pass by, because they're trapped—confined and suffering from wrong thoughts and views. The only thing that can free them is a combination of forgiveness, patience, and love. Pray for them. Never judge. Show them who I am. Refrain from criticism, which exacerbates self-hatred. I can touch every situation with grace and help you lead these imprisoned ones to streams in the desert. And I can lead you to those who'll open their hearts and move with you to new paths of joy. There may be hardship and resistance at times, but I will give you strength and wisdom. Those who listen will be blessed. Watch how I direct you, so you can guide them. Be wise. Observe. I will show you new ways, and tell you who to speak to and when. I'm light and life. I bring you peace and joy and healing. Trust Me. I love you.

That leads me to healing

"Are any of you sick? You should call for the elders of the church to come and pray over you, anointing you with oil in the name of the Lord. Such a prayer offered in faith will heal the sick, and the Lord will make you well. And if you have committed any sins, you will be forgiven."
—James 5:14-15

Me: Lord, a woman I know has been trying to help her mom, who is dying. Would You give me the right words to say to her? I want to offer comforting words that will minister healing to them both. Would You help me to bring them both peace and rest and joy through these difficulties? Pour Your love over them in ways they can't deny. Thanks for wisdom and a greater understanding of how You can work in this situation. Teach me more about healing, Lord. It seemed so easy for Jesus while He was here. Why is it so hard for us to believe that it can happen? Why couldn't my son be healed? Could I have brought healing to him if I'd had more contact with him? If I'd prayed with him more? Could anything have been done differently? How I miss him. Lord, I love You.

God: Dear one, you did what you could for your son. Yes, I can heal, but the circumstances must be right. Remember, it's a battle: spiritually, mentally, and physically. It's often a matter of mindset and acceptance of problems and issues. And often people give up too soon, because they don't feel they have the strength or ability to confront the disease or what is broken. Usually, they've resigned themselves by the time the difficulty or setback occurs. Then, it's even more of a struggle to regain the confidence needed so that healing or deliverance can take place. When Jesus was on the earth, He did the fighting for others. He could help them, because He Himself had won the battle in the wilderness. If He'd lost against the adversary, He wouldn't have had the power to help anyone. People lose these fights first in their minds. That's why it's so important to spend time listening to Me and My voice daily. I can lead you out of any mental battle, whether it's against pressure (mental, physical, family, work, etc.) or weakness that brings sickness or a physical crisis. I can reassure you when the going gets tough. Practice turning your thoughts to Me. Only I have the power to pull you out of any despair, heartache, anxiety, or sickness by reminding you of My ability and that I can remove the darkness and bring light again into your life. I love you.

So I can survive and thrive

"The Lord cares deeply when his loved ones die."
—Psalm 116:15

Me: Lord, You gave me life, and You know the day of my death. You can heal me when I need it, but You also allow disease on the earth. Show me again Your way and Your will. I understand that sickness and suffering were never a part of Your original plan for mankind. But, sadly, people turn their backs on You and having a relationship with You. They want to do things their own way, without consulting You as to what is best for themselves or others. And so, because of selfishness and idolatry and heeding the voice of the adversary, whose only goals are to steal, kill, and destroy, many suffer from bad choices. And I'm disheartened whenever I experience the death of another loved one. But I know You've said that the demise of those You love is costly and precious to You, just as it is to us. Thanks for Your guidance today so I can lead others to a greater understanding of how You mean things to be and how they will be again one day, when Your Son returns for us. How can we survive and thrive until then in this world You made? I love You.

God: Dear one, you're right. I count it very precious, or costly, when one of My beloved ones dies. I never wanted this to happen. For, when a person dies, he or she can no longer walk or talk with Me on earth, or represent My love among people, or deliver My healing message to others. Death of any of My children is always painful to Me. It never was a blessing. My desire has always been that people live forever with Me. But many have turned away to their own devices, and they ignore that vital part of life—spirit. To survive and thrive now, you must be able to minister grace and healing to your mind and body by way of My Spirit in you, which you received when you believed in My Son and what He did for you. Remember, His blood shed for you gives you forgiveness and His body broken for you brings you healing. And you can help others reclaim that spiritual part that was lost with Adam by telling them how to believe in what My Son accomplished for them. The spirit they receive can lead them to all truth, including how to survive and thrive in this life and the next. For I long to live with as many as possible now and forever. I love you.

JUNE 25
As a cheerful child

"I tell you the truth, anyone who doesn't receive the Kingdom of God like a child will never enter it."
—Mark 10:15

Me: Lord, You reminded me of a dream where I peeked into my laundry room and was surprised to see my mother doing laundry there. She squinted her eyes and furrowed her brow as she bent over to gaze down at a basket full of clothes. She seemed burdened by them. Behind her, a small girl swung her legs cheerfully as she sat, propped up on the windowsill. The child asked my mother what she wanted the most, then quickly answered the question for her: "I know! You'd like to be sitting up here! Do you want to sit with me now?" On hearing this, my mother's stern, depressed expression immediately changed, and she sighed and smiled. The child had touched a vulnerable place. I realized from this dream that one can reach others by tenderly touching the one soft spot in their life. Instead of looking for faults and pointing them out, we can reach for what's most dear to them. You do this for us, Lord! Help me to see through Your eyes so I can discern peoples' hearts, and love as You do. It's all about seeing like a small child, isn't it? Thanks for showing me this. Would You help me to remember this simple dream, and how I can help people feel loved and accepted by You, just as You've done for me? I love You.

God: Dear one, My heart bleeds for some who avoid Me, because they feel trapped. Like your mom in the dream, they work their hearts out in a "laundry room," trying to wash away their guilt and shame, like stains they can't remove, and the torn places of their lives that they can't seem to mend or repair. Maybe they were abused or talked down to as children, and so their self-image has been damaged, and they don't know how to restore it. They may want to return to younger years, before they experienced hardship or abuse or sadness, or escape to a place or time far away from their present state. I'll lead you to these people and give you encouraging words to speak to them. When people "sputter" with negativity, it's because they lack what it takes to move ahead. They've run out of steam and have nothing to push them forward. I can help them if they come to Me for help. Be My "child in the laundry room"—the one to bring them light out of darkness. I'll show you how to do this and what to say. I love you.

195

Who understands why good people die young

"Good people pass away; the godly often die before their time. But no one seems to care or wonder why. No one seems to understand that God is protecting them from the evil to come."
—Isaiah 57:1

Me: Lord, teach me more about healing. Why is it so hard for us to believe and receive it? Why do some die so young? Could they have been healed? Help me to see You as You are and be able to understand how I can more effectively fight for Your people. Would You help me to understand why people who are trying to live for You and do Your will often suffer and die prematurely? And then why people who deny Your existence and live miserable, evil lives continue to thrive, while the good ones die early? Help me to understand why You allow these things. Thanks, Lord. I love You.

God: Dear one, I fight for you. Remember that the closer you get to Me, the more intense the spiritual battle grows. That's because the adversary, who doesn't want anyone to know the truth, tries to put up barriers to being able to win the fight. I can deliver you, but you must focus on Me. I can direct your steps, and keep you safe from harm, but you must trust Me to lead you. Why do I allow good and faithful people to suffer and die prematurely? Remember, My purpose for people has always been that they be able to choose freely, not forcibly, to come to Me. My desire was always that people live eternally, and, in this life, abundantly. It was the devil who rebelled against Me and now pursues the destruction of mankind through deception and accusations. As a result of his manipulation of truth and justice, people are lured into making choices that cause harm to themselves and others. Sometimes even good people are deceived. When they fail to heed My warnings, they're often sidetracked. Then others take advantage of them through short term "benefits" that cause or exacerbate disease. I can heal, but undoing bad choices is difficult and requires great trust and reliance on Me. Sometimes deliverance is hindered by a person's belief in what's available or what I can do for them. At other times it's actually more merciful for them to die to avoid greater pain and hardship. My will was never that people die, especially prematurely. Remember that those who do believe in Me and My Son will live forever. And those who've harmed others for their own advantage, and fight against Me and My own, will be judged justly later. I love you.

And never forget

"But Jesus replied, "My Father is always working, and so am I."
—*John 5:17*

Me: I haven't forgotten about You, Lord. You've been in my thoughts continually, and Your presence is always at the forefront of my mind. You've proven yourself to be my best friend by blessing and showing me Your red thread throughout my life and exactly why things happened the way they did along the way. All the things I worried about, thinking they were mistakes or wrong choices, You've somehow woven into this tapestry of my life to make it more beautiful. It amazes me how everything has worked out for good. Thanks for how You've led me to where I belong—by Your side. You've even used circumstances to bring me to where I was needed. Thanks for how You sent Jesus to make things right that once were so terribly wrong. Show me now where You want me, Lord. Speak to me in visions and dreams, and reveal to me more of Your Word, for Your ways are undeniably far above mine. Help me to devote time to what is most important to You today. I love You.

God: Dear one, I don't look on your brokenness. I see the love I have for you and the love you have for Me. These are what please Me the most! They make My heart sing. They make Me glad! Listen to Me, My love, and I'll always give you the right words to say and the best thoughts to have in each moment. I'll give you My insight and promises to bring to others. I'll bring you love, peace, newness of life, and healing as you turn your thoughts to Me. But you must remember Me in your daily struggles. You must remember Me as you go about your business, when you're entertaining, helping, or trying to bring good things to others. Help Me by bringing My message of hope to them. Because it's there, in your heart, ready to be delivered. But you must remember to look to Me for it! My desire is for a greater pouring out of My Spirit. That's My goal. But I need your help. I'll show you who to reach and how to reach them. Just rely on Me for wisdom and direction. I'll supply you with the needed time and the right contacts. Trust Me for these. I'll also provide quiet time to reflect and talk with Me, so I can repair what's been broken and mend what's been torn apart. I desire this more than you do! Come to Me often and listen, for I have so much to say to you! I love you.

JUNE 28
How You make me new

"This means that anyone who belongs to Christ has become a new person. The old life is gone; a new life has begun!"
—2 Corinthians 5:17

Me: Lord, thanks for a brisk, but quiet, walk this morning around the lake. It was so nice to hear the birds before dawn twittering in the trees, to enjoy the cooler air, to look for the deer and the fox, and to watch the ducks and geese near the marina. But mostly, it was wonderful to talk. It's so nice to share my thoughts with You, Lord, and to know that You hear my complaints and my praises, and You actually love to listen to me! Would You bless this day? Would You fling open the right doors? Would You show me how to reach even higher into the sacred and secret places of Your heart? Would You unfold Your plan more and more to me? And my purpose in it all? Would You make new what needs to be renewed? Take the old, rusty parts—the broken or unfit pieces of my life—and remake them the way You see fit. And polish them so they shine! Because only You can redo me, so I'm even better than before! I love You.

God: My love, you celebrate this special time of year, when so many births take place and wedding vows are consummated. It makes you so happy to live in this season of rebirth and renewal, when many memories are made by the young and the young at heart to be recalled later in life. New lives begin, and new ways of life spring forth. Couples begin life together, and they are full of hope, expectation, and anticipation. Speak to those you meet about their hopes and dreams. Are they being fulfilled? If not, why? Tell them that what they always hoped for, and still long to achieve, can come to pass! Explain how, through trust in Me, they can attain their aspirations. They can have the life they always dreamed of, and new meaning to go with it. Through Me, their expectations will always be fulfilled. This is the new hope you can bring to them. The same way I renew you through My Spirit in you, I can also work in all those who come to Me. And you can support and help Me as I make all things new. I love you.

JUNE 29
Because who is like You?

"Don't store up treasures here on earth, where moths eat them and rust destroys them, and where thieves break in and steal. Store your treasures in heaven, where moths and rust cannot destroy, and thieves do not break in and steal. Wherever your treasure is, there the desires of your heart will also be."
—*Matthew 6:19-21*

Me: Who is like You, Lord? Who can ever attain to Your greatness? Who can exalt an inglorious person like me, or bring a haughty person down low? Who can ease pain and suffering, and bring peace amid turmoil? Your Word is clear, but few attend to its message of deliverance and hope. When we turn to You, make You our Lord, and acknowledge Your greatness and power, then we can see what's true. We can see light and life and healing. It's not from this world that peace or joy can come. It's in the world where You abide—a world where we can participate if we believe. Remind me not to put down stakes here on earth, where moth and rust corrupt and where meaningless thoughts break through and steal my peace. Help me to see Your greatness, Your true worth, and Your light that brightens my path to Your Kingdom. Help me to be drawn to Your plan for me. And to clearly see the direction You want me to go and what path I should take, so I'm always embraced by Your healing arms of love. I love You.

God: Child, I love you. Do you really understand this? Even now, I'm preparing you for a place beyond anything you can ask or think. Don't let the trials you endure now cause you to give up hope for the future. Because they're part of My preparation. You can't imagine the gifts I'm wrapping for you now to present to you later. Today, My presence surrounds and engulfs you with peace and joy. All bitterness is gone when you seek Me. You glow with My light from within you. Seek My face, and I'll strengthen you. I'll warm and cleanse your heart as you need comforting and healing. And you can do these things for others by sharing My love with them. Come closer to Me, so I can be your closest friend. Let My words fall on your ears like a soft whispering or a gentle rain. They will bring you rest. And don't be afraid to hold My words out to others. They are like apples of gold on silver platters. They are a delicacy rarely seen or heard. Do your best, and I will work in you a glorious work. I love you.

Who gets me ready for the race

"I have fought the good fight, I have finished the race, I have kept the faith."
—2 Timothy 4:7

Me: Lord, I had another unusual dream last night. In it, I signed up to drive a race car in a contest sponsored by my company. I would need to speed only one lap around a track, but the trick was that all the drivers had to strip down to their underwear while driving. My coworkers were all surprised that I would sign up for something like this! But I had brainstormed a way to be successful: I'd wear super-slick biking shorts and a jog bra underneath a racing outfit with Velcro along the seams, so I could just rip the top and pants off while I was driving. I woke up before I could see how I finished the race. Lord, show me the meaning of this strange dream. What is this race, and what are You asking me to do? Make it clear and show me how to fulfill Your expectations for me. Dress me in Your "clothing" and equip me so I'm not over-burdened by worry about what others might think of me. Help me to be transparent to You and to others. And help me to win this race! Thanks, Lord. I love You.

God: Dear one, you did sign up for a "race"—My call on your life! And people are often surprised when they see the things you're willing and able to do, because they see you as an unlikely candidate who is small, aging, and seemingly insignificant. But women have proven themselves to be faster than men in many cases. And you can change roles in mid-stream and travel light. These are great attributes. To be successful, you can let all offenses and negatives slide easily off you, so they never stick. Transparency before Me is crucial. And underneath that cover of yours lies a secret agent for Me. Like David, you don't need the world's heavy armature to conquer giants. I provide all the light armor and tools you need. Little do people know how much capability you have! Remember, there is power in the name of My Son, Jesus Christ! You can use it for your own benefit and that of others to bring healing, strength, and miracles. It's truly "wonder-working power" and awesome authority over darkness! It's yours to use freely. You can utilize it in your prayers and in your thoughts. It's here and available any time you need it! So you can win the race before you. I love you.

July

FOCUS:
PRAISEWORTHY PATIENCE

"God blesses those who patiently endure testing and temptation. Afterward they will receive the crown of life that God has promised to those who love him."

—JAMES 1:12

JULY 1
Prepare me for that day

"But you must not forget this one thing, dear friends: A day is like a thousand years to the Lord, and a thousand years is like a day."
—2 Peter 3:8

Me: Lord, how fast time goes by! It amazes me to see a day come that I've anticipated or finally experience something I've forever longed for. It's this way with our hope and expectation for Christ's return. I know it'll come when we least expect it. And then, we'll get to see Him face-to-face! Lord, prepare me for that day. Would You help me to be strong mentally, physically, and spiritually, so that, when I finally see Him, I'll be ready to look Him joyfully in the eyes? And I'll be confident to hear Him say, "Well done My faithful servant!" Please be patient with me, and help me to be a good witness for You. I know You only work in us for good. Help me to walk in Your ways today. You showed me recently that it's not the things we think are big, like honors, promotions, and recognitions, that are most important to You. You focus more on what seems insignificant to us to see what we will do. You want to see how we'll respond to those who come our way. And Your rewards are determined by our responses, more than by the things the world deems as important. May I shine for You! I love You.

God: Dear one, remember that I'm timeless. Time means nothing to Me. I'm free from its confines. And I have all the patience in the world because My world is forever. And you're a part of it. Trust Me that I'm leading you to places you've never been, and I'll show you things you've never imagined. My love never fails, no matter how little or big you think you are or how you estimate your own ability. Continue to let this love shine through you. Hold My hand and let Me lead you. But you must listen to Me to be able to release My love. Deal graciously with the people I bring to you. They may seek your love and My light. Take one step at a time and follow Me. I'll lead you to bright paths, and I'll open your eyes so you can see what I see. In My world, love and kindness prevail. It's a wonderful place. Follow Me there. Don't be afraid. Just take My hand. My ways are tender and kind, unlike the world around you. You can't always see My world, but it's there, hidden to those who don't seek Me or My Word. But I'll reveal it to you, because you are Mine and I love you.

JULY 2
When Your train arrives

"But thank God! He has made us his captives and continues to lead us along in Christ's triumphal procession. Now he uses us to spread the knowledge of Christ everywhere, like a sweet perfume."
—2 Corinthians 2:14

Me: Lord, You've blessed me mightily. You've given me every one of my heart's desires. You've delivered me from evil and brought me to Your place of beauty. You've been with me from before I was born, and You've watched over me and guided my steps. Thank You. And thanks for friends with pure hearts who also seek You. Thanks for family members who "get it." Thanks for those who will listen and give support. Thanks for tenderness and mercy and grace all my days. You're awesome. You're great. You're magnificent. Thanks today for great wisdom in my speech and actions. Thanks for opening doors of utterance. You're worthy of all praise. Would You be with me now as I begin a new day? Would You show me where You want me? Lead me to those who need to hear Your words. Let me be a part of Your amazing train, where You are the engineer, and I am Your spirit-filled stoker who shovels Your power-inducing coal into the "heart" bins so that more "joy" cars can be added and pulled forward. As You direct me, I'll hitch on one car after another, and they, in turn, will add others. It'll be a mighty train of rejoicing for You that moves toward heaven and Your high calling! I love You.

God: Dear one, I'll open doors and show You how to attract others to Me. I'll give you greater wisdom to do this. But it will take time, so you must be patient. You desire to see My promises fulfilled, like Abraham did. You love how I spoke to him in the deserts and high places. You see how I showed him things and fulfilled My visions for and through him. You'd like to be a witness for Me in the same way and to be part of the train that I started long ago. I'll help you. Now you see part of it. As you bear witness to strategic ones, they'll hook onto our procession. They'll add to your joy. Don't be afraid to speak what I tell you. I desire strong men and women who'll serve Me and are not afraid to hitch onto My train to reach new places, where I can work through them. From them, I'll create a great new place for people who love Me. Today, bring My hope and peace to those I bring you. Open your mouth and speak My joy to them. Welcome them on board! I love you.

JULY 3
And I see the results of Your light

"Let your light shine for all to see. For the glory of the Lord rises to shine on you."
—*Isaiah 60:1*

Me: Lord, Independence Day approaches, and I think about the pricelessness of freedom. I celebrate liberty in this country, but I sometimes ask myself why we deserve it. What price had to be paid so we could enjoy it? If I look back in history, I see the great faith of the pilgrims who came here. I see the bold stance of those who refused to live under tyranny and were not afraid to stand up to oppression, even though this meant that they would suffer huge losses and, in some cases, die as a result. Thanks, Lord, for leading people who trusted in You to this place and for helping them to have the courage to give up so much to gain liberty for themselves and others. Thanks for their lives, for they are truly a gift to us. I see how we often take liberty for granted. Direct our leaders to a greater understanding of our need for Your presence, Your power, and Your Word. Lord, open their eyes to how we must depend on You to maintain the freedom to worship You now and later. Help me to see how powerful You are and how weak I am without You. Open my heart to hear. Help me today to represent You in new ways. Help me to lead by Your example and encourage others to be bold and brave to seek You in the face of opposition. Give me the strength and wisdom and patience to follow wherever You lead me. May I be a beacon of light and a hand of mercy to others. I love You.

God: Dear one, you are a beacon for Me. You're a light, shining brightly in this world. Just like the pilgrims, your light shines so others can see My presence on this earth! This light is in you, and it seeps through your pores, your skin, your eyes, your ears, your mouth—every part of you! Let it pour from you, because it wants to. It's the light of Jesus Christ within you—His very presence in this world. Let is glow, like a brightly shining star. Don't temper it. Let it out in all its glory! That's how those long ago lived. My Word permeated every part of their being. They lived it, spoke it, and taught it to their children. Even now, the results of their light in this country still shines on. Do you see this? Your light can shine for years, like the rays of the sun that radiate for many lightyears. I want you to understand this! Never hide your light "under a bushel!" Be brave! Let it shine! I love you.

And how You freed me

"So if the Son sets you free, you are truly free."
—*John 8:36*

Me: Dear Lord, today I am thankful for the freedom we have in Christ Jesus. Thanks, God, for this unspeakable gift. We need to thank You every day, because it affects our lives in more ways than we can ever imagine. We're blessed because of You, God, and our freedom comes from You. Many yearn for the liberty we have. You gave it to us freely and without any cost to us! Your Son paid the price with His own blood. And You offered Him to us as Your gift to set us free from lives of bondage. Thank You for this precious gift and for the freedom to worship You. We are ever thankful for this privilege. Today, would You help me to remember my forefathers and mothers, who sacrificed everything to come here, many so they could have a place to seek You and Your Word without persecution? Remind me of the sacrifice of Your Son, who gave His life so that I could come to You freely. Thanks, God, for Your sacrifice of love. I love You.

God: Dear one, freedom prevails when people overcome trials. Testing will come, and sometimes it's difficult to endure. The main test will always be whether you can continue to stand on My Word and what you know to be true. Each day, you'll face new trials. They may be in the form of patience with co-workers, who focus on negatives and can't seem to get past complaining about people or situations. Or the tests may be from family members who are never thankful or grateful for what you do for them and are constantly demanding more. It may feel like the closer you get to Me, the harder the trials become. "New level, new devil," some have said. But you can endure the tests by always bringing your thoughts back to Me. Then, I'll guide and direct you. I'll remind you of the things for which you can be thankful. But you must come to Me and let Me lead you. It's difficult, as you've seen, because the world will always fight for your thoughts. The will of the world is always that you be subjected to it. Sometimes it's hard to turn away, and you must ask Me for strength to be able to do this. I will always give you what you need to win. But you must come to Me with your whole heart so I can give you reinforcement. Depend on Me for all your needs. For I alone can meet them. I love you.

JULY 5
And how You work

"Oh, how great are God's riches and wisdom and knowledge! How impossible it is for us to understand his decisions and his ways! For who can know the Lord's thoughts?"
—Romans 11:33-34

Me: Lord, Psalm 37:1-4 says: "Don't worry about the wicked or envy those who do wrong. For like grass, they soon fade away. Like spring flowers, they soon wither. Trust in the Lord and do good. Then you will live safely in the land and prosper. Take delight in the Lord, and he will give you your heart's desires." I've seen this firsthand—how You take care of us! I've seen how You back me up, and those who love You, and how you protect and strengthen me, when others try to tear me down. Thanks, Lord. Would You enlighten me today and prepare me to serve You in a greater way? Help me to see Your face more clearly and understand what You want for me and for others. It amazes me how You work all things out for good, even when they were meant for evil. Sometimes I need patience to see how You unfold things that I imagined could only bring bad results. I love You.

God: Dear one, you can see how even bad things can somehow bring good results. You see how My purposes work, and how My will can operate out of seemingly chaotic events that you imagined could only bring evil outcomes. You see how all things work toward a purpose, that only I can know, to ultimately bring My Word to pass. When others seek to destroy My people, they themselves are destroyed. Bless those who seek or speak evil, and I'll move them to where they belong. Trust Me in this. I love My people and those who come to Me. I won't tolerate those bent on destroying them. Your heart is good because You come to Me for advice. Seek Me, especially in times when you feel anger rising in you toward people, or when they simply rub you the wrong way. If you let Me deal with them, they'll be dealt with in the best way possible. Watch and see. Commit your way to Me. Then you'll have great peace and joy. I love you. Yes, I chose you from among many because I knew you'd respond to Me. Let Me direct your way to places you could never imagine. The enemy will try to cause destruction and harm, but he can't determine the path to which events will lead. Only I can do that, and I always bring ultimate good, even from evil. I love you.

Despite my frustrations

"Don't be afraid, for I am with you. Don't be discouraged, for I am your God. I will strengthen you and help you. I will hold you up with my victorious right hand."
—*Isaiah 41:10*

Me: Dear Lord, You understand my frustrations. Would You help me to love in a greater way and not to react with anger or irritation when I'm confronted with disrespectful or rude behavior? When I must attend to people whose lives are out of control because they aren't managing what they have, would You give me patience? It's especially hard when I'd like to do something fun or experience a little joy, but then my time is interrupted by a crisis or unexpected resistance. You love us despite ourselves! You support me even in the discouraging times. And, if I choose to give during these moments, You provide me with my own precious time later. Would You strengthen me now, Lord? Would You help me to be mentally aware and physically able to act when You need me to? I seek Your grace, because sometimes I feel like I've had it with people! I need Your encouraging hand of kindness so I can do my best today. Recently, You showed me why Your Son cried when He came to raise his friend Lazarus from death. He was extremely saddened by how people, once created to live full lives free from pain and grief, lived in constant fear and frequent sorrow over the results of death. You never meant life to be this way. Give me Your heart so I can experience life the way You meant me to. I love You.

God: Dear one, know that I work behind the scenes, even in the most heart-rending situations, to accomplish My purposes. I will arrange meaningful times to share with others in ways that change your life and theirs forever. And you will still have precious time to enjoy life with Me! Remember, I have greater plans for you than any you can imagine! I will minister to many through you. Even now, I touch the lives of others because of you. Just continue to speak of Me and demonstrate My love. As you do, I'll give you clearer vision and you'll begin to see more clearly through My eyes. Let My healing words pour over and through you, and they will wash away your worries, concerns, frustrations, fears, and impatience. My Word builds you up and heals your wounds. It brings you peace and direction. It leads you closer to the way life was meant to be lived. Let it bring you strength and meaning mentally, physically, and spiritually. I love you.

JULY 7
As I linger here, waiting for You

"Anna, a prophet, was also there in the Temple...and she was very old.... She never left the Temple but stayed there day and night, worshiping God with fasting and prayer. She came along just as Simeon was talking with Mary and Joseph, and she began praising God. She talked about the child to everyone who had been waiting expectantly for God to rescue Jerusalem."
—*Luke 2:36-38*

Me: Lord, I feel like Anna the prophetess must have felt, after waiting for so many years to see Your Son's face. I've lingered for days in wilderness places, unaware that there were people like me who also wanted to see You. I've come lately to the feast, and I'm just beginning to understand what it means to "dine at Your table." Would You show me how to shift things in my life around so I can move closer to You and sit beside You? I want to absorb every one of Your disclosures and savor Your delights as I taste Your fulfilling fruit. I need Your help with this, Lord. Open my heart even more to receive Your bounty, and then open my mouth as You did Moses's and give me words to say to Your people. I want to know these are not my words, but Yours. Help me to understand You in a greater way. My hands are open. Fill them! Show me more of Your greatness and kindness, mercy and love. Lead me to Your table, where I can relish Your gifts. I love You.

God: Dear one, you're like Anna to me, because you've been patient to seek Me for so many years. You've endured much just to see My face and that of My Son. I know you've longed for this, just as she did. And, one day, like her, you'll experience the fulfillment of My promise and see Me face to face. You'll behold the light-filled eyes of the Lamb and sit with us and know us as you are known. I've always been there for you, although you didn't know it. I've directed your steps. I do this for you continuously. I try to whisper things in your ears so you'll hear me. Sometimes it's hard to get your attention when there are so many distractions, but I'll give you answers when you ask. When you feel unpeaceful, turn to Me again. Then I'll offer My words of peace to you. Then I'll lead you to linger with Me at My special table so you can taste My sweet and fulfilling fruit as we wait together for the time of His return. I love you.

209

July 8
Among foolish people

"'My people are foolish and do not know me,' says the Lord. 'They are stupid children who have no understanding. They are clever enough at doing wrong, but they have no idea how to do right!'"
—Jeremiah 4:22

Me: Lord, the people I have the hardest time dealing with are those who should know better than to act the way they do. These are people who say they are Christians, but then they deny Your power and live in constant fear. Would You give me patience with them, and show me how to respond when they make unwise choices based on fear, emotion, and reactions to bad news or other people's behavior? Please teach me, because sometimes I react with frustration and anger! I think they should be smarter and more aware when they seem oblivious to You and what You've promised them. I hate that they turn their backs on You and deny that You can help or protect them. You are our refuge and strength. You've promised that You will always be there for us. Show me when to speak and what to say. Today, please highlight the ones who really want to hear and understand. Thanks, Lord. I love You.

God: Dear one, I feel as you do, and I'm sometimes frustrated with My people. When they turn away from a belief in Me, or what I can do for them, remember that they answer to Me, not to you. And I may be working on them now for an outcome later. With the words I give you to speak, the goal is always to turn their thoughts back to Me. I will give you the questions to ask, and the answers, to point them in the right direction. I understand how you feel, and I commiserate when you don't get the response you desire, but remember these people are My responsibility, not yours. Appeal to their better nature. Ask Me to be able to see their hearts. I can help you with this. By listening more closely to Me, your heart will be prepared for any confrontation or conversation. Remember that people come and go. They can run hot and cold. But I will bring you the ones who are hungry and want to hear from you. The ones who want to change. Many will come for support, strength, calming, help, and greater wisdom. Don't worry about those who react negatively or walk away. They leave for a reason. They may not be ready to trust in Me. And just because someone reacts unkindly to you now doesn't mean they won't return with questions later. I love you.

Who goad my patience

"Because of the privilege and authority God has given me, I give each of you this warning: Don't think you are better than you really are. Be honest in your evaluation of yourselves, measuring yourselves by the faith God has given us."
—Romans 12:3

Me: God, would You forgive me when I'm impatient with people? Thanks for wisdom to be able to look past thoughtlessness to their hearts and what might be going on in their lives. Lord, sometimes I'm so disappointed with people, who promise to do things, but never follow through. Procrastination causes me exasperation! And gets on my nerves! Would You show me Your perspective on this? Life passes by so quickly, and I want to get things done while there's time. I just don't understand why people wait so long, until it's too late, and then never accomplish what they set out to do! Or, they blame me and others when they fail to complete what they promised. What do You think, Lord? Help me to see Your point of view on this. Help me to see what You see. For You're the One who made us! And I know You can make up for neglectful lacks. Help me to be humble, and show me when my thoughts are not Your thoughts. I love You.

God: Dear one, I love your desire to get things done. I can use this kind of motivation. Just make sure to check in with Me first before you act or speak. I may give you reasons to pause or to wait. But, when I call you to action, then it's time to move! Then you can walk in great power. And you'll find other people who want to walk dynamically with you by trusting in Me. This is My desire for you. Don't let people, who lack this kind of trust, burden your heart. Leave them to Me. It's never your responsibility to change or to push people. They are Mine, and I'll work on them. Leave them to Me. Put them in a spiritual "bucket" and let Me take hold of the handle. I will move them! You'll see, when you trust Me to see things happen, that I can operate even beyond your expectations. You'll think these things are miracles. But they're small matters to me! Trust Me. For it's in your faith that you can find answers, see results, and encounter great and wonderful things every day. It may be beyond your comprehension at times, but I do hear your requests, and I will help you. Seek Me in each encounter with "poky" people, and you'll begin to see My power in your life and in theirs too. I love you.

As I watch You work through me

"I pray that God, the source of hope, will fill you completely with joy and peace because you trust in him. Then you will overflow with confident hope through the power of the Holy Spirit."
—Romans 15:13

Me: Dear Lord, You are great. You're magnificent in Your beauty! Would You help me to always remain in Your presence, so I can become better and not bitter as I grow older? I see so many people getting sad and angry as they age. Would You help me to bring joy and hope to those who seek a more fulfilling way? Give me greater mercy, grace, and patience, especially when I see people receive accolades for the things I myself have accomplished. Help me to forgive when I'm overlooked, or when people strike out in unkind ways and deal unjustly with me or others. I need your help to be able to move on. I feel let down by some I thought were friends, after I entrusted my heart to them, especially when I was betrayed by their words or actions. I'm sure You feel this same way when people You've given so much to turn against You and deny Your existence. Show me how You overcome Your despair in these situations. Open new doors to those who appreciate my friendship and Yours. I love You.

God: Dear child, one day you'll see a return on all your investments of time into people. I'm working even now to bring you wonderful ones who will stick with you through thick and thin. They'll be loyal, and they'll appreciate what you do for them. Just look to Me. When you focus more on Me, and allow Me to fill you with peace, then you'll have fewer heartaches. Your life will be more enjoyable. Let Me guide you every moment. Then, you'll see spectacular results. Leave the complainers and deniers to Me. I'll work on them. Extend your hand of healing and love to those who want to receive what you have to give them. They'll return your compassion to you. Just realize that I may have other purposes for you than what you imagine. The things you pursue may not be part of your calling. I'll place you in front of people in My own way for My own purposes. These will be in specially designated moments, often unplanned, when I can thoroughly use your abilities in unusual ways. Trust Me in this. I'm preparing you. Let Me work in you to will and to do of My good pleasure, which will be your good pleasure too! I love you.

JULY 11
Your warrior watchman*

"He was amazed to see that no one intervened to help the oppressed. So he himself stepped in to save them with his strong arm, and his justice sustained him."
—Isaiah 59:16

Me: Lord, may I be the one who stands in the gap for You? I want to help shorten the distance between where people struggle and where You want them to be. I want to be Your "warrior watchman,"* by interceding for them when they fall short. I want to pray for my country and ask for forgiveness for how we've ignored You in so many ways. My desire is to seek Your face, hear Your voice, and follow Your lead in every situation. Give me grace to courageously come into Your presence and rest in Your arms. Help me to direct others and give them advice that stems from You. Deliver me from frustration, for only when I rest in Your peace can I help anyone. Be the Lord of my words and the supporter of my soul. Be the watchman over my thoughts in days of trouble. Let peace reign over me, even when others don't receive me. Guide me in every thought, word, and deed, and let me be an example of Your love. May I never fear to turn to You or to hear and speak Your truth. Thanks for Your healing hand and how You protect me. Thanks for Your grace and kindness to me and my family. I love You.

God: Dear one, I admire your desire to stand in the gap for Me by bringing mercy to those who suffer and search for truth. Remember that I make all things work out for good, so never allow yourself to feel frustrated when people don't respond the way you'd like them to. They may not immediately receive your message, because they live in a painful place. Sometimes their minds are clouded by the doubt that is rampant in the world. But I will massage their hearts by reaching inside them in ways beyond your imagination, and you can help Me with this process. Sometimes it takes persistent patience. Trust Me, for I will never let you down. I'll place you near those who desire to hear My words. As My watchman, you can stand in the gap for Me. And I'll take you to places you've never been and put you in front of people you've never met. Leave this to Me. I'll soften each blow aimed at you and give you what you need to succeed. I'll lead you to those who seek Me. Wait and see! I love you.

p. 51, Throne Room Prayer: Praying with Jesus on the Sea of Glass by Brian and Candice Simmons

JULY 12
And show me if I should stay or go

"For everything there is a season, a time for every activity under heaven."
—*Ecclesiastes 3:1*

Me: Lord, some days seem to go by so slowly, and then other days go by way too quickly! Summer is here, and I feel the heat rising with the sun. I see the plants drooping and thirsting for water since we've had no rain. I enjoy clipping the herbs I planted in the spring and using them in recipes and drinks. The blue jay nest by our kitchen window sits empty. The time came for the babies to go, and they've long since flown away. This reminds me of my own life, and I wonder about Your plans for me. Should I stay where I am? Is there a purpose for me in this place? I wonder sometimes. Do I need to spend more years here? Or should I move on to some new venture? If I need to relocate, would You make this clear? What's Your vision for me now? Some days I think I need to stay, and then I think You might want me to consider going a different route. I enjoy what I do now, but I think it would be nice to have more mornings to write, read, and spend time with You. And live closer to family members. I see some who give up everything and move to a foreign land to serve the poor and needy. Is that the direction I need to take? Show me clearly Your will and direction for me. I want to follow Your lead! Thanks for Your help. I love You.

God: Dear one, I'll let you know if you need to change your course. I'll always give You clear directions. Just because others change their lifestyles doesn't mean you must follow their lead. Remember, My will is to work in you for My good pleasure, not someone else's! You live to serve My purpose, not the aims of others. Every person has a unique calling. Some respond to it, and some don't. Each one is different. And each person can know his or her own life-purpose. Yours is special to you, because you have your own talents and abilities. I alone know all your unique strengths. I also know your weaknesses. Major and sudden changes may not be the best use of your time. Usually change involves thoughtful planning, with My help, of course. Focus now on what's before you. Follow My lead, and I will make things clear as to what to do next. Take life a step at a time. It doesn't need to be complicated. Just depend on Me to steer your course in the right direction! When it's time to enter a new season of your life, it will be very clear to you. Because I love you.

JULY 13
As I place my feet into Your footsteps

"The Lord keeps you from all harm and watches over your life. The Lord keeps watch over you as you come and go, both now and forever."
—Psalm 121:7-8

Me: Lord, You've pursued me since I was a child. When I survived a fall from a bridge on my 11th birthday in 1963, I realized that I'd miraculously survived. Later, I gazed out the car window on the way to church and asked, "Why? What do You have in mind for me?" In childhood dreams, I felt Your presence and turned to see a man in a hooded cape persistently following me. I realized this was Jesus. I went to a Billy Graham rally in Houston in November 1965, and I walked up to the altar to acknowledge a belief in Your Son. Later, I decided to give my whole heart to Him at a Young Life camp in Colorado in August 1969. Thanks for Your patience with me and for allowing me to experience the great joy of getting to know You. Thanks for helping me see You more clearly through a greater understanding of Your wonderful Word, the Bible. Open more doors to share Your presence and bring joy to others in ways beyond my imagination. You're so precious to me! Help me to see what You want me to do for You. Help me to speak the words You give me. You're my heart. You're my soul. You're my hope. You're my anchor in life's storms. You're my love, my peace, my joy, my breath, my strength. my everything. Be my footsteps as I walk with You. I love You.

God: Dear one, I'm always there for you and always will be. My presence is a certainty in an uncertain world. As you minister to others, I minister to you. I cause you to stand out by making you shine with a glow that causes others to notice. This can motivate people to want to listen to you and heed what you say. But you must refrain from negative thoughts or remarks about yourself or others, for this diminishes the radiance of your glow. No matter what you do or say, I'll always be your savior, your biggest supporter, your redeemer, your lover, your comforter, your guide, your encourager, and your eternal hope. I spare your life from destruction. I pardon you. From falls or failures, I lift you back up. I block you from harm. In a protected place, I keep you safe from evil. Focus on Me as you prepare for the day, and put on every piece of My spiritual armor. This is your protection. Remember that I'm your ready armor-bearer. I love you.

And a few people acknowledge

"The eyes of the Lord search the whole earth in order to strengthen those whose hearts are fully committed to him."
—*2 Chronicles 16:9*

Me: Lord, thanks for reassuring me of Your presence when it's still and quiet, and the doorbell doesn't ring, and few people call. You're always there to reassure and console me. You remind me every morning of Your mercy and bountiful goodness. I think about how You always meet my needs and give me more than I ask for. You've never let me down. People come and go, and I can't always depend on them. A few are faithful and follow through with their promises. But others wave with the wind. They blow here and there, hot then cold, and change directions like a wayward weathervane. Show me those who want to stay put and have a desire to worship You and relish Your love. Would You open my eyes to those whose purpose is firm and whose hearts are fixed on You? I seek those who want to pray purposely and bring Your message of love and hope to the people of this world. Open doors to those who want to spend sacred time together with You. Thanks! I love You.

God: Dear one, I love how you come to Me when you're feeling sad or lonely. When you focus on Me and the words I speak to you, I can ease your loneliness and remove any trace of pain. Remember that all things happen in their own time (Ecclesiastes 3:1). There are reasons for why things happen when they do. You may think things take place because you made a wrong choice and caused a negative outcome. Understand that all things work inside My plan. Sometimes I allow negative things to happen. I don't cause them, but I permit them. But even these work toward a purpose. I may allow a negative impact, but only because I'm seeking a positive result later. Learn to trust in Me. Listen to Me, and I'll lead you to all truth. Sometimes the lesson is painful. And sometimes you feel alone as you spend time patiently pursuing Me, while others chase after momentary pleasures or waste time with short-lived pursuits. They may even avoid you, because they don't want to hear what you're learning. But I'm always by your side. Rely on Me to guide you. I will. You seek to do what's best. I can help you. Look to spend time with wise people who also seek Me. I will lead you to these ones. I love you.

Your aspiring love-child

"But you are not controlled by your sinful nature. You are controlled by the Spirit if you have the Spirit of God living in you."
—Romans 8:9

Me: I'm beginning to see Your purposes for me, Lord, as they are gradually disclosed before my eyes. I see how You want me to be more of a love-child or love-warrior, and I accept the challenge! But I need Your help! I see how You bring me people—many I've known before. And now they want to hear about You and what I'm learning. Thanks. I see how You want me to surround myself with those who also want to grow up in Your Word. Show me how to love and encourage them. I don't want to lead any astray. I want to move in the way You show me. Would You guide me? If You want some doors to remain open, and I need to be more patient with people, show me! But, if I need to move on because of closing doors, direct me in how to do this. Help me to focus on what You're leading me to do, so I don't get sidetracked by the words or actions of unkind or cruel people, who don't understand how You work. I want to do Your will, and I don't want to hurt or offend the ones You're calling. Show me Your path and how to walk in it, Lord. I love You.

God: Dear child, just rely on Me and what I tell you. Yes, everything happens for a reason. And every person you encounter is affected by you in some way. When people treat you unfairly, or speak offensively to you, usually they aren't trying to hurt you. They're reacting to some brokenness in their own soul. Because they don't understand how to apply the healing balm of My Word, or My Son's teachings, they repeat what they see in the world. This involves maintaining a position of power or control over others. When they feel threatened by you, because they think you're infringing on their space, they lash out to hold onto their "territory." Relax and know that I'm the one in control. Things may appear as accidental, but there's always a reason. Don't fret about past mistakes or things you think you should have managed in a better way. Let Me work things out for you. Pray for the people I put in your path. And remember, My Son often upset those who didn't know Him. But those who loved Me were never offended. Some people will be upset no matter what you do. While they choose to be offended, you move with love and acceptance. These will enable you as My mighty prayer warrior. I love you.

JULY 16
As You expand my territory

"He was the one who prayed to the God of Israel, "Oh, that you would bless me and expand my territory! Please be with me in all that I do, and keep me from all trouble and pain!" And God granted him his request."
—1 Chronicles 2:55

Me: Dear Lord, I pray again this prayer of Jabez: "May Your hand be on me today to expand and enlarge my borders." Open more new doors and lead me to those I can reach. Show me the people that most need Your help and seek Your truth amid the world's propaganda, and give me Your patience to deal with them. Whisper in my ears Your sweet words of inspiration. Cover me with Your peace and lift me with Your joy. Saturate me with Your love. Lead me with Your right hand of sweet fellowship. Strengthen me with Your might, and enlighten me through Your wisdom. Talk to me in quiet places, and give me direction during chaotic times. Would You help me to live in the moment? Would You open my eyes to Your truth so I can live it throughout the day? Take me to places beyond my imagination! I love You.

God: Dear one, today is a blessed day because you're in it. Today, I'll bring you up higher and closer to Me. Today, I can expand your influence and your borders, but you must continue to seek Me persistently in all you do. Don't look to people to be what they can't be. Love and accept them for who and what they are. They're often deceived, fallen, fearful, and ashamed, because they're separated from Me and blinded by the world and those who rule it. Many can still distinguish between light and darkness, so you can represent light to them and a way to hope. You can "salt" their meat and create a hunger for peace and healing and a path to My light. Do this by loving them despite their dark ways and by exemplifying a new way to reconciliation and healing. Some will turn to you and listen. These are those whose eyes shine when you speak the truth, because this is what they've longed for but have never seen. Keep speaking and shining the light I radiate through your heart. Don't be discouraged by those who don't respond or those who resist your efforts. I give many chances for people to turn to Me and change their direction. I keep trying. You must keep trying too. Don't give up hope. I'll work though you! Be persistent and patient, and I will continue to enlarge your borders through your capacity to give. I love you.

And crush my concerns

"Keep on asking, and you will receive what you ask for. Keep on seeking, and you will find. Keep on knocking, and the door will be opened to you."
—*Matthew 7:7*

Me: I want to be where You are, Lord. Place me where You'd have me be today. Prepare my way and guide me. Would You help me speak what You want spoken? It's hard for me when I'm around some people. Even a few in the church are challenging at times, especially when I hear them speaking half-truths or saying misleading things. Something rises up in me, and I have to say something! Lord, move within me in these moments and remind me of what words I should say, or refrain from saying, so I can bless them. Those You set in front of me are there for a reason. I understand this. Help me to be there for them as a good listener so I can minister to them in the most helpful ways. Steer me away from evil, lessen my anxiety, and help me to see as You see. I want to be a delight to You, to offer a sacrifice of love, and to fulfill Your purposes for Me. Help me to die to myself and to live only for You. Give me Your strength to be able to do this. I need Your patience and wisdom. Thanks, Lord. I love You.

God: Dear one, I'm fulfilling My purpose in you even now. I'm guiding you and tenderly leading you with great patience. As you turn your eyes to Me, I'll show you wonderful things that are beyond discovering or even understanding in this world. I have many secrets that I'm willing to reveal to you, because you come to Me seeking answers. They are treasures hidden in deep places, so they're not easily discerned. As you continue to seek to understand Me and My ways, you'll begin to unearth them. And you'll be delighted when you see the beauty of My purposes and the magnificence of My designs. As you come to Me with your whole heart, leaving nothing uncommitted, buried, or hidden, your eyes will be opened more and more. As you throw aside every reservation, leave behind every fear, open your heart and mind to Me, let Me lead you to paths unknown to others, and ultimately trust My leading, then you'll experience the fullness of understanding and wisdom. Open your arms wide, and I'll pull you toward Me like a magnet. I'll vanquish your fears, curb your worries, and crush your concerns. No one else can do this for you. So, hold Me in your heart. Hold Me in your mind. Remember Me always. I love you.

So I never give up

"That is why we never give up. Though our bodies are dying, our spirits are being renewed every day. For our present troubles are small and won't last very long. Yet they produce for us a glory that vastly outweighs them and will last forever! So we don't look at the troubles we can see now; rather, we fix our gaze on things that cannot be seen. For the things we see now will soon be gone, but the things we cannot see will last forever."
—2 Corinthians 4:16-18

Me: Dear Lord, You're a God of might and dominion. You reign on high and orchestrate the events of this world. You are love, and You do not harbor hate or unforgiveness. And so, I seek after Your love. Would You help me to never despair or lose hope? You are with me, protecting and fighting for me, even when I can't see or feel You. I seek Your truth, for it alone is real and brings real answers. I need only look for it. With Your help, it can be verified in every word I hear and in every action I see. You bring me peace and joy in times of frustration and sadness, when I hear so many lies. I'll seek You always. Sometimes I look up and see a bright star in the morning, and it reminds me of Your Son. It appears far away, but I remember that You are very near, even when it seems like You're distant. Today, I reach out to You until I can feel how close You really are. When loved ones die, I won't despair, because I understand that their lives are forever. Your love surrounds them as it has enveloped me. And I can embrace them as You've embraced me. There are no fences in Your world. There is no time or space. It's boundless. I'll remember this. I love You.

God: Dear one, I'm so close to you! Nearer than you can even imagine! So, never despair or give up hope. Hope is in Me and through My Son. Peace is in Me and through My Son. Love is in Me and through My Son. Joy is in Me and through My Son. Deliverance is in Me and through My Son. Abundance is in Me and through My Son. Answers are in Me and through My Son. Patience is in Me and through My Son. Kindness is in Me and through My Son. True reason is in Me and through My Son. Understanding is in Me and through My Son. Favor is in Me and through My Son. Come and have it all! I love you.

And watch You deliver me from injustice

"Those who plant injustice will harvest disaster, and their reign of terror will come to an end."
—*Proverbs 22:8*

Me: Lord, forgive me for my impatience and fretful thoughts. Help me to move far away from anger and bitterness in my feelings about others. I don't want to worry about what others think of me or be hindered by other's rejection of my words or way of life. It doesn't matter in the end, does it? Please deliver me from these fears and anxieties. And help me to understand how you protect and deliver me from injustice. Would You strengthen me the way You did Joseph, when he suffered for his honesty but still ended up fulfilling what You'd called him to do? Would You help me to endure with patience, embrace Your love, and be fearless about speaking up when I need to. Make it clear to me when it's my thinking and when it's Yours toward people. Help me to discern truth from error, deception and lies. Show me when it's time to move on in relationships that are no longer profitable or when others won't receive me. Help me get past caring so much about what others think of me. I love You.

God: Dear one, your heart is right, and I admire how you try so hard. But let Me remind you that it's not through your efforts alone that you'll succeed but through your trust in Me. I know you don't always understand, and you often have questions about why things are the way they are. You seek answers, but you'll never find them outside of My Word. You're often very hard on yourself. You sometimes expect too much of yourself and others. Let Me be Your guide and give you strength. Let Me give you courage and wisdom in every situation. I'll teach you what you need to know. I'll show you clearly when people are pushing lies or untruths. Those who build their foundations on these things will suffer later. It's a law. What you give out, you will receive back. But I will keep you safe from their actions. And vindicate you for things done unjustly to you. Don't worry. People with eyes to see will recognize who you are and admire your goodness. They will see the true foundation of any falsity. I will take care of your reputation. Don't worry. With Me, it will remain pure, good, and right. Let Me take care of things for you. I always have. Just trust Me now. Be patient. Let Me show you My great kindness. Lean on Me. I love you.

While I wait to see You face-to-face

"I speak to him face to face, clearly, and not in riddles! He sees the Lord as he is."
—Numbers 12:8

Me: Lord, I want so much to sit with You face-to-face! Sometimes I think that if I could do this, I'd be super-inspired to be the best person I can be and enabled to reach new heights, even the high places You envision for me. Mostly, I need Your help to be able to see others as You see them. I still at times distrust people and their intentions, because I can't see inside their minds. I know many are self-centered and unconcerned about others. Please open My eyes to what is in the hearts of those I meet, so I can reach into the soft areas of their needs. I want to be more effective and aware of Your designs for them and for me. I can only do this if I can see the way You see. Would You help me to have the kind of relationship Moses had with you—one that was "face-to-face." Like him, I want to clearly hear Your voice so I can discern Your thoughts and those of others. Would You increase this ability in me? I love You.

God: Dear one, Moses was blessed to know Me face-to-face, because he listened to My voice. As he listened, his trust in Me grew. And he learned how to do what I told him to do—no more, no less. When he obeyed, he saw great results, as did a whole nation of people. As you heed My voice, you and the people around you will be blessed! It isn't always easy to hear My voice or even discern Me. There are many distractions in the world around you. It takes great discipline, patience, and a willingness to spend time focusing on Me and My words. It also takes amazing faithfulness. It requires daily practice, a desire to lean closer to Me, and a readiness to bend your ear ever nearer to Me. I will help you with this, but you must trust Me. As you do, I will whisper in your ear and warn you of things to come. I will reveal the very hearts of the people you meet. But you must first learn how to listen. Take it a step at a time. Each day, devote moments to just listening for My voice. Start with a small amount of time and build on it every day. As you practice, you will see increasingly mighty results. The more you do this, the more I will speak to you and give you great revelations. I love you.

Through the stream, the fountain, and the well

"For you are the fountain of life, the light by which we see."
—*Psalm 36:9*

Me: Lord, once You revealed three things that You'd always be for me: a stream, a fountain, and a well. The stream represents Your great grace that flows down to my spirit from Your high place. Tapping into this spiritual flow brings greater ability to gracefully move with Your Spirit. The fountain is Your constant source of wisdom that shoots up through me from a hidden spring—the indwelling Christ in me. This force enables me mentally to recall the things God has placed in my heart. The well speaks of a stored life force, a solid source for physical strength and healing, that I can draw from whenever I need it. My past experiences with You fill the well as My trust in You grows. My life is in Your hands, and I need Your help to solve the problems I encounter with good solutions to things I'm unable to grasp on my own. I need Your supernatural ability, Lord, to accomplish what needs to be done. Would You work through my spirit, Lord, and download to me what I need to complete Your mighty works? Help me to overcome the Goliaths I sometimes face. Give me needed endurance and patience so I can succeed. Help me to be where You want me to be. And remind me to draw more of Your strength and ability from the stream, the fountain, and the well as I grow more and more to love You.

God: Dear one, you can always depend on Me to come through for you. True resolve comes from My Spirit in you, and, from this secret spring, your heart can be strengthened. Pull from My fountain of wisdom so you can withstand the temptation to succumb to any frustration that might try to sabotage your efforts. Allow Me to be your sufficiency. I will deliver you. I will sustain you through My spiritual stream of grace. From the depths of a living well, I will give you needed physical rest through understanding. Remember, My light dispels darkness. My Spirit supernaturally flowing through you gives you needed peace so you're able to "download" all the solutions you need. I will lead you to good results if you let Me. My spiritual strength will get you through when your own ability doesn't suffice. You are precious in My sight. Don't try to do these things alone. You can't. Lean on Me. I'll come through for you with the answers you need. But first, you must let your mind be at peace to listen. I love you.

Which are the ways You warn me

"I am warning you ahead of time, dear friends. Be on guard so that you will not be carried away by the errors of these wicked people and lose your own secure footing."
—2 Peter 3:17

Me: You warn us, Lord. I can see it in Your words. You forewarn us of things to come. Help us, Lord, to heed Your premonitions and not be blinded to them. Help us to recognize Your trumpet calls when they come. Sometimes when I walk around the lake, I look up at the clouds and I imagine hearing Your trumpet calls at that moment. And seeing Your Son's face appear in the clouds as He calls me up to Him to live in His presence. Oh, how I long for this! I know the time is short and even shorter until Jesus's return for us. Give me courage to "dare the consequences" and be brave. I want to be courageous and never shrink with fear. Thanks for assuring me that you treasure me, even when others don't. Help me to reach those who are hungering and thirsting for You. Who are they, Lord? Show me their faces. Bring them to me so I can lead them to You. Help me to serve Your people and bring positive light and life to them. Help me to love as You do, because I know how very much You care for me. Let today be a miraculous day—a day that glorifies You—as I wait for His return. I put it in Your hands. I love You.

God: Dear one, you see the birth pains of what will come eventually, in the last days. You hear the rise of the voices of those who are deceived. Many promote false teachings—to love what is false and to hate what is true—that permeate schools so that young people now balk at any belief in Me. They learn to disdain Me and the teachings of My Son. False voices rise, and you see their fruit. They encourage stealing, killing, and destroying what's good. But you must listen to the voices of My prophets, who warn against them. And you must stand up to those who think a belief in Me is a thing of the past. Only an outpouring of love and a movement toward Me and My Son can stop them. And you can help. Some will return to Me as they move away from the false voices, and you'll see great and mighty outcomes. Don't be afraid. Go! I will lead you. I fight for you, and I win My battles! You need never fear. I hold you up during times of trial, and I give you peace. I am with you to sustain you until My Son's return. Lean on Me for direction, love, forgiveness, patience, and strength. I love you.

While You repair the broken pieces

"'Don't be afraid,' he said, 'for you are very precious to God. Peace! Be encouraged! Be strong!' As he spoke these words to me, I suddenly felt stronger and said to him, 'Please speak to me, my lord, for you have strengthened me.'"
—Daniel 10:19

Me: Lord, as I look through picture albums and sort through photos taken over many years, I often feel remorse. Some of the old cards and letters I kept make me feel sad. I think of people I no longer see, relationships that no longer exist, and family gatherings that are no more. I regret choices and question my actions at times. Lord, show me what I need to know and how I should think about these painful memories. Show me how You work good out of bad here on earth, and how You can bring blessings from perceived failures. Teach me how to see things from Your perspective and help me to reconcile my memories and have peace with them. Show me a good end and how my life matters after all. Encourage me by opening my eyes to the lives I've blessed, and how I did direct others to Your goodness. I want to affect every person I meet in ways that lead them to You. You remind me of my role as a prayer warrior and that I may not understand the past or know the future, but it will all be a part of Your plan. "Take it a day at a time," You remind me. "And have patience with the process." I love You.

God: Dear one, you're where I need you to be. And I'll show you day by day how to fill the hours. Know that where you are is where I've placed you! And, yes, I'll always work the events of your life out for good, no matter what they are and who they involve. Some things happen for reasons you don't understand now. But be patient. Because, one day you will understand. I'll place you with those who need to hear your words. They may not listen now, but they'll understand later. Remember your call to prayer. And never lose sight of how important your life is. I'll give you what you need to carry out My will, which involves many lives you will affect and change. I'll even use "mistakes." I use everything, yes, everything, as part of My plan that includes the broken pieces. And I'll always take care of you and your family, as I promised. The adversary will cause you to question yourself by stirring up misgivings, and he'll try to make you think you've made irreconcilable mistakes. But I don't look at anything this way. Every part of your life will be used for good. I love you.

And show me eternity

"Yet God has made everything beautiful for its own time. He has planted eternity in the human heart, but even so, people cannot see the whole scope of God's work from beginning to end."
—*Ecclesiastes 3:11*

Me: Lord, I want You to know how much You are loved! I want You to find the family You've sought for so long. I want You to be blessed by Your children as they rise up and recognize all that You are, because You are awesome, blessed, comforting, delightful, earnest, faithful, generous, honorable, illustrious, just, kind, lovely, magnificent, noble, omniscient, peace-giving, quiescent, reliable, stalwart, truthful, understanding, veritable, wonderful, xenial, yielding, and zealous. My praise extends to every letter of the alphabet! Lord, I celebrate You today. Would You help me to remember all that You've done for me and all the names that stand for You? And remind me that You're near enough to bring me what's needed at any moment. Would You give me strength to do what You want me to do and be able to accomplish all that you have in store for me? I look forward to spending eternity with You, and I anticipate that You must have a lot in store for me and all those who love You. Thanks, Lord. I love You.

God: Dear one, I've prepared this day for you to walk in. I see Your life all laid out before Me, and I see the beginning and the end of it. Because I see eternity. Your vision is limited by time. Mine is not. Rely on Me to tell you what you need to know to live and breathe and have the power to heal and lead others. Rely on Me for good advice. I can give it. Just trust Me. Today, seek Me and My thoughts. Don't be dismayed by evil events or actions around you. See beyond them. I can show you the reasons behind everything. Take things one step at a time. Don't let yourself be overwhelmed by too many things. I can lead you through any maze. I have much in store for you and many things planned. Only be patient with Me and trust in My timing. Take it a day at a time, and let Me fulfill My will in your life. I can open your eyes to wonderful things and lead you to new opportunities that are beyond your expectations. Today, seek My will and My way in everything. I will always make things clear to you. Just listen. Seek the truth and what is right and righteous. There is time to do what you need to do, so don't feel discouraged or impatient. Remember, I can see eternity. I love you.

As the world changes around me

"Only I can tell you the future before it even happens. Everything I plan will come to pass, for I do whatever I wish."
—*Isaiah 46:10*

Me: Lord, where are we now? What's happening in our world, and when will Your Son return for us? Will it be in my lifetime? Or my children's or grandchildren's? Sometimes I glance ahead, and I sigh and pray and wonder just how we will get through this. And I know, with Your help, we can. And I realize that it isn't for me to know the times or the seasons or when and how things will happen in the future. Only You can know these things. And You'll reveal them in due time. In the meantime, I trust and depend on You for my daily needs and the accomplishment of Your purposes in my life. But I pray that this day, the only day I have to live, will be peaceful and that I can accomplish Your purposes and learn more, so I'm able to help others. Would You help me to view others with Your eyes so I can touch even impenetrable hearts? I need to see the way You do so I can help people survive now and later. I love You.

God: Child, I won't tell you when My Son will come, but the day grows closer, and I am using those in power, who think they're in control, to bring that day closer. The world grows darker, but you'll see many come to Me. You'll see and experience a revival in your lifetime, and many will believe in and receive My Son, including your family members. Some will surprise you! Keep praying for each one, for your prayers are powerful! And I will reveal more when the time is right. What matters most to Me is the fulfillment of My Word, including the prophecies that were given over many ages. I know what will happen and what the earth and its people must endure. And often, I grieve in anticipation of future events. Yet, I glory in the outcome, because I know My people will be the winners in the end. My desire is for all people to know Me and understand what My will is for them. I'm often saddened when people reject My message and accept the lies that are handed to them by the adversary. If they could only see the reality—what truly lies beneath it all—they'd understand how I view things. I'm the only true God, and the way to Me is simple—by believing what I've done through My Son. There's no easier way. Come to Me and live! I love you.

And I crave Your caring hand

"I entrust my spirit into your hand. Rescue me, Lord, for you are a faithful God."
—Psalm 31:5

Me: Lord, as I look around me, I see Your hand more and more in everything. And I recognize how You touch those who seek You with their whole heart and acknowledge Your presence in their lives. These are the ones who abound, maybe not always materially, but mentally and spiritually. I realize more and more that the people who are unkind, harsh, unthankful, critical, and unappreciative are afraid. Maybe they fear loss or rejection. It could be any number of things. Would You show me ways to help alleviate their fears, even when they don't respond to me in the way I'd like? So many times, I'd like to just be alone with You and not have to deal with people's moods and negativity that burden my heart. Give me patience and show me how to work with them in a way that brings blessings to them and others. Remind me always that You're near, because I'd die without Your presence. I crave Your caring hand, especially when I'm surrounded by the world's negatives. I love You.

God: Dear one, you know that I love you, and I'm always nearby. You know that I alone truly understand your heart. Others miss out when they don't seek their answers from Me. I understand how you feel, and I do appreciate you. Don't be discouraged by others' neglect and negativity or be surprised when you see them lie or try to take what's not theirs. People apart from Me lack depth, because they neglect their true calling and don't understand who or what they're meant to be. And so, they seek to attain what's not theirs, because they feel like they're missing something. They sense a hole in their soul, so they covet what they see others enjoying. Only I can lift, heal, bless, enrich, remove, or change lives in a way that's permanent. In the end, you know that everyone will answer for what they've done with what they were given. They will explain how they used their "talents." The number of abilities given doesn't matter as much as what they did with them. Those who were given more have more responsibilities. One day, I'll ask, "Did you use your abilities to bless and enrich others or waste what you were given?" If you use your gifts wisely, you will receive much in the next life. Just follow My lead in this whole matter of life, and you'll be truly blessed with peace. I love you.

July 27
In a hidden room

"Those who live in the shelter of the Most High will find rest in the shadow of the Almighty."
—Psalm 91:1

Me: Lord, I had another dream last night. I was with a group of people in a cobbled alley lined with worn wooden tables and benches. I sat at a table with some people, and we exchanged gifts. Each person appreciated what the others had to offer. But a short, pudgy, balding man, not a part of the group, kept edging closer to me with one sly eye on my gifts. He started asking me pointed questions, and I could tell that he wanted to take them away. I felt very uneasy and a little frightened. So, I ducked behind the person next to me and headed for an almost-hidden door near the alley. I found it unlocked and crept through it. Inside, I found a small, peaceful room with a chair full of fluffy pillows. Two men stood talking at the far end of the room. They looked up expectantly when I came in. Then I woke up. The dream reminded me of how the thief eases his way into our space with the intent of stealing our gifts. He wants to take away what's rightfully ours. But, if we'll find that peaceful place to spend time with You and Jesus each day, we can escape his sneaky manipulations. You want us to go to a secret place, away from the world, to sit with You in a comfortable chair full of fluffy pillows. Today, dispel any darkness and bring Your bright light through my door so I can recognize my gifts, fully use them, and offer them to others. Let peace reign in me as I spend time with You. I love You.

God: Dear one, I'm working even now to bring good things to you. Just watch as I do it. There's a refining process going on, and I will orchestrate your life to become something you can only dream about. I'll bring you to a place where people will comfortably come to you for advice and counsel. They will seek your help, because they trust you and see your gifts. I'll also take you in new directions. Just listen for My still, small voice when you enter My presence in that quiet place. Sit with me awhile. Then, peace can reign. Things people say or do, even the way you feel, may cause your thoughts to drift to negative expectations or fears. Resist these thoughts by embracing the power of My Word. Push away evil, and it will flee from you. Don't allow the enemy, through anxiety or intimidation, to enter your heart or mind. I give you power, love, a sound mind, and self-control. I alone. Remember I am real; I am near. I bring peace. Let My peace flow through you today. I love you.

Where I can polish Your boots

"The servant watched her in silence, wondering whether or not the Lord had given him success in his mission."
—*Genesis 24:21*

Me: Let me polish Your boots, Lord. I want to make them shine. And then I want to place my feet in them and track your steps so I can carry Your message to everyone I meet. I want to make them so attractive that others will want to walk in them too! May I carry Your sword for You too, Lord, and wield it as You direct me, so I can defend Your name and be able to strike through the aims of the enemy? Let me wear Your hat, Lord, as a protection from bitter rains that try to saturate and penetrate my thoughts. Teach me, like Abraham's servant Eliezer, to stand in silence, gazing and waiting for the slightest nod from You. Help me to be still enough to hear, and patient enough to wait, for a word from You. Many people seek recognition, power, wealth, and material things. But Your desire is for obedience and faithfulness to Your Word. I may never gain popularity here, but I realize that any stardom will only compromise my fame in the future. You've told me that I'm a hidden gem. And that the world's acclaim is fleeting. But Your glory endures. That's what I seek. I want to walk in Your shoes, wear Your hat, and carry Your sword, so I can reach many for You! I love You.

God: Dear one, remember that a great servant is dependable and trustworthy. A celebrated servant has an excellent prayer life, attends first to the master's business, speaks well of the master, says little about him or herself, and gives the master all the glory. Keep trying to live these qualities, and one day you'll excel in them all. I honor your efforts more than you can know. Gazing at Me and listening for My voice are the most important things you can do. Check everything with Me before speaking, and continuously mirror My thoughts. Then reflect My visage when you go out into the world. Life on earth is difficult. There are many obstacles, especially for those who don't trust or believe or heed My voice. But the next life will be a constant joy and a continual pleasure for you, because you sought Me out and served Me. Then, you'll always be in My presence. As you seek Me, you'll experience amazing joy because of this hope and expectation. Be thankful for this... that You are the apple of My eye. How I love you.

JULY 29
Then soar high with You

"But those who trust in the Lord will find new strength. They will soar high on wings like eagles. They will run and not grow weary. They will walk and not faint."
—Isaiah 40:31

Me: Dear Lord, You are my life, my light, my sun, my moon, my stars, my hope, and my encouragement when things seem dark. Thanks for a haven where I can meet and share with You and reflect again on Your wonderful works. I want to gaze on Your glory and share with You what I'm learning. You are so gracious, Lord. Thanks for the people You've introduced me to. What a blessing they've been to me. Let today be blessed with Your mighty goodness, peace, and joy. Let Your hand reign through the world's chaos and cause me to have great hope for Your promises being fulfilled. Help me to proclaim Your name and expand Your territory today, Lord. Bring me before mighty men and women, and teach me how to stand firm for You in every situation. Give me peace and patience when others are distraught about health, finances, or world events. Help me to be a solid rock. Show me Your way, and let me see You when others fail to. Guide me in my words and actions so I can be used for Your purposes. Open my eyes to an abundance of Your revelation and guide me so I can stay on Your course and soar up high with You! Because I love You.

God: Child, you are the apple of My eye. I love you, and I want the best for you. Trials lie ahead, but I will always sustain you and give you great peace. Just ask me for directions when you feel lost. I'll always answer and direct you. I long to do more for you—to show you more of My good pleasure and to prove My presence to you. Just ask! This week, expect great blessings, for I am working on your behalf. My fruit in your life is always sweet. It never rots or decays like real fruit, nor does it fade away. It is a result of your daily walk as you focus on Me. Your sweet-smelling savor comes from the fruit you eat, mentally, physically and spiritually. And your wonderful and appealing aroma will attract those who are hungry for Me. Patience, goodness, kindness, faithfulness, self-control, gentleness, peace, love, and joy are all evident in your life as you trust more and more in Me. Walking in My Spirit produces a sweetness in you and in your nature. People sense and feel it. Manifest My love more and more and, as you hold tight to My hand, you will soar with Me on My wings of grace to the place of hope I've prepared for you. I love you.

JULY 30
In that moment

"We are here for only a moment, visitors and strangers in the land as our ancestors were before us. Our days on earth are like a passing shadow, gone so soon without a trace."
—*1 Chronicles 29:15*

Me: Lord, the days go by fast, and sometimes I pray they go by even faster. When will Your Son return and take us up with Him to You? I long for this. The world is such a burden at times. You've blessed me beyond anything I could ever ask or even think, but I do get tired of the struggle sometimes. Lord, guide me away from temptations and deliver me from evil. Thanks for how Jesus taught us to pray in Matthew 6:13: "Don't let us yield to temptation but rescue us from the evil one." Bring me nearer to godly men and women, who also long to know You better. And show me how I can work together with them! I realize that often when You bring them near, it's when I don't feel like taking the time, because I feel tired or pressured. Help me to see past my feelings and be reminded that these people come from You to encourage and be encouraged. Give me strength and patience to meet them where they are. Let my "shadow" touch and bless and cover them so that my "territory" can expand to more generations. Thanks. I love You.

God: Dear one, you ask Me when My Son will return. When will the prophecies be fulfilled? Will it be in your lifetime? While you're alive, you'll see changes in the Middle East and throughout the world. Watch and see how things progress. But know that I can protect you, no matter what happens. Today, I'll guide and lead you. I'll give you certainty and answers when you need them. Walk with Me now, and you'll reign with Me one day among the stars. Put on the mantle of peace I've placed on your shoulders and live out your calling—to reach the people of the earth with My message. Continue to intercede for others, praying for them continuously. Continue to teach with words of deliverance—My message of love and hope. Continue to win in the spiritual realm by putting on My armor as you study My Word and listen for My words each and every moment. I'll bring others to walk alongside you. Watch for them. Then, we can all move together to overcome evil forces with the sword of the spirit. And, one day, My Son will place on your head a crown of rejoicing because you heeded My call. I love you.

JULY 31
When I can bask in Your goodness

"For every child of God defeats this evil world, and we achieve this victory through our faith."
—1 John 5:4

Me: It's enough to know You, Lord, to hear You now and then, to bask in Your goodness and love, and to sense that You are near. I am ever thankful to have a relationship with You. You've indicated to me that I must focus on You, not on myself or others, so I can have lasting peace and be able to get along with others. I will endeavor more and more to do this. As I look to You today, would You open up opportunities to speak about You to others and show them Your goodness, Your love, Your joy, and Your peace? It's a torn-apart world, filled with hatred, confusion, anger, apathy, disease, distrust, and negativity. I can reflect the ways of the world, or I can reflect the One who lives in my heart. Help me to reflect Your love, Lord. Show me a way to speak and share what others need to hear. Would You help me to be able to touch their hearts so they can know You as I do? You're the healer of broken hearts. Would You bring miracles to demonstrate Your greatness? You've told me to simply trust in You and let You work things out. Do Your magic, Lord! Bring Your peace, hope and joy to me and to others! Thanks, Lord. I love You.

God: Dear one, there are, as you know, forces working against you and others, but I'm always with you to lead, guide, and help you! The adversary will try very hard to offend or upset you. Will you stay where you're needed, despite the offense? Or will it cause you to desert your post? This will always be the crux of the matter. There will always be reasons to leave, quit, or give up, but can you resist them and press on? This is always the test. Just remember, if someone rejects, neglects, abuses, or leaves you, I will always supply what you need when you need it. Never blame yourself for others' failings. It's not your doing. The adversary will always try to separate and discourage those I'm trying to call. You've remained firm, because you're My lovely "adamant"—a stone that can't be broken. He'll try to break you, but you must continue in your calling and listen for My leading. I'll always guide you through the "noise" and give you needed strength to strive, survive, and thrive. Stay where you are now. Stand firm. I'll give you further directions later. Trust Me. Be patient. I love you.

August

FOCUS:
FEARLESS FAITH

"So be strong and courageous! Do not be afraid and do not panic before them. For the Lord your God will personally go ahead of you. He will neither fail you nor abandon you."

—DEUTERONOMY 31:6

AUGUST 1

May they love You as I do!

"Put on your sword, O mighty warrior! You are so glorious, so majestic! In your majesty, ride out to victory, defending truth, humility, and justice. Go forth to perform awe-inspiring deeds!"
—Psalm 45:3-4

Me: Lord, how You loved David! How You loved his heart for You. He blew it at times, but he always came to You for forgiveness. You loved this about him. He was a warrior for You. Oh, that I and my descendants would have his courage to fight for Your causes! That we would be able to stand for You and win against all odds! May my children and grandchildren be witnesses for You and defend their right to worship, even when God-deniers reign. May they love You as I do! I think of the witnesses in Revelation 11, who served as the counterpart to the false witnesses in the end times. You showed me how my grandchildren will serve You like these two did, and You'll give them supernatural ability to endure and prevail. I pray for this, Lord! May they live for Your purposes! I love You.

God: Dear one, I love those, like David and Elijah, who stand for Me against all odds. I love it when people bind themselves to My Word and what I stand for. Was it easy for Elijah to stand against 50 men who came to kill him? No. He was scared! But he also trusted in Me. What about you? Are you afraid of people and what they might do to you? Do you fear them more than Me? If so, then you are bound to serve them. If you're more in awe of Me, and what I can do, you're at liberty to live without fear. You're free to live as I meant you to—with power and dignity and God-given rights. But you must choose. Elijah proved himself, because he listened for My words and spoke them boldly, and they always proved to be true. This is the proof of validity for any prophet or warrior. True light shines through My Word. It's the source of understanding. Bring it to mind throughout the day. Then, you'll have the strength to prevail. I rejoice in your search for Me, because I've created you to be a powerful prayer warrior. I'll use you for purposes beyond your imagination in places you never thought possible. Never forget My promises, because you're meant to bring light to this world. Someday you'll look back and see how I worked through you and your family to cause change in the world. Without you I couldn't do it. I love you.

AUGUST 2
So we can calm any storm

"When Jesus woke up, he rebuked the wind and said to the waves, "Silence! Be still!"
Suddenly the wind stopped, and there was a great calm. Then he asked them, "Why
are you afraid? Do you still have no faith?"
—Mark 4:39-40

Me: Lord, today You reminded me of when the disciples and Jesus crossed the sea in a storm. The winds blew and the waves raged and, as Jesus slept, the disciples grew more fearful. Terrified, they woke Him up and asked if He cared that they might all die! His answer? "Oh, you of little faith!" Why were they so afraid when He was with them? He immediately stood up and rebuked the storm! Then calm prevailed. You showed me something from this story recently—how to "hunker down" with Your Son in my boat during a storm. If there's turmoil around me, He'll always stand up and rebuke the winds and the waves for me as I trust Him. And I can stay peacefully still, knowing that He will. When I'm feeling torn apart or stressed or confused or rattled, I can turn to the comforting spirit in me to help me focus more on You, Your Son, and Your promises. And You assure me that You'll deliver me and others with Your hope-filled words. You offer help when I need it and calm during stormy times. I love You.

God: Dear one, sometimes you underestimate yourself and the ability you have through what resides inside you! Don't you realize what I've given you? Authority and power to accomplish so much! Trust Me in every situation. Allow me to work in and through you. You know that I will. Today, rest in Me. Rest in My Son. Rest in My Spirit. And I will show you what can be done and how. Don't be anxious. I've given you everything you need to accomplish what's called for both now and later. With My help, you'll get more done than you can imagine. Just trust in Me. My words are healing words. They bring peace amid anxiety. They bring answers amid turmoil. Don't forget to listen for them. They hang, suspended in the air, ready for you to take and absorb. They're as close to you as the air you breathe. And, like air, you can't survive without them. Breathe them in. Then exhale them. Reach up and take them as I offer them to you. Place them in your mind. If you tried to live even for a few moments without air, you'd die. My Word is like this. You must inhale it to live and survive and thrive. Because it's the essence of My wisdom. I love you.

AUGUST 3
And have Your faith

"And it is impossible to please God without faith. Anyone who wants to come to him must believe that God exists and that he rewards those who sincerely seek him."
—Hebrews 11:6

Me: Lord, trusting You isn't always easy. It requires faith when I don't see anything happening, discernment when I can't hear Your voice, empathy when I can't feel compassion, connection when I want to withdraw, and fearless speech when I'm not sure if my words are the right ones. These can only come through a reliance on You. Only You can show me the reality when my mind questions a thing's existence. Only You can make things happen when they seem to be impossible. Lord, help me to see what You see, hear what You hear, feel what you feel, touch as You touch, and love as You love. You're my true guide. Lead me today in the way You need me to go. And open my eyes that are often dimmed by the darkness. I love You.

God: Dear child, let life unfold before you. This means that you must trust Me—the great Architect—to create the most magnificent plan out of any chaos. Be patient, and, one day, you'll behold My design as I unveil it to you. Your life is a marvelous part of this picture—one you can't fathom or imagine now. The challenge for you is that life is made up of so many bits and pieces that seem disorganized, until you finally see how each fragment fits into the greater scheme of things. If you trust Me to make an amazing design out of all the odd parts, you'll enjoy the journey. Remember the dream you had once where you got into a rickety boat with a crazy driver who steered helter skelter over choppy waves and went farther and farther away from the safety of the shore? You wondered where he was taking you, and you grew concerned! It all seemed very dangerous until you found yourself on an exotic island with others who were fishing and enjoying each other's company. And you realized that driver was Me and that your life was like a trip in a flimsy boat over squally waters. And you had to trust Me to get you to the right place through it all. My presence is real, though you can't see or feel Me. You want to see My face and understand more deeply who I am. You think your faith would deepen then. I understand. One day, you'll be in My presence and understand it all. But today, know that I'm with you. Although you can't discern Me, you can sense Me. Reach out your hand, and know that I'm with you. I love you.

AUGUST 4
To be able to live Your light

"You are the light of the world—like a city on a hilltop that cannot be hidden. No one lights a lamp and then puts it under a basket. Instead, a lamp is placed on a stand, where it gives light to everyone in the house. In the same way, let your good deeds shine out for all to see, so that everyone will praise your heavenly Father."
—Matthew 5:14-16

Me: Dear Lord, recently I met a young Chinese student at a restaurant while visiting Oxford, England. Feeling prompted, I remarked about how good his steak smelled. "I am celebrating," he said. "What are you celebrating?" I asked. He told me he'd passed his finals at college. I asked what he was studying, and he replied, "Ancient Asian Art." Where did he plan on using his knowledge? He said he had more opportunity in England than in China and would probably stay here. But he wasn't sure. I asked if he believed in God. He said, "I'm a Christian." That surprised me. I asked how he'd come to believe in Christ. And he explained that he'd worked in a church, but, mostly, it was his grandmother who had influenced him. "She's a Christian," he said. "My parents are Communist." He looked down. His admissions touched me deeply as a grandmother with aspirations for my own grandchildren. I also wondered what persecution he faces from family and friends. I told him how Jesus inside him would guide him to where he needed to be. He nodded. When I got up to leave, he stood up, and my heart went out to this brave young man who faced many obstacles because of his faith. How thankful I was to meet him. I thought of how few young people will admit to a faith these days. Especially when they face persecution. How easy we have it in the U.S.! Yet we take it for granted. Give us courage, Lord, to face our fears. I love You.

God: Dear one, many people tremble at the thought of a belief in Me! They're very fearful, because they don't understand Me or Who I am. They imagine they must give up a part of themselves if they acknowledge My existence. Their minds are filled with false information—the world's propaganda. So, they make gods out of things they can see and seemingly "understand." They find it hard to draw near to Me, because they can't see or hear or feel or touch Me. But you are My eyes and ears and hands and feet to them. My heart is in your heart. People who seek to know Me will recognize your faith. You can share My love with them, as you did. As My light, you can bring them My encouraging message of hope. I love you.

240

AUGUST 5
As a graduate of Your "courage college"

"They do not fear bad news; they confidently trust the LORD to care for them."
—Psalm 112:7

Me: Lord, this week I met with some clients who are continuously filled with fear. Even though the threat of catching a pandemic virus has dissipated, and the number of cases has declined, they've chosen to stay home indefinitely. "We ate out every night during the pandemic," they said, "but now that people aren't wearing masks, we won't go out at all." They were concerned that some weren't vaccinated and, though they were vaccinated, they might still get the virus. As I sat wearing a mask to ease their minds, I wasn't sure how to respond. Fear seems random, I thought. You never know how people, including Christians, will respond when they feel threatened. I'm often surprised by irrationality. I've been in your "courage college" and your "fearless university" for years. You've helped me to overcome so many fears, because You needed me to be available to work for You during times of terror. I think of how Jesus touched and healed the sick, even lepers! What boldness! Help me to be an example of Your bravery in these kinds of situations, Lord. Someday I want to walk down Your aisle and receive my "Courage" diploma from you. I love You.

God: Dear one, you are an example of fearlessness. Others can see this and decide how they want to live their own lives. Some will always fear the unknown and base their choices on rampant anxieties. But you can be a guide to a life of faith and peace. Some will choose to live in the bondage of fear and miss out on life's opportunities. And they will regret these decisions later. What is My desire for you? To be steadfast in your faith in Christ. To lean entirely on Him in absolute trust and confidence in His power, wisdom, and goodness. I want your roots to be firmly planted in Him, so that you are continually built up in Him, established in your faith, and overflowing with thanksgiving. Because of your hope for what is waiting for you, you can be filled with a clear understanding of My ways and purposes. And you can discern spiritual things, because you were drawn out of the dominion of darkness and transferred into the kingdom of my Son through His love for you. In your choice for a life of trust and fearlessness, I will continue to guide you forward. Trust Me to take bold steps forward as the fierceness of compromise continues to cause freedom to evaporate. I'll help you. I love you.

AUGUST 6
Where I can sow into Your garden

"Confess your sins to each other and pray for each other so that you may be healed. The earnest prayer of a righteous person has great power and produces wonderful results."
—James 5:16

Me: Holy Spirit, work in me to carry out Your purposes, so I can be bold to shout out the wonder of Your ways! Give me the guts to push back the evil that's causing confusion through the enemy's hidden agenda. Help me to shine Your light on what's taking place so it's obvious to all. Bring me into Your presence so I can be strong with Your confidence and bold with Your courage. Send angels to help us battle against those who obstruct justice, so we can transform this land. Oh, how I want to see them encamp around us! Bring more of Your supernatural blessings to create a greater outpouring of Your Spirit. Rain down Your peace and heal the broken hearts. Show me how to proceed with Your love. I present myself to You. Give me grace to help bring about an amazing revival. Help me to sow good seeds and plant plentiful possibilities. I've loved the places You've led me so far, where I've crossed paths with those positioned for Your purposes. Allow me more of these amazing divine appointments, when I've been able to "sow into Your garden." I want to serve Your purposes and bring more light to the world around me. Help me, Lord! For I love You.

God: Dear one, your prayers and requests are so weighty with Me! I stand by My people—those who come and ask and desire My help. You see what happens in the areas where people turn away from Me to ungodliness? You see how profound is the hurt when people create their own gods to worship, including themselves, the government, and their own ideologies that are apart from My Word? It's so evident. But your prayers are very effectual, because they are fervent. They are sincere. So, keep asking. Of course, I'll give you the freedom and strength you need to prosper and have health. I'll also give you great courage. I'll always stand by your side and be there for you. And I'll lead this country into mighty revivals as more people like you come to Me. Never fear! I'm a God of strength and power, and I carry the weight of many, because I can. I love you.

And stand up for You

"So we are Christ's ambassadors; God is making his appeal through us. We speak for Christ when we plead, "Come back to God!""
—*2 Corinthians 5:20*

Me: Lord, would You help me to be more like Jehoshaphat, who sought You with his whole heart? I want to have faith like Noah, who followed Your directions, even when he was surrounded by unbelief and disdain in a very hateful and deceitful land. Oh, to be like Abraham, who left his home and family to follow You and seek a new way of life. And David, who praised and worshipped You, even while he was receiving death-threats. Or like Paul, who brought Your messages of love and hope and peace to lands far away, while suffering great persecution for his efforts. I want to be one of Your sent ones, who speak Your Word and gladly stand for You here on earth. Open my eyes more and more to how I can do this for You. Strengthen me spiritually, mentally, and physically, and help me to never forget who I am and who You are. Thanks, Lord. I love You.

God: Dear one, I can make you fearless. I can make you brave in any situation so that, when you experience hardship or pressure, you can face it with greater strength and confidence. You're a survivor. You have My faith. And I can take you to higher places, but you must be patient, for it will take time. One day, you'll be amazed at how you were a part of so many peoples' lives, even when you didn't think you were. You touch many people each day. Continue to bless them, even when they refute your message and despise what you represent. They don't hate you; they reject Me. They blame Me for their lacks. Love them despite themselves. Only love can win over hate. It's the greatest healer of all wounds. So, be a healer. Be a lover. Take time each day to seek My joy and My peace. You can find them in Me and in My Word. My Son brings peace to your heart and offers you protection through the Holy Spirit, who lives in you and serves you. Let your heart be My house and your body My temple. You've tried to represent Me, and My peace lies within you. Let it reign. Let My joyful light shine from you. Offer My kindness and love as gifts to those around you. My Son paid for these. People can see them manifested through you. So let them shine too. I love you.

As Your fearless lover

"Such love has no fear, because perfect love expels all fear. If we are afraid, it is for fear of punishment, and this shows that we have not fully experienced his perfect love."
—1 John 4:18

Me: Why does anyone look elsewhere when You are here, Lord, right in front of us? Why do we seek counsel in people who are blind, deaf, and dumb and can't see beyond today or even what's meaningful in this moment? Why do we watch a screen and determine our fate based on news of wars, terror, trouble, disputes, disease, and death? Why do we become afraid of a mouse, a gnat, a spider, a bug, a virus, or a lie? You made us. And You made the world for us. Why are we so filled with fear and unable to trust You, the One who is greater than everything? The One who loves us. You're all-powerful and all-knowing. You're ready to hear our prayers. You listen attentively to our vapid requests and care about our petty lives. And You still yearn for our fellowship and long for our love. How oblivious we are! Why do we forget that You're ever-present and ever-ready to help us? Let us turn our eyes, ears, minds, and hearts to You! Let us go to You for peace and reconciliation. I want to trust You for deliverance and answers in every situation. Because only You can do these things for us. I love You.

God: Dear one, I'm the true and righteous judge. My Word separates the lies from the truth. My Word divides light from darkness. People are sometimes manipulated by worldly systems and leaders. They seek approval out of fear. They often wallow in praise and become twisted by flattery. They seek substance in false words—lies meant to control and use them for evil or selfish purposes. They see only what's in front of them and don't foresee the impact of these things on their future. They're often blinded by frightful scenes. And their choices made from fear cause great hurt to themselves and others. One day, My true light will surface and confront the world. People will clearly see the cover-ups that caused so much chaos. Then, all the devilish dishonesty will be revealed. Until then, you must live in a world full of deception. You must confront the lies while remaining focused on My truth, which is the reality. Look to Me continuously for understanding on how you can survive and thrive amid deceit. And how you can maintain resounding faith. I love you.

Because You protect me

"Son of man, do not fear them or their words. Don't be afraid even though their threats surround you like nettles and briers and stinging scorpions. Do not be dismayed by their dark scowls, even though they are rebels."
—Ezekiel 2:6

Me: Lord, daily we hear reports of attacks on Your people. We see disasters in the news: vehicles blown up, people shot to death, structures demolished, women threatened and raped, and children killed in crossfire. And I wonder why people think these actions will promote their causes. I sit in my house, and I feel the enemy lurking. I'm inclined to build walls, put up my defenses, and guard against looming threats, because it feels like they grow closer every day. Lord, what's happening in this time we live in? Years ago, we may have observed an occasional attack from terrorists or murderers far away, but it was rare. Now, the assaults come more often, and some are in our own backyard! There's always been war, but now it feels nearer. Protect me, Lord, and give me greater faith in Your ability to provide shelter. Show me how I can live for you and not succumb to the fear around me. Help me to trust in You and Your presence, knowing that one day I'll be with You always. And Your world will be perfect and without fear. You're my succorer and my strength. Give me courage. Help me to know You in greater ways and remember You in each moment. Sometimes I feel like I'm in a spiritual wilderness. Lead me to Your promised land in my mind. Be with me today and every day in my thoughts, words, and deeds. Because I love You.

God: Dear one, don't be afraid of what people might do to you or to your family. I'm always nearby, encouraging and strengthening you and giving you peace. Do you believe that I can protect you? How many times have I promised you that I would? I offer you a spiritual force that can give you all that you need to survive and flourish. Others may try to frighten you, but I've given you every weapon you need to succeed. Trust Me, and I'll guide you through any threatening situation. Do you believe I've set you apart from this world? That I have a hedge of protection around you? Do you understand that you'll spend eternity with Me and that I have a special place set aside for you? So, why be discouraged or disheartened by the things in this world? Through faith in Me you can experience My peace always. I love you.

AUGUST 10
And lead us to Your mountaintop

"Teach your children to choose the right path, and when they are older, they will remain upon it."
—*Proverbs 22:6*

Me: Lord, would You peel back the layers from the hearts of my children, so they can receive Your love and know You more fully? Would You tenderly remove the scales and wipe away the remaining film that covers their eyes, so they can see just who You are? Would You direct them through the dark woods to the brightly-lit paths that lead to Your meadow-embraced mountain of surprise and delight? Would You hold their hands, as they blindly walk, and gently lead them to Your inviting campfire? I can see them sitting with You for a while, gazing over at Your fire-lit eyes as they listen to Your comforting words. I know they'd be in awe of You, if they could only see You like this. They'd see how glorious You are! I so want them to be deeply touched by Your beauty and enthralled by Your love, as I am. But now, please hide them in the shelter of Your wings as You gradually reveal to them Your hidden secrets, which You will one day hold out to them. I ask these things in Your Son's name. I love You.

God: Dear one, do you believe that I work in you to will and to do of My good pleasure? And that, even now, I'm working to bless your children? One day, you'll see just how I touched both you and them. And it'll become clearer to you just how I led them to walk down a path with Me. You've asked for My blessing on them, and I honor your requests. Remember how I honored My commitment to David? I promised him that I'd work through him to bring a lamp to the people of Israel—the promised Messiah (2 Kings 8:19). This promise came through his children, even though some of them didn't walk with Me. I honor your belief, and I hear your heart's request. Along My path are many beautiful sights and wonderful people to encounter. If you stay on it, by focusing on Me, you'll see many signs and wonders. You may think it's a difficult road to follow at times, but it really isn't, if you let Me lead you. Look beyond it. In the distance is a snow-capped mountain that rises up to the sky and touches the clouds. I'll lead you and your children to this place step by step. Together, we'll reach the summit. Just trust Me. From the top, you'll see a spectacular sight, beyond anything you could ask or think. From where you are now, it may seem to be beyond your capability to ever reach the top. But, with My help, you can do it. Just follow My steps! I love you.

AUGUST 11
So I can see a revival

"And I will give you a new heart, and I will put a new spirit in you. I will take out your stony, stubborn heart and give you a tender, responsive heart."
—Ezekiel 36:26

Me: Lord, I'm still so taken aback when people question Your love and goodness and are filled with fear about the future! I guess I forget human nature, and I expect others to know what I know—that You're an amazing provider and that all we have is from You. You are our sole source, and from You alone we have life and breath. Others still don't understand this. I wonder if they ever will! I know I must ask for Your guidance, because You alone can help me. Lord, I pray that You'll work through me to open the eyes of those who are blind. Stone by stone, show me how to remove the obstacles, so their hearts can change. Because I want to help You rebuild Your church, Your temple, as men of God like Ezra once did. Guide me and give me strength. Lead me in Your work and help me speak for You. Everything is in Your hands. Would You help me to serve You in better ways and to see a revival of hearts? I love You.

God: My love, you see what can happen when people turn their hearts to Me. You see how blessed they are! Look at the revivals throughout history. It can be the same way in your land, in your lifetime, when people turn their hearts back to Me! I want to abide among My people, but I can only do this if I'm allowed to be a part of their lives. My heart is to sustain people and to give them everything they need to live and survive and be blessed. I can do this if they come to Me and heed My advice. When they turn from following Me, the results are disastrous! Dear one, keep coming to Me with your requests. Be patient and know I'm directing you, even now. The right doors will open at the right time, and I will lead you to where you can best help Me to build My church. Stone by stone, we'll work together to build a mighty foundation. As you trust Me, we can work with one purpose. When you feel anxious, focus on Me, and I'll bring you immeasurable peace. This work is not forever. I'll entrust you with those who desire the faith they see in you. I'll show you their hearts. I'll open your eyes and theirs to see Me more clearly. And I'll give you the strength you need to work. I love you.

AUGUST 12
And You can reveal real justice

"In the night I search for you; in the morning I earnestly seek you. For only when you come to judge the earth will people learn what is right."
—Isaiah 26:9

Me: Lord, You keep telling me that the things the world promotes and becomes enamored with, or fears the most, are not the things that You view as important at all! Often what the media promotes with megaphones to attract peoples' attention is merely a smokescreen for what's really happening behind the scenes. You showed me that many initiatives are promotions by politicians to gain power and steal control from the hands of the citizens. And these advances are gained one signature at a time! Lord, help us! Would You stir, push, or move people—whatever it takes—so that they can wake up to what others are doing "on their behalf" to "protect" them? Through fear they're being manipulated to act in harmful ways so that they are losing their freedom little by little. Some of these efforts are attempts to steal our ability to worship You. Show me what I can do! Help me to make some impact to preserve a godly way of life in my community and nation. Thanks, Lord. I love You.

God: Dear one, I work through both good and bad situations with the ultimate end being good. My aim is to disclose the hearts and intentions of people and reveal their true nature. Those who say they want to help others, but then take advantage of vulnerable people so they can line their own and others' pockets, are eventually revealed for who they are. As I uncover more corruption, and people grow disillusioned with their leaders, many will turn to Me for answers. The greatest revivals happen when people are fed up with those they once put on a pedestal and revered, only to be disappointed by them. Disillusionment can cause many people to look for a better way to live with some semblance of hope for the future. Rulers may try to steal what was freely given to My people by promising life-altering changes for the better. But when the people follow the words and see the real outcomes, they begin to realize what is really behind the promises. I always listen to the cries of My people, who pray night and day for real justice, which can come only from following Me. And I always shine a light on evil leaders who take advantage of innocent people. Trust Me. I'm working even now on behalf of you and those who come to Me. I love you.

AUGUST 13
Through a mighty tree

"The thief's purpose is to steal and kill and destroy. My purpose is to give them a rich and satisfying life."
—John 10:10

Me: Lord, last night I had an unusual dream. I was visiting a town, and I met a man who was working for a local businessman, who'd posted a "Help Wanted" sign in his storefront. His job was to repair the holes in peoples' shoes. He took me to meet the businessowner, an older man who sat beside a huge tree, carving out the pulp. The tree was almost hollowed out. Only the sides still stood to support the tree, and I wondered how it would survive with so much of its "innards" chiseled out. I asked the man why he was doing this, and he explained that he was cleaning out the rotten parts, so it could become healthy again. When I woke up, I wondered what the dream meant. You explained that the tree was Your church, which needs cleansing so it can survive. The older man was You, with the job of removing the rottenness. "The people in the church are blindly following leaders, who lead them away from Me," You said. And You pointed out that the tree could still survive and flourish if it tapped into its roots again: Your Word. I realized that the man, who was repairing the holes in the shoes of Your people, was Jesus, who wanted them to walk again soundly with You. Lord, place me where You want me. So many people are misled. They suffer and need Your hand of hope. Show me how to lead them to You. I love You.

God: Dear child, you have this great gift, the earth, that was given to you and to all mankind ages ago. I created it for people like you so you could be inspired by its majesty and come to worship Me. Since dominion of the earth was handed over to My enemy, he's been trying to destroy it, and My people, by disrupting My plans. But he can't completely, so he grows more frustrated every day. His goal is still to steal, kill, and destroy as much as possible. His main target is the church and its body. And he's succeeded in misleading and destroying the lives of many of the people I love. Some are led astray by leaders in the church, who place themselves above My Word. But remember what Jesus accomplished. He brought beauty from ashes and healing from hurt. You'll be amazed at what We'll do. Even as the rottenness of the church is removed, see how I will cause many mighty, faith-filled trees to grow up from the seeds of that one huge tree. Though it appears to be dead at times, the seeds have been planted. Remember that a seed must die to itself for a plant to sprout up and live from it! I love you.

AUGUST 14
So I can overcome anger

"Be strong in the Lord and in his mighty power. Put on all of God's armor so that you will be able to stand firm against all strategies of the devil. For we are not fighting against flesh-and-blood enemies, but against evil rulers and authorities of the unseen world, against mighty powers in this dark world, and against evil spirits in the heavenly places. Therefore, put on every piece of God's armor so you will be able to resist the enemy in the time of evil. Then after the battle you will still be standing firm."
—Ephesians 6:10-13

Me: Lord, sometimes I feel frustrated and angry. I still get impatient with people, and I need Your help in dealing with them. I get annoyed and irritated when they speak or act foolishly, or they seem to lack consideration for others. Would You help me to bow down before You in these situations, so I can overcome my negative reactions with Your great goodness? For You are always kind and good. Prepare me to deal with any feelings that trigger these reactions. Give me wise words to say in response to people's unwise choices or comments, so I can best help them. Remind me that hurting people hurt people. I love You.

God: Child, some days will be hard to bear because of mental pressures caused by people. Sometimes you'll feel like lashing out or giving up. But you must press into Me. You can succeed if you trust in Me and not in how you feel. Remember, you're fighting a spiritual battle. Be ready for sudden confrontations by donning My armor to face these situations. This prepares you to resist the pride, prejudice, anger, hatred, and vitriol of people. This equips you with patience. Never be surprised by negative responses incited by the enemy. You can keep your heart pure with the truth of My Word. You can keep your thoughts simple with its simplicity. When you're not sure, turn to Me. I'll make things as clear as light shining through a cloud. There will be doubters, but My path will lead you to those who seek My presence. You'll know them when you see them. They're the ones hungry to hear what you have to say. Tell them about My peace and My love. Memorize scripture so you have the right words to say. This gives you the armor you need. It's your sword to fight the enemy who comes against you. Equip yourself so you're strong for the daily battles you face. I love you.

And leave Your legacy

"For God has not given us a spirit of fear and timidity, but of power, love, and self-discipline."
—2 Timothy 1:7

Me: Lord, when I listened to the memories shared about President Reagan at his funeral, I was impressed by the stories of his optimism and faith. I never realized his strong beliefs and spiritual side. Thanks for giving him to us for a while and for his example of believing. He had a wonderful way of reaching people when others couldn't. Would you please give insight and understanding to our current president? Help that person to deal with other nations to bring peace and negotiate without the cost of more lives. Help all our leaders to use greater wisdom and diplomacy. Inspire them to make good decisions. Work in them to make choices based on Your Word and not on selfish ambitions and pride. Let me be a leader for You, Lord. Lead me to the place You want me to be. Give me strength and courage to serve You in every place I go. I need Your boldness and confidence. Open my eyes and help me to see as You do. And let me leave my own good legacy, as Ronald Reagan did. I love You.

God: Dear one, to leave a strong legacy, you must be courageous. Only I can make you fearless. Only I can make you brave. Valor doesn't come from the heart of a man, but from his spirit. When you see true bravery, it's not a soulful thing, and it doesn't come from the mind of a man or a woman. It's true source is My Spirit within that person. Only I can inspire real courage. Because it's spiritual. When you see a truly brave person, give thanks, because you're seeing a person filled with My Spirit and having a mind and heart directed by it. People's ways are often loathsome and cowardly, because the world is ruled by our enemy, whose aim is to create cowardice in every heart. As a result, people are often directed by fear or greed, which both result from spiritual weakness. But when people accept My Word and My Son into their hearts, they can have a source of strength, boldness, and confidence. Remember how My disciples acted after they were born again of My Spirit? That kind of courage comes from Me. Have bravery now, and remember that it only comes from Me. I love you.

AUGUST 16
As a faithful one

"But you must remain faithful to the things you have been taught. You know they are true, for you know you can trust those who taught you. You have been taught the holy Scriptures from childhood, and they have given you the wisdom to receive the salvation that comes by trusting in Christ Jesus."
—2 Timothy 3:14-15

Me: Lord, this morning as I walked it felt a little bit cooler. It reminded me of Michigan summers on the lake, when mornings were cool and afternoons warmer, but never hot. As children, we'd sun on the fine-sandy beach then jump into the invigoratingly chilly, clear water. Or we'd hop into Grampa's motorboat so he could drive us around the lake. For fun, we'd take out the skis and see how long we could stay up in the water as he pulled us behind the speeding boat. I loved it. I have such fond memories of those times. Thanks for these childhood days spent with grandparents, Lord. What a blessing they were! I can only live today. I understand that. But help me to make the most of my life now, so others can hold cherished memories because of my influence, just as I now think of the touching times spent with my grandparents. I know my choices have an impact on those around me, and I want to bring positive things to their lives that bring them closer to You. May I influence them for good! I love You.

God: My child, I've always been near you, though you were often unaware of My presence. I walked with you as a child, and I surrounded you with My love, even though you couldn't see Me. I was always with you, smiling on you and blessing you. I laughed when you laughed. I cried when you cried. I was elated when you were happy, and I was sad when you had a bad day. Every moment with you was always very precious to Me. You see, I always considered you to be special, because I made you that way. I treasure the sound of your voice, especially when it's lifted up to Me. I love to hear your requests, and I work to meet them diligently. Your praise and thanksgiving mean more to Me than words can say. They bring Me great joy. Remember, I continue to work on your behalf each day, whether you know it or not. And I continuously guide you toward a closer walk with Me so that your life can be an impactful blessing to you and to others, including those in your own family. I love you.

Who's not just a piece of a pie

"And God will generously provide all you need. Then you will always have everything you need and plenty left over to share with others."
—2 Corinthians 9:8

Me: I walked another way today, Lord. It was interesting to see the moon from a different angle. It was full and right in front of me as I set out. And it reminded me of Your fullness and what You make available to us. I remembered the slivered moon I'd seen not so long ago that reminded me of other religions, and I asked You what You thought. Your answer was that, while many could have the moon's "fullness," through an understanding of what You offer them, they've chosen to be content with only a sliver of life. Some religions are based on the teachings of one man, now dead. Because of limited understanding, they don't know how to access Your Spirit, and life for them is confined to earthly things, which can never give them what they desire the most. Any life beyond this one is based on how they live now and if they measure up. Land and family become preeminent, so they squabble and fight among themselves to keep what little they have. They settle for having only a slice of the pie, instead of the whole thing, which would be attainable if they knew and believed in Jesus Christ. Lord, how can I reach them and others with Your message of faith, hope, and redemption? I love You.

God: Dear one, you see how I've blessed you. You see how I bring you peace and joy, love and light. That's because you received the great gift My Son offered to you when you believed in Him. Without this freely given gift, the only way to heaven is through good works. And it's very difficult for anyone to gain My rewards by doing good, since all fall short. When Jesus offered up his life, and rose from death, He made available the key to open the door to heaven, and He paved a way for entry into My kingdom. What a gift! Without having to earn your way through good works, you can simply accept this amazing gift and walk right into My presence! You're at once forgiven by believing in Him, and your shortcomings are dismissed and forgotten. Now you are welcomed without questions about your past. Now you can stand before Me without consciousness of guilt or shame. That's the "whole pie" I promise to all people who believe in Me and in Him. How He loves you! And how I love you.

AUGUST 18
You're my friend

"I no longer call you servants, because a servant does not know his master's business. Instead, I have called you friends, for everything that I learned from my Father I have made known to you."
—John 15:15

Me: Lord, what a friend I have in You! You're my source of inspiration, my guide, my first love, my comfort, and my healer. It's You who sought me out and bought me eternal life through the work of Your Son, who gave His life for me. It's You who stand beside me, guarding my heart and protecting me from harm. I don't ever need to feel despair or fear that people might hurt me. They can't as long as I remember that You're near. Today, I thanked You for the brisk morning air as I walked at sunrise. And You reminded me that You gave me this because I asked for it on a day when the air dripped with humidity, and the heat was stifling, even at dawn. You'd do more for me if I'd just ask, You said. So many things don't happen, because we fail to ask! You told me that no request goes unanswered. And no life is wasted. All lives matter to You, and You use everyone and everything for a purpose, as part of Your overall plan. Remind me to come to You more often, Lord! I love You.

God: Dear one, you're seeing a turning point in your life. You're experiencing the greatness of walking with a purpose by making small requests and then recognizing My responses as they unfold before you. I want you to realize how great My pleasure is in you and how much I want to show you My power through answering your prayers! Renew your strength and confidence in Me by "dining at My table" each and every day. And I'll always give you what you need to succeed in each moment. As we spend more time together, I'll reveal to you the instructions you need to be more than a conqueror in every situation. And you'll begin to realize that the way I talk to you is not always audibly. It's more of a knowingness, or awareness, of what I want you to do. Sometimes you'll just experience My answer, like today when you felt unusually pleasant weather in the middle of a turbid summer. The more you dine with Me, the more you'll be able to hear and understand and recognize My answers. As You walk with Me, You'll see many more breakthroughs, and you'll experience much more of My love. I love you.

Who helps me deal with stupidity

"Avoid worthless, foolish talk that only leads to more godless behavior."
—2 Timothy 2:16

Me: Dear God, sometimes I feel especially tired of peoples' stubbornness, pride, haughtiness, stupidity, and anger. Would You show me how to deal with "entitled" behavior? Let me see as Jesus did—through His spirit and not His emotions. Help me today to see You as You are, to see people as You see them, and to be who You want me to be. Help me to accomplish what I need to, and to be where I need to be when I need to be there. Show me what to do in each situation. Would you help me to know when it's right to sacrifice my time and money and resources for a cause? Show me how and when to release any needless things to You, and when it's profitable to offer what I have to others? My desire is that everything be for You. I need Your guidance, Lord, for I'm weak and ignorant at times, and I need Your strength and wisdom. You're awesome, Lord! Thanks for how You work with me. I love You.

God: Dear one, those who contend against you resist Me. Some think they're fighting for their own rights. They see your strong stance as a personal attack against them and their shaky beliefs. They're threatened by your confidence, which comes from Me! Let Me reveal to you what they're made of, where their hearts truly abide, and how to reach them, if possible. I'll rip off their masks and reveal their true natures. Be My instigator—My one to bring light out of darkness. I know it's hard for you now, because you don't know when My promises will come to pass or when you'll see answers to your prayers. Continue to trust and believe and look for My promises fulfilled. I'll always be there for you. Today, seek My words to bring deliverance to you and to others. My Word is real. Watch and pray. Never give up. Expect answers. Doors will open unexpectedly, and you will see many "suddenlies" occur. Some call these "kairos" moments, or times that are appointed for the purposes of God. I give strength and courage and wisdom, even when others only offer shame, rejection, discouragement, doubt, and despair. People come and go. They are hot. Then they are cold. Most know only hopelessness and lack of trust, because they've been deceived by the negatives that surround them in this world. I am constant and real. Depend on Me for answers. I love you.

AUGUST 20

Through Your Son's love

"The Son radiates God's own glory and expresses the very character of God, and he sustains everything by the mighty power of his command. When he had cleansed us from our sins, he sat down in the place of honor at the right hand of the majestic God in heaven. This shows that the Son is far greater than the angels, just as the name God gave him is greater than their names."
—*Hebrews 1:3-4*

Me: Dear Lord, I love the name "Jesus!" What a beautiful name! He saved my soul, made me whole, and freed me from guilt and shame. Your Son rescued me from darkness, showed me the way, and introduced me to Your truth. He's my hero. He's my Lord, my guide, and my most wonderful friend. He frees me from myself—my unworthiness, fear, loneliness, feelings of rejection, lacks, and my instabilities. He brings me up higher each time I seek the comfort of His presence. He shows a more glorified way to You. Thank You for redeeming me through the work of Your Savior Son. How can I ever thank You enough? I love You.

God: Child, Jesus Christ was My firstborn among many. He has been My "righthand Man" from the beginning of the world as you know it. With My help, He designed the earth and the people who inhabit it. He came to earth to bring My message of hope and deliverance. His story is not a secret, but it's often misunderstood. I want you to understand it now. He grew up as a child and lived as a man, and, while He did these, He submitted himself wholly to Me. He didn't have the benefit of having access to My Spirit until He was baptized by John. He was faced with sin, or disobedience to Me, but He chose to listen to, learn from, and obey Me in every situation. Even though He had the body and soul of a man, He subjected Himself to Me and to My Spirit in Him, so you could come to know Me later. He chose to die a terrible death so you could live through Him. He deserves to be your hero. He accomplished all that was needed to be your Savior and Lord. How I love His willingness! It was all for you. I love you.

That pulls me up from the pits

"And we know that God causes everything to work together for the good of those who love God and are called according to his purpose for them."
—Romans 8:28

Me: Lord, again I come to You with thankfulness for all You've shown and done for me. I realize now how You worked out for good the things I'd thought were terrible mistakes. It's amazing to me how You can fix the things that were once so broken. Be near me now, Lord. I love how You spared me in so many situations, when I should have been terribly harmed or died, because You knew that I'd come to love You. You knew my heart before I was born! You covered me with Your hand of mercy, and You protected me. You pulled me out of pits when I was drowning and set me up in a good place. Thanks. You brought me through disasters and despair, and You gave me hope. You delivered me from self-pity, and You gave me a reason for living. Thanks. Please continue to work through me as You have before. I love You.

God: Child, My desire is that you be a beacon for Me. I want you to be a light shining brightly in this world filled with darkness. Because you've experienced deliverance, you can shine My hope to others, who also long to see My presence on this earth. So shine! The best gift I've given you lies within you, trying to illuminate through every part of you! Let it pour out of you! It's the light of Jesus Christ in you—His very illumination in this world! Let it glow, like a brightly shining bulb. Never temper or hide it. Let it out in all its glory! Be My faithful one. Bring My Word to the people of this world. Be an example of faith and love and the peace of My fulfillment. Don't be afraid to stand against adversity and speak the Word of Truth. Open your heart and take in those in need. Heal them with My mercy! Restore them with My peace! Be courageous with the strength and courage I alone can give. Be My right hand by upholding and defending the truth in this world. Be a sign and a wonder by standing against the odds. I'll reveal to you My strategies and work through you to accomplish them. Then you can relay My wisdom and insight by directing those who come to you. Some will be won by your encouraging words—those whose hearts were once broken and hardened and now seek healing. I love you.

And frees me from fear

"I prayed to the Lord, and he answered me. He freed me from all my fears."
—*Psalm 34:4*

Me: Dear Lord, show me Your amazing hand of deliverance from the fears of this world. I wonder what will happen to our nation if so many continue to turn away from You? If our leaders pull others farther away from Your truth, what will we have to endure? I see so many faithless people walking away from You. This concerns me. Would You show me how to pray for and help those consumed with material worries and stifled by hopelessness? Would You give them spiritual wings so they can fly up and see where You are and who You are in their lives? Open their eyes to see Your greatness and grandeur! Today, give me Your peace, and reassure me of Your presence as I walk among the "almost dead." Guide me with Your grace and mercy as I deal with them. Give me supernatural patience and greater understanding. Guard my thoughts, Lord. I love You.

God: Dear one, My way is precious, or costly. It requires effort. It demands choices that often run contrary to the world's purposes. People cry out for peace and justice, but they may be unwilling to give of themselves or to do what's needed to attain these. They allow others to come against Me and are unwilling to defend My righteousness. They're afraid to take a stand against injustice. Righteousness means to live for what is right. Unrighteousness is the turning away from Me and what is godly to grasp what is unholy and self-seeking and false. It has abounded since the world began. Few will stand against it. I look for those who are willing to fight for Me, to put "self" on the line, speak against ungodliness, and choose My ways over the world's ways. These will inherit righteousness, or a life near Me, and My rewards in the next life, when all is made good and right and just. I've heard your prayers. And I've already put into motion the deliverance of those who will defend Me. Even if your leaders reject Me and cause chaos to gain power, be assured that I'll always fight for you and for My own. Some will never come to Me, but there are people who will hear My words. Don't be afraid to speak to them. Never fear persecution, for I will protect you with My hand of justice. I'll always show you who the true believers are and how you can effectively touch their lives. Because I love you.

So I can see into their hearts

"I will give them hearts that recognize me as the Lord. They will be my people, and I will be their God, for they will return to me wholeheartedly."
—Jeremiah 24:7

Me: Lord, today You told me that You'd show me more of Your mysteries if I looked at the world through Your eyes. I told You that, because of all You've revealed to me through Your Word, I can see things, even the reasons for things, that others can't see. And You said, "I will show you more, if you want to learn, about things like why people are the way they are and what's the true essence of their hearts." I answered, "Sure! Please show me!" Lord, would You also give me peace when there seems to be none? Would You show me kindness when there's none to be found? Would You show me mercy when others seem so merciless? Remind me of Your presence, for my mind goes every which way, and I tend to focus on all the wrong things. Show me my "true north"—my destination and calling—and help me to bring peace through right thinking to others. So many are riddled with fear of the future and burdened by financial needs. Help me to lead more to a belief in Your abundance and a trust in You as their provider. And deliver me from any fear of reaching out to help when it's needed. Most of all, show me their hearts as You promised! I love You.

God: Dear one, as you listen more and more to My revelations about your life and others', you'll find peace, joy, kindness, and mercy. These disclosures will bring you greater understanding and reconciliation. I long to work with you every day, to teach and strengthen you mentally, physically, spiritually, and every way, so you can abound more and more. People suffer, because they focus on their own lacks, circumstances, surroundings, and other people. The farther away from Me they wander, the less attractive and appealing life becomes. It descends into a sort of drudgery that brings disease, disaster, and death. Only I can lead anyone to the life of their dreams. By spending time with Me, you can strengthen yourself in My presence. Then I can speak to you and reveal wonderful things about yourself—what you can do, how you can succeed, and how you can reach others' hearts. I love you.

And know the ones who'll rise up

"In the last days,' God says, 'I will pour out my Spirit upon all people. Your sons and daughters will prophesy. Your young men will see visions, and your old men will dream dreams."
—*Acts 2:17*

Me: Lord, how I yearn to see young people, who seek Your truth and are willing to rise up and fight against evil. My hope is that I will one day see more standing against hate and the princes of darkness, who try to rule this world with underhanded practices, lies, deceit, and fear. Work through my children and grandchildren, and help them to be bold to hold up their hands and stop the evil. Give them courage, as warriors against the enemy and his cohorts, to fight with swords of truth, being covered by breastplates of righteousness, their feet shod with the gospel of peace, and donning helmets of salvation to protect their thoughts. I want to be counted as one of Your leaders, but sometimes I feel discouraged when I see so many young people turning against You. And then, at other times, I'm encouraged to see some who are willing to worship you passionately! Show me more of these and how I can help them today! I love You.

God: Dear one, I understand your yearning. Like you, My deepest desire is that all people would grow into an understanding of My goodness. When they continue to deny the signs I send, it's hard to understand their lack of desire to know the truth, especially when they suffer needlessly. This "stuckness" makes Me sad. Some will never come to know Me. Because of My agreement with mankind, I must honor their choices. Many people fill their minds with the negatives of this world. Then they plead for help, not knowing who to turn to. They surround themselves with "thorns" for protection and don't understand that they've created a harmful barrier from which it's hard to escape. They seek the garden I created but can't reach it. You can show them how to break through the "thickets," without getting hurt, by guiding them to My truth. Some cry out for help. Listen for them. Others will stay trapped, because they're afraid of change. Continue to hold forth My love in the hope that one day they'll respond. The main thing is that the seeds are planted. Some seeds will spring up and give birth to new life later. Other seeds will die without good soil to help them survive and thrive with new growth. And some will be choked by worldly fears and desires. Your only responsibility is to speak. I will bring the good results. I love you.

So they can be freed

"For the Lord is the Spirit, and wherever the Spirit of the Lord is, there is freedom."
—2 Corinthians 3:17

Me: Thanks, Lord, for those who've gone before me and fought for freedom and justice. Thanks for how they gave their time and their lives so that others, like me, could be spared from tyranny and oppression and maintain the right to worship as they choose. Because of them, I can practice my faith and not be afraid to speak. All because they had the courage to stand up for their beliefs. They faced threats without backing down. They spoke the truth courageously. They took up arms and fought when others floundered and backed away from the fight. Would You help me to be brave when I am faced with difficult choices? Would You give me needed courage when I see religious liberty threatened? And protect those who fight for our rights. Comfort and heal and free those who are being oppressed. Be near me now as I strive to do Your will. Show me how I can stand up for You and Your Word. I love You.

God: Dear one, I will always give you courage to fight for the truth. Because only My truth can set people free from tyranny and oppression. And I'll always lead you to the truth if you'll look to Me. I'll never let you be deceived by people who speak lies if you'll come to Me for answers. When you're unsure about others' motives, just ask. Never let people cloud your mind with muddled thinking. They may be fishing in a muddy hole. Go to the crystal-clear waters of My Word for directions. Then, you'll have peace. Don't be distracted by those who try to move your eyes away from Me. Focus on Me and how I can help you. When people don't seek My help, it's because they're filled with pride. People who try to instill fear in you are like wounded lions who stagger around, roaring so they can paralyze and then bring down others with them. Then they'll rip off pieces of their victims to fulfill their hunger. But their appetite for destruction is never satisfied. Don't let these people scare you. The sword you wield is My Word. With it, you can annihilate any ungodly words and actions. You'll have what you need to fight the good fight, and their foolish efforts will soon be nullified. You can make them scatter through the power of My Word. This is how I can help you and others to maintain freedom and peace. I love you.

AUGUST 26

By You who are good

"For the Lord is good. His unfailing love continues forever, and his faithfulness continues to each generation."
—*Psalm 100:5*

Me: Dear Lord, I love our life together! Thanks for reminding me today of how You made all things for Your loved ones. "Everything has a purpose," You said. "Everything was created for a reason!" You reminded me that all of it is good, like You. But now, I wonder what is happening to the wonderful world You once created. I want so much to see it as You meant it to be. It's hard when I watch as the things You created for good are used for evil by greedy, manipulative people who don't respect Your laws or justice. Help me in each moment to use my words and actions and thoughts only for Your good, so I can rest in Your love and be at peace with You and with others. Today, help me to be in Your will. Help me to walk minute by minute with You. Put me in the right place at the right time. You gave us such a great gift—our minds—because you wanted so much for us to be able to communicate with You. And yet, many "do their own thing," apart from You. Now, we see the results in a cruel world that is very different from the one You made. Help us to turn back to You in our hearts and minds. I love You.

God: Dear one, I used My power and might—all that I am—to create all things for good. Because that is who and what I am. And the world I made for your benefit was perfect in its goodness when it was made. Though My purpose was for people to rule the earth with My help, living in a paradise and having dominion over it, they chose to hand this gift over to My arch enemy. And now, this adversary reigns over the earth, because he has the legal authority to do this. Having a choice between good and evil offers a proving ground for all people. And I can see who will come to Me and who will walk away. All must endure the tests of life, and you can lead them to a knowledge of My truth. You can help to open their eyes to what their choices mean both now and later. Many are ignorant. The time is now, and people need to understand. You can explain that the fractured world they live in will not last and that a new heaven and earth will come into existence later, after this world has passed away. Those who pass the test by coming to know who I am, many through a belief in the life and resurrection of My Son, will abide there. You can make this clear to them now. I love you.

As I'm surrounded by faithful friends

"There are 'friends' who destroy each other, but a real friend sticks closer than a brother."
—*Proverbs 18:24*

Me: Lord, You bring me certainty that things will always work out. When I feel stressed about circumstances, not knowing how they'll end up, I can always turn to You for reassurance. Thanks for Your hand in leading me and working things out. Today, give me needed time to accomplish all that's needed. Let everything be a blessing. You're awesome, Lord. You're kind, gentle, and the love of my life. You give me strength when I need it. Thanks for those You've placed in my path, for I look back and realize how often You had people there for me at the times I needed them. Thanks for committed friends who are a constant when life feels uncertain. Thanks for the many blessings You've lavished so freely on me, many through faithful friends. I think of all the wonderful ways You've poured out to me over the years. Everything I've asked for! Bless this day, as You've blessed so many others. Thanks for encouragement, especially from faith-filled friends. I love You.

God: Dear one, I love how you've found good friends who believe and embrace what you do. I love the fellowship of believers who encourage each other and build each other up in faith, so they can stand along with Me. I have always desired this. As times get tougher, you'll need more encouragement, and I'll provide this for you. Now, continue to pray, because I hear your prayers. Of course, I work on your behalf to help you and others to maintain the right to worship freely. I'll bring many together to stand for this right. And their voices will rise and unite against tyranny. The guise for power will always be for "safety," but the real issue is a lust for control and an excuse to maintain it. But I'll always take care of you. Never fear. I'll lead you where you need to go. I'll be with you to meet your needs. Every day's a gift from Me. But there will be days when you wonder how you can survive. You'll wonder how you can deal with stressful situations and angry, demanding, or unhappy people, who try to blame you for their problems. You'll sometimes feel pressured by family members. How can you handle this? By praying for yourself and for them. Come to Me with your concerns, and lay them before Me. I'll take care of you and them! I love you.

Who fight alongside me

"Fight the good fight for the true faith. Hold tightly to the eternal life to which God has called you, which you have declared so well before many witnesses."
—*1 Timothy 6:12*

Me: Lord, I think about 9-11 and how it changed so many lives. Unseen danger has always surrounded us, but the enemy has caused the world to become even more fear-filled, cynical, and bitter. We've always endured threats. Evil has always existed. But now, people are more ensnared in it and threatened by its looming presence because of the media. You're still the same God. You've always been near us, ready to protect and guide us. That's never changed. We must, as always, lean on Your protection, mercy, grace, and guidance. Would You help me to do this to a greater extent, Lord? When I see hateful people attacking Your believers, show me how to win spiritually. How can I demonstrate Your might and power amid this evil? Would You protect me and my family? How can I bring peace and hope and encouragement to others? Show me those with a desire to know You and learn from You. Reveal to me those who seek You with their whole heart. Give me what I need to fight and succeed. People are desperate for You. Help me don Your grace-filled armor now. I love You.

God: Dear one, loving Me alone is not an easy thing, because you're surrounded by so many false gods in this life. The adversary makes sure that you're distracted by other "priorities"—things the world deems as "all important." Then, your attention can be drawn far away from Me and all I represent. Soon hate replaces love in your heart, and your mind reflects what's bad or tainted, instead of what I made and how I blessed the earth immeasurably. I've always been close at hand and ready to guide and reassure anyone who comes to Me. I wish everyone understood how much I love them and want the best for them. I desire protection for My precious lambs, but they're often led into traps by the lures of the enemy, whose aim is to steal, kill, and destroy. My Son's purpose was to bring you abundant life (John 10:10). Remember, I'm always with you, so be aware of My surrounding presence. Know that, despite unbelief and cynicism, I'll guide and lead you. You're My light in this world, bringing hope to others. Focus today on the beauty of life and the grandeur of My creation. Then you'll see your attitude change from bitter to sweet, from anger to awe, and from hate to love. I love you.

AUGUST 29
Because we remember what was done

"Search me, O God, and know my heart; test me and know my anxious thoughts."
—*Psalm 139:23*

Me: Minister to me this morning, Lord, as only You can, so I can minister to others today. Open more doors, and help me to bless those I meet! I know this day will be a special day. I can feel it in my bones. Would You show me how, why, and what to say? Thanks for opening the Scriptures to me in new ways. Thanks for enlightening my eyes and revealing Your heart to me. Getting to know You more each day has been such a blessing, and I am so grateful! I feel as though I've grown so much closer to You over the years! And I've begun to understand Your heart and who You are. I see now how Your Son must have felt during His days here on earth. He cried and got angry at people's insensitivity and thoughtlessness. He fretted as I do, but He knew how to go to You for answers and insight. He spent many hours with You! Lord, show me how to make prayer time with You a bigger part of my life. Thanks for teaching me about following Your lead, about the differences between men and women, and how to not view others as my enemy. Because there's really only one. You teach me so much. Show me more today, because I want to overcome all odds, just like Your Son did! I love You.

God: Child, do you wonder what My heart is for you? I want you to overcome all fears, because I want you to be brave. I'm a fearless God, and I'll show you how to be courageous in every situation. Just trust Me and remember what I've already done for you. You see your purpose more and more and how I have you where I need you. You're an encourager, and people won't forget the hope you brought to them and the reminders of My love. Continue to seek My peace. Others need this desperately. Remember to thank and praise Me. Remember My love and how My Son gave His life for you. Recall the grace that surrounds you because of what He did. Remember the healing He accomplished for you through His bruises and wounds. Remember the peace you have because of what He endured. His fearlessness makes you courageous. I'm your Lord, and I have your back. My strengthening hand is on you even now. Think of My Son as you pray. Remember how much He loved you to do what He did for you so you can be brave. I love you.

Through Your love

"The LORD your God is in your midst, a mighty one who will save; he will rejoice over you with gladness; he will quiet you by his love; he will exult over you with loud singing."
—Zephaniah 3:17

Me: Lord, today I'm reflecting on Your love and the many things You've done to remind me that You're near. I remember a sign of encouragement You gave me years ago, when I lived far from family and friends in a small Michigan town. We'd moved there because of my husband's job, and I knew no one. I felt very alone and foreign as I sat in a restaurant on the outskirts of town. Then I glanced out the window and spotted an especially beautiful rainbow. It made me cry, because I knew You were assuring me that You hadn't forgotten about me. Shortly after this, I met Carole and her son Jason, and we became good friends. After I shared Your message of love with her, she committed her life to You. Your rainbow reminder had encouraged me to seek friendship and share Your hope during a time when I felt deserted. I will never forget it. Thanks for the daily reminders of Your presence and all the things You do to show how much You care for me. Today, remind me again of Your love! Inspire and show me what You're excited about. Open my eyes and ears to see and hear new ways to overcome any feelings of isolation. Make things clear to me so I can be directed to those who seek You. Open doors beyond anything I could ask or think. I love You.

God: Child, you see how I've always been with you. There are so many examples of times I tried to remind you of My presence. And I will continue to prompt You toward a constant awareness of Me. You're a light that can reflect My presence in the world. And My love shines from you to others who seek this same light. Like you, they yearn for it. Shine it out and don't be afraid to tell them from where it originates. Some want to hear your stories of My love reminders. Never be afraid to speak forthrightly and honestly about what I've done for you. The right memories and stories will be there for you. I'll continue to reveal things to you, but you must stop long enough to see and hear them. Then share about them with others! It's hard when there are so many distractions. But keep turning your thoughts to Me. Because I'm your ever-present help, especially in the places where you feel alone and abandoned. And I love you.

To finish what was started

"Go ahead and finish what your ancestors started."
—Matthew 23:32

Me: Lord, my heart yearns for more time to sit and talk to my grandfather. I would love to be able to hear his voice and ask him questions! There are so many things I wish I could understand about him now. He had vision and strength and wisdom beyond so many others. Lord, where did these come from? Did he know you? Did he tap into Your wisdom? Did he understand spiritual things or believe in Your power? He had many talents: husbandry, expertise in lapidary, metallurgic arts, chemical engineering, and knowledge about so many other things. Where did this ability come from? And what about his drive and determination? Lord, You alone give us understanding and ability. Little do we know or comprehend about You or the things You've made. Was Your hand in his life? Enlighten me, Lord, and show me why Your favor was on him. What was his greater purpose? I have so many questions, Lord, and a desire to understand. Help me to see things through Your eyes. I love You.

God: Dear one, you see how I can use a life for a greater purpose, even when the person may not realize that I'm doing this or know who I am. Your grandfather had a zeal, an understanding, and a capability beyond many others. This was innate in him, but I also had My hand on his heritage to bring about his life and then yours. He came for a purpose. I knew he would respond to his calling, which was to use his mind to create things that would help others and change lives. I always need able, capable men and women for this purpose. He might not have attributed his ability or success completely to Me, because he believed that people were mostly self-made. But he responded to My call, and he used his talents successfully and energetically for the betterment of many. That is more than many choose to do. Every day in a person's life is a day I've created for present-day goodness and for potential future glory. Every day is a day I've made to glorify My purpose. Seek My face today with all your might, then look for opportunities to tell others from where your power and ability come. I'll always steer your course by working with your skillset to create goodness and direct you down right paths to future glory. I love you.

September

FOCUS:
GRATIFYING GRACE

"So let us come boldly to the throne of our gracious God. There we will receive his mercy, and we will find grace to help us when we need it most."

—HEBREWS 4:16

Bring me a new song

"Sing a new song to the Lord! Let the whole earth sing to the Lord."
—*Psalm 96:1*

Me: Dear Lord, I know You're calling me to pray more intently for others. Would You show me who You want me to pray for? And stir up my heart so I can feel the love You have for them. Remind me when You want me to pray for those who show no signs of wanting to change and continue to turn away from You through rebellion or apathy or fear. Let me not be discouraged by their unwillingness to respond to You or to me. Show me how I can help You to build Your church. What can I do for You today? And what are You teaching and preparing me for? What's Your vision for me, Lord? Enlighten and give me what's needed to accomplish more for You. Today, give me greater clarity on the direction You wish me to take. Thanks for continuing to lead me and for not giving up on me! Help me to be more positive, kind, expectant, happy, and hopeful. Bring a new song to my heart—one of great grace and fulfillment. I love You.

God: Dear child, I'll make it all clear to you. And I'll give you the direction you need every day. I'll also give you peace and confidence as you lean on Me. Just remember that I do this moment by moment, step by step. Don't fret about past mistakes. I can heal anything that was broken and build bridges that might've been burned. I place you where you're needed, never where your efforts are fruitless. It's true that you can never force your way into peoples' lives. They must open the door to let you in. Or to let Me in. And they will when they're ready. I'll show you where your attempts and prayers will one day pay off and which people will listen to your words and value them, even though it may be at a later time. Through you, I can bring peace and comfort and joy to others. And, with your help, we'll build My church, which is My bride. Watch for this. Don't become frustrated. Trust in My timing. I'll show you where you can bring the most help and healing. I know you feel lacking—incapable when you don't see any results. But you must trust My lead. Remember My Word never returns void. Hold My hand. Accept My grace. Know I'm always with you. I love you.

SEPTEMBER 2
So I can be Your heart specialist

"When I am with those who are weak, I share their weakness, for I want to bring the weak to Christ. Yes, I try to find common ground with everyone, doing everything I can to save some. I do everything to spread the Good News and share in its blessings."
—*1 Corinthians 9:22-23*

Me: Lord, in a dream I visited a counseling clinic and walked past the registrar to wander down a hall to gaze at door plates. I noticed that each door led to individuals who were specialists in helping people. Back in the reception area, all the chairs were filled, so I stood waiting for a seat. I recognized a woman standing near me and said, "Hi," but she reacted angrily. "You weren't so friendly to me before when you disagreed with me." She referred to a time when our political views differed. Not wanting to appear put off by her, I said, "Yes, I voted for so and so! But I want to find common ground with you!" She sneered, but I pursued. "I want to stand with you in the place where we can be united!" She softened at this. Then I woke up. Lord, I know that Your heart is to bring reconciliation where there is none. Sometimes I feel at a loss when people I care about refuse to discuss solutions to problems, pursue answers, or find common ground. Show me how to approach them in a world so divided by opinions. How can I reach bitter ones who walk away? I love You.

God: Child, many people you encounter are seeking Me. They are angry because they're finding so many doors shut to them now that once were open. You can bring many of them to Me, especially when churches close their doors or don't deliver healing messages. People you see at work also seek your help, because they aren't finding what they need anywhere in the world, and they're tired of waiting and hoping for answers that can't be found. Don't get caught up in political debates, because, in the end, this isn't what's important. What truly matters is finding common ground with seekers. Look for the doors. I'll show them to you. Today, spend time listening for Me, and I'll reveal many connections. I'll bring people to you who want to hear your words. Never be offended by what they say, because they only spew what they've heard. I'll give you extraordinary ability to reach them, and show you how to be a "heart specialist" for each one I send. Hold onto My Son's robe because here we go with grace! I love you.

As I place my feet in Yours

"I am surrounded by people who love to argue and fight."
—*Habakkuk 1:3*

Me: Would You help me, Lord? Would You give me Your wisdom when I need it? For I seek it! I'm surrounded by people who speak against Your truths. Please replace their outrageous lies with Your evident reality! Would You envelop me with Your grace? I want to bask in Your kindness. Lift me up, high above them, where I can see Your grace-filled face! There, my mind can find rest and be delivered from the unrest! But while I walk on this earth among the naysayers, show me Your way and how I can walk in it. You remind me that when people attack me or You with their false opinions, they pay a price and suffer later. Those with good consciences and an awareness of others' needs are hit the hardest! The adversary loads them down with burdens of guilt, when they finally realize their error, to stymie their efforts. People who don't care aren't so badly affected, but they still suffer from ill effects, like poor health and economic consequences, though they may not understand why. Show me where to place my feet today so I can walk with You through the heavens, above the chaos and the clouds! I love You.

God: Dear one, I hear you. And I'll always help you fight your battles mentally, physically, and spiritually. Remember, My Son fought these same conflicts! When He lived on earth, He came against many negative thoughts and false sayings. Every day, some spoke against Him: who He was, what He said, and what He represented. And, each day, He still spoke what I told Him, and I reminded Him that He was My Son—the One whose purpose I'd always had in mind. It's the same for you. Each moment, listen for Me as I remind you of your purpose in this life. It's the same as for My Son: to give of your gifts to bring light and life, healing and hope to others. Remember that people who lack confidence in Me are surrounded by the negative influences of this world. Their minds are infiltrated by evil thoughts. You can lead them to My truth. It may take time to turn their minds around, but keep on trying. Remember, your fight is never against flesh and blood. Speak the positives I deliver to you without fear, and you'll see Me in the eyes of some who will come. As you bring My message of hope, I'll reveal Myself more and more to you and to them. I love you.

And see Your goodness in unseen things

"For the Lord God is our sun and our shield. He gives us grace and glory. The Lord will withhold no good thing from those who do what is right."
—*Psalm 84:11*

Me: Lord, I feel like I'm in a whirlwind! Would You place me in the middle of Your stillness, and surround me with Your restful presence? Would You help me to slow down enough to hear Your voice? Remind me of what's most important to You, and whisper what I need to hear and remember. Today, grant me peace, and situate me where You want me. I want to stand with You beneath Your lovely, shade-providing canopy, sheltered from overhanging troubles and covered by Your protective power. Thanks for the little things You do for me to remind me of Your love and constant care for me. Thanks for opening my eyes to how you work on my behalf and for so many others. You even bless those who don't know You. Would You remind me that the things that seem so important and pressing really don't matter? It's the things I can't see that are most important. My future doesn't lie in what people say or how they view me, but in Your promises of a new life. And what lies ahead is beyond anything I could ask or think. Thanks for another awesome day, filled with Your mercy and abundance. Help me to be able to minister to those to whom I am led. May I express Your grace and show this in a greater way. I love You.

God: Dear one, I am ever beside you, speaking to you with My tender words of love. I appreciate you as no other person could, and I am jealous for your love. I am blessed by our conversations and your entreaties. I work continuously to move you in the right direction by steering your time and efforts toward ultimate good. I will confirm My love for you today. Look for My grace in little and in big things. Turn your ear to Me, and let Me whisper in it. You'll see a confirmation of My protective canopy and evidence of My presence through the good things that come to you, the sights you see, and the relationships you have with people who come to you. You'll hear My message to you reiterated in a thousand different ways—through teachings, readings, sharings, conversations, even in nature. I am everywhere—in your mind, in your work, in others who speak good things to you. Listen and learn from Me. I am a God of great grace. I love you.

Especially through my family

"Understand, therefore, that the Lord your God is indeed God. He is the faithful God who keeps his covenant for a thousand generations and lavishes his unfailing love on those who love him and obey his commands."
—*Deuteronomy 7:9*

Me: Lord, thanks for precious time with children and grandchildren. Thanks for fulfilling a promise You made to me many years ago in a dream—that I would have children. Thanks for these ones so dear to my heart! Keep them safe in Your arms, Lord. Teach them as You've taught me. Would You show them how wonderful and powerful You are and how You can meet their every need? Would You fight for them, Lord, as You've fought for me? Thanks for choosing me and for blessing them in Your own great way. I love You.

God: Dear one, place your children and grandchildren (whether physical or spiritual ones) into My hands every day. Then, I can reach into their hearts in ways beyond your comprehension! And you'll see signs, miracles, and wonders through their lives. The reason I made mankind is simple—I wanted a family to love, just as you did. And I wanted to be able to pour out My blessings on them because of My love. I wanted to cover with kindness those who belonged to Me and I to them. I've given many gifts, but you won't see all these blessings until you see Me and who I am. When you understand how I fit into your life, and you into My purposes for you, then you'll recognize what I've done for you. Remember, My main purpose was always to embrace you as My child. Your children and grandchildren are blessed, because you trust in Me. I'm forever, and I will always remember you and the children who come after you. They are with Me in My thoughts and in My arms, and I look after them. Don't fear that when you're gone, they might be forsaken. That will never happen. They are always with Me. Continue to trust. Continue to lean on My Word. Walk with Me in your thoughts and deeds. Know you are blessed by Me, as are your children and grandchildren. I smile down on you, blanketing you with My love and light. I warm your soul with lovingkindness. Relax in Me, knowing that, because I am a gracious God, I squeeze your hand tightly to express My love for you. I do this for your children and grandchildren too. Because I love you and them.

September 6
As I celebrate Your glorious grace

"So we praise God for the glorious grace he has poured out on us who belong to his dear Son."
—*Ephesians 1:6*

Me: Lord, today You showed me something when I read about Hannah (whose name means "grace" or "divine favor") in the book of 1st Samuel. Her husband loved her deeply, but his other wife, Penninah, made fun of her because she had no children. Just as Hannah experienced abuse, I've sometimes suffered at the hands of other women. But You, as a good friend, loved and encouraged me more than I could ask or think. During hard times, You especially blessed my work, my family, and my life. Through sadness, You took me deeper, just like Hannah. Out of ashes came joy, love, hope, abundance, beauty, and understanding. You answered my prayers just as You did hers with amazing miracles. Thanks for reminding me of this. Today, help me to see things even more clearly, so I can look more and more to You. Remind me to be thankful for what You've done, especially when I experience pain. Help me to see the things I could never see on my own. For You're a God of grace. You bless me mightily as You work all things for good. Thanks for Your blessings that are too numerous to count! I love You.

God: Child, how I love you! You truly are the apple of My eye. Today, great grace will abound as I lead you forward, even through hard times, when you're tempted to feel despair. Remember Me as you go about your business. Sing praises, be thankful, and turn your heart to Me. Remember what I've done for you and what I've called you to do. Many still need to hear and see My power in their lives. Let Me work through you to bring them a new message, which is really an old message, but new to them. Deliverance is right around the corner. As I've brought it to you, I can bring it to them. Many will seek you out and bless your life because of My favor on you. Never be saddened by those who don't appreciate you or what you can do for them. They're only disappointed in themselves. Like Penninah, they're sad, because they feel unloved or undeserving of love, never having experienced My tenderness. Show them who I am by seeking My face of grace today. I love you.

When You show me how You did it

"For this is how God loved the world: He gave his one and only Son, so that everyone who believes in him will not perish but have eternal life."
—John 3:16

Me: God, I just don't know how You did it, but I'm grateful for Your extremely gracious sacrificial gift. I'm amazed at Your courage and strength to allow Your Son to die the way He did. How did You do this? I admire how Jesus withstood the temptation to defend Himself and fight back, and how he allowed evil men to mistreat Him. He could only do these things because He trusted in You. Help me to trust You the way He did and to seek You in all I do. I want to submit to You in all my decisions in the same way that Jesus Himself came to You in each situation. Continue to guide me. And disclose to me Your thoughts. I long to hear Your words of encouragement. Thanks for all You do for me. You're my strength and my sufficiency. Without You, I'd be nothing. Please work through me to complete the best plan for my life. I love You.

God: Dear one, you know I had to stand aside and watch as My Son hung on the cross. Of course, I wanted to intervene to prevent His death. It was extremely painful for Me to see Him suffer and not reach out to relieve the suffering. If this was hard for Me, can you understand why it might be difficult for you to watch a family member suffer and die? I didn't want to, but I had to allow His horrific death. I made clear to Him what He must do, and He knew the purpose for His life and death. He understood that He was the final sacrifice. His gift was traumatic for Him and for Me. But, because He was willing to give His life, you don't need to offer another sacrifice to please Me. Many still don't understand this. They torture themselves and think they must suffer to be acceptable to Me. They believe that this is the only way to receive My love and forgiveness. And some run to other gods for the fulfillment that only I can give them through My Son. Look at the terrorists who willingly sacrifice their lives, because they think their self-immolation pleases their god, who might grant them salvation as a result. But even their offering is not good enough to pay the price and bring them before My throne. It's only through acceptance of My Son and the sacrifice of His blood that anyone can ever be worthy enough to stand before Me and receive My gracious prize—eternal life. I love you.

Using threads of a tapestry

"I want them to be encouraged and knit together by strong ties of love. I want them to have complete confidence that they understand God's mysterious plan, which is Christ himself. In him lie hidden all the treasures of wisdom and knowledge."
—*Colossians 2:2-3*

Me: Lord, I saw a glimmer of hope yesterday. A person turned to me for help, and I was able to see into her heart and minister to her need. I was in the right place at the right time. And I realize that no decision I make is ever made in isolation. Everything we do affects many lives like the threads in a tapestry. Help me to make right choices today that help those around me. Guide me in all I do so I can positively affect everyone I encounter. Because I want to see Your grace in a greater way. When I was in Amman, Jordan, I visited a women's cooperative, where hijab-covered ladies created things to sell and support themselves. When I asked someone to take a picture of me with them, the woman on one side of me grasped my hand and the woman on the other side embraced my waist. I was touched by their love. No one needed to preach to them about acceptance. It just happened. I realized then that my main mode of outreach must be through actions of love that show Your great heart for all people. And how You yearn for their love. I am realizing that it's often the least-likely people who show love to others most readily. Lord, touch me so I can refrain from religiosity and rules and rigidity and be able to give more freely by extending Your amazing and embracing hand of love to them. I love You.

God: Dear one, each person is special to Me. And each one has a unique place in My tapestry. See today as a new day, full of promise and hope. See it as a new opportunity to see Me working in your life and in the lives of others. Expect a miracle. Trust Me that I can do this. Through My great grace, I will bring many positive things to pass for you. Expect this. Today, you'll see mighty works. Only trust and believe for them. Because I'm all-encompassing. I bring hope and peace and joy. Continue to lean on My guidance as you traipse along My path, for it will lead you to amazing blessings through the least-likely people. I'll guide you as your chief shepherd. My staff is held out to you. Grasp it, and let Me lead you. No decision is made in isolation. Like the entwining threads in My tapestry, your choices affect many people—more than you'll ever know. I love you.

Never hooked by complacency

"For you have been called to live in freedom, my brothers and sisters. But don't use your freedom to satisfy your sinful nature. Instead, use your freedom to serve one another in love."
—Galatians 5:13

Me: Dear Lord, as I sat in bed reading, I noticed my dog Barney was laying very still by his toy basket. His chest barely moved, and I wondered if he was breathing. I called his name, but he didn't respond. I went to see if he was sleeping. When he didn't react to my touch, I grew alarmed. Then I noticed his tags were hooked onto the basket so he couldn't move. As I released him, I remembered that when he was a puppy his collar caught on a basket, and he was so frightened that he ran around the house yelping. The basket was still attached to him and swung back and forth as he ran, until I could catch and unhook him. Afterward, he ran around the house letting everyone know how upset he was. This time, he just lay still and unresponsive until I noticed and rescued him. We're like this, aren't we? When we're little, we make sure people know that something's amiss. But when we're older, we grow accustomed to things being askew, so we passively wait for someone to notice and make things right, so we don't feel stuck. Lord, remind me to use what You've given me and never become complacent or passive. Help me put my best feet forward so I can help others find release from the traps they find themselves in. Let me never be discouraged from my calling by mistakes I've made. Show me how obstacles can be turned into God-opportunities! I love You.

God: Dear child, your life is in My hands. I've given you eyes to see and ears to hear. Use them for My benefit. By grace, I'll help you to carry a beautiful breadbasket filled with My bread of life—My Word—to feed those who are hungering for an understanding of Me and My Son. Be My special-server, and I'll surround you with a sweet-smelling aroma (imagine the fragrance of fresh-baked bread!) that draws them to you and what you carry. Let Me help you in this moment by moment walk through the world. For it can be hard and strenuous and painful at times. Sometimes it's a struggle to get "unhooked." But you must stay flexible and free, because there are more things to do. Just let Me know when you're ready, and I'll lead you to places where you can bless many others. Just trust Me and don't be afraid of going where I take you! I love you.

But with bravery and courage

"This is my command—be strong and courageous! Do not be afraid or discouraged. For the Lord your God is with you wherever you go."
—Joshua 1:9

Me: Lord, I often think of the story of the good Samaritan. I'm especially reminded of him when I see those most capable of helping and doing things for others step aside, while often the least likely people take the reins and come through in times of trouble or necessity. When I see this happen, it makes me sad and a little angry. I feel affronted when competent people sit by with excuses for not helping! My peace and joy seem to evaporate in the fomented steam of "injustice." I think, "What's wrong with them?" And I look around for the helpers, as Mr. Rogers once referred to them—the people who show up when everyone else flees the scene. And I feel like I can only depend on You to come through for me, especially when I see fewer and fewer people willing to step forward. I am so frustrated by the lack of desire to help. Would You show me, Lord, how to be Your warrior? Would You give me the needed fearlessness to fight like David, when others are too afraid or complacent to stand up for Your people? Show me how to deal with faint-hearted people, who aren't willing to do their part. I need Your help. I need Your grace! Thanks! I love You.

God: Dear one, My grace is always sufficient for you. Remember, you have access to something others may not be able to pull from. Through your spirit, you can reach supernatural levels of peace and courage, no matter what the situation requires or who else is willing or unwilling to step forward. In the trying times, when you feel alone in your efforts, remember to do these things: Renew your mind by putting on My thoughts. Replenish your peace by tapping into the spirit in you. Restore your strength by centering your actions on what you know to be true. Rejuvenate your joy by rejoicing in your fellowship with Me and those who enjoy My company. Reactivate your courage by watching as I bring the right people to help when needed. Remember, to those who are faithful, I am faithful. To those who bless, I give more blessings. To those who act fearlessly out of love, I give tenacious and lasting intrepidity. People sometimes think that what they do makes no real difference. Little do they know. Rely on Me for needed fearlessness when the moment requires a heart that is brave. And your strength will lead others to be more courageous. I love you.

By relying on You

"And the Father who knows all hearts knows what the Spirit is saying, for the Spirit pleads for us believers in harmony with God's own will."
—*Romans 8:27*

Me: Lord, You know my likes and dislikes, and You love me no matter what! You know I love to arrange things so they are pleasing to the sight. I enjoy flowers and colors and magnificent views. Symmetry and some music appeal to me, especially if they aren't chaotic. I appreciate wine and cheese, fresh bread, popcorn, and coffee. I love to travel and see places I've never experienced, where I can meet unusual people. I love birds, turquoise lakes, oceans, and ships. And to walk along white-sanded beaches searching for shells and watching the small crabs make holes in the sand. I love the sound of the sea—how the waves lap on the shore. I enjoy watching dolphins and seeing sails in the distance. I love forests of fragrant pine trees with hidden paths to quaint log cabins or chapels. And walking on cool mornings before the sun rises, when the grass is still dewy and the birds chirp and the raccoons rush to hide after their night escapades. I love to hear the owl early in the morning or to see deer stealthily traipsing near a trail. Spotting the blue heron on the lake as he gazes into the water near the shore brings me delight. And the mother ducks escorting their ducklings down a bank to the water. You know I love these things, and You love me for it. Thanks for Your acceptance of me and my dreams. Thanks for working with me to see my aspirations fulfilled. Show me Yours and how I can help You fulfill them! I love You.

God: Dear one, I see your dreams and I always work with you to see them fulfilled. My dreams work in conjunction with yours. My heart's desire is fulfilled as I work to will and to do of My good pleasure in you. Don't you see that it pleases Me when you're happy and fulfilled and all your needs are met? Wouldn't any father want this for his son or his daughter? My ways are mysterious in that, as I bring to pass what will bless you in your life, My own will is fulfilled. I create aspirations in you and, as you succeed in attaining them, My own longings are satisfied. My joy is in seeing your heart's desires being met. I love you.

SEPTEMBER 12
To direct my sails

"You can make many plans, but the Lord's purpose will prevail."
—Proverbs 19:21

Me: Lord, thanks for how You so obviously direct me to walk in Your steps that are set out before me! While traveling in the Cotswolds, England, my husband and I waited in a bar next to the hotel reception area to be checked into our room. It was taking far longer than we anticipated, so we sat at a table biding our time and trying to be patient. We were alone except for a waiter named Johann, who came over to talk to us. He was from Sri Lanka and told us how he'd ended up in Chipping Campden. He mentioned something about God, and I asked him if he believed in You. His answer was yes, and he admitted to being a Christian, though his wife is a Buddhist. He told us how he listens to the Bible on audiotape every day on his drive to work and that his hope was that his wife would believe one day too. "Have you found a church here?" I asked. "No, none I feel comfortable in," he admitted. We prayed together for that opportunity and that he'd find some other believers in his area. When we left, we felt like we'd made a dear friend. Lord, I love how you lead us unexpectedly to people who need Your assurance of love. How awesome You are! Bless people like Johann who are searching for fellow believers to encourage them. I love You.

God: Dear one, you see how I open doors when you make yourself available! I show you what to ask and how to say it. Your life is an amazing adventure when you're open to the spirit that leads you. You may have one thing in mind, yet sometimes you're thrown a curveball. But then, that interruption turns out to be an opportunity for Me to work through you! Always be flexible to allow Me to guide you. Don't be so wrapped up in your own ideas that you don't allow room for Me to work. I'm never a God of confusion or chaos. But I may direct you in ways "outside the box" or apart from your plans. Sometimes you'll take a detour, and that's ok. Don't be frustrated when I show you a different way. Trust Me at these times and don't be afraid to deviate from your course. Remember, My way is always a way of blessing. It brings good results! It's like sailing. Sometimes you must switch gears, turn the sail, and get off your course a bit so you can head in the right direction. You do this to take advantage of good winds, or to avoid storms. Picture yourself in a sailboat with Me sitting at the helm, while you enjoy the view. Just let Me steer the boat. I love you.

Into deeper levels of the soul

*"He reveals deep and mysterious things and knows what lies hidden in darkness,
though he is surrounded by light."*
—Daniel 2:22

Me: Lord, You showed me recently why people won't go deeper with You when
I asked what prevented so many from seeking Your answers. You showed me the
"levels of the soul" inside of people. While some choose to live in the "shallow
layers," where the breath of life is superficial, others are willing to "go deeper." The
ones who're afraid to go to new levels may've seen others commit themselves to You
and then lose their lives or suffer. So, they're afraid that if they go to these depths,
it'll demand more of them than they can give. They see You as a demanding God,
and they're unwilling to relinquish what they think You might require of them.
Because they can't see what lies waiting for them at these depths, they're afraid to
try. They might have to give up too much of themselves to reach it! So, they refuse
to draw enough deep "breaths" to experience true life! It's like choosing not to love
anyone, because this might result in pain. Lord, help them! And me, as I try to go
deeper with You. I love You.

God: Dear one, remember, Jesus didn't ask everyone to follow Him. How did He
choose His disciples? He looked at their hearts. Even in the womb, I can see the
propensity of an individual. I can tell who'll want to come and who won't. The
adversary also can see this to some extent, and he tries to target the ones he thinks
might believe. But, I send angels to help individuals with a willingness until they
can come to Me. Those I keep calling are those I know will respond. Jesus didn't
call all people, because that would've been fruitless. He knew who'd come. When
people want to stay where they are—in unbelief and pain—you can't move them.
Even when I tell you to speak, some will resist what you say. Their response is not
your responsibility. It's Mine. Some people's hearts are hardened. I keep giving
them chances, but they still refuse to acknowledge Me. You can chip away at their
hardness to reach the softer parts of their soul, but this may be too painful for them.
You remind them of their weaknesses, which they want to hide. Don't be surprised
by outbursts. These are signs that you're penetrating their protective shells. Don't
take it personally. You haven't done anything wrong. Keep trying. I love you.

As I deal with angry people

"We are human, but we don't wage war as humans do. We use God's mighty weapons, not worldly weapons, to knock down the strongholds of human reasoning and to destroy false arguments."
—*2 Corinthians 10:3-4*

Me: Lord, help me to get past this flesh that cries out and gets offended. Forgive my exasperation at times. I'm beginning to realize that when people react to me with anger, it's because I've uncovered a "strong man" or "stronghold" that lurks within. Instead of taking their reaction personally, I need to find out what's bothering them and offer help, if You give me the go ahead. Help me to remember this, Lord. I've been confronted so many times by angry people. And often, I've allowed their explosions to crush me or cause me to stop in my tracks. This reminds me of how lions roar to freeze their prey. Alert me so I can deal as You would with these outbursts. Help me to see clearly what's driving this rage. Help me to see through to the "strong man," who's throwing a fit and demanding a reaction! Thanks for how you lead me and protect my heart. Thanks for Your mercy and wonderful grace. Thanks for Your many blessings, which You've showered on me. You've answered so many of my prayers and given me more than I could ever imagine. You listen when I come to You with my requests, and I will continuously praise Your name! I love You.

God: Dear one, you're my "weathergirl," because you can bring sweet rains of faith and trust to disperse the clouds of doubt and fear. I will provide you with the tools you need so that you're always ready with a response to any "strong man" you face. Trust Me to clothe you with the proper gear—My armor—so you're always prepared for even the stormiest situations. I'm working on your behalf even now to bring you wonderful and eager people who want to hear My message of hope. Be ready to speak, for Mine will always be a wonderful report of deliverance, healing, peace, and grace. Be bold as a lion to speak it, just as Paul spoke fearlessly in every city where he traveled. Never be afraid of the consequences. Remember, I have your back. I'm your rock, your fortress, your refuge, your guide, and your savior. So, have courage! I love you.

While birthing new ones

"For you have been born again, but not to a life that will quickly end. Your new life will last forever because it comes from the eternal, living word of God."
—*1 Peter 1:23*

Me: Lord, I saw a video recently of a man who found a parakeet egg at the bottom of a bird cage in a pet store. The mother had laid the egg before being sold and only the father parakeet remained in the cage. The man asked the owner if he could have the egg. "Sure!" The owner was happy for him to have it. The man took it home and spent countless hours making sure the egg was kept warm under special lights. He watched it day and night until it showed signs of hatching and patiently documented the slow, purposeful process as the tiny, vulnerable baby parakeet emerged, peck by peck, from the shell. Then the work began. He made a feeding solution and fed it to the baby drop by drop. He made sure to stick with a schedule so the bird could survive. The little parakeet lived and thrived and, when it was time, the man went back to the shop and purchased the father parakeet. He wanted his baby to know its dad. He created a parakeet sanctuary in his home and watched enthusiastically as the two "buddies" celebrated the space together. Lord, help me to partner with You to "birth" new ones for you—orphans who are looking for a place where they can survive and flourish. I want to bring them to Your home, where they can be nurtured by the One who cares for them—the father they need! Show me who I can birth for You! Because I love You.

God: Dear one, I've called you to intercede for others—to pray in ways others can't. I'll bring faces to you in the night and wake you at times to show you people I want you to intercede for. You're My intercessor, My prayer warrior, and I can give you supernatural strength to compensate for any lacks or missteps along the way. I see you as a mother hen hovering over her eggs, preparing them to hatch—to be delivered from their shells of bondage by hatching into a new life with Me. I'll bring you into a new season of superior levels of faith and deliverance as you are directed by My love, one step at a time. You're watching an awakening in the culture of your nation and starting to see so many yearn for a return to "normalcy." They seek kindness, love, truth, and a certain belief. Many hunger for peace, which can only come from Me. I'll show you what to do each step of the way. Today, take My hand and follow My lead. I love you.

And I turn to You, my miracle worker

"And I will ask the Father, and he will give you another Advocate, who will never leave you. He is the Holy Spirit, who leads into all truth."
—John 14:16-17

Me: You, Lord, are my miracle worker! You give me peace when there is none. You give me hope when I feel undone. You give me love when people are nowhere to be found. You give me joy when sadness surrounds me. Would You enlighten me as to what's really going on inside the people I encounter, and give me the right words to say to them? I lay before You all my fears. Forgive me for my unforgiveness, impatience, and judgment at times. So many people seem complacent with a low-paying job, a few old clothes, a cell phone, a basement or tiny apartment to live in, and some acceptance by a few "friends." If they have what they need to exist without spending too much effort, they're willing to stay in their "life-rut," like a mouse in a cage that runs around on a wheel and looks out at the world without experiencing it! More meaningful things don't really interest them. But a few do search for something deeper. They see that true rest and peace can never be attained in this world. As much as they seek meaning from things or people, they come up short. And so, they look beyond their lives to find what they feel they lack. They seek a rest. And sometimes they find it. I finally have. I love You.

God: Dear one, I've sent you a wonderful counselor in the form of the Holy Spirit, which you received when you believed in My Son. He's magnificent because of the wondrous things he can do for and through you. When you trust Me with your whole heart, you'll see signs and wonders in your own life and in the lives of others. My light grows brighter as you trust in Me. My power can emanate from your every pore, sometimes in the form of miracles or miraculous deeds. This is because My Spirit can freely work in and through you to bring forth what I desire—good and marvelous things. This includes healings, financial abundance to bless others, people drawing closer to Me, and many other supernatural deeds. There's no limit to what I can do when you trust Me with your whole heart! As you receive and give by allowing My Spirit to work through you, I'll pour out more. So much so that people will see what's available and want what you're manifesting. And you'll see even more of My miracles! All because you were willing to receive first then give. I love you.

SEPTEMBER 17

To know if they are strangers or angels

"Don't forget to show hospitality to strangers, for some who have done this have entertained angels without realizing it!"
—*Hebrews 13:2*

Me: Dear Lord, today, allow me to fall into Your arms and experience a piece of eternity as I recall the visions You've given me of how the world will look one day. I long to sit with You and look out at Your beautiful view of the new earth You've prepared for us. I want to see vistas filled with water and color and life in lovely landscapes—all while enjoying Your presence. I want to ask You many questions about what You did, how You did it, and why You did it, then hear Your voice as You explain it all! I long to fly with You over mountains and lakes and oceans and forests and fjords and waterfalls and canyons and sigh at the sights in Your new world. You're my love and my light, and I long for You. Would You help me now to go beyond anything I can imagine and achieve new heights with and for You? All for Your glory! You're my Lord, my redeemer, my strength, and my help in times of trouble. Be with me, Lord, and bless me with Your favor as I entertain strangers. You know how much I've always wanted to see an angel! May I always put You first in all I do and remember what You've done for me. For You're always righteous. I love You.

God: Dear child, what do I have for you today and for eternity? Always good things. Watch and see how I work for You. See things emerge that you've never seen before. Be surprised by My power and strength as I work to will and to do of My good pleasure in and through you. As You see My good things in your life, remember to give thanks and praise, for, as you do this, I can bless you even more and exceed anything you've asked for or thought about! But you must remember to praise continuously. For this is how you enter My place of grace. I've heard your prayers and I always work on your behalf. I'll bring you many new people to bless—a string of them to lead to heaven. Listen for My instructions, and bless those I bring to you, as I've blessed you. Many will be "strangers" you can entertain! And some may even be angels unannounced. I love you.

SEPTEMBER 18
Because I'm enraptured by Your love

"Let all that I am praise the Lord; with my whole heart, I will praise his holy name...may I never forget the good things he does for me. He forgives all my sins and heals all my diseases. He redeems me from death and crowns me with love and tender mercies. He fills my life with good things. My youth is renewed like the eagle's!"
—Psalm 103:1-5

Me: Dear Lord, I praise You for Your many blessings and I'll never forget all Your benefits! You remind me of how You made all things beautiful for the ones You knew would come. You pursued them through Your love and gave them wonderful gifts to show Your pleasure in them. This was your heart. Not all believed or responded to Your love, but You always were thrilled with those who did come. These are those who turn and see You for who You are and are captivated, not just by Your gifts and what You've made, but by Your beauty. Your amazing love gives me courage in times of stress and strength in times of weakness. You alone can guide me to what I need when I lack understanding and ability. You alone support me. I will endeavor to remember to turn my thoughts to You, and to seek Your face. May I always be enthralled with Your beauty and enraptured by Your love. Let me see more of You as I go about my day today. I love You.

God: Dear one, I've spared your life and given you great grace. I've held you up when you were falling. I've kept you from harm in so many situations when you were least aware of it. Look to Me for support and healing, for I will bring them to you. Remember how Moses was the meekest man on earth? That's My desire for you! I want you to say "yes" no matter what I ask of you! I want you to rely on Me for everything. Because I always have your best interest at heart. It took many years for Moses to become the man I needed him to be. It'll take time for you too. Be patient with yourself and with Me. I'll give you little "checks" in your spirit. These are My reminders so you can grow into a closer walk with Me. Don't fear what lies ahead. Just trust what I tell you. You have nothing to fear. I'll show you My face more and more. And you will see many signs, miracles, and wonders. Prepare yourself for things unlike anything you've ever seen or heard. My words will be there for you. Only listen. Prepare yourself for great things to come. Today. Now. I love you.

Inside Your covered crevice

"As my glorious presence passes by, I will hide you in the crevice of the rock and cover you with my hand until I have passed by."
—Exodus 33:22

Me: Lord, would You heal my heart from hurt and help me to forgive? Would You show me that hidden crevice in a rock next to You, like You did for Moses, where I can hide from all pain and be closer to You? Would You lead me to that place today where I can see Your face and know You're near and feel protected and encouraged? Shield and deliver me from my own suffering—the wounds caused by people's neglect, carelessness, pride, hate, selfishness, anger, or pain. Guard my heart from those who are used by the adversary to steal, kill, and destroy. Strengthen me as I grow older, and give me continual freshness and newness of life. Free me from anguish as I sit next to You in Your cleft of the mountain. Thanks for Your grace and peace and mercy, and for those, like You, who encourage my soul. I love You.

God: Dear one, continue to seek Me, and I will reveal Myself more and more to you. I will bring you wonderful friends as time goes by—people who will be a great blessing to your life. Watch for them. They will be there when you least expect them. They will bring you comfort, peace, and great joy. Some will be angels. I will show you who these are. And they will be for you like the cleft in the rock you seek, where you are freed from past hurt and can learn forgiveness. Life may be hard at times, but I will help you to endure, and I will prepare you for the gut-wrenching times. Lean on Me for comfort and consolation. I will always be there for you. Remember, I am always near you, although you can't see or taste or touch or feel Me. I'm beside you in the cleft of life's mountain. Continue to seek My will, and I'll open doors beyond your imagination. I'll make clear the direction you need to go, so you won't fall into a pit. I'll lead you further up the mountain when it's the right time, and I'll lead you down the mountain when you're needed among the people. With Me, you'll always have peace, whether inside the crevice or as you walk along the mountain path. Because I am a God of grace. I love you.

Where I have a new view

"As the deer pants for water, so I long for you, O God. I thirst for God, the living God. Where can I find him to come and stand before him? Day and night I weep for his help, and all the while my enemies taunt me. "Where is this God of yours?" they scoff."
—Psalm 42:1-3

Me: Lord, I'm trying. You know that. I'm not perfect, but I'm trying. Can I have grace in Your eyes *and* in the eyes of others? I'm frustrated when I try so hard to bless others who don't give back. I've learned to look for kindness elsewhere. But when it's relatives, and I want to maintain a relationship with them, it's hard. They seem to live in a different world, where they expect people to give to them but don't need to reciprocate. They don't see things the same way I do. I seek Your viewpoint. If I need to take another tactic, show me. Yesterday, I saw a white-tailed deer as I walked. He sprang up a hill and watched me curiously from a distance. As I gazed across the street at him, it was like viewing someone in another world, "on the other side." He was a creature unlike me, who thought and felt differently and had a dissimilar perspective. I'm sure it's like that for angels and for You as You view us from another angle and wonder why we do such odd things. Oh, that I could see You like I saw the deer and watch Your eyes as You watch me, and be able to see things, especially people, from Your point of view! I love You.

God: Dear one, although I can see things from a very different perspective from how you view things, I can still work out for good all that you do. And I reward your efforts that are motivated by love. This includes your kind actions that may not be recognized or reciprocated by others. You may not see My rewards in your lifetime, but you will one day, when you stand before My Son. He will acknowledge and reward all that you've done from a spirit-filled heart. Though we're different—you being flesh and Me being spirit—I have the power to work in and through you because of the spirit that resides in you since you believed in My Son. Through this spirit, you can see as I see and tap into My spiritual insight. I can show you a different perspective of things and what is really driving the people who surround you. I can give you the right words to speak so you can still maintain peace, both in your own heart and with them. Embrace this spiritual ability, for it will provide you with a new view of everything—one that is beyond this world. I love you.

SEPTEMBER 21
Away from betrayal

"Even your brothers, members of your own family, have turned against you. They plot and raise complaints against you. Do not trust them, no matter how pleasantly they speak."
—Jeremiah 12:6

Me: Lord, there are times when I've felt betrayed by those closest to me. I remember when I was 10, and I went with my mother to see her friend. She asked about my day, and I ventured to tell her a very personal secret—that I liked a boy in my class. I wanted so much to believe that she was my most trusted confidante. But, when we arrived at her friend's, she winked and blurted out that I had a boyfriend. I was devastated. She'd openly and willingly betrayed my confidence and disclosed what was more important to her—to be "in the know" with her friends. From that point on, I never shared my most personal secrets with her. I eventually forgave her, but any trust was broken. I've felt this way with other relatives and a few friends. Those who wish to be admired by people they want to impress and are willing to belittle even those close to them so they look smart in others' eyes, quickly lose my trust. I wonder if they're aware that their betrayals are hurtful and destructive to themselves? Though I want to develop good relationships, I must also be able to trust before I allow myself to get too close to people. I know this about myself. I think about Moses and how his own siblings spoke evil against him! The result for them was devastating, because You won't put up with the mistreatment and slander of those You love. How can I best deal with people who are willing to betray me? Enlighten me on how to manifest Your amazing grace. I love You.

God: Dear one, yes, even My Son experienced betrayal by His family. Remember when He sat teaching His disciples and someone said, "Your mother and brothers are outside asking for you?" He knew they didn't trust Him to fulfill the ministry I'd called Him to. They just didn't understand what He was doing. Remember when, at 12, He stayed behind to discuss matters with the teachers in Jerusalem? He was a bit baffled that His own parents didn't understand His purpose. He was perplexed by their blindness. But, He also grew to understand that they just couldn't see what He saw. They were oblivious to the spiritual world and what was taking place. They could only see what was happening around them, just as your family members or friends are sometimes "blind-sided" and think that other things are more important than spiritual matters. Don't blame them. He didn't. He understood their failings. I love you.

SEPTEMBER 22
As You give me what's needed

"God himself has prepared us for this, and as a guarantee he has given us his Holy Spirit. So we are always confident, even though we know that as long as we live in these bodies we are not at home with the Lord. For we live by believing and not by seeing."
—2 Corinthians 5:5-7

Me: It's so wonderful, Lord, to see my prayers come to pass and to watch Your strong, powerful, and grace-filled hand in my life, as You work together all things for good. Thanks today for my many blessings and for the things You've so generously given to me. Thanks for my home, my family, my friends, and for the love I share with them. Thanks for answering my prayers. What are You preparing me for now? Would You tell me? What is Your vision for me, Lord? Please enlighten me, and give me what's needed to accomplish Your dreams for me. Today, allow me greater clarity on the direction You wish me to take. And if it's time to move on from my current situation to something new and different, please make it clear! Life is so meaningless when You aren't a part of it. I am thankful that You are! You've given me everything I have. I love You.

God: Dear one, I long to see your desires fulfilled and your prayers answered. I'm with you each day, even during your struggles, and I work to bring you more than what you need to overcome in every situation. Be patient. I *will* bring you your heart's desires. Keep looking to Me for the answers, for through Me you'll find them. Now, during this preparation time, I'll make you ready for the next stage and for life beyond this one. There are experiences and people you'll encounter as I unfold My plan to you. Trust Me in this. As time goes on, you'll see more disclosed, and all will become clearer. Today, sit with Me and let Me give you peace and understanding. You'll gain greater confidence to face each new stage. Don't fret about the past. I've healed the things that were broken and built new bridges for you to traverse. I'll place you where you're needed. Remember, you'll never need to force your way into any God-appointed situation. By My grace, I'll reveal where you're wanted—the places where people value what you have to offer. Through you, I'll bring peace and comfort and joy to many. I'll show you where you can best bring healing. Expect this! Remember, I make up for your weaknesses. With Me, you can accomplish what I lead you to do. Just trust My leading. I love you.

For grace and patience

"When the disciples saw him walking on the water, they were terrified. In their fear, they cried out, 'It's a ghost!' But Jesus spoke to them at once. 'Don't be afraid,' he said. 'Take courage. I am here!'"
—Matthew 14:26-27

Me: Lord, today I pray for patience, grace, and a greater ability to act without screaming in frustration. Sometimes I feel like grabbing my head and running away, because I'm not sure if I have the patience to deal with broken people. Would You please give me wisdom and courage and greater confidence? Lord, I feel angry sometimes when people won't step up to help carry the burdens. I can't do it all myself, and I need Your help in this. I know You implied that whenever our stalls are full, we'll have messes to clean up (Proverbs 14:4). Would You give me the strength to clean up the messes left by people? Today, bring peace to my work. Train me so I can better train others. Thanks for Your patience with me so I can be patient with others. I just don't understand why some don't ever seem to get it or see what's right in front of them. Help me to be Your eyes and ears and to be able to teach them as You would. Thanks for explaining how Jesus walked on water and how it wasn't His "mind over matter," but His use of "spirit over substance," that allowed Him to do this. It's a matter of trusting You and listening to Your Spirit in us. That way, we don't sink or fall. Remind me of this today! I love You.

God: Dear one, I will give you understanding and wisdom. I will be for you peace. I will be for you patience. I will be for you love. I will be for you the friend and father you need. I will be for you joy. I will be for you favor, and I will be for you grace. I will be for you gladness. I will be for you a heart of mercy. I will be for you a godly spouse. I will be for you meekness and humility. I will be for you foresight to see into the future. I will be for you a loyal business partner. I will be for you success. I will be for you the loving eyes, forgiving ears, merciful mouth, and healing hands you need. I will be for you all these things if you will just lean on My shoulder and turn toward My face with your whole being. Seek Me and think of Me. Come to Me and speak to Me. For you, I will be all these things. And I will hold your hand as you walk on the water, so you will never sink or fall. All because I am a gracious and good God, and I love you.

Because I'm Your weathergirl

"The Lord will guide you continually, giving you water when you are dry and restoring your strength. You will be like a well-watered garden, like an ever-flowing spring."
—Isaiah 58:11

Me: Lord, thanks for a great victory! While I was working, I got a call from my husband who works about 45 minutes away. "Well, the thing I most feared happened," he said. "I locked my keys in the car. Can you bring the other set?" I sighed and smiled. If I'd received this call a few years before, I would've responded differently. But this time I looked at my schedule and told him I'd get there before 6 pm. I finished my work and went to a hair appointment. I was done my 4 pm and called him to say I was on my way. We ended up spending the evening at an intimate Italian restaurant. He was grateful, and I saw how you brought wonderful goodness out of a challenging situation. Thanks, Lord, for helping me take things in stride, not over-reacting or getting frustrated, and for helping me to ease into Your plans, which often involve taking detours and always mean making lemonade out of lemons. As Your "weathergirl," help me to be more sensitive to any change in the weather—attitudes, feelings, or situations. Help me to sense a storm coming and to be prepared for it. Help me to see what's needed so I can help myself and others. And to never overreact in a negative way to a change of direction or others' mistakes. Help me to see into people's hearts and be able to help them. I love You.

God: Dear one, the day you were born was a very special day for Me. You've always been one of My great sources of light and life in this world. You've reflected Me and brought glory to My name. You've made mistakes, but you've seen how, together, we can make them right. I've always blessed you and brought you and your family prosperity and peace and needed love and understanding. I've given you mercy when you least expected it. I've given you grace when you were desperate for it. I've showered you with love when no one else would offer you a smidgeon of it! Continue with Me, for I'll never fail you. There's so much more we can accomplish together! Just wait and see! I have many blessings in store for you! Come to Me with your whole heart, and I'll take you to places beyond your imagination! As my "weathergirl," reach for My hand in every situation. Then as the winds blow hot or cold, I can lead you down the right path toward My miraculous mountaintop. I love you.

Bought with a high price

"For God bought you with a high price. So you must honor God with your body."
—1 Corinthians 6:20

Me: Lord, I want to celebrate what Your Son did for me! I wish all people could understand the great sacrifice He made. You went so far beyond anything we could ever ask or think by offering us Your only Son! Thanks! Because of Him, we can now know more about You. We can have a relationship with You. We can be close to You and know that our prayers are answered because, when we believe in Jesus and what He did, we receive Your gift of grace, Holy Spirit, which enables us to communicate with You. Yours was the ultimate sacrifice. What more precious gift could anyone give? Would You enlighten me more today as to what Your gift really means to me? Show me more of its greatness, for I want to see and know and understand just what it enables me to do and how You want me to use its ability and power in each moment. I see in each day how my life is made up of the parts of a puzzle that You're piecing together to design a magnificent portrait. And, one day, You'll show me the full view of what You created through my life. I'm so looking forward to seeing the masterpiece You're making. Despite my mistakes and failings, it will be fantastic, because You're fashioning it. I love You.

God: Dear one, nothing in life is free. Everything comes with a price. Every effort worth making costs something. When people choose evil, or the ways of the world, they pay a price with pieces of their own soul. If they choose the way of My Son, they won't need to pay the necessary price for eternal life, because the payment was already made for them by the blood He sacrificed. Those who choose Him will receive this great reward, but they will never have to pay the exorbitant price necessary to cover its cost. What a remarkable gift He gave for you and for so many! And yet, few people really understand the significance. Tell as many as you can about this great gift of grace that was offered for them. Help them to understand that they only need to accept it to live freely and be able to walk with Me by way of the spirit they receive when they believe. Then, they too can see the grand design of their life unfold before their eyes in amazing ways! I love you.

SEPTEMBER 26
So I can sit with You for awhile

"So there is a special rest still waiting for the people of God. For all who have entered into God's rest have rested from their labors, just as God did after creating the world. So let us do our best to enter that rest."
—Hebrews 4:9-11

Me: Lord, would You let Me see Your Son more clearly so I may at least be able to recognize the outlines of His face and follow in His steps? Because, through His example, I want to seek only You in this world. I yearn for Your presence. I seek Your glory, Your praise, Your dominion, Your calling, Your angels' trumpet sound, Your sword, Your armor, Your hand of mercy, Your peace, Your protection, Your love, Your joy, Your strength, Your heart, Your compassion, Your direction, Your hope, Your magnificence, and Your wisdom. And of Your Son—His beauty, His face, His eyes, His feet, His hands, His robe, His crown of righteousness, His creation, His handiwork, His masterpiece, His new city. Lord, help me to do what is needed for You. Give me the most opportune words—ones that can reach into others' hearts and pluck at their heartstrings as nothing else can. Today, help me to be attentive to the details around me and to see what You want me to see. Help me to be able to behold all aspects of Your work with Your divine perspective. I need Your help with this. Give me Your grace-filled eyes so I can see more clearly. I love You.

God: Dear one, sit with Me awhile. Be still. Let Me whisper My words in your ears. I'll remind you of how much I love you. I'll tell you that you're special and that I've always cared for you. I'll make sure you know that I've always walked beside you, cheering you on, comforting you in your sorrow, and applauding your successes. I'll help you to stand firm when you need support. I'll be your sight when you need to see but can't make out the lines clearly. So, sit awhile with Me, and bask in My light. Be warmed by My presence. Experience My pleasure and joy. Hold My hand. I'll never let you go! Listen to My soft whispers as I give you new insights and direct you through storms and clouds and fierce headwinds. I'll be your way, your truth, your light, and your vision. Just sit beside Me and experience My grace for a while. For I will take care of you now and forever. Because I love you.

With my hands lifted to You

"I fell to my knees and lifted my hands to the Lord my God."
—Ezra 9:5

Me: Dear Lord, thanks for where You place me! Today, as I walked around the lake, I passed a lady in a car parked by the sidewalk. As I went by, she spoke through her window and said, "The power of tears." I stopped and she repeated the words. I saw a police car ahead of her pull away just then, and she explained that he'd stopped her because she was weaving down the road. When she told him tearfully that she'd forgotten her glasses and was suffering from renal failure, he asked her to get out of the car. Thankfully he didn't give her a ticket. I asked if I could pray for her, and she started crying. "Yes," she said. So I took her hand through the window and prayed. Then she asked if I wanted to go to dinner with her and her husband, but then she was conflicted as to how she would introduce me, since she didn't want him to know she was stopped by the police. She waved to me as she drove away. I prayed a good-bye and never saw her again. Lord, my hands are before You. You promised that as I hold them out to You, You'll fill them with more than enough so that the extra would fall between my fingers to those who need Your mercy. You've showed me how my hands represent life and the work I do for You. Those who want to hear will stay inside my palms. Those who don't will sift through my fingers. My hands are Your hands, Lord. Would You help me to use them as You would Yours? I love You.

God: Dear one, I'm ready and available to you, and I'll show you each day how best to use your hands lifted up to Me. I'll encourage and help you. Just listen. I'm ready to pour blessings down to you. I'm ready to lead you to others to heal and to help. I'll work through your hands and your words. Just follow My Spirit in you. I'm always ready to work in and through you. Do you see that? Just be at peace. When your heart is torn or you feel guilty, bring your concerns to Me so I can free you. I'll bring you great joy as you seek My words to bring great deliverance, answers, and healing to others. You see, your prayers can change everything. And life is wonderful when you're thankful and available to Me. Your praise pushes away dark clouds. Seek My mercy and My grace as you seek My face in others. My Word spoken brings you up to Me. It clears the air and breaks through the clouds. It shows My way in the face of darkness. Seek My peace today. I love you.

I present all my failures

"He remembered us in our weakness. His faithful love endures forever."
—*Psalm 136:23*

Me: It's difficult for me, Lord, but I'm learning to rejoice in my failings, knowing that my lacks, mistakes, and shortcomings can bring me closer to You! So many times, I see any success as so far out of reach and beyond my capability. I think of my desire to have good relationships with family members who remain so distant and unwilling to respond. I think of business achievements You've set before me. I think of personal goals for a home I enjoy that I can afford. But You remind me that it's when I'm weak that I depend on You most. Now, I'm beginning to understand the passage in the epistles where Paul says that it's out of his weakness that You produce strength (2 Corinthians 12:9). It's when we need You the most that You can show us Your greatest works! Lord, would You work Your super-ability through me, especially when others imply that I'm faulty or lacking or wrong? I know that, through myself alone, I can never be perfect, and I become frustrated trying. It's only through You that I can ever attain anything worthwhile. Help me now to reach the goals You've set before me. Help me to achieve what You've purposed for me today. Guide me to Your paths, Lord, and direct me to Your will and way. I am in Your hands. I love You.

God: Dear one, think of Abraham Lincoln. He failed many times, yet somehow succeeded to affect many thousands of lives, because he persisted and came to Me for help. He was tested as a child, like Joseph, to remove selfishness, so he could put Me first in his life. His faults were self-indulgence, pride, procrastination, self-pity, and focusing on his own pain. His wife and children often distracted him. Yet he believed in Me, and I loved his willingness to keep on trying. That's what I ask of you. Even when you fail, keep trying! I'll always lift you back up and help you to succeed, but you must overcome pride, self-pity, exasperation, and impatience. If you can move past these things, and still follow My calling, then I can work through you to do mighty works! I'll reveal My plan for you little by little, and you'll be blessed by it. I can work through you as you allow Me to help you. Today, focus on Me. Because I love you.

Then I see Your masterpiece

"For we are God's masterpiece. He has created us anew in Christ Jesus, so we can do the good things he planned for us long ago."
—Ephesians 2:10

Me: Dear Lord, today You showed me that what we perceive as an imperfection is not a flaw at all to You, because You use everything for Your own good purposes. What appears to us as worthless, whether it's bad choices, situations, or people, actually contributes to the creation of a beautiful masterpiece. It reminds me of an artist I watched once who made random strokes on a canvas. When he turned the picture around for all to see, it was a perfect portrait of Your Son! Would You help me see Your design in my life? Open my eyes to what You're creating. I want to watch as You work through the world's events to redirect evil efforts toward good. Help me to recognize the grace in what You're doing and how You maximize every bit of goodness. Thanks for reminding me of Your greatness and what You've done for me. Thanks for reminding me of Your mighty mercy and how You can reconcile anything that was broken. Thanks for bringing me peace, even through confusion. Help me to show Your mercy to those who intentionally or unintentionally hurt me. Thanks for showing me love when I least expected it. And for those who were kind to me in desolate moments. Help me to do this for others. I love You.

God: Dear one, you're a hidden gem. But you're also a bright shining star that only I can see at times. Those who care to see you will recognize your true worth and value. I make use of all your abilities. I'll reveal how I do this as time goes on. I've designed you for specific purposes—Mine. I'm preparing You for the future and bringing you a greater understanding of what will happen and when. You'll play a significant role in how My plan plays out, because My hand is on your life. Obedience may seem like a little thing, but it's a mighty thing in My eyes. As you heed My Word, we can work together, and you'll see wonderful things happen in your own life and in the lives of others. As you listen for My voice, you'll receive greater clarification and instructions. Pay attention, and never take My words lightly. Mine is a still, small voice, but, through My Spirit, you can hear it clearly. My directions will always be precise and accurate. Just do as I say. Then, you'll receive great blessings both in this life and in the one to come! I love you.

SEPTEMBER 30
As You work through my spirit

"If you openly declare that Jesus is Lord and believe in your heart that God raised him from the dead, you will be saved."
—Romans 10:9

Me: I'm not perfect, Lord. You know that. And yet You counted me worthy enough to receive Your Holy Spirit, which is perfect. By this, You brought great blessings into my life. You showed me that when I believed in Your Son and all that He did, and made Him my Lord, You gave me some of what You are—Holy Spirit. Like light, it's composed of energy though, in this case, it's spiritual energy. I can't see Your Spirit, but it fills every part of me and, through it, You can communicate with me. The spirit you gave me is unique and can't be reproduced. It's a part of me that lives on forever. Would You work through me now, by way of my spirit, soul, and body, to will and to do of Your good pleasure? Help me to be more aware of what I need to do and of Your ability to work through me in every moment. Show me how to be sensitive to Your Spirit, so I can help others receive this life-giving gift. I love You.

God: Child, when you receive My Spirit, you gain everything you need to live now and forever. This spirit brings light—focused spiritual energy—and life. The more you tap into this gift, the more strength and ability you have for your own and others' healing and deliverance. Because you have this power-source inside you, I don't need to show up in a visible way or send angels to intervene for you, as I did in the Old Testament. Amazing spiritual potential now lies within you. The Chinese call it "chi." I call it light, because it comes from Me, the One who is light. And, like light, I'm the source of all living energy. Once you hunkered down in a boat and waited out the storms of life with your arms over your head. You felt helpless, but I hovered over you and protected you until you were ready. And, when you were, I placed My Spirit inside you. I'm with you now, residing in you. And together we can step out of the boat and walk boldly across the water toward a peaceful place. One day, you'll reach My shore, and it will be a pleasant, beautiful, and fragrant land full of life and light. Right now, I rest with you and bring you peace, even when things feel shaky, like you're back inside the boat in a storm. Only, this time it's all an illusion. Because My Spirit in you gives you the power to calm any tempest. Now, bring me those things that burden your heart, and we can deal with them. I promise you. I love you.

October

FOCUS:
JUBILANT JOY

"You love him even though you have never seen him. Though you do not see him now, you trust him; and you rejoice with a glorious, inexpressible joy."

—I PETER 1:8

OCTOBER 1
With the gift of a day

"This is the day the Lord has made. We will rejoice and be glad in it."
—Psalm 118:24

Me: Lord, I sit and reflect on a dream I once had: I sat on a beach in the dark with my mother and my son, and we celebrated her birthday. My son proudly gave her an oval-shaped package wrapped in brown paper and tied with rough twine. She unwrapped what turned out to be a wicker frame around a burlap interior with a few artificial flowers adorning the edges. She exclaimed, "Oh, I can't use this!" and my son stood up to walk away, obviously hurt. I grabbed the gift and ran after him yelling, "I'll take it!" We both ended up inside a brightly-lit cottage on the edge of the beach, where an old man and a young man stood together at the head of a long table. I told them what had happened, and the young man, whose face was serene and kind, just nodded. He seemed to understand. He remained calm as he waited patiently for more people to arrive. When I woke up, I wondered what the dream meant then realized that the gift was a day in my son's life—something I wanted more than anything since he'd died. The two men were Jesus and God. They had understood what I wanted. Then I thought about words I'd heard recently about enjoying each day as it comes and not always wishing things were different. How important it is to enjoy the time we have with the people You give us. And not be disappointed in what we're offered or how life has evolved. These days are truly gifts to be appreciated. Lord, help me to savor each moment. I love You.

God: Dear one, each day is a gift. And each new moment. As your father, let Me surround you with joy in every moment—even in the hard or sad times. I'll embrace you and hold you up, as your own father did. I'll kiss and soothe you, stroking your hair as your mother would. I'm all things to you and for you in each instant. Seek Me today, for My joy is boundless—it's a sort of giddiness you can never experience anywhere else. Lean your head on Me. Turn your face to Me. Bring your cares to Me. Today, things may seem stressful and unreasonable, but remember I'm always beside you, whispering in your ear, comforting you and reminding you of how much I love you. Don't allow the pressures to get to you. Focus your eyes on Me. Turn your thoughts to Me. Let Me massage you with My hope and comfort you with My presence. Then you'll rejoice in each moment and appreciate the gift of each and every day you have. I love you.

OCTOBER 2
I want to sit with You

"Her sister, Mary, sat at the Lord's feet, listening to what he taught."
—Luke 10:39

Me: Lord, today I thought about what it must have been like for Mary, Martha, and Lazarus to know Jesus as a friend. They must have loved Him. I wish I could sit and talk with Him as they did! I'd love to linger, like Mary, and savor every word He said. You remind me that, one day, I will sit at His feet. I long for that day. And I wonder what He'll look like. How will His voice sound? What will it be like to gaze up and speak right to Him? You explained to me once that He didn't look like I might expect. What do You mean? I envision His face now, because I can imagine what He might have looked like. But did He have a broader nose than I've seen in the pictures? Or was His hair curlier or longer and His beard shorter or darker? Were His eyes blue-green, as I imagine, or were they dark brown? No matter what, I'd have loved Him. I know it. Because I love Him now. Show me more of Him, and of You, Lord! I want to sit in Your presence and gaze into the beautiful eyes of Your Son. I tremble with joy just thinking about it. I love You.

God: Dear one, even though you can't see Me or My Son, remember that We are nearer to you than you think. Today, hold My hand, and I'll gently guide you through trouble and anxiety to the peaceful place where I abide. Today, listen closely, for then I can help you to envision even more clearly who I am and how My Spirit works in you. Lean your head close, and bend your ear to Me. I will tell you things that you will want to hear. Stand close to Me, and feel My presence, which emits joy and love and gentleness. Walk with Me through situations, and let Me carry you, because I will. Today, let Me fill you with My goodness, My light, and My joy, because I will. Today, hold your arms out and grasp the people who come to hear My words, because I will bring them. Today, know that I'm with you always. I support you. I've told you I love you. I'm working even now to bring abundance to you in every way. I'll show you a deeper purpose in the place where you are. Remember that fearlessness can only come through a belief in Me and what I can do for you. I'm with you now, but, one day, you'll see My presence more clearly, and it will be beyond anything you could ever ask or imagine. It will be pure joy for you! I love you.

OCTOBER 3
And imagine a star

"As God's partners, we beg you not to accept this marvelous gift of God's kindness and then ignore it."
—2 Corinthians 6:1

Me: Lord, maybe I'm running away from the things I don't like! Because, when I need to be working, I schedule other things to keep myself occupied, so I'm not bored by the things I should be doing. I sometimes fill the hours with needless things. Would You show me how to do things in a way that fulfills Your purposes for me? How can I best use the little time I have? Make it clear to me so I don't get sidetracked quite so often. I want to feel joy and excitement from what I do, knowing it's for You. Help me to see what You see. Guide me, and help me focus on what's needed. Your kindness is endless and inexhaustible. It never fades away. And life with You is always exciting, because You give good gifts and open up amazing opportunities to me every day. I can depend on You as You surround me with wonderful things and remind me of Your boundless goodness and joy. I love You.

God: Dear one, whether you see it or not, you do fulfill My purposes, even as you do mundane or seemingly endless tasks. Think of Elijah and all the days he spent waiting by a brook or under a tree before he saw My promises fulfilled! He was sometimes dismayed, overwhelmed, and impatient, but he was still able to lead many people back to Me! Even today, many relish the way he lived out his faith under terrible circumstances in a godless reigning regime. You can too. When your sight is limited, it's hard to sit and wait or do the same thing over and over again. When you can't see the importance of what you're doing, you may not be able to see the impact of your life on others. If you could see it clearly, you'd never feel bored or lacking in purpose. Close your eyes now, and imagine a star like the sun. I'm brighter than this! And I shine through your heart and life. People see Me through you. Think of Brother Lawrence, the 17th century monk who learned to praise Me and practice My presence, even while he washed dishes! If you can remember Me while doing repetitive tasks, you'll be joyful, and the tasks will become meaningful as you do them for Me! Today, be confident in who you are and in what I'm doing through you as your constant friend. Continue to pray as you work, because your prayers are effectual. They mean something. They bring joy. I love you.

October 4
As we laugh together

"Always be full of joy in the Lord. I say it again—rejoice! Let everyone see that you are considerate in all you do. Remember, the Lord is coming soon."
—*Philippians 4:4-5*

Me: Lord, how I look forward to laughing with You one day! I look ahead to the time when I can sit with You and just savor Your words of comfort and joy. I want to sing along with my loved ones as we play music together on guitars, harps, flutes, tambourines, and trumpets, and lift our voices higher and higher to the heavens. I want to drift with You from here to there and explore Your amazing paradise! And never see darkness again or pain or sorrow, but be able to experience Your brilliant light that leads on for eternity. I'm impatient for that day, but I thank You for the opportunities to share about You now. Help me to be able to see through Your eyes in every situation. Help me to have peace, because I have Your complete view of things. Thanks, Lord, for all You've done for me. Bless today, Lord, and bring me exuberant joy as I serve and bless others. Would You show me, Lord, how I can touch the people You lead me to? Would You give me wisdom and courage to be able to accomplish this? You're the author of salvation. Help me see the fruit of all I've planted and the results of the good things I've done. Help me to bring hope and cheer to those around me. You, Lord, are my true love. And I love You.

God: Dear one, how I love you too! How I love your fellowship, your thoughts, and your conversations with Me! How I've desired your closeness all these years. Continue with Me. Earnestly seek My love. The more you turn your heart to Me, the more I can give to you. I have so much to share with you! I know you mourn for loved ones who've passed on. One day, you'll rejoice with laughter to see them! And I'll be there with you to relish and savor every moment. How happy I'll be to see you together again with them! Now, they're safe with Me, in my arms, waiting for your arrival. And you will see My glory and how I live. How glorious it will all be! Your world is beautiful as I made it, but it's becoming more and more corrupt. You appreciate what I've done, and this blesses Me, but wait until you see what's hidden "behind the veil!" Rejoice with Me today. See Me in what's around you, even in people. Look at Me, not at others' imperfections or lacks. See Me as I show you their hearts. Then you can have constant joy! And that joy will extend to many others. I love you.

OCTOBER 5
And experience a joyful season

"Therefore, whenever we have the opportunity, we should do good to everyone—especially to those in the family of faith."
—*Galatians 6:10*

Me: Lord, I love Fall as I feel the evenings growing cooler. I love the sound of the school bus in the morning as children get ready to go to school. It's a reminder that my favorite season is here. I love the colorful, changing leaves and the brisk morning air as I walk. Thanks, Lord, for this time that brings me so much joy! Although I know it's a preparation for harsher, colder days, I focus on the blessings now. There are many things I love about where I am. I enjoy getting to know my neighbors as I walk the dogs around the neighborhood. Each one brings me joy. The single lady across the street has two chihuahuas, and she makes sure to greet me as I walk by. She watches my house when I travel and texts me if she notices anything unusual. The couple next door sit in front of their house and wave as I walk by. Sometimes they come over to pet my dog Barney, who loves their attention! And my neighbor on the other side recently lost her husband. I take her devotional books to encourage her. Thanks for these special ways that I can show Your kindness and remind them of Your love. Today, show me where You want me and who I should talk to. Help me to minister to those who are near so I can bring them greater joy and peace. I love You.

God: Dear one, do you see how you reap what you sow? When you plant good things, like warm words and acts of kindness, you receive graciousness in return. When you're thoughtful, you reap friendly responses. When you're angry or bitter, you receive negativity. It's the law of giving and receiving, or sowing and reaping. This is what life and its seasons are made up of. If you plant a rose seed, then water and nurture it, you'll get a beautiful rose bush. But never an oak tree! You can't get back something you never sowed. It's simple. Yet people are confounded when others respond negatively to them. You may be surprised when the response to your kindness is contrariness. Sometimes people's negative reaction is a result of how they were treated by others. In that case, you can be the "change agent" by doing something good, despite the evil. You can "pay it forward" by creating kindness where there was none before. It's so simple. Yet so many miss it! I love you.

OCTOBER 6
Where we dance throughout the day

"You have turned my mourning into joyful dancing. You have taken away my clothes of mourning and clothed me with joy, that I might sing praises to you and not be silent. O Lord my God, I will give you thanks forever!"
—Psalm 30:11-12

Me: Dear Lord, thanks for peace and joy today! Would You dance with me throughout the day so I can abound in Your blessings, exult in Your strength, and be lavished by Your love? Let me see You in a brand-new way and have many secret conversations with You. For You are my love and the One I worship. Help me to experience more and more of Your anointed adoration! Let me feel Your arms around me, always embracing me in Your strong love-hold. Let me be showered by Your joy. And let me always be the apple of Your eye. I love You.

God: Dear one, how I love you and enjoy our time together! I only desire more of it! Please take moments throughout the day to turn to Me so I can share My thoughts with you. I often have things to say, but I need you to listen! I always gaze on you with eyes of tenderness, because you are deeply loved and favored. I admire you, one who stands with and for Me. You'll always be the apple of My eye! You're chosen, and you're special and unique in this world, especially to Me. Know that I'm ever near and ready to answer any request. I bring you peace and never chaotic turmoil. Continue to rest in My presence. Bask in My beauty, glory in My words, be lavished by My love, and know that, through My endearing embrace, you're fulfilled. Don't be too afraid of being wrong or saying inappropriate things. I'll always work things out for good. But, if you listen, I'll always give you the right words to speak in every situation. The adversary may roar against you and try to take away what's most important to you—your peace and joy. He'll try to magnify your "mistakes" and use them against you. He'll try to weaken you by averting your gaze from My wonderful love, and he'll try to upset you, so you become hurt or offended. Don't fall for it! Come to Me, and I'll lift you up in the sight of others, especially those who try to "put you down." Turn your eyes to Me, and I'll bear you up when others belittle or overlook you. I'll dance with you anytime, My dear partner. Because you're My child who brings me great joy. I love you.

With hands uplifted

"Worship the LORD with gladness. Come before him, singing with joy."
—*Psalm 100:2*

Me: It's me, Lord, seeking Your joy! It's me, Lord, longing for Your love. You present me with peace during times of trouble, uncertainty, and chaos. You encircle me with joy in days when I experience sadness, frustration, anger, or unkindness. You inspire me so that I burst with Your love and sing out loud with Your joy! You grant me grace in days of despair and remind me of Your amazing grace and kindness when the world wields its harsh denials. You are a continual friend, full of mercy and love. Would You nudge me today toward the reality that You're always here for me when I need you, even when I forget so quickly? Would You hold my hand tight and gently lead me to Your world, where I can sigh and breathe Your fresh, exhilarating air? Help me to understand in a greater way that You are the One who gives me what I need, including the capacity to help myself and others. For I desperately desire Your strength to accomplish my daily tasks, which sometimes feel overwhelming. Remind me of Your presence as I lift my heart and hands up to You. You are a great God, a loving God. And I love You.

God: Dear one, just rest in Me. Know that I'm always by your side. Know that some—the ones with eyes to see—can recognize an "aura" of light that emanates from you. The glow of My favor surrounds you, and some will be drawn to it. As far as the others—never be discouraged by those who don't share your vision or see things the way you do. Many will doubt My calling, My authority, My ability, My presence, and My influence, and, because of this, they will suffer because they refuse to acknowledge or hear Me. I will try to warn them and lead them to what's right. And You can help me in this effort. But it's up to them to heed Me and you. Some choose to continue to live in their own manmade "hellhole." But you can remain joyful, because you know what I've done, and that's your strength. Rejoice in Me. Seek Me with your whole heart. Look past the things and people of this world to My Word and what lies somewhat hidden within its pages. This world is temporary. But if you look to Me and My Word, I can guide you through the maze of unbelief, falsehood, and corruption. I'll show you My way, which is a way of forgiveness, peace, kindness, strength, and joy. It's always a way of blessing. Seek it now. I love you.

You cover me with Your hand

"Some will turn away from the true faith.... These people are hypocrites and liars, and their consciences are dead."
—*1 Timothy 4:1-2*

Me: Lord, You're a blessing to me. Help me to trust You and know that only You are perfect and the source of all perfection. Only You are wise and the source of all wisdom. Only You are love and the source of all true affection. You're always there for me. Thanks. When others disappoint, You continuously come through. Today, let me feel Your presence as my source of all joy. Help me to love as You do and to move closer to You and away from sin and the effects of it. Show me how to deal with people, especially how to forgive them when they mistreat me or others. But also, show me what I should say when they're being used for evil purposes. Give me Your wisdom in dealing with them. It's hard to reconcile with people who take advantage of me or others for their own benefit. Especially when they act in hurtful ways that are outside the bounds of love and decency. Show me how to best handle these situations. Cover me with Your hand of protection so that any attempts to harm are hindered. Help me to act in a godly manner and to best represent You. Thanks, Lord. You are my helper and guide. Instruct me in all Your ways. I love You.

God: Dear one, I'm always with you to instruct you and bring you peace, even in times of anguish, when some act out of selfish desires. Sometimes you may be tempted to accuse or be unforgiving and pass judgment. Let me do this. Just live and be joyful, and have My peace. Let Me handle the rest. I'll take care of those who take advantage of good people like you in hurtful ways. Some act this way out of ignorance; others are very aware of what they're doing. But any action involves choices. I give many chances and remind people of what's wrong, but it's up to them if they choose to continue to make mistakes or live in evil ways. Sometimes their conscience becomes seared as if with a hot iron. In other words, they grow hardened to the results of their bad choices that hurt others. Little by little, they let in the evil until they're taken over by it. If they want release from this bondage, they must replace the wrong thoughts with My Word. It always involves choices. But now, you rejoice and be glad in Me, for I give you joy, forgiveness, peace, and abounding love. I protect you in every situation. Remember, no mortal is capable of fully loving unless that love comes from Me. I love you.

OCTOBER 9
As I sit by Your fire

"Didn't our hearts burn within us as he talked with us..."
—*Luke 24:32*

Me: Lord, last night You led me to a peaceful campsite, surrounded by fragrant pine trees, where a fire burned, and its warmth encompassed me. I sat with Your Son, and He began to share His heart. And I knew He loved me, because He embraced me as I am. He encouraged me and gave me new ideas and explained why people are the way they are. And He showed me things to come and how it will be when He returns. He told me about my ancestors and why He chose me and what He had in mind for my children and theirs. And I realized at that moment that I'd ended up in this place because You drew me here. Another person approached and wondered why we were sitting here and what we were talking about. I reached out and grasped his cold hands to warm them, and I pulled up a log for him so he could sit next to us. We shared with him how we came here and where we'd been and how You'd arranged our steps so we'd be here at the right place and time and how nothing was a coincidence. His questioning eyes reflected the light of the fire, and we saw our faces in them as he told us about his life and where he'd been and how he realized why he was here. Then he stopped and asked us who we were. When we explained, he put his face in his hands and cried because he knew that he'd found the place he'd been seeking. Then I remembered what Your Son had gone through for us and why I was there, and I cried too. We all held hands, and I realized that this was what I'd always wanted. Then I woke up and the day began. But the memory of this meaningful dream will always linger. I love You.

God: Dear one, when you turn your eyes to Me today, you'll see My Son right there beside you. And you'll hear His comforting words, which are bright with joy and hope. They'll bring light to your path and clarify the things around you. When you start to feel discouraged, turn to Me again and see yourself sitting by the campfire. Remember, it's sparked by My heart and ignited by My love. Strengthen yourself with My words as you sit with Him. When the day gets challenging, remember that He's gazing lovingly at you. Focus on Him. Then He can encourage you and bring you great peace and jubilant joy. He'll help you to focus more on Me and all I've done for you. People will come and go. Don't let them discourage you. The right ones will come and sit with you by the fire. I'll lead these ones to you. I love you.

OCTOBER 10
Absorbing Your joy

"This is a sacred day before our Lord. Don't be dejected and sad, for the joy of the Lord is your strength!"
—*Nehemiah 8:10*

Me: Lord, let my memories be sweet of the special times, when I sang and prayed and shared and ate together with friends and family. Help me to shed the aches and pains of tired thoughts and hurtful words and painful times. I want to be filled with Your joy! I want to constantly rejoice in You, the One who joyfully made me! I want to celebrate the ways You've triumphed over evil and death, even in my lifetime! I long to see loved ones who've gone before me one day and be reunited with them. I long for Your Son's return. Oh, that He'd come soon and take us to the perfect place He's created for us! I look forward to celebrating forever with You and with those who love You! Your encouragement now, even in sadness, is awesome and breathtaking! Your open doors are beyond my imagination. Thanks for Your leading and Your calling for me. Show me the right doors—the ones I need to walk through. Enlighten my eyes so I can see what You view as I look out at the world. If there are people I should speak to, give me the right words to say. Reveal their hearts, and help me not to judge by their appearance or words. You are so good at this! I love You.

God: Dear one, today is a day I've made. Rejoice and be glad in it! Joy and rejoicing always come from Me. They're the wonderful result of turning your thoughts to Me. Did you know that I love to hear your praise, especially when you lift it up to me during unlikely times, like when you're experiencing pain? I actually long to hear it from you. And as you praise Me, I can lift you up. I wait for these opportunities to bless you. I watch as you go out and as you come in. I watch as you get up and as you lay down. As you minister to others, My heart is thrilled, because I know the blessings you will receive as a result. I cry when you cry, and I'm sad when you're sad. When others receive your words, I'm very joyful. When they reject you, I'm sad. I can work through you to reach the lost and hurting ones. Through you, I can minister to them. Praise Me in your thoughts, your words, and your actions. Let me lead you to wholeness. I can do this when you open your heart to thankfulness for the good things I've done for you. Then you'll have joy, and people will see it and welcome Me into their own lives because of it. I love you.

October 11
So I can skip with You

"Make me walk along the path of your commands, for that is where my happiness is found."
—Psalm 119:35

Me: Thanks, Lord, for revealing more and more who You are to me. Thanks for the relationship I've developed with You over many years. You've been more than merciful and gracious to me. Thanks that when I read about religions, and religious ways that are cruel, oppressive, and enslaving, I can understand that these ways are not Your ways. Would You reveal to me more about Yourself each day? Your way is never a way of doing without or of withholding love, nourishment, trust, caring, decency, or hope. It's a way of compassion, help, strength, abundance, and grace. Thanks for showing me this. Whenever people are cruel or controlling, this is not because of You or from You. It's never Your way. Because You are kind. You are love. You are mercy. You are pure joy. And I long to skip down a path with You one day! I love You.

God: Dear one, My path requires great determination. That's because the world will tell you that a belief in Me is absurd. At these times, remember who the "god of this world" is (2 Corinthians 4:4) and how he tries to blind people to the truth. When you realize Who I am and how much I love you, it's easy to receive Me. My path is full of unexpected encounters, but I always prepare you for what lies ahead. And I'll always show you the answers to life's perplexing questions if you ask. But this requires staying close and listening to Me. My way is not the way of many people, who blow hot and cold and give when they think it benefits them. My way surpasses the smallness of religions that create rules to control their followers. My way is an open way of trust, compassion, hope, and understanding. I walk alongside those who come to Me and want to understand My Word. These are able to comprehend more as they step onto My path. It's easier if you hold My hand and trust Me. Keep in mind that I'm always by your side, and My Spirit works to guide and comfort you. No other religion on earth offers a relationship like this. With Me, you need never worry about what lies ahead or what tomorrow might bring, because I always give you what you need to handle what life brings. Remember, My path leads to immeasurable joy if you let Me guide you. So, lean on My guidance, and I'll bring you great confidence and hope. I love you.

October 12
As You lead me from chaos to calm

"You intended to harm me, but God intended it all for good. He brought me to this position so I could save the lives of many people."
—Genesis 50:20

Me: Lord, I love the story of Joseph. It's one of my favorites! It amazes me how You worked out all the details of his life so that he ended up in the right place at the right time. And You directed the results so that they all worked out for good. It makes me wonder about my own life. How much sway do I have and how much do You determine? How in the world do You make so many crazy, chaotic things work out so well in the end? Please work things out in my life so that everything ends up being a great blessing for You and for those whose lives I touch! Be my captain and guide me to Your ultimate purposes and greatest desires for me. Show me what they are, Lord. I know you want me to pray. I'll continue to do that. But please direct me, Lord. Put right words in my mouth and give me the courage to speak when You prompt me. Through Your grace, surround my heart with Your protective goodness and love—special wrappings to preserve and hold within me Your peace and joy, despite the world's negativity! Make calm out of chaos. I love You.

God: Child, I'm always working on your behalf to shift all outcomes from being unfortunate or disastrous to good and meaningful. But not just that. I also arrange things for My own purposes. And I have a special design for you. You sometimes don't see it, though you have glimpses of it. It's always right in front of you, though not entirely visible. I've led you to people and places, and I'll lead you to others in the future—ones I'm calling. These will include those who know they're being called by Me but don't know how to follow their calling. I'll place them with you so they can learn how to discern My plans, which will become clearer as time goes on. When people disappoint or hurt you, I'll make up for their injurious behavior. But never allow their lacks to hinder your purposes. Some will neglect their calling and choose to do what they think is best, until they realize how they've veered from My path. People of integrity will often make up for others' failures. I can protect your heart from any whose motives are tainted by fear, anger, bitterness, deception, or greed so you can have joy. Little by little, I'll turn every curse into a blessing and surround you with wonderful peace and kindness and love. I love you.

OCTOBER 13
By lifting the unbearable fear-load

"We destroy every proud obstacle that keeps people from knowing God. We capture their rebellious thoughts and teach them to obey Christ."
—2 Corinthians 10:5

Me: Lord, heal our nation from divisiveness, hatred, accusations, and finger-pointing. Deliver us from pervasive labeling and lumping people together into groups. Help us to see others as individuals with hearts and minds and souls. I want to see as You do—into each person's heart. Help us not to judge others or predetermine outcomes and motives. We need your strong arm of guidance and deliverance. At times, I feel like our country is falling fast! Would You hold us up to Your wonderful light so we can see clearly and begin to have Your wisdom in these desperate times? Many are sinking in the mire, and I want to help them. Show me how to reach them, and give me the strength I need to pull them up and out. Only You can save. Show me how to bring them closer to You so they too can see You as I do and experience Your amazing joy and love. I love You.

God: Dear one, do you see how people are swayed by false stories that influence attitudes, beliefs, commerce, nations, and governments? It was the same in Jesus's time. Many enterprises and religions are built on stories passed down by people who follow precepts set by earlier generations. When one comes along to confront an erroneous pattern or belief, and speak the truth, people may grow very emotional. Anything that threatens to undermine their shaky foundation makes them afraid that their leaning tower will come crashing down. Even now, you'll experience this. You'll see this kind of fear in people around you. Some will lie awake at night, because they dread what might happen. They torment themselves with trivia and propaganda. With weary eyes and heaving hearts, they listen attentively to misappropriated lies. And they're unsure of what to do. Be My guide in these dark times. Be My light to bring life to others. Share My love and confidence that brings deliverance. Remember, My joy gives strength. And you can have more joy by focusing on the fulfillment of My promises. You can bring true guidance and direction by living and speaking My Word. You can lighten the heaviness around you and lift the unbearable fear-load. People without hope are afraid—they know they'll die one day. And, because the future is uncertain, they fear it. But you can bring a certain brightness by reflecting My hope-filled Spirit. I love you.

315

OCTOBER 14
So we can thrill at the sunrise colors

"His coming is as brilliant as the sunrise. Rays of light flash from his hands, where his awesome power is hidden."
—Habakkuk 3:4

Me: Thank You, Lord, for all You've done for me. Thanks for how You turned an extraordinarily evil event into a glorious victory for good! It was the gift of Your Son that keeps on giving. His suffering set us free to live without the pain of death. The shame He endured released us from the guilt we inherited from Adam. His willingness to give of Himself was a gift that keeps unfolding before us. It's like a beautiful bow on a package that's untied just at the right time so that ribbons of mercy fall all around us. Then, as we unwrap Your present, layer by layer, we discover a fabulously framed picture that's still being painted, stroke by stroke, by an invisible hand that knows more about us than we do. And we stand beside You and gaze amazed as You finish the work of our life, and we see a masterpiece of beauty with a background of sunrise colors! What joy! Thanks for the gift of this new life, with You as our benefactor—the One who bought and paid for us with His blood so that we might live through Him! And be painted by His magical, light-flashing, rainbow-inspiring strokes for eternity. I love You.

God: Child, you see how much you need Me and how much I can do for you. As each new day passes, you'll begin to see how much more I can do! Just lean on Me, and trust Me to provide for you. Today will be an exceptional day, because I've blessed it. But your future will be even more extraordinary—way beyond your comprehension! As days on earth become darker and less peaceful, remember that My day is soon at hand. The world will never offer you your heart's desires. Only I can offer you these. During your lifetime, there will be threats and fears and wars, but within your heart you can always have My peace. When My Son returns one day for you, your new life will be filled with joy, like the colors of a sunrise morning. Remember this. Let My strong hand lead and help and guide you while you're on earth. I'll open many doors for you. I always have. But you must walk through them. Don't be afraid to enter and go through them. Then I can help you find the "gold" at the end of My rainbow. I love you.

And relish what You've given us

"You made the moon to mark the seasons, and the sun knows when to set."
—Psalm 104:19

Me: Lord, I love these autumn days and the crisp cool mornings as I walk. They remind me of how my grandmother would stay at her cabin in Michigan on the lake just long enough for the leaves to turn into bright shades of yellow, orange, gold, and red. Then, as she sat on a lawn chair under the tall pine trees around the cabin, she'd soak up the beauty as she gazed around the lake at the reflected colors on the turquoise water. She might sigh a few more times as she packed her things for the long ride home, as the turbid, hot, humid Texas air was just starting to wind down to tolerable temperatures. She'd load up the car and drive until she could see the large oak trees limbs drooping with Spanish moss and the orange trees surrounded by fallen fruit. Once there, she'd dream about next year's cool summer days under the fragrant pine trees by the lake. Thanks, Lord, for the seasons and how each day can be filled with wonderful memories. For all Your amazing miracles and wonders—thanks! The more I savor Your goodness with thankfulness for what You've done, the more good things I see in life. I love You.

God: Dear one, every day is a new day. I'm the Lord of light, variance, color, and beauty. My ways never change, but I create variety for your enjoyment. And you can rejoice and be glad, even in this world, as you rest in My love. Release your cares to Me, and let Me lift your burdens. Draw closer to Me, and I will draw closer to you. The world around you is fleeting and temporal, so avoid falling in love with it. Everything in it is nonbinding. Instead, appreciate what I've given you, and try to understand why I created you and what you see around you. It's all because I love you dearly. Yes, I've spared your life many times from being undone by harmful things, even death itself, though you were unaware. Remember, I'm always by your side. So, spend your days remembering Me. Praise Me continuously. Celebrate each season I've made. For this is "the joy of the Lord." As you bring your thoughts to Me, not condescending to the world's ways, you'll find greater joy in your heart. People will try to bring you down with negative thoughts and words. But I bring deliverance and a peaceful way that is full of color, light, and joy. Look through My eyes by reading My Word so I can show you how much I love you.

While we spend time together

"But God did listen! He paid attention to my prayer. Praise God, who did not ignore my prayer or withdraw his unfailing love from me."
—*Psalm 66:19-20*

Me: Lord, more than 20 years ago I started writing in my journals and spending early mornings with You. This time built in me a greater understanding of You and Your willingness to communicate and respond to me. And I've come to know You as my closest confidante and friend. This special time brought me incredible joy and blessings and greater certainty of Your presence. Each day, I've felt closer to You as I've grown more accustomed to hearing Your voice. The fellowship has been ever-so-sweet, and the conversions were always encouraging. Thanks for revealing to me a way to know and understand Your ways. You've shown me so many things I could never understand, like what's in people and how I can best deal with them. You've instructed me in Your ways, and You've given me support, promises, joy, and hope. Your presence has been a wonderful light to me and a beacon during life's storms. Today, give me needed wisdom as I deal with those you bring my way. Show me the right words to speak and help me to forgive when some come against me. Help me to focus on You and the positives You bring, including Your encouragement and strength. Thanks for this special time together. I love You.

God: Dear one, today holds many possible and potential blessings. As you encounter them, remember where they come from, and give thanks. I'll always bring you great joy and peace and love. I'll offer you ways to grow and become great in My eyes. You can fit into the shoes I provide for you. Don't be afraid to put them on. Just trust and have confidence in Me to walk in them. I'll back you up and support you in every situation. I always work in you to will and to do of My good pleasure. Remember that I am a God of accessibility—I am with you as you encounter any situation, place, or person you meet. So, depend on Me to lead you to the right places and people. Trust that I direct your steps. Persevere and push on. Let Me be your source of strength. I'm your confidence-builder. Only I can give you what you need. Lean on Me, and I'll come through for you always. Just take life a step at a time. I love you.

And see the power of words

"I have hidden your word in my heart, that I might not sin against you."
—Psalm 119:11

Me: Thanks, Lord, for a day to rest in You. Thanks for it being free from confrontations and complaints from unappreciative people! Thanks that I can delight in You and in Your presence. Thanks for friends who want to know You and seek You as I do and for people with whom I can share Your hope and joy. Would You give me visions like Your prophets, and show me where You want me and to whom I should speak? I see a sifting going on where You watch to see which side people stand on, and I submit to You and Your will. Bring those who also seek Your will, whose God is You and whose expectations are based on Your truth. Thanks. Today, I thank you for the people You've brought to walk alongside me. I know I need to be Your representative among godless souls, and I put my trust in You to lead and place me where You want me. Help me to be bold to speak Your words that can cut through any clutter—lies or misinformation—so I can acknowledge Your presence and follow more closely in Your footsteps. Help me to come against any bitterness in my soul toward those who mistreat me. Help me to forgive and move on. Today, lead me to Your place of joy and rest. I love You.

God: Dear one, allow My Word to live in your heart. Let it dwell in your mind and flow through you richly to others. Yes, I will lead you to others who want to hear and receive what you can share. Yes, I will speak freely to you as you listen for Me. Yes, I want you to take more time to hear Me as you sit with Me inside My sanctuary. I'm your Lord and your God. I give you grace and love—more than you have room to receive. I give you boundless joy—more than you can comprehend. You're My special, precious child. Remember, your thoughts are powerful. And your words can penetrate hearts. So, you must be careful in how you use them. Never throw them around carelessly. They are swords that can heal, captivate, bring results, and make whole, or cause pain, destruction, sadness, and death. Plant them carefully. Use them to bring joy. Use them to bring people closer to Me. Use them to build on My strong foundation. I'll lead you to mighty men and women who seek My will. Wait and see. I love you.

As I cast Your nets

"Come, be my disciples, and I will show you how to fish for people!"
—Matthew 4:19

Me: Show me, Lord, where to cast my nets. Lead me, Lord, to where I can gather and reap the best results. You are Lord of all. You are wise and mighty. You're above all most powerful. Would You show me, Lord, where to sow Your seeds so they produce the best harvest? I know You can enlighten my eyes in the same way You did the disciples after they'd fished all night with no results (John 21). When Jesus told them to cast the nets on the right side of the boat, they knew it was Him. You alone can reveal things that are hidden to others. You can show me where the hungry people are and how to reach them. And only You can change peoples' hearts. Now, I want to learn more about how not to judge people by their appearances. I want to be able to see beyond the surface. Show me those who want to know You, Lord! They may not be the friendliest, wisest, or most attractive people, but You can show me which of them wants to hear about You. Make it clear to me who You are calling, and help me to see their needs clearly. Thanks, Lord. You are above all. Give me eyes to see and ears to hear. Give me the courage to do what You're asking me to do. You're great, Lord. You give me strength and joy. Thank You. I love You.

God: Dear one, pray for anyone you come into contact with, but never let them steal your peace. The ones who lack peace have made other things besides a relationship with Me their priority, like money, time, jobs, power, control, reputation, status, or other people. They rely on things in the world to give them what they need, and, of course, these things can never last. Your job is to show those I bring to you that, even when they're surrounded by turmoil, they can be peaceful. Some will balk at this. These aren't the ones who will listen. When people reject your message, shake the dust off your feet, and move on! Watch for the right ones. They'll be evident. They will want to hear. Today, seek My glory in the ones I've chosen, the ones who respond to you. You'll see how My glory shines in their faces as they experience My joy. You'll see how they have My peace and can rest during chaos. These are My precious called ones. I love you.

OCTOBER 19
  And feel Your joy

"Dear brothers and sisters, when troubles of any kind come your way, consider it an opportunity for great joy."
—James 1:2

Me: Lord, I want to experience Your joy today! I feel like I've been in your "Peace Class" for quite some time now. And I'm finally able to recognize when I've lost my peace and see how to get it back again. I've learned how to move my mind back to that quiet place, where I can sense Your presence and hear Your voice. And You show me clearly what's trying to steal it away. Now, would You teach me about joy and how I can have it all the time? I look at the week ahead, and my stomach churns when I see all the things on my calendar. I don't look forward to some of them. I long for time to do the things I really enjoy, like reading, writing, watching my favorite programs, and spending quiet time with You. But I know this is not Your will for me now. I must meet with people, including some I don't care to spend time with. Sometimes it's discouraging, even with Your encouragement, when the people I try to help refuse advice that could change their lives! Show me how to deal with stubborn people, who don't want to change. It's hard when I see them suffer hardships, because they neglect Your simple laws that mean the difference between abundance or scarcity, life or death. Thanks for patience, Lord. I love You.

God: Dear one, My words are always life-giving. They bring peace and joy and a refreshing calm. They bring needed healing to those who seek them. They bring what's needed in your life and others'. Come to Me with your whole heart, and open up your tenderest parts to Me. Then I can heal them and give you strength and peace. Don't be afraid to come to Me. When you do, you'll gain access to amazing amounts of joy, and this joy can flow through you to others. Open your heart to Me, and allow Me to heal your mind and body. My Word never returns void. Even when some refuse to hear it, others will respond. And those who walk away now may heed it later. Don't be discouraged. Know that I have your back. I love how you keep trying. Some will listen and change. Keep trying to reach these. Precious child, My love goes beyond anything you can experience. Open your heart to Me, and join Me on a joy journey! I love you.

OCTOBER 20
Again and again and again

"Taste and see that the Lord is good. Oh, the joys of those who take refuge in him!"
—*Psalm 34:8*

Me: Lord, I enjoy time alone with You. I love the quietness and the opportunity to hear Your voice, and to be able to speak with You about so many matters. I love this time when I'm undisturbed by all the demands on my life. Thanks for great peace in my heart today, knowing You will come through for me again and again and again. Would You lead me to Your place of rest, and show me more about how You view things? I desire You and Your presence. Let me be like Joseph or Moses, whose hearts You sought and won, and whose lives You led to help so many others, because You loved them and they loved You. Show me how I can walk in Your powerful ways. Often, I don't understand why people are so unkind and cruel, or why they betray and dishonor Your honorable and righteous ones. It's hard for me to relate to this. I want to be Your light, Lord. Thanks for Your strength and guidance. Thanks for Your insight when I have no answers. But most of all, thanks for Your peace and joy. I love You.

God: Dear one, you are so very special to Me. Your voice is sweet to My ears. I love our conversations. Just keep handing your cares over to Me in the quiet moments. Lift them up to Me, and I will take them from you. Let Me bear your burdens and bring you lasting peace and overflowing joy. I know how to solve your problems, and bring you answers. Only let Me. You often feel burdened, but you don't need to feel this way. Hand your concerns over to Me. Then, you'll be freer to think, act, and help others. Your heart will be so much lighter! Then, you can be a greater blessing to those you encounter. I want you to know that many people live in fear of what others think of them, of what might happen to them, of being betrayed, and of not having enough. The more fear they have, the less able I am to work on their behalf. Some have learned to move past their fears so they can trust in Me. But few will do this. Most blame others for their qualms, instead of facing and overcoming them. Never take it personally when people attack or slight you for your beliefs. If you remain steady, those who truly want to understand and have peace will come to you for help and advice. These will acknowledge your strength and admire it. These are your true allies and friends. I love you.

OCTOBER 21
And look toward my dream

"May he grant your heart's desires and make all your plans succeed."
—*Psalm 20:4*

Me: Dear Lord, I reread the book, *Pollyanna*, a few years ago, and I remembered why I always loved this story, referred to as "The Glad Book." It reminds me of a desire I had long ago, when I was eight years old and watched the movie that was based on the book at a classmate's birthday party. Like Pollyanna, I wanted to change people's lives for the better. That became my dream. My desire was to bring a message of joy and hope to every person I met. Now, I still aspire toward this goal. Help me, Lord! Even today, show me how to touch those in need and be able to bring Your essence of joy to them. Open new doors, and help me to succeed in ways I never dreamed of by spreading Your Word across many boundaries and borders. This is my hope. And my dream. I love You.

God: Child, you've been blessed, and you're a blessing. Do you see how, so many years ago, I set before you this desire, which was also My vision for you? Do you see how I put that dream in your heart because I just wanted you to be great in My eyes? Walk with Me now. Let Me lead you, and I'll guide you to new and wonderful places, where people are eager to hear your words and learn about Me so they can hope and dream, like you. I'll show you where to go, how to get there, and what to do once you're there. Remember Joan of Arc—a small girl with a big heart and great trust in Me? She was a little like Pollyanna. She had a vision to help people. It's always through what people consider "insignificant" events and people that I show myself the strongest. To many, matters may seem very unimportant. But to Me, they never are. I care about the small things—how you treat others, the things you do for people, when you listen to Me, and when you do what I tell you. It's during these moments when I do My best work, for it's the little things that add up to big things in the end. As you listen to Me, and follow through with your inspirations, you'll begin to see how these minor things end up being life-changing to you and to others. Let Me show you the way to My mountain—My place of peace, joy, hope, and beauty. The view there is breath-taking, beyond anything you've ever seen. There you'll find a world that's beyond recognition. There you'll find Me. And you'll experience great joy. I love you.

OCTOBER 22
By drinking Your water of life

"The Spirit and the bride say, "Come." Let anyone who hears this say, "Come." Let anyone who is thirsty come. Let anyone who desires drink freely from the water of life."
—Revelation 22:17

Me: Lord, I realized as I read the gospels how Your Son often chose the seashore as His place to minister and teach. And You confirmed that, like me, Your Son loved the sea and enjoyed being near water. Water symbolizes life and peace and purity and closeness to You. It's through water that we feel refreshed, and, with it, You bring absolute refreshing and newness of life. Jesus must have loved walking by the water and on it! It restored His soul, much like it does mine as I walk around the lake each day, sharing my thoughts with You. I bet that was the time when He felt closest to You, as He sat on a mountain overlooking the Sea of Galilee, praying or teaching. He loved the sea more than the city, because there He could find so many who wanted to hear Him and absorb His words. And this brought Him great joy! Today, as I walk along the water and enjoy the brisk morning air, would You remind me of Your Son and His love for the water of life? I love You.

God: Dear one, My Son does love water, just as you do. And I do. I made it as part of this world and the next—just for you. It's a source of life, just as I am. Remember that, before vegetation could spring up, water had to exist. Nothing on earth can live without it. Besides representing life itself, water symbolizes My Spirit. Remember how My Son revealed Himself first to the woman at the well. And He promised her living water, which signified the spirit He'd make available to her and to many. In Revelation, He revealed that He'd give water from the spring of the water of life, and the river of the water of life would flow from My throne and His throne one day through the new city. It would bring eternal life to all. How important is water on the earth today and in the new heaven and earth I'll create one day? It's essential to bringing forth life. So, as you walk near the water of a lake or a stream or a river or a seashore, remember the wonderful promise from My Son that, one day, "to all who are thirsty I will give freely from the springs of the water of life." (Revelation 21:6.) And never forget how much I love you.

When others disappoint me

"A friend is always loyal, and a brother is born to help in time of need."
—Proverbs 17:17

Me: How I love the special, joyful times with You, Lord! I'm thankful for the happy hours, when I'm reminded of Your presence. I treasure similar times with family and friends. Knowing that they appreciate these moments too and want to spend precious time together means a lot to me. Thanks for good memories of family times. I felt hurt today when a family member, who'd promised special time with me, chose to spend that time with others instead. Would You help me to accept things like this when they happen and be able to trust You during disappointment, knowing You'll work things out for me in other ways? Help me to forgive those who show a lack of consideration and be able to move on and experience Your joy despite defeat. Help me to be guided by Your hand and Your wisdom as I deal with people, especially when they let me down. Help me to know that, when others are disloyal, You are faithful. Let me be the joyful light that You are for me. I love You.

God: Dear one, it's very important that you check in with Me before making commitments. Because some will be loyal and show you respect, but others won't. Some will encourage you by bringing you great joy and peace and kindness. These are the faithful ones who will be there for you when you're in need of comfort. But others will not be good allies. Goodness is returned for goodness. It's the same for kindness. I orchestrate beneficial results for those who bless and give of themselves to My people. My heart is touched by heartfelt giving. When you reach out to bless others, going out of your way to help them, I'll always reciprocate your kind-heartedness. But when people cause harm to My own, they bring bad repercussions on themselves. Loyalty begets more loyalty. Faithfulness brings more who are faithful. Let Me lead you in choosing good friends and show you how to best use your time. I see your life as a beacon of hope. If people seek Me, they'll move closer to you. If they don't seek Me, they'll move away and make excuses for their absence. When people resist time with you, let them go. Leave them to me. I'll direct you so you won't lose your peace or doubt yourself. Because I want you to be strong in My joy always. I love you.

But I see Your mysterious plan

"I was chosen to explain to everyone this mysterious plan that God, the Creator of all things, had kept secret from the beginning. God's purpose in all this was to use the church to display his wisdom in its rich variety to all the unseen rulers and authorities in the heavenly places. This was his eternal plan, which he carried out through Christ Jesus our Lord. Because of Christ and our faith in him, we can now come boldly and confidently into God's presence."
—Ephesians 3:9-12

Me: You're awesome, Lord. You're mighty beyond words. I find it incredible how You're fashioning a magnificent mosaic, piece by piece. You're preparing Your divine pattern out of thousands of puzzle pieces until we see Your powerful plan and purpose! It makes me realize, more and more, Your greatness and might. Thanks for revealing this masterpiece little by little to me. Thanks for showing me Your way when I'm sometimes confused. You walk beside me continuously and help me by holding my hand. Thanks for Your constant guidance. Help me to see Your plan more precisely, so I can better exemplify You. Would You help me to display Your character in all I do? Help me to bring light and life and joy to my work so I can lead others in the best way. You're my leader. Take my hand now and direct me, Lord. I need Your help. Today, open doors beyond my expectation. Guide me to the people You want me to speak to. I love You.

God: Dear one, relish the days and times and hours. Just don't forget Me in them. As the days go by, you'll see more and more how the puzzle pieces of your life fit into a wonderful masterpiece I'm creating. I love to watch you happily going about your days, bringing people new light and life. And I share in your joy. Talk to Me and think of Me, for I love your praise and thankfulness. These are the things I delight in. I'll open more doors for you. Just wait and see. These "beyond your expectation" experiences will contribute to My masterpiece. Be ready, for I'll ask you to do things you've never done. But I'll prepare and guide you as you go. Don't be afraid of what others might say. People come and go. Only My Word lives forever. Let it prevail in your life. Then, I'll bring mighty things to pass! In time, you'll behold My finished masterpiece. And discover how much I love you.

OCTOBER 25
That makes up for the insensitive

"Oh, what joy for those whose disobedience is forgiven, whose sin is put out of sight! Yes, what joy for those whose record the Lord has cleared of guilt, whose lives are lived in complete honesty!"
—Psalm 32:1-2

Me: Lord, would You give me wisdom when I want to be what's needed, but I feel lacking? Help me see the good in others and not be hurt by their absence of love or responsiveness. Help me not to be devastated by others' criticism or failure to see what's in my heart. It makes me feel like I'm standing on a precipice, looking down at an endless abyss of unkindness and cruelty. Help me to see clearly what's going on at these times, to choose my words wisely, and to have the courage to close the doors that need to be slammed shut. Prop the doors open when situations are ripe for forgiveness and mercy. And set me free from bitter, unhappy people, who try to steal my joy! If I can help them, show me how! If not, place them in another's hands. Remind me that the things that upset me: peoples' insensitivity, complaining, and faultfinding, are temporary and meaningless. Then I can maintain Your joy today. I love You.

God: Dear one, it's hard to love the unlovable and deal with their thoughtlessness, neglect, negativity, anger, hatred, etc. It's hard to forgive or bless those who return only insensitivity and unkindness. Do you see that those who act like this are most miserable and vulnerable to attacks, because they refuse to arm themselves against negativity by receiving My Word into their hearts? Often, they're very broken people. When you struggle with them, fall into My arms. Let Me lift you up and give you wisdom and patience. I can direct you as you come closer to Me. Let Me protect and heal your heart so you can reflect My joy in every situation. For you're My beacon. Let My love inside you bring others, even the unlovable ones, to My truth. Just remember that one day all these things will be forgotten. They'll fade away as we stand together and rejoice forever in a place beyond your wildest dreams. Release the negativity to Me, and let me deal with it. Remember, it's Mine to deal with, not yours! And I'll help you maintain your own joy and peace, even when they can't. I love you.

Because I'm comforted by Your nearness

"Because you are my helper, I sing for joy in the shadow of your wings. I cling to you; your strong right hand holds me securely."
—Psalm 63:7-8

Me: Lord, let my day be sweet, because it's touched by Your hand! Let it be one of my very best! Let me be swept right off my feet, because I'm in love with You! I want to be overcome by Your presence and glamoured by Your beauty. I want to be comforted by Your nearness and captured by Your lavish love. Lord, can I see and feel and taste more of You so that nothing bothers me in the least? Let me huddle with You, and feel Your warmth, as we stand with our arms around each other. Let me embrace You in the snowstorm as the flakes fall all around us, but every sound is muffled by our whispers. I can feel Your heartbeat as we snuggle away the cold, and I laugh out loud as we're completely surrounded by thickly falling flakes but warmly oblivious to them. I want to be bound together with You as one and never separated from Your comforting company. I long for this—a solace apart from the world's hurts and harms. You, Lord, are my comforter and my surrounding peace. You are my hiding place. I long to be near You today, Lord! You bring me such sweet joy. I love You.

God: Dear one, because of your love for Me, you're blessed beyond anything you can imagine. Wait until you see what I have in store for you! You won't believe it! Only I can describe its greatness or know what's ahead. You've loved well, and I'll reward you now and later for your kindness. You've followed My lead by speaking My words to others when I've opened the doors to you. And I'll continue to open doors for you to walk through. Only follow My lead. I'll have you in the right place at the right time, for I'm your defender, your advocate, your Lord, your love, your father, your source of all joy, your strength, your life, and your very existence. I'm always present and always near you. I'm stable—a rock to lean on. Be comforted in this: I will always have for you what you need when you need it. When people come and go, I'll remain beside you. Even in the storms, I'll clear the way for you to go so you're never lost. I'll even make new paths for you to walk on. And I'll embrace you as we walk the paths together. Today, let Me fill you with My love through joyful, whispered words that can overflow to others. I love you.

OCTOBER 27
And encouraged during despair

"To all who mourn...he will give a crown of beauty for ashes, a joyous blessing instead of mourning, festive praise instead of despair."
—Isaiah 61:3

Me: Lord, the air is still and quiet as I sit and pray. And I'm thankful for all You've done for me. I am thinking of a time long ago when I studied under a ministry where I worked and lived with other Christians on a 150-acre community farm. My nine-month-old daughter was with me, and I wanted to serve in childcare so I could be close to her. I was allowed to do this for three months. But the woman in charge of the nursery was very demanding, and she required me to read a book about childcare during the morning work hours. Sadly, I was often exhausted, since we attended late night classes, and my sleep was interrupted nightly by my daughter's need to nurse. I still had to meet everyone at 5:30 each morning to jog together. And I had about an hour to get ready for breakfast at 7:30. When I went to the library at 8:30 to read my assignment, I inevitably fell asleep at the desk. My boss, who didn't participate in the night classes or morning rituals, went home to sleep for eight hours, and she didn't understand my inability to focus or finish the book in her timeline. So, she fired me. I was devastated. I was reassigned to a job in the kitchen, where I cooked meals. And my heart broke each day as I dropped my crying baby off at the daycare. She would cling to the screen door and cry and call out to me as I walked away. This was a hard lesson for me, but somehow I survived the ordeal. Lord, show me why I remember this now. What lesson do You want me to learn from it? I don't want to be hard-hearted and unforgiving of people who sometimes seem so cruel. Thanks for Your mercy. I love You.

God: Dear one, your heart is sometimes troubled, because you feel grieved that you and others have fallen short, and you realize how imperfect people really are, including My people, the ones you expected to be loving and merciful. Just come to Me in these times and ask for forgiveness when you feel bitter or angry at other's hard-heartedness. When you ask Me to pardon them, I will. But you must cleanse your own heart first by clothing yourself with the purity of My love. Wash your heart in the crystal-clear springs of My mercy and grace. Only this will help you feel right again in your heart about yourself and others. As you forgive, you will be healed. Then you can move on and feel My overflowing joy. I love you.

October 28
By Your beautiful words

"The Lord made the earth by his power, and he preserves it by his wisdom. With his own understanding he stretched out the heavens."
—Jeremiah 51:15

Me: Dear Lord, I love how You hear me and how You bring magnificent days to enjoy! Would You make more of my days even sweeter with the nectar of Your words? May each fresh word bring me greater understanding and meaning and joy. May I pay attention to each one as they are infused into my soul. Instill in me more of Your creativity and imagination as I encounter each new discerning discovery. Direct my ways to Your heart, and cause me to prosper in a greater way spiritually, mentally, and physically. Enlighten my thoughts, and help me to see everything as You do. Give me more time to read and hear from You and a greater ability to absorb like a sponge whatever You need me to heed and understand. Place in front of me people to help me to learn more about You, and show me how to best benefit from their insight. Let Your peace wash over my soul, even as I grow older and days grow more challenging. Guide my thoughts so I can find Your joy in every situation. I love You.

God: Dear one, you are a joy to Me! You bring me great happiness. I celebrate who you are! I remember you in your goings out and your comings in, and I have always rejoiced over you. Allow Me to bless you more than you could ever imagine. By beautiful waters, you will one day recline, surrounded by sweet-smelling trees and plants as you enjoy peaceful rest in Me. This is My promise to you. Now, as you walk through life with Me, reflect on what's around you. Don't focus so much on where you've been or where you're going. Concentrate on the beauty I unfold around you. Appreciate the things I've done, but, even more, enjoy what I'm doing with your help. You'll see amazing things as you glance around at your surroundings and the people I bring you. And you'll gain a greater appreciation for your life and how I've orchestrated it. It's good to stay on the "right" path, but sometimes you will lose your way, and you will focus on the thorns and thistles. At these times, gaze instead at what's available—what I am doing through you! Then you will have greater joy. Then the nectar of the words I speak to you will be sweet, and you will feel embraced by My lavish love. I love you.

October 29
During a peaceful and precious time

"One day soon afterward Jesus went up on a mountain to pray, and he prayed to God all night."
—Luke 6:12

Me: Thanks for a time of rest and recuperation, Lord, and for precious moments to read and reflect on Your love. Thanks for a "breather," when I can collect myself and refocus on what I can do and how I can do it. My special request today is that You work through me as Your gift of love to others—those you bring to me. As Your gatekeeper, show me the ones You'd have me bring through Your gates. I can see why it was so important for Jesus to go up to the mountain to pray alone early in the morning. I can see why He had to get away from the "maddening crowds," with all their demands on Him. Help me to avoid the demands of people that result in mindless efforts and fruitless results. I need to spend more time with You, Lord, praying and reflecting on Your words. Would You help me to remember this, especially when I feel pressed by too many demands? I know I'd see greater and more beneficial results if I did. Remind me to come to You and take time to talk to You and ask for Your input. How I love this precious time that brings me joy! I love You.

God: Dear one, it's imperative that you set aside time with me each and every day. This time is life-giving "bread" for you. It will help you achieve things you never thought possible. You'll see mighty results in your life, and the lives of others, when you take this time with Me. Your days will go so much smoother, and you will have greater peace, joy, and a healthier life if you will do this. During these times, you'll learn to recognize My voice—when I'm whispering to your heart and trying to tell you something important. Then, I can breathe strength and courage into your soul and expand your spiritual awareness to a much higher degree. I can encourage your heart with gladness and bring you great joy. I can squeeze you with hugs and cover you with kisses as a loving parent would do. Then, I can place your feet solidly in My footsteps and direct you down peaceful paths to greater things. But you must set aside this rare and precious time for Me and for you. I love you.

In a sunny space

"How great is the goodness you have stored up for those who fear you. You lavish it on those who come to you for protection, blessing them before the watching world."
—*Psalm 31:19*

Me: Lord, last night I dreamed that I went to add dirt to some seeds I'd placed in a pan full of small pebbles with the intention of planting them later. The pan was in a warehouse that was attached to a plant store. When I went to scoop up the pebbles from around the seeds, I realized that the seeds had already sprouted long shoots that reached up toward me! I was surprised, and I carefully placed dirt around the sprouts among the pebbles. I looked around the warehouse for a sunny place to set the pan, knowing the sprouts would need some sunlight to keep growing. And I noticed a small, separate room at the back of the warehouse. Light streamed into the room through a large window that opened to the store. Inside the room, a double bed with sheets sat neglected and covered with debris. The room was dirty and cluttered with objects left behind. I decided to tidy it up. So, I cleaned off the bed, moved a small table with a lamp next to it to make the room feel cozier, and organized the clutter around it. That way, it would be more inviting for whoever needed to rest there. As I pondered what I could do to leave the room in better shape, some kids popped through an opening and caused a disruption with shouting and laughing. I told them to play in the other parts of the warehouse. Then I woke up. And I wondered what it all meant. Help me to understand, Lord! I love You.

God: Dear child, your desire to make things better than you found them is obvious in this dream! Your life goal was always to leave a legacy—a space in life that was made more beautiful than before. You sought out the "sunny" places to plant new life and watch it grow. And you wanted to work with Me to clear away the clutter and organize things to create spaces of healing and peace and joy. You also wanted to make places where people could come and see beauty and feel welcome. At times you've experienced disruptions that felt like they distracted you from your purpose, including caring for children. But these actually brought you closer to your own goal of beautifying life and leaving it better than you found it. This has always been your goal and your purpose. And I've helped you along the way to accomplish both. I love you.

OCTOBER 31
As I experience Your amazing grace

"Surely your goodness and unfailing love will pursue me all the days of my life, and I will live in the house of the Lord forever."
—*Psalm 23:6*

Me: Thanks for Your amazing goodness today, Lord, and for taking care of all my needs, even as I hide myself in You moment by moment. Let me sit in the cleft of Your mountain, guarded as You stand with me and shower Me with Your kindness. Replace what has been stolen from me, and multiply many times over what is good. It's calm outside now, but last night the winds and rain and hail tore through the trees, pounded on the roof, and beat against the windows. Thanks for Your hand of protection during the storm as I prayed. Would You always bless and take care of my home, the plants and trees, the birds and animals, our pets, and the people nearby? Thanks for reminding me of a picture I saw once of a bird in a tree that clung to its nest as a storm blew the branches and limbs around it. It sat calmly, knowing it was somehow safe. Thanks that I can feel this way during any tempest. Let today be a day of peacefulness, blessing, favor, and joy. Guide me as I direct others to Your safe and comforting arms within the crevice of Your mountain. I pray for Your favor in unexpected places—grace that moves mountains, opens doors, and gives me access to what You want for me and for others. I love You.

God: Dear one, you see how you need never worry about your safety. Don't you know I'm always available to hear your requests and protect your interests? Get ready now, because, just like the abundant rains that wash down suddenly, I'll pour you out a blessing that you'll not have room enough to receive. As you give, I'll give you even more! Remember this. Allow Me to work to will and to do of My good pleasure in your life. My way is a well-rewarded way, a way of joy and laughter, peace and mercy, love and kindness, even in the midst of storms. Allow Me to have My way in your life so you need never worry or be anxious about the things around you! I'll bless and protect what you have, including your own life. Just turn to Me when others are full of fear. Let Me work to bring you even more peace and joy to share with others. For I want to bless you in mighty ways! I love you.

November

FOCUS:
POWERFUL PRAISE

"Give thanks to the Lord, for he is good!
His faithful love endures forever."

—I CHRONICLES 16:34

As a passenger on Your ship

"Devote yourselves to prayer with an alert mind and a thankful heart."
—Colossians 4:2

Me: It's hard for me to focus sometimes, Lord. Would You help me to keep my eyes directed on You? I'm often distracted by things like what I'll wear or eat, situations at work, or people I need to see. I want to stay on Your path and go in Your direction. Would You help me with this? Help me to keep pace with You and to accomplish what I need to get done for You. I'd like to hand over the steering of my life to You and be able to just live in the comfort of Your arms, knowing every detail of my life is taken care of by You. I want to be consumed by Your thoughts about everything! What do You think about that food or those clothes or that situation or these people? I'd love to hear Your view of all the things I see and feel. Would You help me with this, Lord? I want to trust in You completely. Today, help me to speak into others' lives with the right words. My life is in Your hands. Please steer me in the direction You need me to go! I want to be a passenger on Your ship. I love You.

God: Child, you are precious. I adore you and always have. I see you as you were at 16—full of life and vigor. Someday, you'll see yourself as I do. You often feel heavy with responsibility. Let Me assume this for you. Let Me take your cares and give you constant peace. I can give you great joy too. Just trust in Me. Today, when peace eludes you as the world demands so much from you, turn your thoughts of Me. I'll remind you of My grace-filled presence. I long to help you! Just let me. I'm opening doors for you even now to things beyond your imagination! One day you'll see My floodgates opening to you! For now, rest in Me. Don't worry about things to come or let your mind be distracted by what you think you need now. Do you believe I'll take care of you in ways beyond anything you can ask or think? As you trust in Me, you'll find what you seek. Be thankful for what you have now, and focus on praising and rejoicing. These get My attention! Seek the things of the spirit by focusing on My Word, then I'll steer your life, and you'll rest aboard My ship. You can have My love, peace, and joy every day by turning your eyes to Me with thankfulness! Because eyes focused on Me reflect these qualities. I love you.

  I want to join with You in singing

"He has given me a new song to sing, a hymn of praise to our God. Many will see what he has done and be amazed. They will put their trust in the Lord."
—Psalm 40:3

Me: Lord, last night in a dream I was standing with a group of people under a highway ramp, and I started to sing a song that I made up. A young man near me joined in and added his own lyrics. Soon, others joined in until we were all singing the same tune together. I was surprised to see my son, who died years ago, approach and join us. He took off his shirt and I could see the scars on his back where he'd had many lung surgeries. He looked so good now, and my heart rejoiced to hear him singing with us! Then I noticed a band behind him setting up under the ramp, getting ready to perform more songs. My son gave me some flyers to hand out with pictures of people on one side and a scripture verse on the other. As I handed them out, he read the verse from Psalm 40:3 out loud: "He has given me a new song to sing, a hymn of praise to our God. Many will see what he has done and be amazed. They will put their trust in the Lord." Some people stayed to listen; others walked away. I felt proud that he didn't care what they thought. He was bold for his God, as he always was in life! How happy I was to hear his voice again as he read the words! I woke up praying that I'd have his courage. Help me to be bold for You, Lord. I love You.

God: Dear one, just follow My steps, for they'll never lead you astray. Let Me guide your thoughts and share tender moments with you, sometimes through dreams. For that's my greatest desire. How I love you and mean only good for you. You see how I've released your son from his earthly body, and now he rests in peace. I've freed him from hurt, pain, and all of life's struggles. One day, you'll rejoice and sing with him all the songs you love and miss singing with him now. He loves you so and is thankful for all you did for him, mostly how you led him to Me. As time goes on, you'll see more and more how I use the broken, the feeble, even sinners, to bring about my intent for this world. Never let others' lack of desire for Me lessen your joy in singing for My glory. I'll bring God-lovers alongside you to join in with praise and thanksgiving. The ones who choose to walk away now are short-sighted and live only for the moment. Though they reject you now, it'll be different later. Then, they'll ask for your help. Wait and see. I'll show you who'll heed your words and join you in singing My songs. I love you.

November 3

As we stand at a precipice

"I wait quietly before God, for my victory comes from him. He alone is my rock and my salvation, my fortress where I will never be shaken."
—Psalm 62:1-2

Me: Dear Lord, these are important days because, every few years, we get to vote for our leaders. And often, our nation stands at a precipice. Lord, would You guide each person as he or she votes? Reach into each of our hearts, beyond our opinions and prejudices, to direct us to do what's best for our country by looking beyond vapid promises to what our choices will entail or precipitate, and how they will affect what we face as a nation. Lord, give us courage to turn to You for guidance. I pray that, before we vote, we seek leaders who will work with You to bring healing to our nation. We need freedom, Lord. Elevate those whose desire is to preserve this for us. And open the eyes of those who are blinded by power and control. Obstruct those who want to destroy what You've built. May our nation be in Your hands, and may people arise to stand for You. I know You're in control, even when hope seems lost. Stir our hearts to have confidence in You alone. Give us courage to rise up and speak the truth, undaunted by fear and uninhibited by perceived threats. Give us boldness to be guided by You in all things. In hard times, give us strength to move in the direction of Your loving hand. I love You.

God: Dear one, on special, designated days you can choose your leaders—those you want to represent you and your nation. I can guide you in this process. Be thankful for this right. And never forget the brave actions of people who went before you to fight for this privilege. In many lands, the citizens have little or no choice as to who leads them. Their liberty has been stolen away by people seeking power, and the result is that many must pray in secret, hide their persuasions to spare their own and others' lives, and can only covertly speak the truth. Their lives are in constant danger. Many suffer for their beliefs and are tortured and persecuted for holding onto them. Those who persist in their stance for Me and My Son under these dire circumstances must live with the threat of harm or death. But they will receive rewards for their bravery later, when My Son returns. Be thankful for what you have now. But you must be willing to fight for the maintenance of your freedom so that you and others can worship me freely in spirit and in truth! I love you.

NOVEMBER 4
But I decide to ride high with You

"You lay out the rafters of your home in the rain clouds. You make the clouds your chariot; you ride upon the wings of the wind."
—*Psalm 104:3*

Me: You astonish me, God, with Your amazing ways. Thanks for the appearance of an extraordinary rainbow yesterday to remind me of Your presence. The double rainbow established that You are there and that You hear my prayers. What a wonderful reminder of Your love! It was the most beautiful one I'd ever seen. Thank You! You are truly marvelous. Thanks again for Your blessings and mercy. They go beyond my imagination. Often, I'm far too concerned about myself. I don't think enough about others' grief or sadness, because I'm so aware of my own problems. Lord, give me a bigger heart to understand and empathize. Would You help me to sift through pride and relinquish self-pity by replacing them with love and mercy and understanding? Help me to flee from judgment and criticism once and for all. You're awesome and mighty—a great God above all gods in this world. Thanks today for being with me and for directing and giving me peace. Thanks for reminding me again and again of Your wonderful presence. And for blessing My children and their children. Thank You for Your love. I love You.

God: Dear one, I surround you like a cloud. I swirl around you, massaging you continuously with My love. You can't see Me, but I watch over you. Yes, I smile on you. And I whisper things to you. My words become your works as you listen to them then follow My leading. My hand is always on you. And I protect you as you reach out to Me. Never be afraid. Life on earth now is tough, but it won't last forever. Life with Me will. And although you can't see it yet, My world is wonderful and beautiful and liberating and amazing! Because there are no boundaries or fences. There are no limitations or fears. No sadness or sorrow or anger or bitterness. One day you'll see it—when My Son comes for you. Then you'll ride with Him through the clouds on the wings of the wind! Watch for Him, because His time to come draws near. He loves you with an awesome and burning love. He cries for you when you suffer and mourns for you when you feel alone. As you walk with My Spirit in you, you'll have greater freedom, peace, joy, and a way that surpasses all others. I love you.

November 5
My masterful maestro

"David continued to succeed in everything he did, for the Lord was with him."
—*1 Samuel 18:14*

Me: Dear God, You're my agent of light and love, music and magic, excitement and enjoyment. You're my precious poet, my awesome artist, and my chief conductor. You lead the way to wonderful things in my life. Would You help me to depend on You for everything? And help me to see You as You are and where You are—in the middle of my life. Help me to focus on Your greatness and Your ability to love through me. Lead on, masterful maestro! Play Your strokes with brightness and beauty. For You are perfection and prowess and praise. You are my shining example. Help me to love You for who and what You are, and to better envision what You want to do through me. Would You help me to see You in a more dynamic way? For I long to know You as David did. I'm so pitiful at times—so very lacking. Without you, I'm nothing. David saw You for who You are and for all that You are. He understood what You'd done for him, and he glorified and praised You for it. You placed him in high places, because he placed You high in his heart. Everywhere I turn, I'm reminded of You. I see You in the beauty of the trees and birds and flowers. You're my best friend. David felt the same way. Help me to have a heart like his. Not just today, but every day. And let this be the first day, but not the last, to see You as he did. I love You.

God: Dear one, you know I'm with you always. I've anointed you with a special grace and favor, as I did My beloved David, and no one can take this away from you. Let no one steal My peace from your heart. It's My gift to you. I continue to work My wonderful deeds through you. I bless you mightily and can bring you a life beyond anything you can imagine. I will restore what's been taken from you over the years, even returning to you double what was stolen. This is My promise. Trust Me, and let Me work amazing things in and through your life. Continue to speak and to serve. Listen to My words, and then follow them. Remember, My words are very real. They bring light and life and a refreshing. They always come from My heart to yours. Today, let Me bring you joy unlike any you've ever known. Today, let Me bring you love unlike any in this world. For I love you.

Who gives me songs of praise

"In that day you will sing: 'I will praise you, O Lord!'"
—Isaiah 12:1

Me: Lord, today I rejoiced as I walked among the things You created. And I asked You about the birds and why You made them the way they are. "Why do they sing in such different ways, and each song is so beautiful?" I asked. "Because I love to hear each one's very unique song of praise!" You answered. And I realized how much You must love to hear each of us singing our own special praise songs to You! "How sorrowful it must be for You, though," I thought, "to soar over the earth and see so many people turning away and ignoring You." "Yes. It hurts My heart immensely," You said. "But I have great joy, like the shepherd who found the one lost sheep, when I see anyone turn to Me and come to trust Me. I especially love to hear their songs of praise." You see us as lights as You soar above. You see us as stars on the earth, like the stars in heaven. You recognize us by the glow coming from our hearts—the light shining from us. Help me to be more of a light in this world so others can know that I'm Yours and come to know You in a greater way. And help me to remember to lift my voice in praise to You. Because it brings You such great joy! I love You.

God: Dear one, many have the right wraps for the wrong reasons. And being religious is not what I want at all from people. I long for hearts filled with My love. Most people are far more concerned about how they look or if they're doing things in the most acceptable way. They want to fit in with those who appear to have the most power or control. Often, these are not the ones I approve of and accept. Why do you think I picked David? While others tried to appear religious or more acceptable, their hearts were far from Me. Saul made every effort to look good in the eyes of others. But David didn't care what others thought about him. He loved to sit and sing praises to Me! That's what I loved about him. You see, people will choose leaders who look good or say the right things or come from a prestigious family. But I never promote people pleasers or people that are lauded by others. You can always tell the motivations of people by asking Me. Some may seem like they're good, but just because they look good doesn't make them so. I seek the ones who praise, like David. I look for the ones who seek My love above all else. As you enjoy hearing birdsongs, I love hearing peoples' unique songs of praise. I love you.

And thankfulness for this day

"Praise the Lord with melodies on the lyre; make music for him on the ten-stringed harp. Sing a new song of praise to him; play skillfully on the harp, and sing with joy. For the word of the Lord holds true, and we can trust everything he does. He loves whatever is just and good; the unfailing love of the Lord fills the earth."
—Psalm 33:2-5

Me: Dear Lord, thanks for this new day. I'm so blessed and thankful for all You've done for me! Thanks for my family and friends and for blessing the work of my hands. Thanks for opening my eyes to Your great blessings and for the strength to receive them. You're awesome and magnificent. I worship and praise you in this day. Thanks for answering my questions—all of them! Thanks for a joyful day, filled with Your wonder! Thanks for peace this morning as I walked and observed the ducks, the lake, the deer, the fox, and even the clouds overhead, which reminded me of how Your Son will one day return to the earth in them. What a sight it will be! I long to stand in Your presence. And I know I will one day. You told me the tree, whose leaves rustled in the wind as I walked by it was clapping, not for You, but for me! Because it loved my praise! Thanks for warming my heart and soul, even on a chilly morning! I love You.

God: Dear one, today is a special day. Receive it as a great blessing from Me! Live and enjoy it, because every day is a gift. Treat each one as something very special. Rejoice and be glad in it, as My Word has said, because I made it for you. When you treat the days as unique blessings, your life becomes more enjoyable. And this attitude of praise prepares you for another life later. Living in joy and thanksgiving for what I've done helps you to bask in My goodness and light and to see Me more clearly. Remember that whatever you aspire to do in this life will determine your assignment in the next life, after My Son's return to earth. Your responsibility then will be determined by your choices now, and your rewards will be shaped by what you achieved in thankfulness to Me. Today, remember Me in everything you do. Take time to share your heart and your concerns, with Me. Be blessed in this day. Because I will walk with you through the details—all the details! I love you.

November 8
Through a tender heart

"I will give them singleness of heart and put a new spirit within them. I will take away their stony, stubborn heart and give them a tender, responsive heart..."
—Ezekiel 11:19

Me: Lord, would You remove our stony hearts and give us new, responsive hearts that are sensitive to Your touch? Would You help us to feel what You feel? Your Son once wept because He understood the pain others felt. Help me to love as He loves. Give me an enlarged spirit that I can go out and come in freely in Your presence! I want to be able to converse with You as a child with its father, because Your insight is amazing! Continue to open doors and bring me to those who desire Your love as I do. Only Your love. Open my eyes to the newness of Your ways, and help me to be more responsive to You in every way. Today, remind me how near You are, and help me to savor the time I have, so I can enjoy each and every moment. Let nothing disturb my peace. And let me see as You do, through crystalline eyes, with no presence of shame, remorse, unforgiveness, bitterness, or anger to obscure my vision. I want to see as You see and feel as You feel. I love You.

God: Dear one, allow Me to continually fire up your spirit with My touch so that your heart never becomes cold or hard, bitter or brittle. Let Me enlarge your love with My love so that you can always feel things as powerfully as I do. Let Me illuminate your vision with the light of My Spirit so you can always envision what I see. It may feel like a hard thing to look to Me continually, when you are surrounded by so many distractions. But it's the most important and life-giving thing you can do! The more you turn your thoughts to Me, the more I can help you throughout the day. It will always be hard to resist the temptation of complaining or criticizing or focusing on what's wrong with people and things. But don't get caught up in these. I'll help you to curtail these thoughts and any speech relating to them. And as you focus on praising and thanking Me, you'll know the enveloping power of My presence in ways beyond your imagination. Oh, how I love you.

While I sit in the shadow

"He will cover you with his feathers. He will shelter you with his wings. His faithful promises are your armor and protection."
—Psalm 91:4

Me: Lord, You're awesome and amazing! You've freed my heart from so many worries and burdens. Little by little, You've shown me how to be fearless and courageous, how to love and be loved, and how to bless and accommodate others without fear of personal loss. You've given me so many great blessings and healings! Let my life be an example and a witness for You. How can I best work for You now? Set my heart where it needs to be—on You and Your ways. Help me to not be so concerned about what others think of me, but, instead, to be more concerned about the state of my soul and the souls of others. Give me fresh words to speak and vital insight into people's hearts, so I can offer both prophetic and anointed words to bless them. I'll wait on You for these. You're so merciful and gracious, Lord. Help me to be more like You and Your Son. Please stir up the hearts of those in my family so they might know how much you care for and love them. Ignite Your fire in them so they can behold Your brightness and feel the warmth that only You can exude. Heal them of their doubts and fears so they can recognize what You've done for them. I love You.

God: Dear one, you're so precious to me. What a blessing you are! How wonderfully you're made! You know, I made each cell, even each fingerprint, unique to you. Every part of you intertwines and fits together to make a meaningful whole. My Word is like this. It's fearfully and wonderfully made for your benefit. Study it to find true meaning. Learn it to find answers to life. For it's written just for you. You bless others as you live and speak it, and you see how powerful it is in your life and the lives of others. The more of it you grasp, the greater your ability to minister to others and bring them My loving care and mercy. I can deliver power through its ability to work in and through you to bring answers, healing, love, deliverance, and understanding to those around you. Remember, it was written for this purpose! And, even when others will not say so, know how much I value and treasure you. I'm always near you. I hover over you like a heron that spreads its wings to take flight. I extend My wings to protect you, so that you're always in My shadow. I keep you from evil and harm. Trust Me that I direct your steps. I love you.

Of my ever-ready teacher

"Give thanks to the Lord, for he is good! His faithful love endures forever."
—Psalm 136:1

Me: Oh, how I give thanks to You, Lord, and love Your name! You are my father forever and ever. You bring me wonderful things and make my heart glad in times of trouble and distress. I can look to You to meet my needs, for You alone are holy and powerful. You alone restore my strength and enable me to survive, even when there is so much injustice and evil in the world. I can look to You to give me salvation, wholeness, and life everlasting. This life on earth is only a grain of sand compared to Your forever, which is like an endless beach. Would You constantly remind me of this? For I depend on You to be with me, to heal me, and to support me at all times. I want to be transformed by Your love, Lord. Would You show me how, and help me to be all that I can be for You? I will never forget Your mercy, Your kindness, or Your grace. You're my father. I'm Your child. And I'll admire Your wonderful works today as You bring me before receptive people and give me the courage to speak. Today, I'll listen for Your voice, and You'll give me clear directions. You'll warn me before any impending disaster that might affect me or those you bring to my mind for prayer. Yes, I'll listen and learn from You. For You are mighty to save. I love You.

God: Child, remember, it's nothing for me to do a big or a small thing for you. I can stop or start a rain shower when it's needed, for I created the heavens and the earth. I made you. Don't you realize how much I want to bless you and bring you joy? Oh, how I enjoy your praise and worship! I bask in your love and in hearing your voice, your songs, and your prayers. You're my child, and I love you more than words can express. You give Me great joy and happiness, just as your children and grandchildren touch your heart when they thank you and tell you how much they love you. I don't want you to suffer from unforgiveness, pain, or remorse, so I'll show you the heart behind any words spoken. That way you can discern and make wise choices regarding people. Continue to walk and talk with Me, and I'll always guide you. You're My student, and I'm Your ever-ready teacher. I love you.

November 11
Who flows through me

"Always be joyful. Never stop praying. Be thankful in all circumstances, for this is God's will for you who belong to Christ Jesus."
—*1 Thessalonians 5:16-18*

Me: Flow through me, Lord. Let my life be a continuous witness of Your life-giving power. When I feel like I'm under attack, or flustered and frustrated, remind me to reach up to You for help and seek answers from You. May I never forget that You're always there to provide for me. Help me to see through people whose agenda is their own self-promotion and to react with Your love and wisdom. Let me be a light for You in the darkness so I can encourage others in their walks and bring peace and fearlessness and hope to everyone around me. Help me to stand firm on Your Word, undefeated by negativity, pride, unkindness, and anger, or attempts to manipulate and misrepresent what You've done. May I always promote Your will in this life. You remind me that I'm still Your "weathergirl," and I must pray against any "bad weather," or movement intended for evil. I know that, as Your prayer warrior, I can ask that what the devil means for evil can be used for good. Remind me today of those people and things I need to pray for. I love You.

God: Dear one, spend the day thanking Me for all the good things around you. Praise Me continuously, for this is how you can maintain joy, which is your strength. Remember to bring your thoughts, even the negative ones, to Me. Never let people bring you down or discourage you through their self-centered and thoughtless words or actions. My path is paved with hope and joy—always. Look toward Me as you walk, and see how I can set a protective barrier around you, so that life's annoyances just bounce off you. Negatives will be directed toward you, like darts from the enemy, who'll try to penetrate your protective barrier. His purpose is to divert your attention from your real purpose, because he's annoyed when your focus is on Me. Don't let him distract you. I want you to show My power through you so you can demolish his evil purposes! Over the years, you've seen this in operation when tornadoes, hurricanes, and storms were averted after you prayed against them. Few people realize how powerful their prayers really are. But you do. I love you.

And allows me the privilege

"Put on your new nature, and be renewed as you learn to know your Creator and become like him."
—*Colossians 3:10*

Me: Thanks, Lord, for choosing me as one of Your own. Would You allow me the privilege of fulfilling Your call for my life? Would You enlighten and train Me for Your purposes? I praise you, Lord, for Your unspeakable gift, which You gave me so freely. Your gift brought me deliverance from evil, sickness, hurt, fear, and self-pity. I praise You for life and love, hope and peace, and a mind free from worry and fear. I praise You for joy and laughter, the freedom to love others, and for knowing Your love gives me what I need. How I want to be deserving of Your call! Let me always be pleasing to You and a shining example of Your amazing gift. Oh, that I could be a magnet to those who are searching for Your truth! Surround me with new brothers and sisters, children and parents to encourage. Would You place around me those who love You with their whole heart—people who desire You as I do and want to do Your will? Guide me as I reach within my spirit to use Your authority to speak and act. Give me clear vision so I can see into peoples' hearts and understand their hopes and fears and be able to communicate more effectively with them. How I love You.

God: Dear one, it's a new day of promise. It's a day I've given you to compound what's good and expand on your gifts that you will use for eternity. It's a day of fellowship and forgiveness. Use this day to glorify Me by offering your heart to Me. As I send people to you, allow Me to direct your conversation. I'll bring the right ones and give you the words to say. Speak to them with My authority. It won't always be easy, but I'll give you peace and joy along with the words. And many will become your sisters, brothers, fathers, mothers, and children. Rest in Me. Let Me do the work for you. Sometimes people will ask you to do things that you think are unreasonable. Their requests will rub you the wrong way or irritate your flesh. You'll ask, "Why can't they do this?" or "Why are they asking me to do it?" Let Me show you how to respond, and, in the end, you'll receive great rewards for what you do. It may seem unfair or inconvenient at times, but allow Me to be your sufficiency. Then you'll never have lack or regret. You'll always have an abundance to give. Let Me show you how to work using My power and ability. I love you.

To see You pour out more and more

"From his abundance we have all received one gracious blessing after another."
—*John 1:16*

Me: How amazing You are, Lord! Recently I walked early in the morning down sidewalks barely lit by a few hovering streetlamps. The sky felt like black velvet studded with diamonds. You pointed out the Big Dipper and its many glittering points above me, and You reminded me of what it symbolized—how You've "poured out" to me in prolific ways. You've answered so many prayers by providing a family and friends to love. You've led me to situations where I could help others by speaking into their lives. You've taught me about Your Word and answered so many questions about its meaning and how I could use its principles to prosper and be in health. Thanks for all of this. Would You help me to see You in a greater way today? I read in Matthew how Jesus fed multitudes with a few loaves of bread and fish. And You showed me how You're able to go above and beyond our needs, because Your ways are so much greater than ours, and Your means are unlimited. Show me more of Your bounty! You never had to do any of this for us! Thanks for doing it anyway and for Your wonderful willingness to do it. You're a great God, worthy of praise. I love You.

God: Child, how people often misunderstand who I am! How they invent concepts and suppositions and imaginations that turn out to be false, instead of simply reading what's been revealed about Me! I inspired people to write down My thoughts, revelations, and insights so that anyone could come to know Me. Nothing about Me is completely hidden. It's hard to understand why people choose to ignore the truths disclosed over thousands of years so they can understand My purposes and heart! It's all there for those who want to know! I'm a loving God. And I can bring you amazing grace and powerful peace as you trust in Me. I alone provide plentiful mercy. Only I can fully minister to your needs and give you lasting financial abundance. Depend on Me today and every day. Look to Me for answers. They're there for you when you need them. Future events will shake the world, but I'll prepare and show you what to do so that you can survive and thrive. I'll open doors, but you must focus on Me, especially in the trying times. Joy and peace are always available to you, but you must trust Me to show you how to access them in each moment. I love you.

NOVEMBER 14
As I wait for You

"As for me, I look to the Lord for help. I wait confidently for God to save me, and my God will certainly hear me."
—*Micah 7:7*

Me: Dear Lord, sometimes I wonder, "Are You happy with me and what I'm doing?" Then I ask You whether I should stay where I am or go somewhere else. I hear of people who give up their careers to go to foreign lands as missionaries, and I think that sounds so admirable. But I don't know that this is Your calling for me. I've come to believe that my "mission field" is here in my home, in my neighborhood, through my church, and in my place of business. You've opened many doors for me to walk through, and these openings have led to people I could bless, joy I could share, a better understanding of life, as well as health and prosperity. Show me if You need me to proceed down another path, and remind me to trust Your leading if I need to stay on this one. Help me to understand more how You see things. I'm confident that You hear me, and I wait patiently for the day Your Son will appear and show Your awesome power in this broken world. I praise and thank You for the many ways you've blessed me. Thanks for Your gift of life. Thanks for the world You've made and for the seasons, each one beautiful in its own way. Thanks for Your Son. I love You.

God: Child, of course I'm pleased with you. I called you, didn't I? I've told you, "You're the apple of My eye!" And now I remind you, "You're where I want you to be." If I need you to move or to change, I'll make it clear. But, for now, stay where you are. You feel at times like you're missing something, like you're not doing enough. You blame yourself for "mistakes." Don't you see? All things are for a reason. When things happen, they're a tool for you to learn and grow. If you stumble and wallow in self-pity or blame, it's like falling into a mud-puddle that grows thicker and harder to escape from the longer you lay there. Take My hand so I can pull you up when life feels uncertain. Don't fret about things you wish were different. Let Me arrange things for you so you're joyful at the outcome, which will be far beyond anything you could ask or think. Rest in Me, and know that you'll be amazed at what I'll bring to pass in your life, especially when My Son returns. For now, I'll show you ways to make the most impact on the world around you. I love you.

And relish Your freedom

"Jesus said to the people who believed in him, 'You are truly my disciples if you remain faithful to my teachings. And you will know the truth, and the truth will set you free.'"
—*John 8:31-32*

Me: Dear Lord, it's a great day to praise You! Because You've always shown me that You're here for me. Today, You showed me how, with Your help, I could know how to answer any misguidance. I received an email from a friend who shared a message from her minister who claimed that many Christians are white supremacists and nationalists, and that Christianity was only one among many religions. I responded that I'd recently heard from a client who's a Christian, but she's neither a white supremacist nor a nationalist. She's just one who's concerned that our nation is on a road to accepting many regulations that restrict our freedoms so we can be "safe." The bent seems to be to inhibit free speech and hinder our right to worship freely. I told my friend that when I took a high school class on religions, You led me to a belief in Your Son as the only one who could overcome death and offer us a way to live freely and not be overly controlled by mandates and rules. Now, we can walk by Your Spirit because of Him. Lord, I'm so thankful that Your Son gave His life so I could know the way to You and walk in it freely. I love You.

God: Dear one, all things are in My hands. In the days ahead, you'll hear more radical ideological arguments, but remember that I work out things, all things, to attain My end results. The enemy will even try to steal, kill, and destroy by working through some who claim to be Mine. You must know the truths in My Word and stand by them. This is your power. Encourage others to know them too! People will come to you with questions. They may repeat what others say to see your response. Give them My answers. Accusations are abhorrent to Me—like fingernails scratching on a blackboard. People who act out of religiosity and criticize those who courageously stand up for Me are far from My heart. Those who are thankful for what I've done, who honor My name and believe in My promises are blessed in this life. They can walk in My freedom. I love you.

As I find my way to Your feast

"In Jerusalem, the LORD of Heaven's Armies will spread a wonderful feast for all the people of the world. It will be a delicious banquet with clear, well-aged wine and choice meat."
—Isaiah 25:6

Me: Lord, I want to sit and sup with You forever! Would You let me taste of Your goodness and savor Your favor more each day? Let me be like Your finest wine—aged, rich, and rare. Let me be blessed and a blessing to You and to those around me. Let me be as Your choicest food for others, so they can be filled with Your great contentment and satisfaction. Thanks for Your amazing wisdom so that my words are like a precious ointment that soothes and eases pain and sadness. Pour out Your finest oil all over me so that I may be a sweet fragrance oozing Your delight to others. Like a willow tree, let my branches swing and sway gently with the wind so that they can reach and touch those above, beneath, and around me to bring them great comfort. And let my trunk be supple enough to withstand any wind or storm. Water me continuously with Your life-giving, liquid love. And help me to feel Your presence and be fed by Your generous hand. May I always honor Your name. I love You.

God: Dear one, I love your heart and your desire to be My partner and friend. And, one day, we'll sit together, you and I, and we'll enjoy the great feast prepared for all My beloved ones! Now, I observe your every move. I watch as you go out and as you come in. I watch as you get up and as you lay down. I watch as you minister to others, and I love it! I cry when you cry, and I'm sad when you're sad. When others receive your words, I'm joyful. When they reject your advice, My heart hurts for you. I work through you to reach the lost and the hurting ones. Remember this. Today, I'm with you as you bring them hope. When you feel unsure as to how to pray or what to say, I'll help you. In time, knowing how to pray will be "third nature" to you—part of your body, soul, and spirit. Now, I'll remind you of your desire and show you what to do. For I've made you a blessing, and you're blessed as you live in the light of My Word. Through it, I guide you to what's true. My Word issues in wisdom, but it also brings healing and peace and joy. My words will become more real to you as you trust My Spirit to guide your understanding of it. My Word lightens your path so you can see where you're going—on your way to My feast. I love you.

Along with my friend Nelle

"The LORD helps the fallen and lifts those bent beneath their loads."
—Psalm 145:14

Me: Lord, thanks for those with whom I can share my love for You. Thanks for my friend, Nelle, who turned 101 this week and appreciated going to lunch with me on her birthday. She loves You as I do and has lived a long life, because she's thankful for all she has. She has no close relatives, because she's outlived them all! Yet she lives with great thankfulness for each day. I appreciate the time we shared. Thanks for showing me others like her I can bless. These older people are so precious, Lord. Please show me how I can help them. Give me revelation and insight into their hearts. May they remember the good things done and the helpful words spoken to them. Help me in my littleness to do big things for You. Give me a boost, like a father helping his child up onto a tall stool. I need a step up so I can view things from Your perspective and be able to see what lies ahead for me and for them. Would You open my eyes so I can discern what's right and profitable and what's wrong and hurtful? Be my sieve to filter what I hear, so I can sort the bad from the good. Give me discernment. Thanks! I love You.

God: Child, I'll bring more people like Nelle to you, who need your encouragement and love. Remember, I'm always here for you. I'll lift you up when you need a boost or just need some support. I hear you. Remember, My voice is just a whisper away. Just listen for it. I'll tell you when to extend a hand of love or when to warn people with words they need to hear. I'll give you a heads up if someone needs your help. Listen for My whispers. Some days will be easy days filled with unexpected blessings that seem to just rain down. Other days will be hard days filled with struggles. Life is made up of both. The hard days can give you confidence and courage if you let them. They can remind you to look to Me for answers or needed boosts. In the good days, it's easier to give thanks and praise. But if you can thank Me in the hard days, this is especially precious to Me. Remember that each day is a gift from Me. I don't cause you hardship; I can deliver and protect you and bring good things from any difficulty. Remember Me every day with praise in your heart, even during the tough times. And that I love you.

November 18
And be able to enter Your gates

"Enter his gates with thanksgiving; go into his courts with praise. Give thanks to him and praise his name."
—Psalm 100:4

Me: Lord, would You help me to refocus on the things of today and on the matters most important to You and Your kingdom? Help me to see each day through Your eyes and to behold the beauty of Your magnificent presence as You work through me and others to carry out Your plan in this world. Help me to only see You and Your truth in the words and actions and events that surround me. Help me to remember, Lord, that all I have is because of You. Help me to recall this fact in each moment and to know that everything I do can be attributed to You. I can rejoice in this: You are my every-need-supplier, my fortress, my strength, and my guide. Help me to worship You as David did, with my whole heart fervently. I want to be thankful, grateful, and to praise Your name continuously. I want to recognize You as my constant sufficiency. For You are my all in all! And I want to enter with You into Your gates. I love You.

God: Dear one, today is a day I've made. Remember to be thankful for all that's in it. Rejoice in who you are and what I've made you. As you praise, you'll receive greater healing and health. As you give thanks, you'll receive more of My abundance. As you rejoice, you'll become more spiritually-minded. Remember these three things: praise, thanksgiving, and rejoicing. These are your keys to receiving from Me all that I've promised. These will open the gates to My courts and lift you higher so you can step up to My throne. Remember that I'm ever by your side; and I have much more planned for you. Continue to pray for others, for that is My calling for you. Your prayers are powerful, and I honor them. I hear your every word. And none of them will return void, or without results, just like My words. Never be discouraged by what you see around you. I'm always at work, even during the trying times. Let me continually renew your spirit with My loving touch so you never become hardened or burdened or unpeaceful or unkind. Let Me renew Your love day by day. I can do this as you rejoice in Me. I love you.

354

As You arrange the clouds

"For your unfailing love is as high as the heavens. Your faithfulness reaches to the clouds."
—Psalm 57:10

Me: Dear God, I love how You watch over me day and night. You keep me safe from evil and help me to follow Your light. You make me aware of Your beauty by arranging the clouds in patterns to remind me of Your presence in the heavens. You're like a pleasant wind. You gently remind me that You're all around me. Like the flowers, You bring me joy, and You nudge me with Your beauty. You remind me of the sun as You warm my heart with Your love. Like the mountains, You tower over me with Your majesty. You whisper in my ears, and You tell me wonderful things that I could never understand on my own. You place me with people who enlighten and help me to sort out the puzzle pieces of my life. Mysteries are solved by Your revealing words. Thanks for Your great goodness. You bless my children and grandchildren in ways I will never know in this life. Today, may I glory only in You. I love You.

God: Dear child, in My foresight I saw you take your first breath. I watched as you took your first steps. And, as you walked over each path of your life, I stepped up beside you and guided you toward My goodness. Even when you sensed uncertainty, or felt fear or dread, or went in what you imagined was the wrong direction, I sighed, because I wished you could know what I know and what I'd already done for you. One day, you'll see the goodness I've worked out through you. And you'll see how wonderfully you were led. And you'll be amazed at the miracle of it all! Today, remember how much I love you. Have joy in Me. For I'll always direct your steps. Yes, you're where I want you to be. So be thankful for what you have and the many things I've already done for you. Revel in My love and how I've sewn its sinewy threads through every fabric of your life. Hold My relationship with you up high. Relish it. And, one day, you'll see how it brought you great satisfaction. Because of your faithfulness to Me, your physical and spiritual children will be blessed beyond measure. They'll thrive, as will their children, for I will bless them. Shine My love to them, and they'll never forget it. I love you.

NOVEMBER 20
And I gaze at the waves

"O God, you are my God; I earnestly search for you. My soul thirsts for you; my whole body longs for you in this parched and weary land where there is no water."
—Psalm 63:1

Me: Lord, today, remind me of how ever-present You are! Give me signs of confirmation to stir me up and get me going! At times I feel unsettled and out of sorts. Show me why, Lord. Is there someone or something I need to pray for? Sometimes I just long to feel the breezes and breathe in the smells of my grandparents' cabin in Michigan. I want to wake up and see the sun shining on the turquoise water and hear the splashing waves of the bracing lake. I want to gaze at its beautiful, crystal-clear expanse that extends out to the island as I swing in the hammock beneath the pine trees. I want to daydream and listen for Your voice and spend rainy days just sitting in front of the fireplace, listening to my favorite songs on my grandfather's stereo. Oh, to drift off to sleep in the fragrant loft beneath the log rafters as I listen to the waves lapping the shore beneath the window. Such pleasant thoughts and sweet memories! I know that my time with You will be like this one day. Give me visions to propel me toward peaceful moments as I walk along the peaceful path with You. I love You.

God: Dear one, you long for moments with Me, just as I long for time with you. Like you, I want intimacy and fellowship—shining days filled with sweet thoughts. I desire, as you do, a time when you will see My great works and be able to recognize what I've done for you and be thankful for it all! The reason you're unsettled at times is because you long for the day when the world will be at rest, when people will recognize who I am and who they are in Me. Now, you see hatred, corruption, selfishness, and evil. When you sense these, you ask, "Why do I feel so unpeaceful?" It's because you feel the unfulfillment around you as you watch people rushing headlong toward disaster and death. I can help you through this time and give you lasting peace. But you must listen for Me, heed what I say, and look for ways to praise Me. Then I can bless and protect you and your family. Set aside special moments each morning, when we can sit and swing together for a while in that lovely hammock under the pine trees and have overflowing thankfulness as we watch the peaceful waves that extend to that island of hope. I love you.

And remember how blessed I am

"The Lord is my strength and shield. I trust him with all my heart. He helps me, and my heart is filled with joy. I burst out in songs of thanksgiving."
—Psalm 28:7

Me: Lord, isn't it funny how those who have the least to be thankful for are often the most blessed of all? I watched a young woman on TV who was born without arms and legs, yet she grew up to be a world-famous wrestler, because she believed she could! I've also listened to an inspirational speaker who was born without arms and legs and draws thousands of young people who want to hear him speak. They recognize his joy and life-zeal, and they realize that they have no reason to feel hopeless, helpless, or incapable. When I watch his audience, I see young women weeping as they gaze up at him and realize that their own problems are pretty insignificant. Yet I know so many people with plenty who are bitter, hateful, resentful, angry, and demanding. They're easily offended because they're unthankful. It amazes me. Help me to always be grateful, Lord. I praise You now for what You accomplished through Your Son for me. I praise You for Your love, which You freely give me in each moment. I praise You for Your mercy, which You abound toward me continuously, even when I don't deserve it. I praise You for Your grace, Your divine favor, which You shower on me every day! I praise You today with my whole being. Because I love You.

God: Dear one, long ago there were people who had a passion to serve Me and follow My Word. They sacrificed their homes, families, creature comforts, and all they owned to go to an obscure place where they could worship Me freely and establish a worshipful way of life. Their desire was to be free from tyranny and oppression. Like Abraham in the Bible, they were pilgrims. I loved them for their willingness to worship Me. They gave of themselves in ways you can't even imagine. Many of them lost all they had on their journey. Yet, despite the hardships, they were thankful and blessed to be in a place where they could freely live for Me. Because of their willingness and commitment, I not only blessed them, but also their future generations with prosperity, peace, joy, freedom, and more. Today, remember these praise-worthy pilgrims and the sacrifices they made as you celebrate Thanksgiving. Their willing life-offerings are a great gift to you. I love you.

November 22
Because I can never forget

"My child, never forget the things I have taught you."
—Proverbs 3:1

Me: God, I can never forget all that You've done for me! Lord, You are so very compassionate! Your love is past understanding and past finding out! Would You show me more of Your wonderful mercy? I turn my face to You, because I want You to enlighten and strengthen me. You give me courage in times of distress and help in times of fear and concern. You sustain me and hold me up when I feel weak, lacking in strength or ability, or confused and frustrated by the people around me. I must remember to always turn my thoughts to You and seek Your face, especially during the times when chaos and uncertainty seem to swirl around me. Send Your angels to watch over me, my business, my home, and my family. Let this Thanksgiving be the most memorable for me in a very wonderful way. Heal the people I know who are hurting. I pray for my family members, especially those who struggle with who they are and how You fit into their lives. They can't seem to see You, and they're caught up in the confusion that surrounds them. Let Your love be the centerpiece on the table this year. Let Your forgiveness be the focal point and the main course for the meal. Thanks, Lord! Touch my lips with Your kindness. I love You.

God: Dear one, I'm with you and your family. As I promised in Exodus 20:6, I'll bless your descendants to 1,000 generations because you've loved Me! So don't worry. Even if mistakes were made, I can make things new again. I can bring joy out of tragedy and despair. I'm a God of all comfort. I bring renewal. People can be short-sighted. They may not see what lies ahead. But I do. Even though the enemy seeks to destroy what I created for good, I give life more abundantly. From death, I can make life spring up. Trust Me, even when life seems hard or unfair. Be thankful for what you've been given, and turn your heart to Me with praise, remembering what I've done for you and what I've called you to do. There are those who still need to hear and see My greatness and power in their lives. Let them see it through you. It's a time of thanksgiving that you can use to bring meaning and hope. Let Me work through you to offer others this message by meeting them where they are. I did this for you. I love you.

November 23
What I know

"Now all glory to God, who is able, through his mighty power at work within us, to accomplish infinitely more than we might ask or think."
—*Ephesians 3:20*

Me: Lord, my heart abounds with thanksgiving for all You've done. Thanks for all the wonderful people You've placed before me and all the places You've led me to. Thanks for all the doors You've opened for me. I lay my life before You. I've longed to know You since I was a child. I remember sitting on a log at the beach near my grandparents' cabin looking up at the stars and wondering where You were and wanting to see Your face. Later, in a dream, I glanced back and was shocked to see Jesus following me, His face partly hidden by the hood of His cape. I couldn't make out His features, but I knew it was Him and that He had my back. I realized then that He wanted me to turn and wait for Him, so He could walk beside me. Over the years, I've reached out to You many times with questions, prayers, and requests. And You've answered them all. You always come through, even when I imagine my requests are impossible. Thanks for Your friendship, love, and guidance over the years. Many people might think that the things that happen are just coincidental. But I know different. With You, all things have some meaning. I love You.

God: Child, remember that, as your Father, I'll always lead you to a place where you can have permanent peace. I back you up and forgive your faults. I hug you and hold you up as your own father would. I kiss you and comfort you. Because I am Spirit, I must do all these things through the spirit in you. And you can only know that I'm working for you by reaching inside to what resides in your heart. I'm all things to you. I'm your coming and going. Seek Me today through the spirit in you, and I will give you greater peace and joy. My joy is boundless. It's a sort of giddiness you could never experience from anything else. Lean your head on Me. Turn your face to Me. Walk with Me. Today may seem stressful. People may not agree with you, but I work from within you, whispering in your ears, comforting you and telling you what to think and how to speak. Don't allow the stress to get to you. Focus your eyes on Me. Turn your thoughts to Me. I will bring you to safe places. Let Me massage you with My hope and comfort you with My joy. Because I love you.

NOVEMBER 24
As I ask about the stars

"He counts the stars and calls them all by name."
—Psalm 147:4

Me: Lord, teach me about the stars. What do they mean for us? Are they significant as signs? Do they represent us in some way? Are they types of life? Are they alive? Are they spiritual? Do they watch over us like angels? Can they come to earth? Why do they burn up? Do they take other forms? Can they show us something? Why does Your Word say that you count and name them? Are they that important to You? What is their significance to us? How did the wise men know that that one star pointed to Your Son and His birth? I have so many questions about the stars. Please show me, Lord. Lead and teach me with Your truth. I know they must somehow sing Your praises! I love You.

God: Dear one, the stars were put in their places to teach and to lead people. They were always meant to be signs and guideposts to Me. They tell a story—an unfolding description of My Son, who would come once and again. They explain enough about His birth, His life, and how it all would lead up to what I'd do one day so that people could be saved after Adam's fall. They were placed there to show the way to Me. In form, they're merely concentrated balls of energy and light. I created light. I live in light. Remember, My Son came from light and exists in all of it. Angels are also made up of light. They can be in light or bring light. The stars were placed in the sky to tell a story—a message that communicated My truth and deliverance from the enemy. You can discern this story in the patterns of the stars. Many have deciphered it by studying their designs. Even unbelievers can see and understand the meaning of these signs. Some stars may be more meaningful to certain people. There may be a particular star or pattern of stars that speaks to you. You have often been drawn to Orion. I will show you those that remind Me of you. Just as I do the stars, I've hand-picked names for My beloved ones, like you. And, one day, as you stand before My Son, He'll hand you a white gemstone with your special name engraved on it. I love you.

NOVEMBER 25
And I wonder at Your secrets

"The secret things belong unto the Lord our God: but those things which are revealed belong unto us and to our children forever, that we may do all the words of this law."
—Deuteronomy 29:29

Me: Lord, I love the stillness of the mornings, and I long for more of these times with You. Today, I listened to the quiet. In the background I could barely hear the sounds of people: cars on the highway, trains whistling in the distance, and planes buzzing overhead. So I bent in closer to hear Your still, small voice, which I've grown accustomed to discerning in the lull and, now, even when I'm surrounded by the world's chaos. Is heaven very still and quiet? Or is its silence sometimes broken by the thunder of clouds colliding, lightning bolts charging toward the earth, or water crystals crackling through the air? Do You live in these things or is Your habitat more ethereal and evasive? When we are with You there, will Your voice be more audible, or will we just perceive it because we're spirits, like You? Will we be able to look at You and just know what You're thinking? Or will we hear a thunderous voice and words that flow to us like rippling water through the air? I have so many questions, Lord. And I know You have the answers. But I also know that You reveal what I can understand at the right time and place. Thanks for all You've showed me. I revel and delight in what I know of You. Show me more! I love You.

God: Dear one, My voice grows more distinct as you get closer to Me. That's because the more spiritually aware of Me you are, or in-tune with My Spirit, the more receptive to My voice you become. You are made up of flesh and blood, but when you receive My gift of Holy Spirit by believing in My Son, you can tap into, or discern, My voice via the spirit in you. As you tune into My unique "wavelength," you have access to Me spiritually. When I call you to Me one day, and you become a wholly spiritual being, then you'll be far more able to recognize My voice. And you'll see Me as I am. Now, the distractions make it hard. And life seems difficult, because you have so many questions. Don't focus on what you don't have or don't know. Remember that My promises will come to pass. And, one day, you'll be with Me. Now, focus on this: you have so much to be thankful for, and you can see how I've blessed you in so many situations in so many ways. Focus on this. Focus on Me. I love you.

NOVEMBER 26
While seeking Your refuge

"The Lord is good, a strong refuge when trouble comes. He is close to those who trust in him."
—Nahum 1:7

Me: Lord, people can never determine the fate of the earth. They can't force the planet to exist forever so they can sustain mankind. That's up to You! We can follow You in our words and actions. But it's up to You to determine outcomes. You alone mandate the fate of the earth. Help me to serve You in powerful ways while I live on this planet. And let me take refuge in You in times of trouble. Help me to trust You in each moment and remember your promises of peace and hope no matter what is going on around me. May I do Your will as I trust in You. May I be as one of Your devoted ones, so I can stand in Your presence and be praised as one of Your most beloved. Oh, to behold the beauty of Your Son as I look into His eyes! I long for that time—to be forever with You and those who've loved You as I do. I turn my eyes and ears to You now and wait patiently for the day when I'm with You and can walk and talk with Your Son. Guide me now with Your hand of mercy. You alone give me refreshing and ease my cares when others are filled with fear. You give hope to those who know You. You're a great God, worthy of all praise. Your Word gives light to those who seek it. You alone protect me from the world's evil. Guide me now with Your kind and loving hand. I love You.

God: Dear one, the loftiest goals require the most patience and perseverance. Sometimes they require blood, sweat, and even tears. But, then, their attainment becomes the most precious of all. This is what I want you to see. When My Son gave His life for you, it required His all—everything He had to give! But see how precious a gift it was and what the result was? Now, we have a family—a brother and sisterhood we share with those who understand the value of that gift. If you will offer your all, it will be returned immeasurably. You can reach new heights and see a future beyond your comprehension. I'll show you how, but you must listen in your weakest moments, when it's the hardest. Trust Me that I'll bring you great rewards that will please and bless you. This includes time with Me. Continue to love others and bring them love, hope, and a reason to receive My Word, even as their world seems to be crumbling around them. This brings a blessing to Me and to you now and later! I love you.

   As I seek Your Son's face

"You must pay close attention to what they wrote, for their words are like a lamp shining in a dark place—until the Day dawns, and Christ the Morning Star shines in your hearts."
—2 Peter 1:19

Me: I praise You, God, for Your many blessings and for Your ways, which are above our ways. Thanks for Your voice that directs me and Your hands that lead me. I praise You for Your love and tenderness and Your many mercies. You are above all, and I look up to You and Your Son, whom You sent to be Your voice, Your hands, and Your feet on this earth. I praise You for offering Him as a sacrifice for us—to live and die for us so we could have eternal life. Our entrance into Your presence is through Your Son, and if we persevere and have faith, we can stand in Your presence now and forevermore. It's a place of peace, glory, wisdom, and love. It's a place of forgiveness and blessings. Would You help me to seek and find the face of Your Son in this life, Lord? Would You open my eyes so I can see and understand Him as the Morning Star? Help me to discern and know You as the dazzling light that You are. You showed me that, when You created light, Jesus came into being, because He also is light. You showed me that receiving healing requires persistence and determination. I think of the woman with the issue of blood, blind Bartimaeus, and others. In any hardship, You will always make a way out, because You are the light. And I love You.

God: Dear one, how I love you and enjoy our times together—the walks and questions and ponderings! How I cry for you when your heart aches for others or when you experience pain and hurt. How I long to heal you! I can, when you turn to Me with a thankful and trusting heart. I often wait for you, and I exult when you remember Me during the day and ask for My help. These special times bring Me great pleasure. Let Me help you more often. I can. I will as You come to Me with praise. Let's be partners and plan life together. You'll be surprised at what we can come up with! Listen and turn to Me more often during the day. I'll speak to you as often as you turn your face to Me. And you'll discover that the more you come to Me, the more you're able to recognize the face of My Son and feel His presence. I love you.

Through Your faithfulness

"And this same God who takes care of me will supply all your needs from his glorious riches, which have been given to us in Christ Jesus."
—*Philippians 4:19*

Me: Lord, how good and how faithful You are! You're there for me every moment. You stir my heart with gladness, and You remind me of Your good works. You see and touch me with miraculous views. Early this morning, I looked up at the sparkling stars as I walked, and I was so aware of Your presence! You filled me with joy at the sound of the wind rustling through the autumn leaves not yet fallen! You showed me a deer, a possum, and geese that lingered near the lake. I remembered how, yesterday, You unfolded a rainbow in the sky to let me know that I'm special and unique to you. I think about how You gave me children and grandchildren to love and brought me friends who offered me kindness on a love-filled platter. You've supplied a wonderful house and food for my table. You've often healed me and given me needed strength. You've supplied me with endurance, patience, goodness, and abundance when I needed them. You've given me success in my endeavors. Thanks for these things, Lord. You're so good to me. I love You.

God: Dear one, see how good life is when you consider all that you have and what I've done for you? You know that life can be difficult when you focus on the wrong things. But you're beginning to understand how, when you praise and give thanks for what you have, even when the world reminds you of what you don't have, you're filled to overflowing with joy while others experience sadness and remorse! Remember, in every situation, that I mean what I say, and I say what I mean. And My promises to you will always come to pass, even when others deny them. In other words, I'm always there for you! Never fall into the pattern of focusing on what is not. Continue to see what is. You have so much to be thankful for! Focus on this. If you look back on your life, you can see how I've worked in so many ways to bless you and how you yourself have impacted so many lives over the years. Focus on Me, then no lack will matter. Let Me be the One who creates goodness from all you've done. Give, and you'll receive back more than you ever gave. And the return will usually come from the least-likely people. You plant the seeds, and I bring the increase. So it is. So it will ever be. I love you.

And soar with Your joy

"It will happen in a moment, in the blink of an eye, when the last trumpet is blown. For when the trumpet sounds, those who have died will be raised to live forever. And we who are living will also be transformed."
—1 Corinthians 15:52

Me: Lord, how I long for that day, when this corruptible body will put on incorruptibility, when I get a new spiritual body and can fly away with You into the air! I'll defy gravity by becoming like You. I'll soar into the heavenlies and see all that's in every universe! I'll behold every star up close, see all You've made, and be awed by Your power. I'll never look back, only forward to eternity. I'll be able to share Your joy and celebrate with You what You've done. What an amazing day that will be! How I look forward to it! Lord, even now, I want to know You as You know me. I want to gaze into the Your Son's face and see His eyes and brilliant smile and amazing beauty. As I whisper Your name, would You remind me of Your presence and this hope I have in You? Remind me of Your love that always abounds, of Your grace that is unmatched, and of Your joy that can't be described. Show me how I can overcome any challenge in this life when I work in unison with You. I love You.

God: Dear one, sometimes you want only to get through this day and move on to the next! You're anxious for the next stage to begin. But I've called you to peace in this life. And your purpose is to love. This should be your focus. You may want to move on, because some of the people you must deal with are difficult to love, but you must love nonetheless. Because that's what others will see in you, and this will produce change in their own hardened hearts. That's the only balm that can heal. Remember this. Love is your defense and your shield from harm. Today, have joy in who you are and what you have, knowing that I can work through you! And, one day, you'll experience non-stop joy in My presence, and you'll be rewarded for your love. Remember, My angels surround you and lighten your path so you can see more clearly. And every day that your life exudes praise and thanksgiving will be a joyful day for you. Thankfulness allows you to see My greatness, My presence, and My fullness of joy. Then, you can live life as I meant it to be lived while still on earth. Don't blame yourself for mistakes or shortcomings. Instead, live freely with continual praise and thanksgiving. Then you can move mountains. I love you.

Above the mishmash

"You guided my conception and formed me in the womb. You clothed me with skin and flesh, and you knit my bones and sinews together. You gave me life and showed me your unfailing love. My life was preserved by your care."
—Job 10:9-12

Me: Lord, would You bring favor on all who associate with me? Would You bring blessings on those who come close to me? Let it be evident that these blessings are because of You. Let others say of me, "God has been with her!" Today, You reminded me that what I think of as imperfect is not at all that way to You! When I looked down at the sidewalk, I saw a marred surface filled with pockmarks. "That's how you see yourself," You said. "But it's not how I view you! I see what's perfect in you, your spirit." Everything is used for Your purposes. What appears to us as a mishmash of things—bad decisions, imperfections, crises, and all the paraphernalia of life—is used by You to create a beautiful pattern or picture in the end. Show me Your grand design for my life and for life in general. Open my eyes to what You're creating today and where You are in it all. I'd love to see how You work through all the world's messes to make something good! Help me to understand what You're doing. I love You.

God: Child, continue to be thankful for all I've done for you, for I've already blessed you and your family. You may sometimes wish your life was happier, better, or more satisfying, but I've blessed you in ways you can't even imagine now. One day, you'll see how many times I was involved in your life, and how I worked behind the scenes to arrange things on your behalf. In years to come, you'll be aware of many whose lives you touched in amazing ways. And your blessings, and theirs, will abound because you trusted in Me. Rest in Me now. Remember, I give you all things, even needed time. Don't worry, thinking that others have wasted your time. Be patient with those I send your way. Treat them as you'd treat Me or wish that you were treated, including when you're older. Your time will be rewarded in ways you can't even imagine now. I love you.

December

FOCUS:
HEAVEN-BOUND HOPE

"I pray that your hearts will be flooded with light so that you
can understand the confident hope he has given to those he called
—his holy people who are his rich and glorious inheritance."

—EPHESIANS 1:18

DECEMBER 1
I may have earthly regrets

"And so, Lord, where do I put my hope? My only hope is in you."
—Psalm 39:7

Me: Dear Lord, as the year draws to a close, I ask myself, "What have I accomplished?" and "Did I do enough?" I turn again to You for answers. I want to live inside Your will, but many times I feel like I've fallen short. Maybe I didn't say or do enough. Maybe I wasn't there for some when I should've been. Is there more I could've done? Would You cover any shortfalls? Would You forgive me for my impatience at times? Thanks for how You've tried to direct me. My life is in Your hands. Would You prepare me for the years ahead? Would You show me how You see my life and what it means to You? Only You can reveal how You view things. I'd love to have Your perspective, because it's all guesswork to me! Prepare me for what lies ahead. Put a hedge of protection around all that I have and all You've given me, including my family. I love You.

God: Dear one, in this life you'll always have questions, because all you can see is what's in front of you. For most people, who see life as purely material, life is a disappointment in the end, because they always feel like they could've done more. It's the heart yearning for more time and greater fulfillment, which can never be achieved in this life on earth. This regret is inevitable because the enemy corrupted what I originally made available and twisted the good things to make them evil. People can never be fully satisfied with what they've accomplished in the here and now. And they'll always feel like they could've done more and failed to reach their targets. It's only through Me that anyone can "hit the bullseye" or qualify for more life. Only I can make you "good enough" by making you whole and complete with My Spirit. Your life is in My hands. I've given you breath and blood, bone and sinew, and now I've given you eyes to see and ears to hear. Continue to use them for My benefit! Let Me work through you to bless others and bring them the silver platter of a forever life—My Word. Let me cover you with My sweet fragrance of love to draw others to you. Let Me work through you to feed the minds and bodies of those hungering and thirsting for Me. Be My sweetbread for them. I will burn up the things that don't fit in with My purposes. I'll guide you so that all your doings work for My good. And, through Me, you will be fulfilled and full of joy and hope. I love you.

369

DECEMBER 2
And feel grief in the tough times

"Why am I discouraged? Why is my heart so sad? I will put my hope in God! I will praise him again—my Savior and my God!"
—Psalm 42:11

Me: Help me, Lord, to remember that You're here beside me, even in the tough times! This morning, I saw a red truck turning a corner, and my heart leapt with joy, then sank back into grief as I thought of my son and how he loved his red truck. It was horribly painful for him and for me as we drove together to the bank for the last time to get the title, because he had to sell his beloved truck before he died. At that point, he was in the last stages of lung cancer. I think of him now, and I miss him terribly! Looking back, I wish I had more time with him. Sometimes I can hear him singing and playing his guitar. But, with time, the sound of his voice grows more faint. He brought so much joy to my life as someone who loved You so much, Lord! Just as I do. I miss sharing with him and listening to his voice. Lord, give me hope today. Help me to rejoice in Your Word and to remember that life with You is eternal. Thanks for blessing my family and for Your promise that my grandchildren will rise up and fulfill their callings. Inspire and set mentors before them, who will lead and teach them in Your ways. Give them spiritual eyes to see so they're never lost and can find and know You, even in the toughest times! I love You.

God: Dear child, you miss your son. I understand your sadness and regrets. But I have none. I saw what he did in his life—how he made beautiful things and strove to follow Me and understand My truths. He applied what he knew, and he showed many young people My way of life. Even in death, he loved Me. His was a grace-filled existence that touched and changed this world for the better. And it will never be the same because of him. Let this understanding dry your tears. Today, listen for My whispers as you go about your work. I'm right by your side. I'm taking care of your children and grandchildren. I'm ever with them, though they aren't always aware of it. How I love them! Did you know that your son's heart is in each of his children? He got it from you! So, though he's gone, you'll come to see how I made the most of his life. As I've told you, no one had a heart like his. He loved with a tenderness rarely seen in others. He saw others' hearts like you do. I embrace him now as we wait for a time to come, when we will all be together! I love you.

But I can replace the dead leaves

"For we died and were buried with Christ by baptism. And just as Christ was raised from the dead by the glorious power of the Father, now we also may live new lives."
—Romans 6:4

Me: Lord, in a dream last night, I was on a trip with my family, and we walked together along a beach. When we got back to the hotel, I went to get some clothes from my suitcase, and I found it filled with dead leaves. This upset me, because I had to remove most of them to get to my clothes, which were now covered with leaf-bits. As I dug through the debris, I was surprised to find a brand-new, beautiful bathing suit at the very bottom of the suitcase! When I awoke, I wondered why it was there. Lord, show me if there's something to reflect on here or anything I need to know. Do I need to dig through or remove any "dead" things in my life? Lord, You have the words of eternal life. Thanks for this life you've blessed me with, but remind me that this flesh means nothing except that it can bring You glory. Only spirit can live on. And we were always meant to be spiritual beings. Through Your Son, we're now able to embrace Your Spirit. Thanks for this amazing gift, Lord. I love You.

God: Dear one, I love how you're writing down dreams and memories. One day, your grandchildren will want to read or hear about them. They will, like you, yearn to know the One who adores them. One day, they'll turn to Me and understand the great love I have for them—a greater love than anyone on earth can offer. The dead leaves are hurtful memories that you need to move past, because they cause you pain. I never intended for you to experience sadness as you sometimes do. When I made people, I wanted them to live eternally and enjoy the bounty of the earth with joy and thankfulness. Sadly, the adversary entered the garden and expropriated My gift of life. Now, many lives are cut short, and I mourn to see the devastation that results from the enemy's deception. One day, this will all change when My Son returns to form a new world, where people can live as I intended—forever. Until then, remove the dead leaves, or sad memories, through what I've clothed you with, Holy Spirit. Like the beautiful new bathing suit, this gift brings you joy, peace, and healing. It makes you into a new person—a spiritual being once again. Through its power, you can remove the "dead" past and live in newness of life now. I love you.

DECEMBER 4
And learn to walk on water

"The Lord is slow to get angry, but his power is great, and he never lets the guilty go unpunished. He displays his power in the whirlwind and the storm. The billowing clouds are the dust beneath his feet."
—Nahum 1:3

Me: Lord, help me to walk on the water. Bear me up and support my steps, so I can walk safely over tumultuous waves and stormy seas. If I hold onto Your hand, I know I can stand firmly with You, even when I'm pelted by fierce winds and rain! You alone can help me face the day. You can show me the way to walk. Help me to be strong by trusting in You today, knowing You'll provide for me and my family. Help me to leave a hope-legacy for others, who also struggle in this life. Help me to focus on what I need to do to accomplish this. Give me guidance, for I long for it. Help me to see outside of myself to what is really happening around me. Give me true vision and insight. Show me where to place my feet so I don't sink or wander from Your path. Then I can lead others in the right direction. Shine a bright light on my path, so I can see clearly where You want me to go. I need Your help. I love You.

God: Dear one, I plead your cause and fight for you against evil forces, even when you're asking, "Where are You?" I have My way in the whirlwind and in the storm, and the clouds are just dust under My feet. I can use the things I've made to come against those who work for evil purposes. I can dry up rivers and seas and cause floods when necessary. I can make mountains tremble and melt away hills. I can cause the earth to move in My presence, if I choose to. I'm a stronghold in troubling times for those who take refuge in Me. I pursue your enemies and, one day, you'll see peace published to the nations. In that day, you'll see One come to reign, and many will come to see the light I bring through Him. Because He'll be the promised lamp of hope. And you'll celebrate His arrival, because He'll bring an end to evil. Only those who don't know Him will be afraid, because they'll see just who He is. They'll be amazed and terrified at how He fights against those who try to sell out nations, use people for profit, and cause great destruction to the planet I created. But My own chosen ones will clap their hands and sing for joy when He comes, because they'll gather together on My holy mountain to celebrate with Him and Me forever. I love you.

December 5
With Your angels

"For he will order his angels to protect you wherever you go."
—*Psalm 91:11*

Me: Thanks, God, for the unspeakable gift of Your Son given freely and unselfishly to bring us deliverance from sickness, fear, sadness, death, and so much more. When I watched the movie, *The Passion of the Christ*, I saw Mary following Jesus to the cross. Her flashbacks of him as a child made me cry, because I thought of my own son who had died. Like me, she wanted so much to save him, but she felt helpless. I thought of how I'd feel as a mother looking on as they tortured my son. The name Mary means "bitterness," and Simeon's prophecy to her at the temple, when Jesus was dedicated, was that a sword would pierce her soul (Luke 2:35). You sent an angel to her, and You remind me that You send angels to those who must endure great hardships. These messengers bring hope and strength when needed. I know that angels have protected me in the past and, though I've never seen them, You promise that I'll see many one day! I long for that day, when I'll see Your world and all that's hidden from me now. Lord, teach me more about these things that bring me so much hope. I love You.

God: Dear one, I keep My hand over all you do. I'm with you in every situation, and I take care of your every need. I also place you where I want you. I live and move through you. You want so much to see into My world. One day you will. You want My Son to return. He will! It will be at the right time, and you'll be ready! Then, you'll embrace your son again and see the family and friends who have passed before you. I do have a special place for you, where you can behold Me and be near My Son. There, you'll watch how We see and embrace all those who love Us. Thanks for your heart. Thanks for your desire to know Me. Thanks for how you persist when others give up. One day, you'll be rewarded for this. Don't feel sad that you never received acknowledgement for some things you've done, or that you lost precious time with loved ones. One day, you'll see how I make up for these things in ways beyond your imagination. The next life will far surpass anything you can think of now. Don't worry about aging or providing for family members. You'll always have what you need, because I'll always be what you need. And I'll take care of your family too. I appreciate so much about you. Rest in Me, and remember that I hold you up when others forget you. I love you.

DECEMBER 6
So I can go where You go

"How precious are your thoughts about me, O God. They cannot be numbered! I can't even count them; they outnumber the grains of sand! And when I wake up, you are still with me!"
—*Psalm 139:17-18*

Me: Lord, You've blessed me so much! You are so wonderful, and I'm forever grateful. Everything I've ever asked for, You've provided! I don't know how You do it, but You always answer my requests. When I thought I wanted children, You blessed me with two. When I prayed for a nice house, You supplied me with one beyond my expectations. When I talked to You about having my own business, You made it happen! Trips abroad? Somehow, You worked every one out. You've given me good friends, success, abundance, grace, love, mercy, peace, and hope. Thanks for a beloved church family and a husband who loves me. Thanks for brothers and sisters who care about me, grandchildren to adore, clients to cherish, and mornings to worship You. You are precious and the source of great joy. Let today and tomorrow be as blessed as yesterday. Take me ever farther down Your path to places I've never even dared to dream of going and to people I've never imagined I might meet. Spread out Your carpet before me, and lead me down Your corridors. I want to follow You. I want to go where You go. May our journey together extend into heaven, where the light always shines and the doors never close, where people are always good and kind, and where love always abounds. That's where I want to be—right next to You. Please lead me there. I love You.

God: Child, you are precious to Me. You're My gorgeous gem, My vibrant diamond. You shine like a brilliant light in the darkness. People around you can see who you are, if they have spiritual eyes to see. Your arms extend kindness and hope to those who are lost—people who don't know their way or where to go or what to do. But you guide them. I will always lead you to right paths as you turn your thoughts to Me. I will always guide your steps to the most desired places, where My light shines and no evil exists. One day, you'll walk hand in hand with My Son, and you'll see the world as I always intended it to be. It will be a place of indescribable beauty and unspeakable joy. Just wait and see! I love you.

And see Your favor on my family

"And having chosen them, he called them to come to him. And having called them, he gave them right standing with himself. And having given them right standing, he gave them his glory."
—Romans 8:30

Me: Lord, help me with my family. They need hope and peace and a greater sense of joy, as the world around them gets more tumultuous, chaotic, and confusing. So many schools now promote false teachings that deny Your existence, create confusion, and obliterate our nation's history and any memory of those who fought so hard to preserve a land where we can worship You freely. Would You lead my children and grandchildren to Your truth? Can You assure me of their salvation, or at least give me some hope for this? Please remind me of how You choose Your sons and daughters? Do You know before they're born? Why did You pick me? I know now that You've often guided me so I could lead others. Now, help me with my words, Lord. Often, I speak without listening to You first. Remind me to go to You when I'm not sure of what to say. Give me peace in any life storm. Thanks for encouragement and wisdom above all. Thanks again for assurance of my family's salvation. You always lift me up! How I love You.

God: Dear one, I know ahead of time who will receive Me. These are the ones My angels watch over, even before birth. That's how the devil sometimes recognizes My elect—by watching My angels. He may send his "troops" to try to destroy those I've set My sites on. He may even attack their family. That's why it's so important for people to know the power that's available to them and how to use My Son's name against his schemes. You won't see as many attacks directed against unbelievers and those the adversary has "under his thumb." He doesn't need to use his devices to entice or manipulate them, because they're already within his grip. When the enemy tries to hurt a person I've called, he knows he can't destroy them, because I hold them in My hand. And I will always use his evil intentions for good. Remember that prayer is powerful in these situations, and claiming My promises is absolutely life-giving. Many of My assurances are for your children (Isaiah 44:3, 49:25, 54:13). Never forget that I will always show My favor to the progeny of those who love Me. I love you.

DECEMBER 8
And cause blind eyes to see

"You will open the eyes of the blind and free the captives from prison. You will release those who sit in dark dungeons."
—Isaiah 42:7

Me: Lord, in the book of Isaiah, the prophet foretold of a Messiah who'd come and suffer and die for us. He gave enough details, or breadcrumbs, so that anyone who was looking for answers, or a path to follow, would be able to see the signs. How can anyone not notice that Jesus was that promised One? The signals are so clear! Where He'd be born, what He'd do, how He'd live, what He'd suffer, how He'd die, and where He'd be buried—these were all predicted in Your Word! Only a blind person could deny the fulfillment of these prophecies. Lord, let blind eyes see Your means of deliverance today. Enlighten my own eyes more and more to my own ministry and calling and how I can bring Your love and light to others. Lead me today, and give me strength and wisdom to do what You ask me to do. You are with me now. You've always been here. Thanks for guiding my steps. I didn't always make the best choices, but, somehow, You've worked out everything for good. I love You.

God: Dear one, each year brings you closer to the return of My Son and a new kingdom on earth. Refresh your thoughts with My Word. Cleanse your heart and mind with My love and light. Come to Me with your requests, and expect miracles today! As you face the days ahead, set your vision higher. Prepare yourself for new things and fresh opportunities by becoming more familiar with the promises and prophecies in My Word. As time goes on, you'll see even more of them fulfilled—right in front of your eyes! I'll bring you people to lead and to bless. Minister to them by teaching them what you know from My Word. My love supersedes any affection in this world. It alone can heal and bring new light to others. Don't worry about how people respond or what they think of you. It's Me they reject if they don't accept you or what you share with them. It's Me they push aside. Don't take it personally. Continue to persevere, and think the good thoughts I've given you from My Word. Let My peace embrace your heart, so My love can flow freely through you. I love you.

As voices ring out

"And I assure you that the time is coming, indeed it's here now, when the dead will hear my voice—the voice of the Son of God. And those who listen will live."
—John 5:25

Me: Lord, we need just judges in our land. We need leaders with courage to stand up for You. Send Your angels to whisper in the ears of people who will demand leadership with our country's best interests at heart. We need ones who will defend Your principles, laws, and justice! Send wise men and women, and awaken people to the reality of what they could face if they turn a blind eye to what's happening behind the scene. Open their eyes to the truth and to what is corrupt and false in our land. Bring righteousness to the forefront. Let voices ring out to reverberate Your words, and show us how to echo Your words in all we do! As I raise up songs of praise to You, let me see Your greatness as I proclaim Your message of hope. Show me Your will and how I can best resonate Your greatness. Help me to have peace amid any trial and be able to express strength and courage, even when others have none. Bring me before people who want my help, Lord. Help me to discern their needs and be able to show them what You can do for them financially, mentally, and spiritually. Give me Your answers and solutions to their problems, so I can best help them. You're a gracious God. Thanks for all you do! I love You.

God: Dear one, heaven and hell can't get in the way of My purposes! Nothing can prevent My design for you and My children in this world. Only I can control the outcomes. No one else! So don't worry about your life or the lives of those you love. The enemy may try to cause harm. He may try to squelch and silence the voices of My children. But My purposes and power will always rise to the forefront, even when they were seemingly suppressed. And I will bring you peace. I'll restore wholeness where it's needed. I'll bless you beyond your expectations and demonstrate My great mercy and justice. Don't hesitate to heed My words or to speak them. They'll bring light and life to others. They'll usher in hope in times of trouble. My words, spoken by My people, will bring deliverance. I'll give you wisdom and enlighten your eyes as to what is false. Trust Me, not your feelings, to give you direction. Today, I'll bless you in ways beyond your imagination. And, one day, you'll thrill to hear My voice ring out as I call My children home! I love you.

DECEMBER 10
And we are released

"All creation has been groaning as in the pains of childbirth right up to the present time. And we believers also groan, even though we have the Holy Spirit within us as a foretaste of future glory, for we long for our bodies to be released from sin and suffering. We...wait with eager hope for the day when God will give us our full rights as his adopted children, including the new bodies he has promised us."
—*Romans 8:22-23*

Me: Lord, how amazing You are! Yesterday I watched a documentary about *The Hidden Life of Trees*, and I realized that there is so much I don't know about Your creations. Nothing is too hard or too wonderful for You. I see Your face in each day's dawning and each sun's setting. I see You in the masterful way You've taught all creatures to know their unique parts in this world. I see You in the intricacies of life and how we ourselves are made. Teach us, as You have all of Your creation, so we may turn to You with all our hearts and instinctively know who You are. Your presence of light and life is a constant reminder of all You've done. Reveal to me today those who desire to know more about You and to understand how You work. Lead me to touch the ones You're calling, so I can draw them into a greater understanding of You. Show me the light in their eyes and the glow in their hearts, then give me the right words to say. Raise up leaders and mighty ones, Lord. And if I can somehow help You do this, show me! Let my children's children bring others to You with hearts offered up to and for You. One day may I gaze out to see how my love for You was multiplied through many others. Thanks for this. I love You.

God: Child, wherever you find yourself, remember that I watch over you day and night. I'm with you as you sleep and when you're awake. Your ways are My ways as you turn your thoughts and actions to Me. Remember, I'm your father, and I always care for you. You may be awed by the things you see now, but, dear one, there are miracles ahead that are beyond your imagination! These wonders are meant for you and for those who believe. One day, My Son will return, and what a great day that will be! Until then, seek My promises, and claim them as your own. Seek My presence through My words, which bring peace and love and reconciliation to everyone who heeds them. I love you.

DECEMBER 11
At just the right time

"For God says, 'At just the right time, I heard you. On the day of salvation, I helped you.' Indeed, the "right time" is now. Today is the day of salvation."
—2 Corinthians 6:2

Me: Lord, it's amazing how fast the weeks go by. It'll be truly astonishing when You create a new heaven and earth, and we see what eternity looks like compared to the world and its limits now. Thousands of years here may be but a moment then. I want so much to understand time, to watch the history of events, and to know how You view them. What is Your perspective? I want to fly from here to there, to see the world from Your viewpoint, and to be able to soar with Jesus through the universe. I want to hold His hand as I fly, to glance over at His shining face, to see His approving smile, and to hear His voice "like many waters" as He speaks. I want to be enlightened by His wisdom and to gain His insight. I want to hear Him explain the reasons behind what He's done and to describe the world as He meant it to be. How gorgeous it will be one day, with crystal clear waters, mountains with lush forests, and animals who live alongside us. Treasures beyond my imagination. I want to see it all. One day I will, Lord! Thanks! How I love You.

God: Child, what is time? What meaning does it have? Do you live for time? Or do you live for yourself? Or for Me? Do you serve time? Time is just a means. Like money, it serves a purpose. It can help you achieve certain ends. But it cannot provide for you. It's only a means to an end. I am your Lord, the One who loves and sustains you. I've anointed you, and I've called you out to be My child—a special part of My family. I've given you time now to use for your benefit and to accomplish My purposes. Use it as I lead you, so you can succeed in reaching the goals I set before you. I'll show you how. Then, one day, You'll see time as I see it, and you'll understand the full meaning of eternity. In My world, you'll have no need to tell time, because it won't exist. It'll be an unnecessary part of eternal life. It won't be needed as a measure, because life will be limitless. My new heaven and earth will be perfect places, without the necessity for time or space. "Property" will be nonexistent. It will be a wonderful world beyond your expectation. And you'll share it with Me forever. Because I love you.

379

DECEMBER 12
When You finally come for us

"He who is the faithful witness to all these things says, 'Yes, I am coming soon!' Amen! Come, Lord Jesus!"
—Revelation 22:20

Me: Dear God, I say, "Come soon, Lord Jesus!" and I look forward to Your Son's return, when the heavens will open to receive us. But I know there is still work to be done. I see "every man doing what is right in his own eyes" (Judges 21:25) and only a few leaders who will stand up for truth. Most are afraid to hold forth what's right out of fear for reprisal or retribution. We need guts, Lord, so we can be courageous in the face of what others provoke. We need to care more about what You think! Would You help me to step forward fearlessly for You? Lord, would You give me supernatural strength to stand for You today? Would You help me to recognize those with a gleam in their eyes, who are searching for You? How may I help You fulfill Your vision for a revival on this earth? Work through me to will and to do of Your good pleasure! Enlighten my understanding so I may see clearly. Help me to listen to You and heed Your voice. Show me how best to work for You and Your people. Prepare me for the glorious day of Your Son's return! I love You.

God: Child, My Word gives you understanding and true enlightenment. You may seek wisdom elsewhere, but you can only gain it from My Word. People come and go. They think they can bring answers to the world's plights and chaos and confusion. They believe they're able to solve every problem. What they don't understand is that they are dealing with spiritual things and a realm they can't fathom. They try to fix things physically that can only be reconciled spiritually. And, because satan is the god of this world, he will not allow them to "straighten things out." Only when My Son returns will harmony be restored to the world, so it's truly peaceful. Only then will people see My love and mercy manifested throughout the earth. He will create a new world—full of light and life. Then, My love will shine in the faces of people, and their lips will utter praise and thanksgiving continuously. It will be a magnificent place of peace and joy. And you will see My mercy abound. But now, you can only see frustration in people's hearts, because they don't understand why they're here and what is their purpose. These things are hidden from them until they come to know who I am. But you be my hands and feet to reach them! I love you.

And I experience the greatest adventure

"He will wipe every tear from their eyes, and there will be no more death or sorrow or crying or pain. All these things are gone forever."
—Revelation 21:4

Me: Lord, You abide in the heavens, or that space above the earth. Lift me up to where You live, and help me to remain there by Your side, but never to look down on others. When I wonder why someone doesn't do what they promised, help me not to judge them unjustly. When others criticize me, help me to forgive them. Lord, I want to be merciful, like You. Help me to be a good example of this. I never want to have a hardened heart toward anyone or anything, but to have a child-like, trusting heart toward You and others. Sometimes I want to see myself as a majestic steed, when I'm still learning like a lamb. Teach and train me, so I can stand proudly near You in Your kingdom. I may not be worthy, but I want to be one of Your mighty warriors. I'm ready to fight for You and lead others to Your truth. I may not be completely capable, but I'm willing! Only You know what I can do, Lord. I just want to be close to You. And I want to be one of Your guides, who can lead others up to Your holy place, where death has no hold, where tears don't exist, and where we can see You as You are. What an adventure, Lord! Today, draw me closer to You. And show me Your plan for my life. Make it all clear to me. You are more real to me now than ever! I love You.

God: Dear child, this world is not your home. Always remember this. This place can be cruel and pitiless. It can be stark and striving and lacking in love. Come to Me with all your heart. Let Me lead you to new places. Let Me open your eyes and ears to what you can do and what truly exists in a world beyond this one. Don't depend on people to meet your needs. They'll disappoint you. And this world will end one day. When My new world emerges, it will be perfect in every way. It'll be beyond anything you can imagine. You'll have no fear or worry or stress. There will be no more famine or war or sickness or hunger. No more tears. People will thrive on love. It will be a place that is filled with praise and worship, instead of hate, resentment, pride, power-lust, and anger. There will be only love, but not love as you know it now. It will be perfect love—My love. This new land will come one day. And you will be an integral part of it, because you're willing to help me prepare for its arrival. I love you.

And wonder no more what eternity looks like

"Yet what we suffer now is nothing compared to the glory he will reveal to us later."
—Romans 8:18

Me: Lord, time passes by faster and faster, and I wonder what eternity will feel like. I watch each day for Your Son's return, and I look forward to listening to Him as He unfolds the earth's story. Then I want to look over His shoulder as He remakes it. I want to view eternity through His eyes and see beyond this universe. I want to travel with Him to places I've never seen and be amazed by it all! I long to bow before You and look up to see You shining in all Your glory. I want to be touched by You and crowned by Your grace and mercy. I want to sit with You and hear You speak and explain more than I could comprehend now. I long to watch as You reveal Your mysteries and allow me to see through a clear glass into the world You've desired. I yearn to hear Your Son's voice falling on my ears and to feel His healing touch. I long to walk and talk with Him as I listen to His wisdom. Guide me now with Your loving hand, for You alone refresh me and ease my cares. You bring blessings and hope to me and to those who know You. You're a great God, worthy of praise. I thank You for Your many blessings. I love You.

God: Dear one, what you see now is a fleeting moment. Time passes quickly, even as many days seem to slip through your fingers. You see a shadow of things to come, and you can't even fathom the glory to be revealed when My Son returns for you. Your eyes are veiled now so you can only see vaguely what really surrounds you. This present world holds beauty in the things I've made. But it's only a shadow of the things to come. My new heaven and earth will be more than magnificent. It will be glorious! For you'll see the reality of My greatness and that of My Son. The new earth will be a paradise with trees filled with life-giving fruit and streams flowing with living water. You'll be united with your true family and your body will be incorruptible. Sadness, sickness, destruction, and death will not exist. Spread My message of hope for this new life. Tell people about the deliverance available to them from the evils of this world and about this future place where they can have joy for eternity. Rejoice now in what you know and what you have in Me and through My Son. This is the true rejoicing, where you'll find healing peace and joy. I love you.

As I prepare for what's coming

"But in that coming day no weapon turned against you will succeed. You will silence every voice raised up to accuse you. These benefits are enjoyed by the servants of the Lord; their vindication will come from me. I, the Lord, have spoken!"
—Isaiah 54:17

Me: Lord, only You can make a person great. Only You can make anyone worthy of Your acclaim. Thanks for how You've raised me up and supported me all these years. Give me grace and strength to continue and victory over all opposition and obstacles. Show me the best use of my time today. I know I'm always in training. Help me to accomplish what You need to have done in the time that's left. Thanks for bringing together all the elements I need to be successful. Would You show me more about the end times and how I can prepare for these? I want to know the signs and the seasons and how to warn others. Open my eyes to what lies ahead. I love You.

God: Dear one, in the days ahead, things will change dramatically on the earth. My Son will return for you, but there will be trials first. People will not have so much abundance, and they will be driven by a greater fear of lack. The adversary will manipulate many by blinding them to My truth. But you can prepare yourself by putting on My armor and making yourself ready for the battle ahead. Do this by coming to Me throughout the day and asking for My direction and leading. I will separate out My own army and determine how each person fits into the scheme of things. Even now, I'm making determinations and preparing My troops for the times ahead. I'll be able to use those who are prepared and ready in even greater ways. Your willingness and ability to use your mind for My purposes will determine your unique spot in this mighty force. After the final battle on earth, at the end of His thousand-year reign, My Son will create a beautiful and new planet. The waters will be crystal-clear, and the rivers will run freely. The forests will be green and thriving, and animals will coexist with mankind. It will be beyond your imagination—a place where true freedom exists. As a righteous ruler, My Son will bring peace, joy, hope, and justice, which have never prevailed on this earth. You'll see the love My Son has for those He gave His life to save. Remember, His love goes way beyond any love you'll ever experience on this earth. I love you.

DECEMBER 16
With hope-filled expectation

"Faith is the confidence that what we hope for will actually happen; it gives us assurance about things we cannot see."
—Hebrews 11:1

Me: Search my heart, Lord. Reveal to me my true self and what that means to You. Help me to understand my shortcomings and how I can move beyond them. Why is my memory so short that I forget Your goodness and the things you've done for me? I see you in each page of Your Word and in each corner of my life. I see you in the people I meet and in my daily connections. I see Your hand in history—in the lives of people who overcame obstacles and moved to bring needed change to the world. Show me how I can reach the levels You've chosen for me so I can pass on something greater to many others. Show me what I must do to be one of Your mighty ones. And forgive the years when I was so far away from Your presence. Help me to make up for lost time by expending my best effort and expanding Your influence. Help me to prepare others so they can be mighty spiritual warriors for Your cause. I love You.

God: Dear one, watch and be ready! As time goes on, you'll see more trouble in the world. Find your quiet place, where you can maintain peace, even when you're surrounded by turmoil. Learn how you can "batten down the hatches." How can you prepare yourself for hard times that may come in your lifetime? I will show you how financially, mentally, and spiritually. Then, you'll be ready. Just listen as I direct you. For I'll whisper to you the words you need to hear, and I'll always warn you before trials come, and give you needed courage. Even in the hardest times, remember that you have hope, because you know My Son. Hope is for things to come—the things you can't see yet. Hope is what you believe for, trust in, and expect to come to pass, because you have faith in Me. Hope brings you deliverance from evil and a reason to act in the right place at the right time. You hope for the return of Your Savior, Jesus Christ. One day He'll come for you, and He'll pull you up to Him in the clouds. He'll swoop you up in His arms and carry you away with Him to a new life. This is your hope. This will bring you cheer amid trouble and trial. Have hope in Him! I love you.

While filling jars with Your oil

"For we speak as messengers approved by God to be entrusted with the Good News. Our purpose is to please God, not people. He alone examines the motives of our hearts."
—*1 Thessalonians 2:4*

Me: Lord, how You surprise me with the appearance of people who are willing to serve You with their whole hearts and stand up for You! Thanks for introducing them to me! I'd love to be like the widowed wife of a prophet, who was approached by the prophet Elisha. She believed his words and filled her jars with oil so she could pay off her debt and save herself and her son. Thanks for people like Your great messenger Elijah, who delivered Your promises at a time when life seemed small, and every resource was shrinking. People of faith reveal more to us about who we are and what we can do because of what You've already accomplished. Thanks for those you bring into my life, who remind me of the gifts I possess and how I can use them to carry more "anointed oil" so that more people can survive and thrive in this life. I'm amazed at Your goodness and how You send these people at just the right moments. When we feel like we're falling back, You show us how to move ahead with jars filled with oil to sustain us! You're a good God, and I thank You for Your love and favor on my life and for how You lead me constantly through the good and bad times. I love You.

God: Dear one, you see how I'm always with you. And you understand how I bless you and give you peace and joy, sometimes with the help of My special messengers, whom I send to bless and help you. You see how, as you direct your gaze more and more to Me, you can maintain greater peace and calm. There are extraordinary miracles ahead—things which you cannot even imagine now. There are wonders and signs meant for you and for others who believe and expect the results of their faith. Look forward to these. Know that I'm with you now, and that My Son will return for you. What a great day! Until then, claim what I've promised to you. Look for ways to use your gifts to expand your capabilities as a special messenger to others so that your blessings can spread to them and seep into their hearts. There are great days ahead. Only seek My presence, and let your words be wise, because they're based on My love. I love you.

DECEMBER 18
Through heavenly dreams

"He speaks in dreams, in visions of the night, when deep sleep falls on people as they lie in their beds. He whispers in their ears...."
—Job 33:15-16

Me: Lord, I remember an especially meaningful dream You gave me once. I was on a journey with my family when my son asked me to take a special side-trip with him. First, we sped raftless down a spectacular waterway—a wide, rushing river that wound through forests of pine trees. We floated around bends, speeding past people who were swimming. Then, we flew from a cliff over beautiful mountains and valleys. "Let's go there!" my son shouted. And we soared up to a log lodge at the top of one mountain. We entered a room where people danced and sang with their hands raised high in praise. We joined in, and I realized I was wearing a colorful skirt that moved and flowed as I danced. Then, in another room, a man behind a counter pulled a tap and handed us drinks in pilsner glasses. We went to a booth and sipped what tasted like honey or ambrosia. After we finished, my son said, "Let's go!" and we left the lodge to soar away. When I awoke, I realized that You'd showed me a taste of paradise. This vision gave me joy and hope for the future, especially after my son died, because I knew I'd spend endless days like this with him! I love that dream. Would You bless me with more like this one to remind me of what's ahead? I love You.

God: Dear one, trust Me to bring you what you need when you need it. I'll give you visions and dreams when I want you to see things more clearly or to bring you needed hope. They'll give you a greater ability to focus on My promises by helping you turn your thoughts away from anything negative. Through whispers and dreams and visions, I'll give you hope and the ability to absorb more of who I am and what I can do. Time spent with Me will open many doors. But it takes a willingness to recognize the meaning of the messages I give you and a desire to follow through with what I try to communicate to you. The Apostle Paul spent years in the desert absorbing these things. Only by isolating himself away from people could he accomplish this. As I direct you, others may not understand why you do what you do. Trust me anyway. And I will always provide not just what you need now, but so much more for a later time. I love you.

386

As a harbinger of hope

"God is our refuge and strength, always ready to help in times of trouble."
—Psalm 46:1

Me: Dear Lord, would You remind me of Your love today? Would You breathe on Me Your breath of life, and include with it forgiveness, mercy, and peace? Do you remember the things You promised to me long ago? Please fill my thoughts with hopefulness for the future. Let my habitation be a place of hope, where people can come to receive grace and feel loved. Open new doors to waiting hearts. Reveal to me what I need to know for upcoming times, so I can be expectant and best able to lead those You bring to me. What is Your plan, and how can I be a part of it? Show me, Lord. I also ask for rest for my soul, so I can be strengthened to face another day. Give me wisdom and confidence to be able to help in the best way possible those who seek Your advice and counsel. I seek Your integrity. Help me to be joyful, peaceful, calm, and ready to answer anyone who asks about You. I look to You to work in me to will and to do of Your good pleasure. Help me to abound more in Your great grace, love, and hope. I love You.

God: Dear one, you are the apple of My eye. When you feel weak, plant your feet on top of My solid rock. It will give you needed strength. I see you now as a child splashing through a puddle and laughing happily as storm clouds hover over you and rain pours all around you. I've never neglected those things that are deep in your heart. I'll never forget all your hopeful dreams or the things you overcame as a child. Go back to these dreams, for they are your gifts from Me to keep forever. Remember, I'm your help and your strength. I'm your Lord, and you can look to Me for solace, peace, and refreshing. Look to Me for answers. I am your God, and I'm almighty. I can bring you help and hope in times of trouble. Be at peace and let your heart be at rest. Don't weary yourself with anxious thoughts. I'll bless you today. Only look to Me with praise and thanksgiving. I'll meet your needs and bring you needed rest and peace. Remember your childhood hopes and dreams, for I will always honor these. And I never forget My promises to you. I love you.

December 20
Looking forward to the time

"Since we are surrounded by such a huge crowd of witnesses to the life of faith, let us strip off every weight that slows us down, especially the sin that so easily trips us up. And let us run with endurance the race God has set before us. We do this by keeping our eyes on Jesus, the champion who initiates and perfects our faith. Because of the joy awaiting him, he endured the cross, disregarding its shame. Now he is seated in the place of honor beside God's throne."
—Hebrews 12:1-2

Me: Lord, I look forward to when I get to meet Abraham, Moses, David, Mary, Peter, Paul, and Your Son, Jesus! I want to see again the people I love too, who have predeceased me. Lord, it'll be amazing to be surrounded by these people and those whose lives were changed when I shared Your message of love with them. And I want to thank the ones who enlightened me with Your hope. We'll all rejoice and dance and praise You! We'll hug each other as we hear You say, "Welcome home!" We'll cry for joy, because we get to spend eternity together in Your glorious world after finally getting to meet You face-to-face. We'll look up at Your Son on His throne and bask in His presence and ask Him many questions about all the things we never understood. How amazing it will be! I look so forward to it. Now, while we wait for His return, help us through this day as we don our armor and fight once more for You against the wiles of the devil. How I love You.

God: Dear one, remember how eager and excited you were to go to your grandparents' cabin? Remember the smell of blueberry pie as you walked in the kitchen door? Or the taste of the molasses cookies your grandfather brought fresh from the bakery? Remember how excited you were to see your grandparents and how you felt when they hugged and greeted you? You wanted them to love you as much as you loved them. Well, someday you'll feel this same way, but even more so, and your heart will skip again. And the excitement will mount as you climb the steps to meet My Son. You'll be overwhelmed by your new home, which will be more fragrant than the pine trees that surrounded your grandparents' cabin. My Son will greet you, and His love will surpass their love. You yearn to experience love like you once felt. But you'll encounter something greater! You'll be surrounded by a love beyond anything you've ever known! I love you.

DECEMBER 21
When I can gaze up at You

"For we have heard of your faith in Christ Jesus and your love for all of God's people, which come from your confident hope of what God has reserved for you in heaven. You have had this expectation ever since you first heard the truth of the Good News."
—*Colossians 1:4-5*

Me: Lord, how I look forward to Your Son's return for us! I've told You that My greatest desire is to one day sit in the front row gazing up at Your face! I still long for this. I want to be counted among those whom You deem to be special and loyal. I want to hear Jesus say to me, "Well done, you good and faithful servant!" I would even love to be rewarded as one of Your spiritual "great ones." Only You can determine this. Would You show me how I can be honorable in Your sight? What can I do today? Help me in each and every moment to choose the right words and identify the best thoughts and actions. As Your warrior, train me in the best use of Your spiritual gifts, so I can continuously walk in Your knowledge, understanding, and wisdom. I want to be able to tap into Your discernment, so I can be an effective minister for You. I love You.

God: Dear one, when My Son returns for you and finally reigns over a new heaven and earth, you'll see things very differently. Time will not matter. Titles and ranks will be meaningless. All the people in My kingdom will be considered worthy, and you will live among "the greats," unaware and uncaring about where you sit or who you stand next to. Because everyone will be considered extraordinary! My glory will be ever-present, and you'll behold the magnificence of an unimaginable world. It will be a place filled with brilliance beyond anything you've ever seen. Forgiveness, grace, mercy, joy, and peace will abound. Even the animals and plants will gleam with light and favor. Remember that the earth is a temporary place. Seek Me and what I tell you, because the world as you know it will one day fade away. Look forward to the day My Son returns, because, until then, this world will deteriorate and degrade. People will suffer, and there will be no peace among the nations. War will prevail and change the face of the planet. Teach your children now how to have peace and rest in Me, no matter what's happening around them. Show them that I'm the only thing solid in this world. Through Me, they can be safe and secure. I love you.

As this world changes

"However, no one knows the day or hour when these things will happen, not even the angels in heaven or the Son himself. Only the Father knows."
—Matthew 24:36

Me: God, I always feel joyful at this time of year when Christmas approaches. I love the lights, the decorations, the food, and the music. But many people seem to be in a frenzy because of others' expectations or their own self-imposed stress. Many are sad to be reminded of lost loved ones. Would you help me to bring Your peace and joy to these people? Help me to show Your love, Lord, and to be patient when some say hurtful and unkind things because they are stressed-out and don't understand that You can relieve any anxiety. I often wonder, when the world seems to move farther and farther away from You, if the "Day of the Lord" is fast approaching. We are seeing so many changes in the world, as leaders proclaim evil as good and good as evil. Will Christ come back for us soon? I hear and read so many things, and I wonder. Can You make it clearer? Would You prepare me? I seek Your wisdom and insight. Reveal to me what I need to know, Lord. Prepare me for that day. I love You.

God: Dear one, My Son will return for you, but I can't tell you the day or time. No matter when it happens, you can be prepared for that day. I'll help you with this. And I'll meet your needs and take care of you. The more time you spend with Me, the more I can do for you. Come to Me and worship Me only. Continue to trust in Me, for I am there for you. Yes, many things in the world will change quickly. More true worshippers will line up with Me versus those who worship false gods. Forces will align. In the Middle East, you'll see prophecies fulfilled. Watch for people to make plans to destroy Israel, and worldly forces will align with them. Be prepared to stand up for your beliefs. I'll give you the needed strength and wisdom to do this. You're in My hands. I'll deliver you from evil. You can help Me to prepare your children too. Teach them My ways so that they understand how I can protect and bless them. Only My Word gives direction and answers to what lies ahead. Don't judge whether a person is worthy of My Word or My blessing. Only I can determine this. Just speak. I will give you the words to say. I'm a Lord of strength, blessing, power, and enlightenment. I love you.

December 23
And I rejoice in what's to come

"After all, what gives us hope and joy, and what will be our proud reward and crown as we stand before our Lord Jesus when he returns? It is you!"
—*1 Thessalonians 2:19*

Me: Lord, I glory in Your name and the promises You've declared in Your Word. As I read, I rejoice in what's to come because of Your love for Your people, Israel, and those who follow and seek a chosen Messiah. I may be adopted into Your family, but I joy in being included, and I seek Your will and how I can serve You. Thanks for Your help in seeing what You have in store for me and how I can serve in Your kingdom now and later. Would You continue to give me insight? Bless me with Your wisdom so I may serve You with my whole heart until Your Son's return. Of course, I want to be in the front row, to gaze right up at You on Your throne, and to be as near to You as possible! I also want to sit among faithful believers like Billy Graham, Oral Roberts, George Müller, Mother Teresa, and Brother Andrew. Help me to live a life that's worthy of this—a life that's centered on You and Your Word and glorifies You. I fall at times. I stumble because I'm human. Would You help me to be more like You in all I say and do so I can stand tall when others fall? I look to You for courage. I love You.

God: Dear one, remember how the mother of James and John came to Jesus and asked if they could sit on His right and left hand when He became king (Matthew 20: 20-28)? His answer was that only I (God) can decide who will be in these places. Where your place is in paradise will be the best place for you. It will suit you in every way and be based on your life on earth and how you lived day by day. Let Me decide what suits you both now and later. What I choose will always be the best for you. It will always be pleasing, because I alone know your heart. You're precious to Me. I love how you are courageous and how you fight to overcome fear. Because you do these things, I can fulfill My desires through you. I can use you in remarkable ways to reach, touch, teach, and bless others. As you've seen, your ministry is to those who've been silenced and need to be heard—people who've hoped and believed and pressed on, despite great hardships. The stories of these living examples must be shared! Their words are mighty swords of light to help others to be able to trust and have faith no matter what. I love you.

DECEMBER 24
Because You're a star

"I am the bright morning star."
—*Revelation 22:16*

Me: Dear Lord, it's Christmas Eve! My heart joins with so many others' in celebrating Your Son's birth, life, and presence here on earth. How thankful I am for His love and for His willingness to die so I can live. I remember the first Christmas that meant so much to me. It was the one after I asked Jesus into my heart. When I drew Him in, I understood for the first time what He'd done to show me who You are and what You did for me. I was so touched by the harps, the songs, the music, and the reality of it all. For the first time, I really understood the meaning behind the words of the songs. I began to realize what life was all about, and this meant so much to me! It seems like there are few people, even among Christians, who truly "get it" and understand how and why Your Son came and just what He did for us! How many know what was accomplished to allow Your light to penetrate the hearts of people? Your Son waded through heaps of unbelief to reach people in dark places, so they could live again! Because He was willing, He's a star. And I long to see His face. I'd love to be able to look back and see Him in the arms of a very young mother, who loved Him before He was born and believed in who He was. Thanks for sending Jesus. I love You.

God: Dear one, as you enjoy time with your family, remember Me. And think about My Son and what He did. Like Him, I see you as a shining star! You sought Me out, and I love you for that. As you follow His Star, like the wise men, to the place of His birth, I'll pave a path for you. I'll show you how to proceed and how to abound with joy. Never forget that I bless your family because of you. They will seek Me in ways you can't imagine because of your life. Know that I care for them, just as I care for you. And I'll reveal Myself more and more to them and to you through dreams, visions, and conversations. My hand is on their lives, as it is on yours, and they will stand before My throne one day. I'll show you, in the days ahead, how to reach others who seek Me as you do. I selected you for a purpose, and I'll show you what that purpose is. Live for My glory so you can shine it to others. Let them see My love through you and how I can comfort, heal, and reconcile what's been torn apart. Where there once was despair, I can bring hope. I love you.

A child once born

"For a child is born to us, a son is given to us."
—Isaiah 9:6

Me: Today, Lord, as I listened to Handel's Messiah, I cried, especially when I heard, "Unto us a child is born...." What a joyful time it was when Jesus was born! The circumstances were tough for Mary and Joseph. After traveling many miles to Bethlehem, Mary had to give birth in a stable, even after enduring months of being disparaged by people for having a child "out of wedlock." Very few understood or accepted what You were doing, though it was an amazing miracle! And it reminds me of how every great effort of Yours, or ours, is always accompanied by great difficulties. Just so, hardship surrounded the birth of Your precious Son, our king! One day, I'd like to see what it was like firsthand. I want to behold Jesus as a child and watch Him as He grew up. I want to have a greater sense of the wonder surrounding His birth and life! I've seen the miracle of how You melt our hearts with Your love. Thanks that my own family may experience this and have a greater awareness of Your presence. I pray that they can find peace and hope and that they might understand Your greatness and what a gracious gift You gave us through Your Son. I lift this Christmas time with family up to You now in prayer. Let there be peaceful moments of wonderful sharing. And open hearts to receive Your blessings. I love You.

God: Dear one, it's a special day for those who understand the true message and meaning of Christmas: that "a child is born to us." Many think something special occurred, but they celebrate their traditions blindly and without hope, because they don't understand what really happened. Remind them of My Son and what He did for them. He lived His life as a sacrifice for them. Just as you mourn tragic things that happen to your own children, I grieved for what I knew He must endure. But I also knew that many sons and daughters would come as a result. And you are one of them! Rejoice today that you are My child and that I can give you the things I promised so long ago—all because of a Son born humbly in a manger. I love you.

DECEMBER 26
Whose beauty will be revealed

"For all creation is waiting eagerly for that future day when God will reveal who his children really are."
—Romans 8:19

Me: Lord, I bow before You, my face to the ground. Then my eyes gaze up at You, because I want so much to see and serve You. Thanks for forgiving all my shortcomings and for removing them far from me and making me whole with Your Spirit. Thanks for cleansing me with Your love and beautifying me with Your favor. Would You make me glow and glimmer because I'm pleasing to You? Open my eyes to how You fight for me, and enable me to help others when there seems to be no hope for them at all. Help me to see why You've placed me here. What good can I do for the people around me? You've led me along Your path all these many years. You've shown me Your good way time and time again. You've revealed to me little by little the unfolding of Your masterpiece in my life. I see glimpses of a pattern, but my vision is still cloudy. I look forward to seeing Your work when it's finally unveiled. You've been faithful to answer my prayers, even more than I could ask or think. Work through my weaknesses, Lord, and make good out of every error that results from my blindness. May my commitments exemplify Your purposes and Your unfolding will in my life! I love You.

God: Dear one, life is a continuous wonder and a celebration. Rejoice in it. But life does not end here. Through My Son, your reward will extend to a new life—one beyond this one. You can't imagine it now or comprehend its greatness. I can give you a vague idea, but no words can express what lies beyond this life. Have hope in what lies ahead for you. Life is short. It's a fleeting moment in time. One day, you're young and full of life; the next day, you're old and nearing life's end. But life is eternal for those who believe and trust and know that I am real, who seek to understand My Word and what My Son accomplished. For those who want to know Me and My ways, the colorful bits and pieces of life are woven together into an intricate and glorious pattern. This beautiful design will be revealed when you stand before My Son, who will unveil the masterpiece that was created from the moments of your life. Tears will come to your eyes when you see how I worked within each instant to weave together every detail for good. Because I love you.

  ### At a wedding

"I am overwhelmed with joy in the Lord my God! For he has dressed me with the clothing of salvation and draped me in a robe of righteousness. I am like a bridegroom dressed for his wedding or a bride with her jewels."
—Isaiah 61:10

Me: Dear Lord, I dreamed that I was alone in a room preparing for a wedding as guests arrived outside. I gazed down at my gift-clothing laid out, and I spent hours trying things on to see how I looked. Someone peeked in to remind me that I should go out to greet the guests. Then it occurred to me that the wedding was Your Son's, and You wanted me to attend to the guests as the celebration approached. In another dream, I was dressed up in a pretty, turquoise-colored dress as I mingled with women who were beautifully attired. We huddled around tables of jewelry to select sets to match our dresses. I looked over shoulders trying to find a necklace to go with my dress. A kind woman smiled and handed me a beautiful blue-green satin choker with a dangling cross to wear around my neck. I thanked her for the perfect match to my outfit. Then we all lined up to go in to meet the king. Lord, the dreams reminded me of how much I want to stand before Your Son in gleaming attire and look up at His shining face. I want to feel overwhelmed by His beauty and love and know that my life was lived for Him. I want to be adequately "dressed" as He places the Crown of Life on my head. Prepare me for this moment, Lord. I love You.

God: Dear one, today, do your best by focusing on Me. I will guide and lead you. Many I'm calling have minds clouded by shrouds of fear that prevent them from coming to My Son's feast. Some cower under clouds of remorse and regret that prevent them from stepping forward. Fears of death, loss, failure, and rejection—all of these keep people imprisoned in a room with no view of what lies ahead. These fears create barriers and prevent deliverance. Only My love can free them. As you speak of My kindness, truth, peace, and joy, they can be freed. Some will see and understand and decide to come and learn from you. Use the gifts I've given you to do this. I've given you what you need to help them. And, through you, I can work supernaturally to enlarge upon what you do naturally because of My Spirit in you. But you must focus on Me and not your gifts. I will make sure you are covered with My special clothing, so you are acceptable. Then we can work together to bring many more to the celebration. I love you.

DECEMBER 28
In a spacious place

"There is more than enough room in my Father's home. If this were not so, would I have told you that I am going to prepare a place for you? When everything is ready, I will come and get you, so that you will always be with me where I am."
—John 14:2

Me: Lord, so many times I wonder what this place You're preparing for us will be like. Will I live close to You? Will I have a room in a house with others or live in my own home? Will it be inside the new city You describe in the Book of Revelation, or will it be outside the gates? I've had dreams of homes, and I wonder if any of these are a picture of my abode in paradise. In a recent dream, I followed my son along a path through the woods, because he wanted me to see a project he was working on. I cried as I went, and I told him that I loved and missed him. I followed him into a basement, where he showed me a large balsam replica of a house he was working on. It was exquisite—very detailed. It reminded me of something he'd create, and I realized it was a model of a living space he wanted to build so his family could live together forever. And I remembered sitting at the kitchen table with him before he died and hearing him say how he wished all his family could be there with him, because he loved spending time with them. He looks forward to it now. I do too. I love You.

God: My child, I love how you seek Me through your thoughts and dreams. I love how you ask Me what I think as you puzzle over things. You miss your son. Your heart aches at the loss of his presence. I understand how you feel. My heart aches too. But he is at peace, and he waits to see you again and share all he knows. That will be a glorious day, when all My beloved children are reunited with each other and with Me! I love your questions. Yes, My Son and I are preparing a place for you now. I could try to describe it to you, but it's beyond anything you can imagine. Your "house" will be unlike anything you've ever seen. In contrast to the home you're in now, it will have no walls and be without limits because, in the spirit world, there are no bounds. Space and time have no boundaries. In this new world, you can move in ways that are limitless. When My Son said that there are more than enough rooms in My Father's house, He was expanding your understanding of a home without walls, where we can all live and move together. I love you.

DECEMBER 29
Where I can look out at a land

"Your eyes will see the king in all his splendor, and you will see a land that stretches into the distance."
—Isaiah 33:17

Me: Today, Lord, I look forward to living in the place that You've promised. I long for it. I even visit it now and then in my dreams. I seek it in my thoughts and envision it in my prayers. I can see it now—a place filled with primeval forests and clear mountain streams full of smooth stones and water that ripples along beside winding wooded paths. Between the lush-green, pine-filled hills, many colored fish thrive in crystalline lakes surrounded by white, silky-sand beaches. The fine sand filters between my toes as I step from the beach into the refreshing, clean coolness of the turquoise-watered lake. I breathe in the sweet fragrance of the nearby pine trees, and I'm warmed by the light as I gaze at brilliant blue-azure skies above me. Then I swing in a hammock placed between two tall evergreen trees just for me, and I gaze out at a distant island in the middle of the lake, just as I did as a child. I enjoy the solace and comfort of cool breezes and the pleasant background chatter of chipmunks, squirrels, and birds. The sounds are soft and harmonious and pleasant, like You, Lord. How I long for this time of joy and peace! I look forward to this place that reminds me of my grandparents' cabin. Today, I'm refreshed by Your constant presence. I love You.

God: Dear one, today, celebrate and be glad! Today, rejoice in what I've already done for you! Today, be thankful, because you know you can look forward to a time when peace will reign on a new earth created for you. Your most vivid imaginations can't even compare to what lies ahead. And, even if you can't find such a place of peace on earth now, you have this one to look forward to. You have this hope, because of what My Son did for you. It's the promise of a new place and time, when war will be no more, and evil purposes and determinations will come to an end. All creatures will co-exist in love and harmony. And everything will center around Me and My Son. This is the hope you can bring to others so they will also look forward to it. When the world offers hardship, pain, suffering, and death, you can look ahead to a time when My Son reigns, and you will experience a new way of life that lasts forever. Until then, have joy as you look forward to His coming. I love you.

That I can't even imagine

"Those who are victorious will sit with me on my throne, just as I was victorious and sat with my Father on his throne."
—Revelation 3:21

Me: Lord, You know how I long to sit in the front row and gaze at Your Son, with His flashing, flaming eyes and glowing, bronze-like feet (Revelation 1:15), as those around Him play their heavenly instruments and hold bowls full of prayers! And to see Him as He holds that scroll and gives instructions for how it all will transpire. I long to see the new Jerusalem in all its glory. I can see myself one day entering the gates to the new city and gliding along those gold-paved streets. I know I'll be welcomed by those I've loved, and I'll walk and talk with them once again. To see their faces once more.... Oh, how I long for this time! Thanks for bringing it to pass. I love You!

God: Dear one, close your eyes and imagine a world filled with light without any darkness. A world where evil cannot exist. Where only kindness and love and mercy abide. A world where you can walk or fly to new places, and where times doesn't exist. You'll gaze at the hills filled with beautiful trees unlike any you've ever seen—lush with leaves for healing. After you glide past streams of crystal-clear water that's pure enough to drink, you'll come to a gate and find people you've known and loved. Because you wear the white robe that's yours because you believe in My Son, you'll be greeted and escorted into the new city. An angel will nod to you as you enter. Beyond the gate you'll walk along a golden street that leads to a tower of steps. You'll climb them to reach the top, where a glowing, many-colored, bright beam beckons to you. Near the summit, the radiance will be overwhelming. But you'll continue. Your eyes will adjust, and you'll make out a huge shining orb on a throne in front of you. To its right another form will greet you. This One will have a face that shines like bronze and hair that glistens like snow. At first, His eyes will appear to flash like fire, but, as you come closer, you'll see that they actually glimmer and sparkle like the refection of light off of a crystal pool. Even His feet will glow under a translucent white robe that flows all around Him. He will reach out to you, and you will go directly up to Him, because you recognize His face. And you'll cry, because you'll feel His great love for you. He is real. He will embrace you and, finally, you will feel like you are home. Remember how much I love you.

DECEMBER 31
And behold Your face

"All praise to God, the Father of our Lord Jesus Christ. It is by his great mercy that we have been born again, because God raised Jesus Christ from the dead. Now we live with great expectation, and we have a priceless inheritance—an inheritance that is kept in heaven for you, pure and undefiled, beyond the reach of change and decay. And through your faith, God is protecting you by his power until you receive this salvation, which is ready to be revealed on the last day for all to see."
—1 Peter 1:3-5

Me: It's the last day of the year, Lord. Thanks for how You've blessed me with such remarkable gifts! Thanks for what You've given me and all that You've done through me this year! When You return, I'll sit at Your feet and praise You as I see Your face before me continually! Bless my children and their children so they know You and Your wondrous ways and mighty works. Because I want them to sit with me at Your feet! I see Your blessings each day, especially in Your answers to my prayer. Thanks for holding my hand through good and bad times and for making the good times more numerous and memorable than the bad. And for how, even what I considered to be bad has worked out for good! Thanks for teaching me how to have joy in all situations and how to love the unlovable. Thanks for hope when all seemed hopeless. I love You.

God: Dear one, it's only the beginning. As you move, I'll move with you in very powerful ways. See through My eyes, and listen with My ears. It's a season of great awakening. You'll see many young people called to Me, and You'll see old people proclaim their beliefs in ways you can't imagine. Look and see the glory of the Lord before you! I'll show you what you need to know. Those who believe in My Son will be saved from destruction, and they'll be woven into the fabric of a better, more lasting spiritual life to become a significant part of the eternal tapestry of My new world. They'll know Me as I am known. Everything else will pass away. This is the most important news you can give them. This is Your calling. Talk to as many as possible, including your children and grandchildren. Tell them you don't know day to day what will happen, but you do know what the end result will be. Give them this message of hope and deliverance today! I love you.

Read other books by Lele Beutel, sign up for
her newsletter, and follow on social media by
scanning the QR code or going to the URL below:

linktr.ee/authorlelebeutel

About the Author

Lele Beutel and her husband, Mike, enjoy traveling to new places. They have found that with each excursion come opportunities to make a difference in people's lives and have their own lives changed by others. Walking on the Camino de Santiago was one such adventure for Lele. She considers herself to be "secret agent" for God because of how He often leads her into unexpected situations where she's able to connect with others. Before retirement, she spent 25 years as a financial advisor and was able to encourage many people mentally, spiritually, and financially through her faith-based advice. Now, she and her husband spend time with their two dogs, Andey and Barney, with grandkids, and as volunteers at their church. They also share experiences with their life group members and the neighbors they meet while walking the dogs.

Other books she has written include: *What God Wants You to Know*, a 365-day devotional that reveals God's heart relating to passages from Genesis through Revelation; *Lele's Selah*, a book of poetry; *The Reignbreaker*, a young adult fantasy; *Flora's Story*, about a young German refugee who miraculously escapes and survives the Nazi and Russian regimes of WWII Germany; and three books of poetry: *Lele's Lovesongs: Words of hope for the ones we love; Lele's Sighs: Reflections and Recollections;* and *The Camino Connection: Connecting with Life and Commemorating a Death While Walking on the Camino de Santiago*.

To reach her, you can find her on Facebook or email her at: *apedersen6@comcast.net*

She would love to hear from you!